D0206454

CHARLES J. SYKES

DUMBING DOWN OUR KIDS

■ Why America's
Children Feel Good
About Themselves but
Can't Read, Write, or Add

St. Martin's Griffin
New York

Design by Pei Loi Koay

Library of Congress Cataloging-in-Publication Data

Sykes, Charles J.
    Dumbing down our kids : why America's children feel good about themselves but can't read, write, or add / Charles J. Sykes.
        p.   cm.
    ISBN 0-312-14823-2
    1. Education, Secondary—United States—Evaluation.   2. Academic   achievement—United States—Evaluation.   I. Title.
    LA222.S95   1995
    373.73—dc20   95-31522
                                    CIP

First St. Martin's Griffin Edition: September 1996

10 9 8 7 6 5 4 3 2 1

To my children and their teachers

CONTENTS

PREFACE

America's schools are in deep trouble, not because they lack men and women who care about children, but because they are dominated by an ideology that does not care much about learning.

This book is not, however, a wholesale indictment of American education. There are dedicated teachers and effective schools throughout the country. In many cases, however, they are an endangered species. Whether it is called Outcome Based Education or "holistic learning," much of what passes for "reform" among educationists today represents a continued flight from high academic standards and expectations. Feel-good learning has little room for teachers who think schools should be about acquiring knowledge.

When I first began writing about education in the mid-1980s, I focused on the problems of higher education, in part because I came from an academic family (my father was a professor), and in part because the crisis of the American university—its flight from teaching, the collapse of academic integrity, the rise of political correctness—carried a special urgency. But even as I wrote *ProfScam,* and later *The Hollow Men,* and *A Nation of Victims,* it was obvious that the decline of higher learning had not taken place in isolation. The roots of the problem were deeper.

It does not take anything away from the gravity of the crisis in our universities to say that the stakes may be even greater in the nation's secondary and elementary schools. As incendiary as the battles over political correctness on campus have been, I have become convinced that the defining cultural and political debates of the decade will center around the so-called school wars, which will be fought out in elementary, middle, junior high, and high schools. Those debates will result in a wave of new reforms, more extensive than anything we have seen in more than a century, replacing old and failed "reforms" that are now the status quo of our schools. If this book provides even a small impetus to that movement, it will have been worthwhile.

I owe a special debt of gratitude to those friends and colleagues who encouraged me to write this book, especially Jim Miller, the president of the Wisconsin Policy Research Institute, whose support and faith have been unflagging. I am similarly grateful to James Piereson and the John M. Olin Foundation whose funding made the research for this book possible. My research assistant, Beth Brooks, was tireless, dedicated, and tenacious in her work and was a valuable sounding board throughout the writing. Michael Hartmann provided valuable advice and counsel as a reader and editor of early versions of the manuscript. My editor at St. Martin's Press, George Witte, was—as always—unfailingly gracious and helpful. George has been a consistent champion of this book and it would certainly not have been possible without his loyalty. My agents Lynn Chu and Glen Hartley immediately saw the potential for a book about America's schools and lent me their enthusiasm at a crucial stage in its development. My wife, Diane, and my children Jay, Alexander, and Sandy also had to endure a great deal during the writing of this book, and I appreciate their patience, faith, and support. And without the understanding of Carl Gardner and Steve Wexler, this project would have been far more difficult than it turned out to be.

I also owe a debt to those critics who have gone before me, and whose works remain an inspiration to anyone who takes on the educationist Blob (to use William Bennett's memorable phrase describing that establishment). I drew sustenance along the way from the work of Arthur Bestor, John Keats, and Richard Mitchell, all of them eloquent and incisive skewerers of the educational status quo. Since they launched their own attacks on the various cults of educational dumbness, little has changed except the cost and the various new labels for the old bad ideas.

But I am especially grateful for the many parents, teachers, school board members, and even administrators who have provided me with their insights, suggestions, and, in many cases, documentation of the trends that appear in this book. Their stories capture the human dimension of the crisis, and their commitment to changing their children's schools will be the engine that drives the coming transformation of American education.

—CHARLES J. SYKES
February 1995

DUMBING DOWN AMERICA'S KIDS

■

"MERE FACTS"

I n Littleton, Colorado, the school district's new "goals" required that students be able to speak and write. But it wasn't exactly clear what they would have to write or speak *about*. "They won't be asked to demonstrate knowledge of important historical figures and events," remarked one parent. "They won't be asked to identify famous writers, artists, scientists."

Until a revolt by voters sent the school board packing, Littleton's school district was under the sway of a new academic theory—Outcome Based Education—that not only de-emphasized grades and competition, but also the content of the various subjects. While many educators tend to waffle over the consequences of the new curricula—replete with "outcomes" and portentous "performance goals"—educators in Littleton were candid to a fault. James Ferguson, the erstwhile principal of Heritage High School, insisted that it was not important for students to learn any specific historical fact. He specifically denied that high school students needed to be able to define either the Holocaust or World War II. When pressed, the educational leader would not even agree that a high school graduate should know something about the Great Depression. In one interview he implied that there was something unfair about singling out some historical landmarks as more important than others, a selection that was arbitrary, judgmental, and impertinent. Nor did he think it was really all that important that students knew the location of Florida. (In a later interview, he changed to "Nepal," probably on the ground that it was farther away and therefore more obviously obscure.) "It is more important for me," Ferguson opined, "to have students know how to read a map than for them to have any one bit of information about that map. Rather than knowing where Nepal is, it's more important that they know how to find Nepal." In other words, students can be taught something called "map reading skills" or "geographical thinking," which does not require knowing where anything is.

While Ferguson's views were not held by every rank-and-file teacher in his school, they were shared by other administrators who also embraced the "outcomes" philosophy then in vogue in the area's schools. In May

1992 Jean Torkelson, an editorial writer for the *Rocky Mountain News*, interviewed the assistant superintendent of the nearby Jefferson County school district. Administrator Vera Dawson explained that in the past the schools had focused too much on "knowledge" and not enough on what she called "the application of knowledge." (This formulation has become so common that almost no one bothers to raise awkward questions about how to apply something you don't have.) So, Torkelson wondered, where does the knowledge of history fit into all of this? Should children study, say, the American Civil War?

In response, Dawson complained that she had been forced to learn all sorts of irrelevant and burdensome details about the Civil War. And, anyway, she asked, what good does it do to learn the dates of the Civil War? Could Torkelson, for example, remember what she was wearing a year ago?

The question astonished the writer. "You're surely not equating the dates of the Civil War with what a person wore a year ago?" Torkelson asked her. But Dawson was doing exactly that. She regarded historical facts as trivia, the effluvia of an outmoded curriculum, useless, worthless knowledge on a par with the color of her blouse the previous season. When did the armies of the North and South engage in mortal combat over the fate of the Union? That, Dawson said, was "unimportant information." (Dawson was not alone. In a 1990 survey of college seniors, 42 percent couldn't name the dates of the War Between the States within half a century.)

Torkelson wanted to make sure that she was not misunderstanding or misconstruing the assistant superintendent. Pushed on the issue, Dawson conceded that it would be difficult to understand the conflict without knowing when it happened. But as a later critic recounted, "in a final trivialization of the great conflict, Dawson said it should be used primarily as a means to study conflicts 'in this classroom, in this community, in this state.' "[1]

Why didn't Sherman and Stonewall Jackson feel good about each other? Do you sometimes feel that way?

Compare the disputes of the Union and the Confederacy to the last time Brenda and Tiffany couldn't agree on when to go to the mall.

The administrators of Chinook Middle School in the Seattle area felt that they were in the vanguard of educational reform with their new science curriculum's hands-on approach and its involvement of students as "active learners." Like educationists around the country, Chinook's curricular visionaries had decided to inject "creativity" into the dreary business of teaching science. They had gone out of their way to hire brightly polished young ed school graduates who shrank instinctively from suggestions that children should be burdened with "mere facts" and scientific trivia. The new curriculum emphasized *doing* instead of merely *knowing*. Administrators and school board members assured parents that this brave new world of hands-on science represented a toughening of the district's academic standards. They might have gotten away with it, except for Andrea Richardson.

Andrea was an eighth grader at Chinook. Her academic record was nearly spotless and she was accustomed to getting A's, even in difficult courses. But the real problem was her attitude toward science. She actually liked it. She didn't just want to feel good about science; she wanted to *learn* science. That's what started it all.

The principal of Chinook would later describe Andrea's science teacher as "one of the best science teachers I've dealt with. This teacher is highly motivating and sometimes they may do some extraordinary things in terms of creativity."[1]

Andrea didn't see it that way.

She was not especially motivated by the three weeks the class spent picking up cereal with tongue depressors, an exercise that was supposed to simulate the way birds feed. As part of the project, students used toothpicks, spoons, and even clothespins to pick up peas. They also spent class time hunting for paper moths on a wall.

For homework in the science class, students created collages and drew pictures of scientists. (This was presumably easier than studying their *discoveries*. As one writer of a letter to the editor later remarked: "Are we to believe that Charles Darwin excelled due to his proficiency at scribbling uncanny portraits of other scientists at work?")[2] One month-long project had Andrea copying a picture of a town in a textbook and drawing in several new buildings. "That's stupid," she later told a local newspaper. "You can't tell if the structures are well built. You can't see if there's a foundation. And especially the way I draw, you can't tell." She received an A.[3]

During the entire semester, the class had only two tests and three homework assignments and managed to cover only two chapters of the textbook. Other classes covered more than twice as much ground.[4] Andrea's frustration was not confined to the new science curriculum. In her math class, students were given A's just for answering the homework problems—whether or not they got the right answer. Just trying was enough; accuracy was apparently optional.[5]

But it was the science class that most annoyed her. She had done more experiments as a fifth and sixth grader than she did as an eighth grader, and the school year had descended from farce, to wasted time, to insult. Finally, she decided to speak out. In a letter to her science teacher, Andrea poured out her complaints:

> I've been in this class for almost a quarter, and I haven't gotten a single thing out of it. Unless you count learning how to be a bird, making imitation cereal or finding out if I can roll my tongue to be valuable learning experiences. Maybe you do, but I don't. . . . I would be better off in my sister's fifth-grade science class.

Andrea, who had complained to her mother about the class, showed her the letter before sending it. Her mother had looked over the science materials and thought them cartoonish. She approved the letter. "We raise our children to stand up for what they believe in," she told the *Seattle Times*.[6]

The letter, however, came as an unpleasant surprise to the novice teacher, who regarded it as "rude and disrespectful." She took her complaints to the principal (who was himself a champion of "creative," "motivating," "hands-on" education) and he agreed. When Andrea's mother declined to come in and discuss the infraction with school officials, Andrea was suspended. When she refused the suspension, the school sent Andrea home with an "emergency expulsion." She was permitted to return to class only after her mother agreed to meet with the principal. "It's between the teacher and the student," her mother explains. "My daughter did not do anything wrong. It was never intended to be rude and disrespectful."[7]

School officials continue to back the teacher. The interim district superintendent at the time dismissed the controversy over the class and Andrea's letter as a "two-bit deal that got escalated into a mountain." The school board decided that the principal had acted appropriately. The vote was unanimous.

In the fall of 1994, Andrea enrolled in John F. Kennedy Catholic High School, rather than the district public high school. "I really don't have much of a choice," she told the *Seattle Times*, "if I want an education."[8]

DUMBING DOWN OUR KIDS

f you can read this," reads a popular bumper sticker, "thank a teacher." It is a touching and often accurate sentiment. But if Americans *can't* read or do sums or find England on a map, then whom do we thank for that? The public education establishment insists that it is not their fault. Don't blame us, they argue, for the dumbing down of America's kids, pointing the finger of blame at parents, poverty, television, family breakdown, and the insufficient generosity of the taxpayers. They have a point, of course, because education never occurs in a vacuum. Parental indifference, changing family structures, and the mental swamp of television also contribute to declines in achievement.

But this is a book about schools and their responsibilities.

There are probably a number of valid explanations for the failure of American students to know geography and elementary facts of history. But one reason for their ignorance is that their schools no longer feel it necessary to teach them such knowledge.

Educationists can advance painstaking reasons for the spreading stain of illiteracy among the nation's elaborately and expensively educated students. But one reason students write and read so poorly is the indifference of educationists toward such details as the mechanics of reading, writing, grammar, and spelling. (Witness the ingenious notion of "invented spelling." It's not wrong, it's *creative*.) Similarly, the fashionable education philosophy that insists that children no longer have to learn the basics of computation may have something to do with the number of youngsters unable to add up a column of numbers without a calculator.

Educationists frequently point to societal attitudes about learning to explain slumping test scores, but they cannot escape their own responsibility for helping to shape those attitudes. They have encouraged Americans to settle for watered-down standards and to be suspicious of any education that demands hard work and intellectual challenge. Indeed, Americans often seem more worried about depriving children of self-actualization and self-esteem than whether they will graduate dumb.

But such attitudes don't form the whole picture. Opinion polls show the public wants schools that provide an orderly environment and a curriculum focused on "the basics." The vast majority of Americans think that "schools should hold students accountable for doing their best," which they define in starkly traditional terms. Nearly nine out of ten parents do not think that students should be able to graduate from high school "unless they can demonstrate they can write and speak English well," and more than four out of five want schools to set up "very clear guidelines on what students should learn and teachers should teach in every major subject."[1]

Why then are so many schools moving in the opposite direction? Because too often the schools are operated not by society's standards, but by those of the educationist establishment that has dominated American schools for six decades. Few of the ideas now being offered as "reforms" and innovations are, in fact, new. Most are retreads of notions fashionable in the 1920s, the 1940s, and the 1950s, repackaged and renamed to obscure their discredited ancestries. The persistence of such ideas, however, reflects the pattern of reform and counterreform that has characterized the decline of American schools in the last half century.

In this book, I will argue that:

- The dumbing down of America's students is a direct result of the dumbing down of the curriculum and the standards of American schools—the legacy of a decades-long flight from learning.
- American students are unable to effectively compete with the rest of the industrialized world, because our schools teach less, expect less, and settle for less than do those of other countries.
- As Arthur Bestor noted four decades ago, a sound education involves a command of the "essential intellectual tools," "a store of reliable information which the mind can draw upon," practice in "the systematic ways of thinking developed within the various fields of scholarly and scientific investigation," and finally, but only finally, "the culminating act of applying this aggregate of intellectual powers to the solution of a problem."[2] American schools fail to provide these qualities in a systematic or meaningful way. In their place, educationists offer what they call "higher-order thinking skills," but are seldom clear about what it is that students should *think about.*
- The decline of the reading and writing abilities of American children is directly attributable to the way those skills are—and are not—taught in American schools. American children are not learning many of these basic facts of history, geography, and science because their schools often are uninterested in teaching them.
- It may get worse. Under the new New Math children are no longer required to master long division, multiplication, addition, or subtraction by hand, but are permitted to use calculators as early as kindergarten. This campaign to dumb down the teaching of mathematics will result

in an epidemic of mathematical and scientific illiteracy with disastrous consequences for higher education and the national workforce.

- Even as evidence mounts that American students are lacking in basic academic skills such as writing, reading, and mathematics, schools are increasingly emphasizing so-called "affective" learning that deals with the feelings, attitudes, and beliefs of students, rather than addressing what they know or can do.

- The emphasis on "feelings" means that schools frequently usurp the prerogatives and invade the privacy of families. This includes offering courses that encourage children to report their parents' attitudes and behavior if they make the child "uncomfortable." Equally troubling, American schools have become backwaters of amateur psychologizing practiced by teachers who are often unqualified and unprepared for such responsibilities.

- The ongoing dumbing down of the nation's schools is reflected in the rapid spread of a host of faux reforms throughout the nation's schools in the 1990s, including Outcome Based Education, cooperative learning, so-called alternative assessment techniques, and the reliance on vague, impenetrable, and unmeasurable "goals" such as: the "Integration of physical, emotional, and spiritual wellness," "Interpersonal Relationships," "Adaptability and Flexibility," "Environmental Stewardship," and "Positive self-concept . . . ," in which "Students demonstrate positive growth in self-concept through appropriate tasks or projects." Although they use the language of reform, these innovations amount to a counterreformation aimed at undoing much of the progress made by reformers in the 1980s.

- As both standards and achievement have fallen, American schools have inflated grades, adjusted or fudged test scores, or dumbed down the tests altogether to provide the illusion of success. When those measures have been insufficient, they have changed their definitions of "success."

- In the name of "equity," "fairness," "inclusiveness," and "self-esteem," standards of excellence are being eroded throughout American education. Educational levelers have become increasingly aggressive in their attacks on ability grouping, programs for the gifted and talented, and distinctions, such as graduation honors, for the best and brightest students.

- The ethical illiteracy of American education has contributed to a moral dumbing down of America's children every bit as grave as the dumbing down of academic standards. Too often America's schools substitute self-indulgence for moral reasoning, and narcissism for concern for others.

- The politicization of higher education—which has drawn so much criticism and publicity—has been reproduced at the elementary and secondary levels of education with little publicity or opposition, even though in many ways it is more toxic. Children in elementary school are especially defenseless against the appropriation of their education by propagandists, since they lack even the modest ability to debate and dissent that college students occasionally still retain.

- American education continues to be dominated by an educational oligarchy that has been aptly called The Blob—a self-interested, self-perpetuating, interlocking directorate of special interest groups that dominates the politics, bureaucracy, hiring, and policy making of American schooling. Sclerotic in its rigidity and bitterly hostile to criticism of any kind, The Blob is both the architect of the status quo and its enforcer.

- American education is facing a historic crisis because the economic, cultural, and political consequences of educational failure are greater than ever before. At one time, it was possible for our society and for individuals to get by with minimal literacy skills, but global competition has raised the stakes permanently. Until recently the system responsible for preparing children has been largely insulated from the consequences of its failures, but in the twenty-first century society can no longer be protected from the fallout from our educational bankruptcy. Conditions, therefore, are ripe for a reformation as sweeping as those that have felled other monoliths that had seemed impregnable and impervious to change . . . until they vanished.

The Politics of Education

If all politics is local, then the most intense local politics in America is school politics. Emotionally pitched battles over Outcome Based Education have dominated the school wars in Virginia, Pennsylvania, Colorado, California, Oklahoma, Wisconsin, and Minnesota, while the struggle over books like *Heather Has Two Mommies* toppled the superintendent in New York City. The school wars are so bitter precisely because the stakes are so highly charged. It is no exaggeration to argue that the education debate of the next decade could be the defining social struggle of our times, for when Americans debate our values or our definition of the good life, or when we argue about what it means to be an American, we are debating what kind of schools we should have and what we should teach in them. Conversely, when Americans debate what kind of schools we want we are debating the central questions of politics and culture.

These debates are not new. But as the national consensus over values, culture, and the purpose of education frays, the questions become more urgent and the pressures on the schools more concentrated. Over the last half century, the schools have been asked to assume (and have asked to assume) extraordinary burdens; they are expected not merely to educate children but to deal with and help resolve society's race problems, to eradicate poverty, to be on the front lines of economic competitiveness, environmentalism, AIDS, multiculturalism, child abuse, drug addiction, sexual harassment, to mediate our ambivalence about family life and sexuality, and to provide children with a moral compass.

Today, American education is breaking apart under the strain, both academically and politically.

Politics, of course, is entwined with education in other countries. But here, as Hannah Arendt has observed, political and social crises are focused on the schools with particular intensity, because education in America "plays a different and, politically, incomparably more important role than in other countries." America used public schools to assimilate immigrants with official ideas of what it meant to be an American. But Arendt argued that our special attitude toward schools also arose from Americans' "extraordinary enthusiasm for the new," including our belief in the limitless possibilities of our "newcomers by birth," our children. A new nation that created a *novus ordo seclorum*—a new order of the ages—believed that if there was a problem, there must be a solution. As often as not, Americans turned to the schools. But as Arendt recognized, there was more than a touch of utopianism in the belief that we could make miniature communities of virtue, tolerance, and compassion that would blossom into an equally virtuous, tolerant and compassionate society.[3]

For nearly a century, educationists have made promise after promise of social transformation and consciousness raising. But Arendt warned that far from transforming society, the utopian schools would increasingly be out of touch with the real world and the course of study they offer increasingly useless to children, who would find themselves prepared for a world that hardly existed except in the imaginations of professors of education and committees on curriculum.

Failure Redux

The most persistent (and damning) conservative critique of modern educationism is that its "reforms" are untested and experimental, the fruits of faddism rather than practice or research. But this criticism is only partly accurate. While it is true that many of the specific gimmicks of the age (the latest being Outcome Based Education, which comes under a variety of names) are untested, it is not true that they are innovations. Ironically, many of the same educationists who contemptuously dismiss critics as nostalgists for the world of *The Adventures of Ozzie & Harriet* are themselves pushing educational "innovations" that were in vogue years before Ozzie was even a gleam in a producer's eye. Indeed, many of the theories now being passed off as path-breaking are merely refried versions of "reforms" in fashion when our grandmothers were still in grade school. Far from being untested, their ideas have been tested and retested for decades in thousands of schools. And they have failed.

Despite superficial differences between progressive "child-centered" education in vogue in the 1920s, Life Adjustment education in the 1950s, the "schools without failure" in the 1960s, and Outcome Based Education in the 1990s, the debate over educational philosophy essentially has remained unchanged. It is a debate over both the methods and aims of teaching, between those who believe that education should concern itself with intellectual discipline and the succeeding waves of innovators who offer the "child's interest" or the well-adjusted personality, self-expressiveness, or self-esteem as more attractive alternatives.

America's school wars inevitably turn on fundamental questions: What is the goal of education? What do schools intend to teach? And what do they expect their students to learn? A school that sees its ultimate product as the well-adjusted teamworker with a healthy sense of self-esteem is unlikely to adopt the same means as a school whose goal is to create individualists. But the jargon of the educationists is particularly unhelpful in sorting out such questions. One of the current buzzphrases, for example, declares that "All children can learn." But that begs the question: Learn what? Trigonometry? Advanced Physics? Or some watered-down stew packaged under a label like "sound environmental stewardship"? Does the phrase "all children can learn" mean that all students have the same capabilities? (In which case it is false.) Or that all students will be able to meet the same standards? (Which is fanciful.) Or, rather, does it mean that the standards for learning are set so low that they can be met by all students?

These questions are not new.

Nearly forty years ago, in *Schools Without Scholars*, author John Keats described the new educational philosophy of American public schools as "compounded of the pragmatic thoughts of the late John Dewey plus a dollop of sentimentality and a generous helping of the oversensitive conscience of the social worker whose life is chiefly spent among those who do not seem able to help themselves." He noted that the educrats of the time masked the dumbing down of the schools by filling their public statements and journals with words like *enriched, meaningful, real life, happy,* and *with zest and zeal.* But what they really meant, Keats charged, was that "there are no absolutes, hence no objective standards in education. The mind cannot be disciplined by means of assigned tasks." His critique is disconcertingly up-to-date. For educationists, Keats wrote in 1958, "There is no a priori knowledge; hence there are no eternal absolutes; no timeless objective goals. Everything, truth included, is relative. Moreover, the present is the only reality we can ever truly know and use."[4] He had no idea how far the educationists would take such ideas over the next half century.

Our current debates tend to obscure this long-running argument. Much of the energy of the educationist establishment is devoted to discrediting critics, who are characterized not as heirs to an intelligent and hard fought struggle over basic principles, but as extremists and opponents of sound educational practice. Contributing to this attitude is the remarkable lack of open debate *within* educational circles. The uniformity of opinion and intolerance of open dissent provides the illusion that those who know and care about education all agree with one another, and that disagreeable outsiders don't know or care about good schools.

The existence of a party line has meant that the burden of opposition has fallen on outsiders, including parents who make do as best they can with their limited backgrounds in educational matters, but whose zeal is occasionally extreme and exaggerated. Thus, the absurd charges by some critics that Outcome Based Education is part of a plot to impose a New World Order (rather than the product of educationist mediocrities trying to avoid being held accountable), or the naive belief that "critical thinking skills" are perhaps unnecessary. In the school wars, disputants often rage against one another across an abyss of mutual incomprehension. This abyss has been widened by the ill-disguised contempt that many educationists have for parents, and by the considerable armory of mind-fogging jargon that obscures the educationists' goals.

Documenting the Crisis

Throughout the pages of this book, I cite examples of classroom practices from schools across the country. Inevitably, educationist critics will cavil at the use of such "anecdotes" because they are unfair to the spirit of their initiatives. But ideas—especially in education—need to be judged not by their intentions, but by their realities. The failure of educational reform can be defined precisely by the size of the gap between wishful thinking and actual practice in the classroom. Educationists, of course, would like to have their ideas judged by how well they sound on paper. Unlike practitioners of other academic disciplines, educationists often offer little or no research to justify the most sweeping changes in classroom practice—insisting that innovations be implemented before there is any data one way or another to determine whether the idea works. With equal ardor, they cling to favored notions of what works long after actual practice has proven them to be abysmal flops. This is a crucial aspect of the educationist culture, because it bears on the problem of verifiability and falsifiability. Ideologues insist that their ideas be judged on the purity of their intentions, rather than on their actual success in practice. Scientists, on the other hand, test their ideas and reject hypotheses that are not supported. As Karl Popper pointed out, this is the essential difference between the ideologue and the scientist: An ideology can *never* be disproved. For the ideologue, a failure is dismissed not as proof that the original idea was wrong, but rather as an indication that the effort did not go far enough, or was badly implemented.

The fundamental problem, however, of devising new schemes from scratch—whether it is a New Man, a new society, a new economy, or a new school—is the question: Will it work? Are flaws in its execution mere accidents, or are they inherent in the idea itself? Was a classless society a good idea that simply fell short because of poor management, bad timing, or historical flukes? Or was it a hopelessly unrealistic daydream that ignored the realities of human nature?

Similarly, when reformers discard traditional curricula and demand that teachers assume radically different roles, or when power and responsibility are shifted from grown-ups to children, what happens in the classroom? How does the romantic blueprint play out in a fifth-grade math class? When I have chosen such stories—some of which are called "Scenes from the Front"—I have done so not because I think they tell the whole story, but because I think that they are representative of trends that are both significant and widespread in American classrooms. By themselves, however, they do not prove that a crisis exists in American education. We need to look elsewhere to see just how far the dumbing down of America's kids has gone.

LOSING THE RACE

While critics tend to rely on the three-decades long decline of the Scholastic Aptitude Test (SAT) to document the dumbing down of American education, more alarming is our performance against the students of other industrialized countries. By virtually every measure of achievement, American students lag far behind their counterparts in both Asia and Europe, especially in math and science. Moreover, the evidence suggests that they are falling farther and farther behind. As educational researcher Harold Stevenson notes, although "the U.S. is among the countries expending the highest proportion of their gross national product on education, our elementary school and secondary school students never place above the median in comparative studies of academic achievement."

Part of the reason is that neither our schools nor our students spend very much time at it. The National Education Commission on Time and Learning found that most American students spend less than half their day actually studying academic subjects. The commission's two-year study found that American students spent only about 41 percent of the school day on basic academics. Their schedules jammed with course work in self-esteem, personal safety, AIDS education, family life, consumer training, driver's ed, holistic health, and gym, the typical American high school student spends only 1,460 hours on subjects like math, science, and history during their four years in high schools. Meanwhile, their counterparts in Japan will spend 3,170 hours on basic subjects, students in France will spend 3,280 on academics, while students in Germany will spend 3,528 hours studying such subjects—nearly three times the hours devoted in American schools.[1]

By some estimates, teachers in Japan give elementary students three times as much homework as American children are given by their teachers, while teachers in Taipei give their students seven times as much homework as children in Minneapolis.[2] By fifth grade, children in Minneapolis are getting slightly more than four hours a week in homework, while fifth graders in Japan get six hours and students in Taipei, thirteen hours.[3]

Our Best and Brightest

The academic crisis is not confined to low-achieving students. Besides the overall drop, the SAT scores show evidence of a rot at the top—a decline in the number of high-scoring students. Even though the number of students taking the SAT rose by more than 50,000 between 1962 and 1983, for example, the number of students scoring above a 700 on the verbal section dropped from 19,099 in 1962–63 to 11,638.[4] Although the number of high-scoring students in math has risen in the last decade, our best students do not stack up well in comparison with their foreign counterparts. According to the National Research Council, *average* students in other industrialized countries are as proficient in mathematics as America's *best* students. The Second International Mathematics Study found that the "performance of the top 5 percent of U.S. students is matched by the top 50 percent of students in Japan." When the very best American students—the top one percent—are measured against the best students of other countries, America's best and brightest finished at the bottom.[5]

When tests compare achievement levels in advanced algebra, for example, twelfth graders in Japan and Hong Kong earn mean scores of nearly 80 points, *twice* the American mean of 40. The same gap appears in scores for the elementary functions of calculus, where Chinese and Japanese students earn mean scores of more than 60, while their twelfth-grade American counterparts score only around 30.[6] Asians, however, are not the only students to outperform us.

In tests measuring the mathematical ability of eighth graders in 20 countries, American students finished tenth in arithmetic, twelfth in algebra, and sixteenth in geometry. High school seniors fared just as poorly. In comparisons with students from 143 other countries, American students finished in the lowest quarter in geometry and ranked second from the bottom in algebra. Stevenson reported: "On no test did American students attain an average score that fell above the median for all countries." A test of thirteen-year-olds in Korea, Spain, the United Kingdom, and the United States found American students dead last in math competence.[7]

Another study of children born in 1974 documents the growing disparities between the performance of American and foreign students. Supervised by the Educational Testing Service (ETS) of Princeton, the international study monitored 24,000 children from twelve countries. When the test was published in the late 1980s, the students were just entering high school. They are now entering the workforce. Seventy-eight percent of the Korean children born in 1974 tested at the 500 level in intermediate math, as did 73 percent of children from French Quebec, and 69 percent from British Columbia. In contrast, only 40 percent of American children achieved at the 500 level. Forty percent of the Korean youngsters scored at the 600 level, which requires a higher level of conceptual understanding, compared with 24 percent of students from British Columbia, and 22 percent of students from French Quebec. Only nine percent of Americans scored at this level.[8]

Apologists for American education often complain that such comparisons are unfair because high school attendance is not as widespread in other countries as it is here. It is therefore unfair, they say, to compare the performance of the exclusive foreign secondary school with the inclusive and democratic high school of this country. But test scores of elementary students gives the lie to such arguments. Elementary education is compulsory worldwide and the same gaps in achievement are found in the tests of younger children.

Comparisons of math scores tend to be mixed for children in the first grade here and abroad. But by the time children have reached the fifth grade, the scores have diverged dramatically. Even when culturally fair tests are used, American students still fail to perform up to the level of their Asian counterparts. As Stevenson reported: "Even the best American schools were not competitive with their counterparts in Asia on mathematics achievement. . . . The *highest*-scoring American school falls below the *lowest*-scoring Asian schools."[9]

One factor in this international learning gap seems to be that we simply ask less of our students than other countries. While one fourth to one third of the high school students in other industrialized countries pass high-level achievement tests in biology that require in-depth knowledge and reasoning skills, only one in twenty-five Americans students (4 percent) passes such tests. A study by the American Federation of Teachers (AFT) found that between 30 percent and 50 percent of students in other countries take advanced, subject-specific exams and that 62 percent to 96 percent passed those tests. In contrast, only 7 percent of American students take Advanced Placement Exams and less than two-thirds pass. The AFT reported that "Entrance to most universities in this country is not dependent upon achieving mastery of rigorous science content (or, for that matter, virtually any other subject-matter content)." In other industrialized countries exams requiring extensive knowledge and skills "*must* be passed by students who want to go on to study in colleges or universities," and "since the exams are well aligned with the school curriculum, students understand that working hard in school will pay off."

The study's author concluded: "In England and Wales, France, Germany and Japan, where students, teachers and parents all know what is expected of the college-bound and what is at stake, a significant number of youngsters rise to the challenge and achieve high standards. . . . we are asking too little of too many of our students, and we are giving them very few incentives to work hard."[10]

The Usual Excuses

Confronted with this dismal record, the educationist establishment relies on a grab bag of excuses and rationalizations. Americans, Stevenson noted, often blame "poor physical facilities and excessive numbers of students" for low test scores and mediocre academic performance. But he concluded: "Our data, especially from Taiwan and China, go a long way toward dispelling such interpretations. Large schools, large class size, and old-fashioned school buildings do not necessarily limit children's academic achievement."[11] American teachers also turn out to have higher levels of formal education than their Asian counterparts.[12]

Other defenders of the status quo have found comfort in blaming our educational problems on television and working parents, but neither excuse works. Indeed, Stevenson and his colleagues have found that Japanese fifth graders "watched as much, if not more, television each day as American children."[13] Their studies found that the average Japanese child watched two hours of television a day, while the average American child of the same age watched 1.8 hours a day.

If television cannot account for low achievement, neither does the prevalence of working mothers in American homes. In the international comparisons cited above, researchers identified the family background of the test takers. They found that while 35 percent of the mothers of Minneapolis students were working mothers, so were 30 percent of the Japanese mothers, 33 percent of the mothers in Taipei, and 97 percent of the mothers in Beijing. [14] Stevenson also notes that Americans comfort themselves with stereotypes in which Asian children are pictured as being under great stress from early ages; that Asian children are somehow "easier" to teach than American kids because they are more docile; that there is little to emulate in Asian teaching methods because they stress rote learning and rely on endless, mindless drill of basic skills. While these false stereotypes "allow us to maintain a view of ourselves as relaxed, successful, effective individualists who are creative, innovative, and independent," Stevenson wrote, they are "largely inaccurate."

Asian students may work hard, but researchers have found no evidence that they "suffer greater psychological distress or a greater incidence of suicide than exists in Western children." Nor is there much support for theories that attribute higher levels of Asian achievement to genetically superior intelligences.[15]

If demographics, television, IQ, and money do not account for the differences, attitudes certainly do. Americans have very different assumptions than do their Asian counterparts about the appropriate role parents should play in the education of their children. Asians, according to Stevenson, expect schools to develop academic skills, while they believe it is up to the home to support the schools and to provide a "healthy emotional environment." In contrast, Americans expect more of their schools and less of themselves. Stevenson says that many Americans "seem to expect that schools will take on responsibility for many more aspects of the child's life," including family roles, sex, drugs, minority relations, illnesses, nutrition, and fire prevention.

The Legacy of Dumbness

The result is a tragic legacy of educational mediocrity:

- More than a decade after *A Nation at Risk* drew attention to the nation's educational mediocrity, the reading proficiency of nine- and thirteen-year-olds has declined even further.
- The 1994 National Assessment of Educational Progress found that a third of American seventeen-year-olds say they are not required to do homework on a daily basis.
- Only one high school junior out of fifty (2 percent) can write well enough to meet national goals.
- Less than 10 percent of seventeen-year-olds can do "rigorous" academic work in "basic" subjects.[16]
- In the United States today, only one in five nine-year-olds can perform even basic mathematical operations. According to the 1990 National Assessment of Educational Progress (NAEP), only one in six nine-year-olds reads well enough to "search for specific information, interrelate ideas, and make generalizations." Only one in four nine-year-olds can apply basic scientific information.[17]
- Among American thirteen-year-olds, only one in ten can "find, understand, and summarize complicated information." Only one in eight eighth graders can understand basic terms and historical relationships. One in eight understands specific government structures and relationships.[18]
- Only one in eight thirteen-year-olds can understand and apply intermediate scientific knowledge and principles. The NAEP found that the percentage of American thirteen-year-olds who understand measurement and geometry concepts and can analyze scientific knowledge and principles "was among the lowest of many countries in the developed world."[19] The 1990 NAEP concluded that "Large proportions, perhaps more than half of our elementary, middle, and high school students are unable to demonstrate competency in challenging subject matter in English, mathematics, science, history, and geography. Further, even fewer appear to be able to use their minds well."[20]
- The writing ability of American students is little short of appalling. American schools, according to the NAEP, produce few students who can write well. *Only 3 percent* of American fourth, eighth, and twelfth graders can write above a "minimal" or "adequate" level, according to the 1992 "Writing Report Card." The test, which rated students' writing

abilities on a scale of one to six, found that fewer than one in thirty American children earned a score of five or six, which meant they could write effectively and persuasively. Only one out of four students even managed to write at the "developed" level, which earned a score of four. "Even the best students who could write effective narrative and informative pieces had difficulty" writing persuasively, the study found.[21] In 1988, only 3 percent of American high school seniors could describe their own television viewing habits in writing above an "adequate" level.[22]

- A "reading report card" finds that 25 percent of high school seniors can barely read their diplomas. A standardized test given to 26,000 Americans sixteen and older "concluded that 80 million Americans are deficient in the basic reading and mathematical skills needed to perform rudimentary tasks in today's society."[23] A 1993 study by the U.S. Department of Education found that 90 million adults—47 percent of the population of the United States—demonstrate low levels of literacy. The level of literacy among adults had fallen by 4 percent since 1986.[24]

- Only 15 percent of college faculty members say that their students are adequately prepared in mathematics and quantitative reasoning—a lower proportion than among higher-education faculty in Hong Kong, Korea, Sweden, Russian, Mexico, Japan, Chile, Israel, or Australia. Only one in five faculty members thinks students have adequate writing and speaking skills.[25]

- A Washington, D.C., grade-school teacher reports that many of the fifth- and sixth-grade students in her geography class were unable to locate Washington, D.C., on a map of the United States, even though they lived in the nation's capital themselves.[26] A survey by the Gallup Organization found that one in seven adults can't find the United States on a blank map of the world. This shouldn't be surprising. In one college *geography* class 25 percent of the students could not locate the Soviet Union on a world map, while on a map of the forty-eight contiguous states, only 22 percent of the class could identify forty or more states correctly.[27]

- Despite the growing importance of scientific knowledge, surveys have found that Americans are woefully ignorant of basic scientific facts. A majority of Americans, for example, do not know that the earth and sun are part of the Milky Way galaxy, and a third of them think humans and dinosaurs walked the earth at the same time. A 1994 survey by Louis Harris & Associates and the American Museum of Natural History found that only about one adult in five scored 60 percent or better on a test of basic knowledge of subjects like space, animals, the environment, diseases, and earth.[28]

- Teachers report that the fall of Communism and the demolition of the Berlin Wall was greeted with blank indifference by many students who knew too little about history to understand or care about the events. "I'm sorry," one high school senior asked during a class discussion of the Eastern Bloc, "but what is this talk of satellites?"[29]

- In the late 1980s, a national survey of high school seniors found that fewer than half could define even basic economic terms. Nearly two thirds of the seniors were unable to correctly define "profit," and less than half could define a "government budget deficit." Most seniors were also baffled by the concept of "inflation." The author of the "Report Card on the Economic Literacy of U.S. High School Students" concluded that "our schools are producing a nation of economic illiterates," and that the level of economic knowledge of students who had the benefit of twelve years of education is "shocking."[30] Especially damning was the finding that even students who took basic high school economics answered only 52 percent of the questions correctly. Students who took "consumer economics" got only 40 percent of the answers correct, while students who took social studies courses were right only 37 percent of the time.[31] A 1992 survey by the National Center for Research in Economic Education and the Gallup Organization yielded similar results. High school seniors answered basic economic questions correctly only 35 percent of the time.[32]
- SAT verbal scores have dropped from a mean of 478 in 1962 to 423 in 1994—a drop of 54 points. The SAT mean math score has fallen from 502 to 479—a drop of 23 points. While math scores have risen 8 points since 1984, they are still below 1974 levels. The national verbal average has fallen 3 points since 1984.[33] During the same period (1960–90), spending on elementary and secondary education increased more than 200 percent, after inflation. Class size has decreased by one third, enrollment has declined by 7 percent, and the number of teachers has increased by 17 percent. Moreover, the decline in test scores came at a time when average teacher salaries and the percentage of teachers with advanced degrees both tripled.

There are obvious real-world consequences for this decline:

- American businesses are now spending $30 billion on workers' training and lose an estimated $25 to $30 billion a year as result of their workers' weak reading and writing skills.[34]
- A survey by the National Association of Manufacturers found that nearly a third of American businesses said the learning skills of their workers are so low that they are unable to reorganize work responsibilities. A quarter of American businesses say their ability to improve their products is limited because of the inability of their employees to learn the necessary skills.[35]

- In a recent year, the Bellsouth Corporation in Atlanta found that fewer than 10 percent of their job applicants met minimal levels of ability for sales, service, and technical jobs. At the same time, MCI Communications in Boston reported that some of its jobs were going unfilled because the company could not find enough qualified applicants.[36]
- In late 1992, executives at Pacific Telesis found that 60 percent of the high school graduates applying for jobs at the firm failed a company exam set at the seventh-grade level.[37]

The Cost of Dumbness

It is hard to put an exact number on what the dumbing down of American education costs the economy, but it is possible to make some approximations. One recent study of job skill requirements found that the average twenty-one- to twenty-five-year-old American was "reading at a level significantly below that demanded by the average job available in 1984 and are even further below the requirements of jobs expected to be created between 1984 and the year 2000." The researchers ranked language skills required for various jobs on a scale of one to six, with a level of six required for scientists, lawyers, and engineers. The vast majority of jobs required a reading skill level of three and four, the requirement for sales and marketing positions. But the study found that *97 percent* of young adults had skills only at the two and three levels, suitable for farming and transportation work.[38]

Economist John Kendrick of George Washington University argues that "the knowledge factor" may account for as much as 70 percent of a nation's productivity trends, either up or down. The skills of our workforce, and their ability to adapt to a knowledge-based economy seem certain to be critical factors in our ability to compete. Kendrick's thesis argues that much of the decline in productivity in American society can be linked to the decline in education and to the resulting gap between the requirements of the economy and the reality of the workforce.

Cornell University Economist John H. Bishop does not go quite as far as Kendrick, but confirms the link between economic growth and the "knowledge factor." At least 10 percent of the "unexplained" slowdown in productivity in the 1970s can be attributed to the decline in achievement scores that began in 1967, Bishop concluded. But the effects of dumbing down will accelerate over time. He projected that the decline in what he called the General Intellectual Achievement (GIA) accounted for 20 percent of the decline in productivity in the 1980s and a full 40 percent of the decline in the 1990s. Writing in the *American Economic Review*, Bishop noted that productivity growth and the test scores dropped almost simultaneously.

That decline, which was severe and unprecedented, meant that students graduating in 1980 were more than a full grade level behind graduates of twenty years earlier. Our schools had produced lower quality workers, which in turn depressed both wages and productivity. If test scores had continued to grow after 1967 at the same rate as they had the previous quarter century, Bishop estimated that the nation's gross national product would have been $86 billion higher than it was in 1988 and $334 billion higher in the year 2010.[39]

This would seem to make a compelling case for spending more money on education, if any link could be shown between higher spending and higher achievement. But national education spending rose more than 25 percent in real terms in the 1980s. And since 1967—when the decline in test scores began in earnest—spending per student had risen faster than it had in the twenty years prior to 1967 (4 percent a year in real terms versus 3.3 percent).[40] In the lower spending years prior to 1967, as Bishop notes, "student test scores had been *rising* steadily for more than 50 years."[41]

In 1989, economist Eric Hanushek published the results of his study of the relationship between spending and academic achievement and refuted one of the central dogmas of the educationist establishment:

> Since the mid-Sixties, there have been around 200 studies looking at the relationship between the inputs to schools, the resources spent on schools, and the performance of students. These studies tell a consistent and rather dramatic story. Result 1 is that *there is no systematic relationship between expenditures on schools and students' performance.* Result 2 is that *there is no systematic relationship between the major ingredients of instructional expenditures per student— chiefly teacher education and teacher experience, which informally drive teacher salaries, and class size—and student performance.*[42]

If the usual scapegoats of educationists—parents, society, and money— cannot account for the decline of American education, then we have to look to the schools themselves and the values that dominate American education in the 1990s.

n June 1993, the Georgetown, Delaware School Board fired veteran math teacher Adele Jones because she gave out too many failing grades. Officially Jones was fired for insubordination. But her real offense was placing education ahead of self-esteem, and it cost her her job. For a while, before she was reinstated, she worked as a waitress.

Jones admits she is a tough teacher. "When students enter my classroom, they know they'll have to earn the grades I give them," she wrote. "I tell kids from the start that I'm not out to fail them, but they've got to understand certain concepts in order to go on to college. If they do four things, they'll do fine: pay attention in class, do their homework, study, and ask questions." Even though her course was demanding, Jones's students also knew that she was available to help them. They knew "that I'm willing to be in at 7:15 every morning and until 6 or 7 every night. That I'm willing to give up my planning period, willing to schedule review sessions just before tests, willing to be accessible by phone.

"But when children are absent 50 to 60 days a year, don't do the homework, and don't perform well on quizzes, do I help them by passing them? I set my standards high so my kids can do likewise."

The high standards were the problem. Adele Jones expected her students to do the work and when they did not, she refused to let them pass her class.[1]

Administrators were troubled by the high number of poor grades she handed out. "The message I kept getting from my supervisors was: 'Keep the kids happy, even if you have to lower your standards.' But it doesn't do any good if we keep passing students on when they get to college and find they can't do the work."[2]

Jones's principal ordered her not to give so many F's to students in her high school algebra class. He wanted her to "have a failure rate consistent with the rest of the school and/or math department."

"What did that mean to me?" Jones later wrote. "It meant grading on a curve, counting class participation more heavily, changing instructional methods I knew challenged the students.

"In other words, it meant I had to change the way I thought about the classroom and the standards of excellence I wanted my students to meet. It meant lowering standards, a move I thought would have been a disservice to my students. I wouldn't be helping them. I'd simply be passing them through the system without giving them the tools they needed to do well at college or in the world of work."[3]

"I believe in hard work and don't accept excuses. I just couldn't pass kids who were failing my algebra course," she told writer Ron Grossman. "I couldn't do that and still sleep at night."[4]

In her first year at Sussex Central High School, Jones had flunked nearly 60 percent of her students; by the second year (as word got out about her demanding standards), the number of failures had fallen to 27 percent. By the middle of the year in which she was fired, the failure rate had dropped to 22 percent. That was still too high for school officials.

In other classes, teachers were not handing out grades based on algebra tests. Instead, other teachers gave students credit for class participation, keeping notebooks, and outside projects. In the new educational parlance, this is called "alternative assessments," and it allowed students to receive passing grades while knowing no more algebra than the students who received failing grades in Ms. Jones's class.

At Jones's dismissal hearing, another teacher acknowledged that if he had used the same standards as Jones, more than two thirds of his students would have gotten D's and F's. Instead, they received passing grades, often A's and B's, which made students, parents, and the administration happy. Adele Jones provided no such solace.

"The smoking gun in this case is her grades," the school district's attorney told a hearing officer. The district's lawyer rejected Jones's argument that the reason for the low grades was the fact that so many students entering Algebra 2 had not been adequately prepared for the advanced work by previous courses. If that was the case, he said, Jones should have readjusted her standards—downward. In fact, he suggested, the answer to the problem should have been for Jones to "start at Algebra 1½."

Besides, administrators argued, Jones's standards and grades were making students feel bad about themselves. Explaining his decision to fire Jones, the school's principal said it was important to provide students with "unanxious expectations." High standards created anxiety. "My goal," he explained, "is to use positive reinforcement to improve the self-esteem of the kids." The school board voted 6 to 4 to uphold his decision to fire Jones.

After her firing, the student body of Sussex Central High School walked out in protest. Many of the students carried signs that read: I FAILED MS. JONES'S CLASS AND IT WAS MY FAULT and JUST BECAUSE A STUDENT IS FAILING DOESN'T MEAN THE TEACHER IS.

Jones was seemingly unaffected by the hoopla. Junior Aimee Karr attended the hearing on Jones's firing to show support, rather that finishing homework for Jones's class. Some students told Karr they thought Jones would cut her some slack at least this one time. "I told the kids, if they thought so, they didn't really know Miss Jones," Karr told a reporter. "Sure enough, she gave me a zero for not having my homework."

Other students came forward to testify to Jones's dedication. Kevin Brittingham, a freshman at the University of Delaware, recalled that he had been one of the students flunked by Jones as a high school student. "After I failed algebra, Miss Jones got in touch with me. She said I'd no reason to fail because I was the brightest kid in the class. So I took the course over, did the work this time and got a B-plus. If she hadn't spoken to me like that, who knows if I'd have gone on to college." Another student testified that the reason so many students failed the Algebra 2 course was their lousy preparation in classes like geometry. Brian Pettyjohn told school board members that his geometry teacher had taken a casual approach to the subject, often sitting on his desk rapping and brainstorming with kids in the class. "The guy was still living in the sixties," Pettyjohn said. "He had us making tie-dyed T-shirts in class."

Other students directly addressed the question of Ms. Jones's impact on their self-esteem. "I'm proud of my 92 average," wrote one student. "Why? Because I actually earned it. Probably it's the first time I had to earn a grade."

Editorializing on the case, the *Chicago Tribune* noted: "It's clear that Jones's students didn't learn only algebra. These kids figured out that pride in accomplishment, not empty flattery, is the necessary equation of self-esteem."[5]

Jones was eventually reinstated after a judge ruled that she had been denied due process. After two members of the school board were ousted in an election, the new board voted 6 to 3 against firing Jones. She returned to class in April 1994.

CHAPTER 3

THE AMERICAN
WAY OF DENIAL

Despite the mounting evidence of an educational crisis, most Americans do not think there is anything seriously wrong with their own children's schools or the education they are getting. However bad things might be elsewhere, most Americans are sure that the dumbing down of American education does not include their own children.

Americans also are likely to rate their own skills far higher than objective evidence would seem to warrant. In 1993, as cited earlier, the U.S. Education Department found that 90 million adults—about 47 percent of the population of the United States—had a low level of literacy. Even so, the report found that the vast majority of Americans describe themselves as being able to read and write English "well" or "very well." This gap between reality and perception, the secretary of education remarked, "paints a picture of a society in which the vast majority of Americans do not know that they do not have the skills they need to earn a living in our increasingly technological society and international marketplace."[1]

They are unfazed by headlines about dropping test scores and unmoved by international comparisons showing Americans lagging far behind the rest of the world. They know there may be problems elsewhere, but they are ... elsewhere. Whatever may be happening in other communities, most Americans are convinced that their local schools are doing fine and confident that their children are doing well in math, science, and reading.

It may seem odd to talk about a national complacency regarding education at a time of such fierce contention over school issues, when newspaper headlines routinely report new studies casting doubt on the quality of the nation's schools. But the gap between those reports and the complacent assurance of Americans explains both the lack of widespread outrage at the decline of educational achievement and the failure of widespread efforts at reform.

In his international comparisons, Stevenson was struck by the degree of complacency among Americans. While 91 percent of Americans said their children's schools were doing a good or excellent job, only around 40 percent of the Asian moms rated their children's schools favorably. Given the level of media coverage of the nation's educational problems,

Stevenson said, those findings were "particularly startling."[2] Stevenson and his colleagues "found little evidence that Americans acknowledge the academic weakness of our nation's children. Despite articles in the press and reports in other media, Americans persist in believing that nothing is seriously wrong—that there is no crisis. When they are confronted with data indicating that American children do poorly in academic subjects compared with children in other societies, they dismiss the results and criticize the studies."[3]

A 1994 survey by the American Association of School Administrators, for instance, found that nearly 90 percent of parents of children in public schools gave the nation's schools an A, B, or C; more than half gave them A's and B's.[4] An Associated Press poll the next month found that 62 percent of Americans rated the quality of their local schools as "excellent" or "good," up from 53 percent in 1989. Only 10 percent of those surveyed rated their local schools as "poor."[5] When Americans were polled in the twenty-sixth annual Phi Delta Kappa–Gallup Poll of the Public's Attitudes Toward the Public Schools, only 8 percent of parents mentioned "standards" or "quality education" as among the biggest problems facing public schools. (They lagged behind "violence," "discipline," "lack of proper financial support," and "drug abuse.")[6]

American students are equally confident of their own academic abilities. In 1992, a Louis Harris survey interviewed high school graduates four to eight years out of school. Overwhelmingly, the graduates said they had been well educated. More than two thirds (68 percent) said they had learned math well in school. Sixty-six percent gave themselves high marks for their writing abilities. An even higher proportion—78 percent—said that they had been taught to read well. Across the board, the recent graduates had high opinions of their own abilities and talents.[7]

So did their parents. The same Harris survey asked parents whose children went into the job market how well their school had prepared them for the world of work. Sixty-five percent of the parents gave their children's school favorable ratings for math, 56 percent for writing, and 67 percent for reading.

A very different picture, however, emerged when employers were asked how they would rate the same skills among the high school graduates they had recently hired. Only 22 percent of the employers thought that the graduates they hired had sufficient math skills. Only 12 percent thought their young employees had been taught to write well. And only 30 percent were satisfied with their employees' reading abilities.[8]

Colleges and universities also are not impressed by recent products of high schools. Only 27 percent of those in higher education said that recent high school graduates had adequate math skills, only 18 percent rated their writing abilities highly, and only 33 percent said that graduates had been taught to read well. None of that dissatisfaction was reflected in the ratings given to schools by the parents of college-bound high school graduates. If anything, the parents of college track students were even deeper into denial. Seventy-one percent said their children had been taught math well, 77 percent gave the schools favorable ratings for teaching writing, and 82 percent gave them positive ratings for reading.[9]

Such attitudes pose a considerable challenge to educational reformers, since they are unlikely to lead to any sense of urgency to change the way schools are run or children are taught. "The results," Harold Stevenson notes, "add up to a very disturbing picture: highly satisfied American parents who apparently have little motivation for improving the quality of American education."[10]

The Complacent American

Why are Americans allowing themselves to be satisfied by educational mediocrity? The answer to that question, so essential for any understanding of the current educational debate, has several elements. The first may be cultural. The 1990s are a difficult time for families and for children; many Americans are sensitive to any suggestions that might further burden children or wound their self-esteem by setting what may seem to them to be unreasonably high standards. But those parents who want their children to do well in school seldom receive any warning signs from the schools telling them if their children are floundering. Educationists have become adept at turning both grades and standardized test results into instruments of public relations and reassurance rather than dependable measurements of actual achievement. During the last few decades grades have been so watered down as to be virtually meaningless and test scores have been skewed to give the impression that everyone is doing quite well—certainly above average. When failure could not simply be covered over with a fresh coat of happy talk, educationists have redefined the rules of the game. As schools have fallen short of traditional measurements of academic achievement they have lowered their goals, or rewritten them into such vague terms that it becomes impossible to measure whether or not those goals are successfully being met. When this tactic has proven insufficient, and critics have demanded more accountability, educationists have fallen back on a decades-old habit of vilifying the critics themselves or flatly denying that there is a crisis in education at all.

Grade Inflation

Grade inflation is both a product and a symptom of dumbing down.

More than two thirds of American eighth graders say that they get mostly A's and B's. According to the College Board, the percentage of students reporting that they had an average grade of A rose from 28 percent to 32 percent between 1987 and 1994. At the same time, their average SAT scores fell by 6 to 15 points. "Teachers want to raise the self-esteem and feel-good attitude of students," explained Howard Everson, a senior research scientist for the College Board. "They want to use grades as a motivator, and they try to placate parents, education administrators and other education stakeholders in the communities."[11] Giving out ever-higher grades for ever-more mediocre work reflects the collapse of standards throughout the educational system. But the inflation of grades also exacerbates the problem, because inflated grades are so useful in covering up the root causes of the collapse.

Since grades no longer credibly reflect academic performance, the floods of content-free A's have become tools of affirmation, therapy, and public relations. High grades reassure parents that all is well with their children's education; they make students feel better about themselves, and are a symbol of the persistence of excellence to the wider community. While disputes over grades continue and are often fiercely contested, it can be argued that the fight over grades is already over, at least de facto, if not de jure. The opponents of grades have succeeded in destroying the grading system as an instrument of reward, punishment, and accountability. Their victory has not been frontal. Indeed, parents still often campaign vigorously against attempts to replace letter grades. But Americans have tacitly accepted that no one should fail or receive a D, or even a C, at least in the case of their own children. Even a grade of C is likely to draw parental complaints, putting renewed pressure on the system to further puff up the rewards. In a survey by the New York State United Teachers, 85 percent of the state's teachers reported that they were pressured by school administrators to give students higher grades. Nearly two thirds said they had been pressured by parents to raise the grade.[12]

See No Evil, Hear No Evil

The lack of any reliable feedback from the schools means that many parents have a hopelessly inflated notion of their child's performance. Chester Finn notes that "most American teachers and principals strive to give students and parents only positive feedback, encouragement and reinforcement." When the former education department official examined 150 student reports, he found that "When it comes to academic performance . . . almost never did I encounter any comment designed to alarm parent or child about the youngster's performance to date. There were no statements calculated to stop them in their tracks, to rattle their complacency, or to demand—with all the authority of teacher and school looming in the background—that a whole new leaf must be turned immediately or dire consequences will follow. To the contrary. It was as if teachers had practiced how to avoid giving offense, raising blood pressure, or causing mom and dad to confront Junior about the sorry state of his schoolwork." The consequences of this feel-good policy fall heaviest on poor and minority youngsters, who bear the brunt of what Finn calls "this unholy marriage of low expectation and high marks."[13]

The evidence is not merely anecdotal. A 1994 study, "What Do Student Grades Mean? Differences Across Schools," found that students in all socioeconomic groups seem to be "beneficiaries" of grade inflation. But the implications are most troubling for students from poorer schools. The study found that many students in schools with high rates of poverty report receiving above-average grades—mostly B's. Unfortunately, those grades seldom reflect high levels of actual achievement. Students in high-poverty schools were given A's for work that would have earned C's or D's in more affluent schools. Defenders of the system argue that the grades simply reflect student performance relative to each school's standards—but they also send a message of reassurance where none is warranted. Far from sending out alarms that students' reading and math abilities are woefully inadequate, the grading system implies that substandard work is actually "above average."

This system makes some sense if the students will always, throughout their lives and careers, be measured against the standard of their schools. But that is not the case; eventually they will have to confront a world where their A- and B-level skills will be revealed as inadequate. Ironically, the students most likely to suffer will be those with the best academic prospects. Rather than challenging them to live up to higher expectations, the system is satisfied with mediocrity or perhaps less. The educational ideology traps them in mediocrity as surely as their schoolmates are trapped in poverty.

This appears to be especially true among minority groups. A study by three academics of the attitudes and academic achievement of black, white, and Hispanic children found a disturbing gap between what parents thought their children were learning and the reality of their actual performance. When Harold Stevenson, Chuansheng Chen, and David Uttal spoke with black mothers of elementary students in Chicago, they found that mothers rated their child's skills and abilities quite high. They thought their children were doing very well in reading and mathematics. So did the kids. They told the researchers that they were working hard in reading and math and were doing well. But, the researchers later wrote, "their self-evaluations of their skills in reading and mathematics were unrelated to their actual level of achievement." The gap between their optimistic perception and the rather dismal actual performance, they wrote, "seems to indicate that the children had not received, or had not effectively incorporated, reliable and appropriate feedback about their performance in school."[14]

In other words, they were drifting toward failure. And no one had ever bothered to tell them.

Lashing the Critics

There are also larger political explanations for America's state of denial. When it is attacked, the educational establishment speaks with nearly a single voice. Wisconsin's teachers union, the Wisconsin Education Association Council, circulates fact sheets titled "Setting the Record Straight: Confronting Myths of Public School Failure," which dismisses criticism as "simplistic" and "distorted." Researchers for the National Education Association have set out a similar party line: There is no decline. Send money. Joining that refrain is the interlocking directorate of teachers colleges, boards of education, administrators, PTAs, and school boards—a vast network that is self-monitoring, self-verifying, and self-congratulating. Whatever differences in emphasis or style they might have, educationists turn as one on outsiders who question their competence or their judgment. Likely as not, those critics will find their character, their intelligence, and their morality questioned, while their substantive arguments are dismissed or ignored altogether. Writing in the mid-1950s, John Keats noted that his criticisms were likely to be brushed off, since "I have noticed that when a layman writes or speaks about public education, our professional educators tend to react in [several] ways. First, they may ignore him. Second, if they are sufficiently stung by his words to disagree, they may say, 'You are either uninformed or dishonest.' Third, if they agree with him, they may say, 'Your point of view is very interesting, but, shall we say, perhaps a little superficial?' "[15]

During the past century, this has become a familiar pattern. When Joseph Mayer Rice, an early education muckraker, documented the political manipulation and flat-out corruption of the schools of the 1890s, the reaction of the education establishment ranged from "chilling disdain to near-hysteria," according to historian Lawrence Cremin.[16] Using language that seems quite up-to-date in our latter-day school wars, Boston's *Journal of Education* accused Rice of sensationalism and depicted him as a carping journalist. A chorus of educationists attacked Rice for his "lack of classroom experience, inadequate evidence, and anti-public school bias," all of which "rendered him unfit to judge American education."[17]

This pattern has continued remarkably unchanged for the last century. The only form of comment that is acceptable from lay persons or parents is uncritical affirmation and enthusiasm for whatever policy happens to be in the ascendency at the moment, from the richness of diversity to "hands-on" science. When traditionalists criticized the emphasis of progressive educators on "life adjustment" in the 1950s, the educationists portrayed their critics in the most sinister light. In their public statements and journals, the educationists depicted outside criticism as evidence of a "calculated, far-reaching plot." Cremin recalls that this approach was "quickly taken up by progressives, and became the leitmotif of their counterattack during the next few years." The educationist establishment of the day put out pamphlets "directing attention to a new genre of ultra-rightists, frequently rabble-rousing citizens' groups that had entered the arena of educational policy making." In both language and approach, the attack on critics of "life adjustment" echoes current efforts to discredit critics of Outcome Based Education and other innovations of the 1990s. While Archibald Anderson, the editor of *Progressive Education* during the 1950s, acknowledged the existence of some "honest and sincere critics," he labeled others as "chronic tax conservationists," "congenital reactionaries," "witch-hunters," "super-patriots," "dogma peddlers," "race haters," and "academic conservatives."[18]

Arthur Bestor, who was by far the most influential critic of public education in the 1950s, noted nearly four decades ago the almost reflexive refusal of educationists to take their critics seriously. Even then, they sought to silence critics with the accusation: "You are an enemy of public schools."[19]

"It is a curiously perverse argument, which belongs to dictatorship, not to democracy," Bestor wrote. "When the citizen of a free state criticizes the policies of a political party, he is not attacking government itself. When he denounces a bureaucracy as incompetent, he is not saying that the work of the bureau ought not to be done and done well. We are fools if we allow a politician to tell us that we cannot attack him without undermining government. We are no less fools if we permit professional educationists to tell us that we cannot criticize their policies without becoming enemies of public schools."[20]

Bestor was also struck by the lack of internal debate among educationists and by the silence of educators in the face of wave after wave of failed fashions and fads. "To the scholar from an established discipline, one of the most shocking facts about the field of education is the almost complete absence of rigorous criticism from within," he wrote in the early 1950s. "Among scientists and scholars, criticism of another's findings is regarded as a normal and necessary part of the process of advancing knowledge."[21] But this was not true among educationists despite their pretensions to "expert" status. Educational journals, he wrote, were "almost devoid of critical reviews."

"The paean of praise that greets every novel program, the closing of ranks that occurs whenever a word of criticism is spoke from outside, is a symptom of the fact that independence of thought has ceased to be a virtue among professional educationists. The monolithic resistance to criticism reveals the existence and influence of what can only be described as an educational party-line . . ."

Hostile to internal dissent and reluctant to engage in honest self-criticism, educationism had developed an almost morbid antipathy to critics, which was reflected in their tendency to deny dissenters any semblance of legitimacy and in the viciousness and malice of their attacks. "The extreme unwillingness of professional educationists to submit their proposals to free public discussion and honest criticism," Bestor observed, "frequently assume the even uglier form of showering critics, no matter how upright and well-informed, with vituperation and personal abuse." Even eminent scholars who publish critiques could expect to be dismissed as "a peripatetic hatchet man," "a demagogue rather than a scholar," "a master of the pointed phrase rather than the finished thought," or tarred with guilt by association.

"This hushing up of criticism is an attitude that belongs, not to a company of independent scholars," Bestor wrote, "but to a bureaucracy, a party, a body united in defense of a vested interest."[22]

The refusal of educationists to admit the legitimacy of outside criticism has led to a situation in which critics who point out that children are shortchanged by shoddy educational practices are accused of "bashing" schools, while those most responsible for the mediocrity of the educational system are labeled . . . "child advocates."

In four decades, little has changed except the size and power of that vested interest and the identities of the "enemies of public schools." In the meantime, public education has increasingly turned away from the business of learning as it has embraced the feelings, attitudes, and personality adjustment of America's children.

DUMBING DOWN OUR SCHOOLS.

HOW DID EINSTEIN *FEEL?*

The California Learning Assessment System (CLAS) is perhaps the nation's widest-scale test of so-called "performance based" and "outcome based" learning. Nearly a million and half of the state's fourth, eighth, and tenth graders took the test in 1994. Students taking the test are graded on a six-point scale. On the writing section, a score of one would indicate that the student's sample was "brief, incoherent, disorganized and undeveloped." A student could earn a score of six for writing that is deemed to be "confident, purposefully coherent and clearly focused."

In May 1994, the *New York Times* published three eighth graders' answers to this question on the state's reading test: "Think about Einstein as a person and a scientist. In the split 'profile' and below it, use symbols, images, drawings, *and/or words* to give your ideas about Einstein the person and Einstein the scientist."[1] [emphasis added]

Students worked with two pictures of Einstein's head in profile (one head was labeled "scientist," the other "the person"), like a drawing in a coloring book, with space left blank to fill in their ideas. The California Learning Assessment System, in other words, is a test of *writing* skills with a test that *does not require students to write complete sentences* (much less paragraphs). By eighth grade, students should theoretically be able to express ideas and thoughts without drawing pictures, but the California test lets students use "symbols, images, and drawings" in place of language.

In the examples cited by the *Times*, one student who described Einstein "the scientist" as "smart, hopful [sic], commonsents [sic], and easy going," and Einstein "the person" as "sad, lonely, happy, postive [sic], loving," was awarded two points for his analysis. Another student who described Einstein as "smart" (next to a picture of a lightbulb) was awarded five out of a possible six points.

Another student drew pictures to illustrate Einstein "the scientist" as "trapped" and "blind." Another picture, apparently intended to be a sheet of music, illustrates "a masterpiece such as a syphony [sic]." The student also describes the scientist as "determined." Einstein "the person" is depicted as "peaceful" (accompanied by a hand-drawn peace sign);

"open-minded" (illustrated by open windows); "beautiful inside" (a butterfly); "conscious-alive" (depicted by what looks like a picture of an electrocardiogram) and "a grain of sand" (pictured as a dot).

This student was awarded the highest possible score—a perfect six out of six—in spite of the misspellings and the absence of any reference to Einstein's scientific contributions. His role in the nuclear age, his theories of time, matter, energy, and relativity are all ignored in a test that asks junior high schoolers how Einstein *felt* rather than what he *thought* or *learned.*

California's educationists defend the tests by comparing them with multiple-choice tests for which students can be easily coached. But that, of course, is not the only alternative. Knowledge can be measured by tests that require written answers, including essays. Such tests are, however, time-consuming to prepare and grade. But the politics of testing is driven by the politics of teaching. An official with the Association of California School Administrators told the *Times* that the test could be a powerful tool to change the entire educational system in the state. "Tests drive curriculum," one educationist told the paper. "By changing the test, that is one of the surest ways to change what goes on in the classroom."

CHAPTER 4

FEELINGS

The course is officially called "Human Interaction," but is referred to by its cheery acronym "Hi!" in places like Petaluma, California, where it is used to help nudge "students to declare their values in front of peers, giving them a safe environment for testing their choices." It is a course that warns kids against "denying your feelings" and urges them to "share" intimate details of their lives with peers.[1]

Handout sheets ask students whether a "close relative" has ever been an alcoholic or suffered from mental illness, how much money their parents make, and whether students "feel OK about crying" and "allow" themselves to do so. Were they "happy most of the time?" Students are also asked: "What presidential candidate did your mom vote for in 1980?" and "Which of these can't your father do: touch his toes, do a head stand, rewire a lamp, replace the spark plugs, sew a shirt?" Did students "walk, bike or use public transportation whenever possible?" Did they recycle? What did they eat when their families "stop for lunch at a fast-food restaurant?"

School district officials insisted that personal questions were not meant to be aired in classroom sessions, but they also admitted that this message has not always been clear. At least two teachers required students to fill out such "work sheets" complete with names and answers. The district's assistant superintendent admitted to columnist Debra Saunders that once such "work sheets" were distributed, it was quite possible that such questions would come up in class for discussion.[2]

A school publication explains: "Besides the handouts, one of the major activities of this section is what we call a 'Media Quilt.' Students are given a blank piece of white paper. They go home and cut out from a magazine all the images of 'male' and 'female' (depending on the student's own sex). We assemble the quilt in class and discuss the media messages. We also explore 'negative space' by discussing what is NOT portrayed by the media." The school explains that this is a "power activity for looking at values that we might not even consciously want!"

Some educationists might describe this sort of things as an example of "higher-order thinking skills" or even "critical thinking." But calling pasting up collages of fashion models a "higher-order skill" might strain the credibility of even a veteran educrat. So the officials in Petaluma have raised the stakes. The assistant superintendent explained to Saunders that the school board had approved the "Hi" curriculum because its members "felt this was a matter of life and death." The recycling habits and the income of their students' parents were issues freighted with mortal significance. "If students don't have the tools to deal with the pressures" and dangers of life, he told Saunders, the school board fears they "would make the wrong choices and it would be fatal."[3] Not only do children have to be self-actualized and put in touch with their feelings, but if we don't do so, *they'll die.*

A number of parents predictably objected to such activities, arguing that the course invaded the privacy of families and sought to usurp some of the functions of parents. "They want to be surrogate parents," complained one. School officials, however, brushed off such complaints, while confirming the substance of the objections. The assistant superintendent told Saunders that it was "pretty generally believed" that parents did not do a good job of communicating with their children, so the schools needed to intervene to get "communication" going again. So ninth-graders are given a "work sheet" on "Family Systems," which describes "open" families as "pure democracy," while "closed" families are labeled "hierarchical," a homework assignment which one can easily imagine generates all manner of "communications" between teens and their parents.

Such programs express the widely held assumption among educationists that kids are frail and easily damaged psychological growths that are in constant danger of being crushed and therefore need to be freed from an excessively disciplined or stifling environment, within their own families, in schools, and in their own feelings.

The message is similar in the popular self-esteem/antidrug program known as Quest. Quest insists that "The Family SHOULD Be Like an Elephant—All Ears." In one Quest activity, students keep track of their feelings over a twenty-four-hour period with an "Emotion Clock." Another exercise, entitled (not surprisingly) "My Emotions," asks students to record "everything that makes you feel good or uncomfortable for one day." Other activities include a "Mood Continuum" and a "Rainbow of Feelings." To help them deal with parents who might not be in touch with their own feelings (or not especially eager to honor and celebrate the emotions of their teenagers), Quest provides helpful guides in the form of scenarios of family discussions and disputes. Students are encouraged to play roles in these vignettes. Professor William Kilpatrick quoted one mother of a student in a Quest program observing that "It seems as if the parents were always put in a bad light. The story would be about a father and son, say; and the father was *always* overbearing, *always* too strict, *always* unfair."[4]

Kilpatrick explains that this is not an accident. "Any parent who has traditional ideas about right and wrong and the conduct of family life is likely to suffer by comparison with facilitative teachers," he wrote. " 'Your parents don't understand you, but we do' seems to be an implicit message in the affective classroom."[5] Also not surprisingly, such programs tend to be quite popular with many youngsters since they focus on their favorite obsession (themselves) and their favorite preconceptions (that it's their life and adults can't tell them what to do).

In academic terms, such classes are hardly difficult. But then, they are not supposed to be difficult. Their message is that there are no fixed standards against which kids should be used to measure their shortcomings, no arduous choices to be made to grow in moral stature.

You are fine the way you are.

The Psychological Classroom

The mother of a Michigan fourth grader describes an exercise in her son's class: "In this lesson, the teacher instructs the students to empty their thoughts, close their eyes, place their finger in the center of their forehead, sit up straight with their feet flat on the floor and breath deeply in through the nose and out from the mouth. The breathing is repeated several times. At the end of this, the teacher no longer prompted the students but instructed them to follow along with a tape recording she provided. On the tape, a man's deep, slow voice instructed the students through basically the same breathing techniques. The tape taught the children how to take a mini-vacation. They were instructed they would be leaving and visiting a beach with waves and ocean sounds. They were told they could smell the air and feel the sand beneath their feet. There they met a special friend (a lifeguard). They are told they could return to this friend anytime they needed him."[6]

After the meditation class, the mother complained that her son, who had been a good sleeper, began to be afraid to go to bed alone and woke up in the middle of the night. Whatever the consequences (and they probably were not usually traumatic), the most obvious and important question is, what is something like this doing in the classroom in the first place? Although educationists would deny that they are practicing formal psychotherapy, many of the exercises bear an eerie similarity. Dr. Harold M. Voth, a faculty member of the Karl Menninger School of Psychiatry, who has reviewed programs such as "Skills for Living" and the "Quest Skills for Living Program," concluded that they were effectively ersatz therapy in the hands of educators whose credentials and qualifications were, at best, questionable. "The questions which are asked by these exercises," Dr. Voth wrote, "are designed to stimulate associative and introspective processes, which without any question will bring to the surface suppressed and even repressed mental content. To introduce such practices in such a large and unstructured scale, and to have these exercises administered by persons untrained in the profession of psychology and psychiatry is dangerous and should not be done. . . ." Moreover, he warned, "There is no assurance that all teachers are free of psychopathology. Exposing the child to the broad issues introduced by the Quest exercises and orchestrated by teachers of unknown mental health and stability places the child in a position of great risk."[7]

Despite such concerns, children are frequently taught that they should turn to the schools' many "experts," rather than parents, when they are faced with difficulties in their lives. Perhaps most troubling of all for many parents is the tendency of schools to encourage children to report family problems to peers, counselors, social workers, and school psychologists. The Michigan select senate committee found that the so-called Michigan Model "is peppered with examples where students are steered away from their families as their first line of defense in life situations. Instead, they are directed to their peers, counselors and other health care workers as providers of advice and direction."[8]

And Other Nuggets of Wisdom

Such courses are increasingly common in the schools, and they are likely to become even more widespread as educationists insist that schools need to be as concerned with a child's emotions as his or her mind. As one educationist proclaimed in the 1960s: "Historically the school has taught the three R's and it has left much of the process of socialization and the development of values—at least officially—to the home, church, and community. It is conceivable that we may someday see the home formally assuming the student's intellectual education, with the school becoming primarily a center for socialization."[9] The notion that the schools should become substitute families/churches/communities and concern themselves with the psyches of their students is as deeply ingrained in educationist lore as any doctrine.

In 1938, the Educational Policies Commission listed four objectives for education, including education for "self-realization" and for "good human relationships." In the 1950s, educrats insisted that the schools' main job was helping children become well adjusted. In 1962, the influential Association of Supervision and Curriculum Development devoted its yearbook to the theme of *Perceiving, Behaving, Becoming*, which proclaimed the importance of the learner's "self-concept" and its enhancement through exercises in self-actualization and self-enhancement, such as encounter groups. The new ideas, labeled "humanistic" by their supporters, were enthusiastically seized upon by the growing ranks of guidance counselors, school psychologists, and educationist psychobabblers who wanted to expand their roles in education. In 1960, a Canadian visitor to American teachers colleges, Charles Anderson, noted the growing popularity of the new field of "guidance," which struck him "as a hybrid melange of watered-down child psychology, mental health, tests and measurements, and non-practical clinical psychology." He also noticed an interesting corollary: "The less distinguished an institution, the greater was the proliferation of courses in guidance."[10]

Another critic, James Koerner, was appalled when he sat in on education courses, in which "Cases of disturbed individuals ranging from deep psychoses to mild neuroses are often discussed by instructors and certainly by students who have no competence in the subject and no business toying with it." The implication of the courses was that the teacher-trainees, "most of whom will not go beyond the master's degree" in education, would now have the "right to engage in psychological diagnosis and perhaps even therapy in public schools." Koerner charged, "The utterly nebulous nature of the entire field of guidance counseling encourages an amateurish attempt in the course work to probe into areas of human motivation, guilt complexes, sexual adjustment, and the like in search of the true reason why Johnny sassed his teacher." Koerner was also struck by the "distressing lack of respect in these courses for the rights of privacy of both parent and student. Too much time is spent in fruitless and questionable attempts at the psychological analysis of student behavior, as well as impudent speculations about parents and home life."[11]

But Koerner had glimpsed only the beginnings of a huge industry within the schools, as well as the ongoing shift away from cognitive learning to a focus on the "affective domain." By 1977, the Association of Supervision and Curriculum Development's yearbook was devoted entirely to *Feeling, Valuing, and the Art of the Growing: Insight into the Affective.*[12] "If education is concerned with the total development of the individual," one of its authors insisted, "then it must go beyond the facilitation of cognitive development. Education must become involved in the child's personal development—his feelings, emotions, values, and interpersonal relationships. This aspect of humanistic education is becoming known as affective education. . . ."[13] The yearbook described affective education in language that is a cross between a pitch for a cruise ship and an encounter group: "It is our contention that schools can help persons become feeling, valuing, and growing individuals. Schools can provide settings designed to evoke feelings—settings in which persons can experience pleasure, passion, delight, and spontaneity. . . . Schools can provide settings designed for the art of growing—settings in which extending ideas, commitment, striving, revising, transforming, and developing wholeness are evident."[14]

The yearbook goes on to make it clear that schools should no longer be in the dreary and limited business of simply teaching children how to read and write. "Literacy is not good enough," it declared. "More is needed to live a personally satisfying life." Not content with math, science, history, geography, and literature, the educationist authors of the yearbook declared their preference for an alternative philosophy in which students are educated in "*perceiving* from many and varied perspectives; *communicating* thoughts and feelings in reciprocally open, honest, and constructive ways; *loving* by spending oneself in trusting, empathetic, and mutually enhancing relationships; *problem solving* and *decision making* which consider varied alternatives and their consequences; *creating* for the generation of innovative possibilities in all facets of human thought, feeling, and action; and *valuing* to continually determine one's own livable code of ethics."[15]

Their vision of the new education was a stew of self-actualization, mixed with psychobabble and a dash of rhetoric about diversity. "We believe," they insisted, "that for maximum learning and for maximum richness of living, each person must be valued for himself with his uniqueness recognized and not only respected but revered: *I am a self and you are a self and I don't want to be made to feel guilty if I am not like you nor should you be made to feel guilty if you are unlike me.*"[16] [emphasis added] When children would actually have time to learn anything remained unclear.

One of the earliest exercises in the new curriculum of feelings was the rap session or encounter group, in which students with "no assigned subject matter" or agenda would sit around and "talk about themselves or whatever is of concern to them." Educationist Cecil Patterson insisted that from these meaningful experiences, students could learn:

To listen to others
To accept and respect others
To understand others
To identify and become aware of one's feelings
To express one's feelings
To become aware of the feelings of others
To experience being accepted and understood by others
To recognize basic commonalties in human experience
To explore oneself
To develop greater awareness of oneself
To be oneself
To change oneself in the direction of being more the self
  one wants to be
To help others accept themselves
To help others understand themselves and each other

Patterson explains that in such groups, "learning occurs without the input of external content...."[17] In other words, it is totally self-indulgent. No ideas are offered by adults, no role models presented. No arguments about what might constitute the "good" are considered, nor is the possibility even entertained that such a "good" might exist and that the students might wish to strive for it. Neither literature nor history are offered as guideposts, only the apparently infallible compass of each youngster's "feelings."

THE RELIGION OF SELF-ESTEEM

Visitors to the school are greeted by a cheerful poster covered with pictures of clapping hands. It declares: "We Applaud Ourselves." For Lillian G. Katz, a professor of early childhood education, the poster symbolizes the new culture of American schools. So does the class project she observed in which first graders from an affluent suburban school prepared booklets titled "All About Me." The first page was devoted to the child's family, but the second page was headed: "What I like to eat"; the next, "What I like to watch on TV"; the next, "What I want for a present"; another was "Where I want to go on vacation."

As Professor Katz later wrote: "The booklet, like thousands of others I have encountered around the country, had no page headings such as 'what I want to know more about,' 'what I am curious about,' 'what I want to solve,' or even 'to make.'"

Instead, the focus of the project was on self-gratification. "Not once," she noted, "was the child asked to play the role of producer, investigator, initiator, explorer, experimenter or problem-solver." Like the poster that celebrated self-applause, the booklet reflected the almost obsessive focus of modern educationists on the self-esteem of children, on making them feel good about themselves. While both poster and booklet were intended to raise students' esteem, they did so, Katz wrote, "by directing their attention inward. The poster urged self-congratulation; it made no reference to possible ways of earning applause—by considering the feelings or needs of others."[1]

In another school, a classroom of fourth graders repeats the mantra of self-affirmation: "I am me and I am enough," the slogan of a socially challenged therapeutic dragon named Pumsy. The "lovable young dragon puppet," who is used in roughly 17,000 elementary schools across the country, encourages children to learn "positive thinking skills" and to avoid "negative self-talk" as they move from their "mud" minds to their "sparkle" minds in which they are creative and feel good about themselves.[2]

Among educationists in the 1990s, self-esteem is an article of faith with almost limitless application. California's Task Force to Promote Self-

Esteem, for instance, declared that a good self-concept "inoculates us against the lures of crime, violence, substance abuse, teen pregnancy, child abuse, chronic welfare dependency and educational failure." It left out acne and athlete's foot.

Perhaps because the fear of working children too hard has become a preoccupation both of parents and educationists, self-esteem has virtually become an official ideology of American education: All children must feel good about themselves no matter what. Asian cultures, Harold Stevenson found, have an unambiguous attitude toward what they expect from their schools: "to teach children academic skills and knowledge—how to read, to write, to apply mathematics, to know something of history and government, and so on." But Americans have no such clear ideas about the role of schools. Instead, "many Americans place a higher priority on life adjustment and the enhancement of self-esteem than on academic learning."[3] Among many educators, the importance of self-esteem is treated as an article of faith. David Dewhurst, a philosopher, recalls a seminar he attended where participants "took it to be the case that one of the maladies of the school system is a pervasive lack of self-esteem among school pupils."

"How did the teachers know that their pupils, some of them, or many of them, lacked self-esteem?" he asked. "Not, apparently, on the basis of the students saying so. It is an interesting fact that those to whom a low self-esteem is imputed are unlikely to say, 'I lack self-esteem' or 'I have low self-esteem.' Typically it is the teachers who say of the students that they lack self-esteem; the students do not say it of themselves."

Indeed, there is little empirical evidence that American students suffer from a crisis of self-esteem. To the contrary, international studies would suggest that American students not only feel far better about themselves than their foreign counterparts, but that they feel far better about themselves and their abilities than reality might warrant. (American students who rank last in international comparisons of math abilities, for instance, rank first when asked how they feel about their math abilities.)

But it is impossible to understand America's public schools without appreciating the extent to which educationists will go to enhance, protect, shield, and inflate the self-image of the nation's students. This therapeutic mindset (which often has more in common with the self-help movement than the academy) underlies much of the hostility toward what educationists imagine was the excessive intellectualism of traditional education. It also drives the attack on grades, on academic standards, and increasingly defines the peculiar personality of American education.

Exactly as They Are

Like so many similar programs, the focus of *Just Because I Am: A Child's Book of Affirmation*, is on feeling good about yourself.[4] The authors advertise the book as "a complete course on self-esteem." As the authors write in the introduction to the *Leader's Guide*, "Every child deserves to believe that she or he is truly a wonder. Every child *needs* to believe this." To the authors, self-esteem is not only an entitlement, it is a necessity— and not just one necessity among many, but *the* necessity for childhood, the *ne plus ultra* of health and happiness. "Nothing," they declare, "is as important as self-esteem to a child's well-being and success."[5] Absolutely nothing. Not their parents, not their economic status, and certainly not the ability to read and write. The authors seem genuinely to believe they have found the Rosetta stone to human satisfaction, the one formula for social reconstruction and personal salvation. "Positive self-esteem," they explain, "increases a child's ability to be happy, healthy, and well adjusted. Children's feelings about themselves affect all the choices they make and shape their plans, hopes and dreams for the future. Many social and psychological problems can be traced to a lack of self-esteem."[6]

Such statements would not be regarded as controversial among educationists of the 1990s. The authors of the self-esteem course argue that self-esteem, like maternal love, should be unconditional. That means, they write, that it should have nothing to do with the behavior, attitudes, or performance of the child. Nothing the child does to himself or others should forfeit or undermine his/her sense of themselves as a "wonder." Among the "core beliefs" laid down by the authors is that "all children have the right to feel good about themselves *exactly as they are.*" [emphasis added] If that is not clear enough, they add as a separate and stand-alone "core belief": "That a child's value is unconditional. Nothing the child does, says, or chooses can change it."[7]

Self-esteem is therefore not the product of achievement, or hard work, or the mastery of a difficult task. It is a given. No matter what. Taken to its extreme, that would mean that laziness, venality, dishonesty, and disobedience should have no effect on one's self-esteem, although the authors would probably insist that if kids had high self-esteem, they would not be guilty of any of those things. A child who was dishonest, they would argue, was dishonest because of low self-esteem. The argument thus becomes circular and can never be disproved.

Like many educationists, the authors of the self-esteem course believe that any attempt to link feeling good about oneself to achievement is both counterproductive and potentially damaging to the child's psyche. They therefore devote the first chapter to teaching children "that it is who they are, not what they do, that is important."

Teachers are told to discourage children from saying "I'm a good soccer player" or "I'm a good singer," because "The danger in letting children define themselves in terms of what they are 'good at' is that we can't all be good at everything, nor should we try. . . . We want to anchor self-esteem firmly to the child himself or herself so that no matter what the performance might be, the self-esteem remains high." The emphasis, therefore, should be on feelings rather than performance. In place of "I'm a good soccer player," children are to be encouraged to say, "I like to play," and in place of "I'm a good singer," "I like to sing."

Class activities include making a banner declaring: I LIKE ME! on which a child can "celebrate his or her own uniqueness."[8]

Throughout the book, the pattern remains the same: The child is encouraged to focus on himself, his feelings, his needs and instincts and not allow himself to be influenced by any external standards. Chapter 2, entitled "This Is My Body," is designed to "make children aware of their instincts and teach them to honor their needs in appropriate ways."[9] Children read: "My body talks to me . . . To tell me what I need."[10] The chapter makes no suggestions that the child should ever talk back to his/her body, nor does it suggest that at times it might be better to encourage a young child to control his needs rather than "honor" them. All of his instincts are not, after all, infallible and all of his appetites not worthy of being "honored." But the authors of *Just Because I Am* insist that children be put in touch with their strong feelings and to affirm them because "These feelings belong to me."

"Children," write the authors, "need to have access to the complete range of their feelings. They need to be taught that all of their feelings are important signals." They suggest that teachers make use of a "feelings jar" in which children are encouraged to put "items symbolizing various feelings: crushed pieces of aluminum foil or cut-up pieces of ribbon for anger, sequins for tears," etc. The goal of this activity is to "reinforce the childrens' right to have and feel their feelings." Teachers are also encouraged to affirm their own feelings by sharing "with the children your own strong feelings about situations in your life."[11]

Subsequent lessons are designed to "familiarize children with their anger." Parents are advised of various ways they might want to handle an angry child. Rather than telling a child to get a grip, parents are urged to say things like: "Anger is a part of living," "Wow, you sure are angry," and "I understand how you feel and that's okay." When dealing with sadness, the authors suggest that parents tell their children, "It's important to listen to your sadness."[12]

Other lessons include "I Can Make Decisions" and "I Have Needs." In the former, the authors write that "Children need to have a sense of power over some of the things that affect them directly. . . . When we let them make decisions, we are showing them that we trust them and their abilities."[13] The ideology that underlies all of this is thoroughly romantic: The child creates values, the child sets standards; the child is naturally good and far wiser than adults would imagine. Seldom, however, has child worship been taken further. The mavens of self-esteem declare that "Children often know what feels 'right' and 'wrong,' 'good' and 'bad.'" So instead of setting limits, or rules, or assuming that adults occasionally do indeed have greater insight, knowledge, and prudence than a child, parents are told that children "need us to honor their experience and intuition."[14]

Children are told the same thing:

> I can make decisions.
> Sometimes I say "yes."
> I say 'yes' to playing and dancing.
> I say 'yes' to laughing and singing. . . .
> When it feels right to me.[15]

When it feels right to me. There is no other standard other than the self; and within the self, apparently, no higher standard than their feelings.

In the lesson on "I Have Needs," the authors argue that it is necessary to "introduce children to the concept of needs" and "to help children become aware of their needs"[16]—as if this would, indeed, be news to most youngsters. Young children, after all, seldom have to be told to be aware of their instincts; they *are* their instincts. Nor do they usually have to be told that they have strong feelings. All children are egotists, who genuinely believe the world revolves around them. As infants, they could be described as being comprised solely of needs, to which the world caters. It is only later they discover the rest of the world, a world that is not part of them and that is not controlled by their wants or desires. This used to be called growing up.

Children who emerge from twelve years or more of such courses may or may not have a healthy "self-concept," but it seems possible that they will also be self-satisfied egotists. When *Just Because I Am*, for example, lists fifty ways "to Take Care of Yourself," only two refer to doing anything for anyone else; the rest are a litany of self-indulgence: "play with your favorite toys," "get a hug," "give yourself a big hug," "wrap yourself in a blanket," "say nice things to yourself," "learn how to talk about your feelings," "be angry when you need to be," and, of course, "Celebrate You!"[17]

Such lists illustrate what Lillian Katz calls the confusion between self-esteem and narcissism. For all their expansive claims, the programs are curiously stunted in their focus and almost inevitably get tangled in their own inanity and trivia. One popular exercise for enhancing self-esteem among kindergartners, Katz notes, "consisted of large paper-doll figures, each having a balloon containing a sentence stem that began 'I am special because. . . .' The children completed the sentence with phrases such as 'I can color,' or 'I can ride a bike,' and 'I like to play with my friends.'" This was all reassuring, noted Katz, but "these children are not likely to believe for very long that they are special because they can color or ride a bike. What are they going to think when they discover just how trivial these criteria for being special are?"

Katz also contrasts the atmosphere in a rural British school she visited with the typical therapeutic American kindergarten. A bulletin board display in the British classroom read: "We are a Class Full of Bodies. Here Are Our Details." Katz reported that the display was "filled with bar graphs showing birth dates, weight and heights, eye colors, numbers of lost teeth, shoe sizes and other data of the entire class." The students themselves worked to take measurements and prepare the graphs, Katz found, as well as learning about concepts like "averages, trends and ranges."

In contrast, Katz wrote, the American kindergarten she visited had a bulletin board displaying student comments about a recent visit to a dairy farm. "Each sentence began with the words 'I liked.' For example, 'I liked the cows' and 'I liked the milking machine.' No sentences began 'What surprised me was . . . ' and 'What I want to know more about is. . . .'"[18]

Beyond the grimly absurd attack on academic values in such programs is the baseness of their values, emphasizing needs but not obligations, feelings but not thoughts, self-gratification rather than self-sacrifice, self-indulgence rather than restraint, self-satisfaction rather than self-knowledge—all of which adds up to a particularly undiluted form of self-absorption. The child is taught to focus on him or herself almost exclusively; the needs of others are somewhere over a distant horizon. The child and his appetites—his emotions, feelings, impulses—are the center of this universe and the requirements of family, community, and others are decidedly secondary.

Despite their enthusiasm for self-esteem, educationists really know very little about the relationship between self-esteem and academic achievement. Quite a number of studies show that students with high levels of achievement generally feel good about themselves, while students who do poorly have a more negative self-image. But here we run into the difference between *correlation* and *causation.* Merely because there is a correlation—or because there is some relationship—between two events does not necessarily mean that one *causes* the other. For example: There is a correlation between increases in the consumption of ice cream (in summer) and the increase in rapes. But there is no evidence that one *causes* the other. Other factors obviously come into play.

In the case of self-esteem and academic performance, the picture is even more clouded. Before leaping to the conclusion that self-esteem results in high performance, might the reverse not be true? Could it be possible that high achievement leads to self-confidence and a healthy self-image, while failure and lack of achievement leads to low self-esteem? Was Michael Jordan a superstar because he felt confident in his self-worth? Or did he feel good about himself because he was a superstar? Would a survey that found that members of the Dallas Cowboys had high self-esteem tell us the secret of *how* they won their Super Bowls? Or would it tell us the *result* of winning the championship game? Could it, in fact, work both ways? Could high self-esteem be both the basis of achievement and its result?

The answer is that educators simply don't know. Studies that measure the relationship between self-esteem and achievement are unable to untangle this puzzle. Nor can studies rule out other factors, such as value systems, family relations, worth ethic, or intellectual capacity that might account for the way high- and low-achieving students feel about themselves. As one researcher noted: "Bright students typically hold themselves in higher regard and perform better than do students who are less bright. Thus, self-esteem might be a simply a by-product of ability status and may exert little influence on school performance."[19]

What does the research tell us about the effects of self-esteem on motivation? That failure depresses some, while it may stimulate others. Defeat may discourage one youngster, while providing the next with the necessary goad to greater effort. A setback that depresses student B may energize student C. Researchers have also found that while high performance results in high self-esteem in some people, the result is not universal. In other words, we really know very little about the interplay between self-esteem and achievement. What we do know is that the link may be delicate and there may be considerable danger in tinkering with it.

In particular, there is little research to justify the heavy emphasis on self-esteem among very young children. Most studies have found that preschool children and those in the early elementary grades have robust self-images. Psychology professor Thomas Moeller writes that children of this age "tend to exhibit what we might call the 'Superboy/Supergirl Syndrome.' They believe that they are wonderful and that they can do anything."[20] One study has found that children's achievement in arithmetic begins to affect their "academic self-concept" by second grade, indicating that the image that children have of themselves is formed by how well they do, rather than the other way around.

The picture becomes much more blurred as children get older. While numerous studies show a correlation between self-esteem and achievement, there is little evidence that a high self-concept either leads to higher academic achievement or that self-esteem is necessary for academic success. Theoretically, it might be possible to conduct experiments to try to determine whether high self-esteem in and of itself helps students do better in school. But such studies are rare and as usual with the social sciences the evidence is incomplete or inconclusive. Some people with low self-esteem can be both creative and successful, and their success may stem precisely from their insecurities and lack of self-confidence. On the other hand, there is ample evidence that some students have a highly developed sense of self despite mediocre accomplishments.

There are other reasons for caution as well. Even though there have been volumes of studies showing a correlation between self-esteem and achievement, most research has found that the correlation is of generally low magnitude. For example, a 1982 review of 20 studies involving 48,000 students found a "quite modest correlation" between self-esteem and achievement. In fact, the researchers found that "only four percent of the variation in school achievement is accounted for by variation in self-concept."[21] A 1980 study looked at 300 different studies of the relationship between self-esteem and achievement and once again found only a very modest relationship.

When another researcher added a measure of self-esteem to other predictors of academic achievement, including social class and intelligence, self-esteem was found to account for only an additional 3 percent of the variation in academic performance. As another researcher explained: "This means that most of the variation in achievement we observe in classrooms—97 percent of it . . . can be explained by influences other than those traditionally associated with the notion of self-concept."[22]

Summing up what researchers know about self-esteem, Professor Thomas G. Moeller drew four major conclusions:

1. The definition of self esteem is "vague, often misunderstood."
2. "There is little direct evidence that U.S. children suffer from a lack of self-esteem."
3. There is little "if any evidence that children's academic performance is causally determined by their global self-concept." Noted Moeller: "There may indeed be benefits to helping children feel good about themselves but improving academic performance is not likely to be one of them."
4. That "research consistently indicates that children's academic self-concept seems to be determined, at least in part, by their academic performance, especially in the early elementary years. It thus seems important to help children do well academically during those years."

"All of this indicates," Moeller concludes, "that massive efforts to improve the global self-esteem of children (particularly in the early elementary school years) are misplaced. The research suggests that rather than worrying about developing programs to improve self-esteem, elementary teachers would profit more by focusing their efforts on devising better ways of teaching children basic skills and on helping young children develop higher levels of achievement motivation."

At a minimum, the uncertainties, gaps, and flat-out contradictions in research on self-esteem would seem to argue for a good deal of caution in implementing sweeping policies regarding competition and self-esteem.

We know that in some cases, anxiety causes failure and losing the race may result in dejection. But anxiety can also lead to success, and losing may merely be prologue to victory. In the one case, it is possible that eliminating anxiety may encourage achievement. Likewise, abolishing defeat may raise spirits. But it may also dull ambition that leads to effort and success. This would seem to suggest modesty in formulating policies that tinker with the reward systems in the schools. But humility runs counter to the impulses of educationists.

The Lotus-Eaters

The educationists' approach to self-esteem is also based on an oddly narrow and naive view not only of motivation, but of what it means to be human. Such courses raise self-affirmation to a position of absolute dominance, eclipsing other values, ambitions, and aspirations. The child is absolved of guilt or shame, or at least any guilt that might affect his self-concept or his self-valuation. But he is also deprived of any reason for growth or change. Such courses do not encourage children to think in terms of goals they might wish to reach or things about themselves and others they might wish to improve.

Indeed, if you are absolutely and unconditionally satisfied with yourself regardless of what you do, why do anything? Why write books? Paint masterpieces? Build cathedrals? Launch enterprises? Perhaps men and women did push the limits of knowledge and human freedom and creative endeavor because they felt so good about themselves. But perhaps some of them did so precisely because they felt incomplete without the struggle. Perhaps some of them did not regard themselves as unconditionally wonderful without accomplishing something worthy of their ambitions. Who knows, for example, how many of the great novels or poems or masterpieces were written by people who had high self-esteem "no matter what they do"? It seems easier to argue rather that microbes were discovered and rivers spanned by men and women who were in some way or another driven to prove something, who were not satisfied that they were "truly a wonder" without doing something wonderful. Try to imagine *The Trial* written by a Franz Kafka who believed that he had "the right to feel good about himself exactly as he was."

All of this is part of the mysterious alchemy of human striving. As harmful as the suggestion might seem to educationists, insecurity can breed remarkable beauty and insight. Even a cursory knowledge of history would indicate that it is precisely that itch of self-doubt that provides the spur to human advance. Take away the struggle, the doubts, and part of the chemistry of humanity is dissolved. A nation of explorers, discoverers, and freedom fighters becomes a nation of lotus-eaters and navel admirers.

Whether the programs of self-esteem are motivated by a romantic view of childhood, by adult guilt, or simply by a desire to spare children pain, it is increasingly obvious that these eminently well-intentioned efforts often have unintended consequences. Members of the generation that braved the Depression and World War II were so anxious to spare their own children the deprivations of their youth that they created the pampered generation of the baby boomers. The boomers (and Generation X), in turn, seem determined to spare *their* children the emotional and psychological privations they imagined that they might have suffered in their own youth. While the Depression generation hastened to make sure the boomers would never lack material possessions, today's parents seem anxious to spare their children the stress, anxiety, and pressures of their youth. Neither of the elder generations seem to have foreseen what such indulgence might mean for the younger generations which not only have been deprived of the adversity of the previous generation, but also of the opportunities to test themselves against those challenges.

Trying to understand the courage and character of the English miners of the 1930s, whose lives he had been observing, George Orwell speculated about the source of their strength and dignity in the face of adversity. "The truth is," he wrote in *The Road to Wigan Pier*, "that many of the qualities we admire in human beings can only function in opposition to some kind of disaster, pain or difficulty; but the tendency of mechanical progress is to eliminate disaster, pain and difficulty."[23] While no one would argue that every effort should not be made to reduce disasters and pain, Orwell's point about the moral consequences of dealing with difficulties is a crucial insight into the way the human soul develops and grows. The notion that parents and teachers can (or should) create an environment in which children always succeed, observed educational psychologist Sylvia Rimm, is a "fallacy."

"Children who learn to lose without being devastated and use failure experiences to grow," writes Rimm, "will achieve in the classroom and in society. Learning to compete is central to achievement in our schools."[24]

Self-Esteem versus Confidence

Such moral and mental strength is not what the educationists call "self-esteem." A far better term would be *confidence*. Rather than beginning with the child's obsession with himself and his feelings, confidence begins with effort and grows by overcoming challenges. In the great education debates, the alternative to "self-esteem" is not a callous disregard for children's attitudes. The alternative to a vacuous obsession with feeling good about oneself is the idea of confidence built on achievement. Here we find one of the great cultural divides in American education: Schools that are intent on building *confidence* will insist on high academic standards; schools concerned with *self-esteem* will fear to ask too much. This is precisely what Los Angeles' legendary math teacher Jaime Escalante was talking about when he said:

> Our schools today ... tend to look upon disadvantaged minority students as though they were on the verge of a mental breakdown, to be protected from any undue stress. ... Ideas like this are not just false. They are the kiss of death for minority youth and, if allowed to proliferate, will significantly stall the advancement of minorities.[25]

Escalante is one of the gifted and committed teachers who knows that a child who masters a difficult problem or surmounts obstacles does not simply feel good about himself, he develops something far more powerful. Confidence is the knowledge that one can accomplish one's goals; it is a faith that is based on achieving something tangible. Such faith grows with the knowledge that a task can be accomplished more easily as one becomes more familiar with it. A student who discovers that sounds can be decoded into words with meanings or who solves a complicated math problem lays the foundation for a sense of himself that is both enduring and solid. *Strive, succeed, build confidence, and strive again.* No one has ever managed to improve upon that formula. The Greeks defined happiness as "The exercise of vital powers along lines of excellence in a life affording them scope." That could also be a working definition of confidence—a far cry from the self-indulgent, no-strings-attached narcissism of what passes for self-esteem in America's public schools.

The Problem of Competition

But the emphasis on self-esteem is not simply about education, or even about the psychological health of children. It is also about equity, one of the parallel obsessions of the American school. Unlike many of those implementing the self-esteem programs in schools across the country, educationist Martin V. Covington is familiar with what the academic research shows and does not show about self-esteem. Indeed, he has the rare good grace to acknowledge that many of the studies of the relationship of self-esteem and academic achievement do not support the educationist dogma on the issue. Taken as a whole, he writes, the research is filled with "inconsistent findings, counterintuitive outcomes, and downright gaps in our knowledge."[26] He admits the "lack of conclusiveness" about whether self-esteem causes achievement or achievement causes self-esteem and notes that "the most disquieting feature of these studies is the generally low magnitude of association found between self-esteem and achievement." Because Covington supports dramatic and sweeping changes in the educational system to enhance self-esteem, he acknowledges that these findings present educationists with "a dilemma."

"If feelings of self-esteem are so important to achievement," he asks, "then why is the demonstrated relationship between self-esteem and academic performance so uniformly low?" And "Why do many students with low self-esteem perform at their best when the odds against succeeding are at their worst? . . . why should failure—which is known to elicit shame, guilt and lowered self-esteem—actually mobilize some students to greater effort?"

There is, of course, another way of looking at this. If we use the scientific method (rather than wishful thinking, for example), we might conclude that rather than a "dilemma," the evidence is trying to tell us that his hypothesis simply is not proved. It is only a puzzle if you insist on clinging to the hypothesis even though the evidence isn't there. Covington acknowledges that sometimes "a lack of a sense of worth is a more powerful stimulant to achievement than self-confidence is" and that high self-esteem "may not always promote the continued will to learn."

But despite the doubts and hesitations suggested by the research, Covington proposes sweeping changes designed to eliminate competition, equalize rewards, and generally raise the self-esteem of students. The contrast could hardly be more striking between the evidence he cites and the conclusions he draws.

For Covington, the issue is competition. He acknowledges that competition "appears to be almost inevitable, generated in part by a minority of students who define their worth in competitive ways." While this might suggest that competition is a natural process and that kids *will* compete, regardless of what grown-ups say about the joys and consolations of cooperation, Covington calls for vigorous efforts to stamp out the competitive spirit. It is not enough, Covington declares, "simply to oppose classroom competition in the abstract. Rather teachers must actively restructure classroom learning incentives to encourage other, more beneficial reasons for learning." His agenda includes what he calls "equity structures," which equalize opportunities and rewards. One "equity structure" he endorses is "cooperative learning" in which students are all rewarded based on the performance of the group, rather than on their individual achievement. Cooperative learning has the advantage of shielding slower students from unpleasant comparisons with others.

He acknowledges possible "downsides" to the elimination of competition, such as undermining the motivation of some students and giving others an inflated sense of their abilities. Despite those doubts, however, he insists that efforts "to promote more equity structures in school should be seriously considered." His goal is not strictly educational; it is at least in equal part an ideological attack on certain values in American society as a whole. Eliminating a competitive environment in schools will require eliminating the competitive environment in society. Schools won't be noncompetitive until American society is made noncompetitive; and vice versa. "To most Americans," he writes, "achievement is everything: it is our badge, our national identity. . . ." And that attitude about achievement—in schools and in society—is, ultimately, Covington's target. The instrument to transform both society and the schools is not class struggle, but self-esteem. "Perhaps only for the sake of self-esteem," Covington declares, "would we be willing to carry out policy recommendations that seriously question two of our most cherished beliefs: the cult of achievement and the myth of competition." In practice, that also translates into an attack on the idea of excellence, and its weight falls most heavily on gifted students.

THE MISSION STATEMENT

n 1885, eighth graders who wished to win admission to Jersey City High School needed to pass a test that asked them, among other things to:

I. Define Algebra, an algebraic expression, a polynomial. Make a literal trinomial.
II. Write a homogeneous quadrinomial of the third degree. . . .
III. Find the sum and difference of 3x-4y+7cd-4xy+16, and 10ay-3x-8xy+7cd-13. . . .

What is the axis of the earth? What is the equator? What is the distance from the equator to either pole in degrees, in miles?

Name the four principle ranges of mountains in Asia, three in Europe, and three in Africa.

Name the capitals of the following countries: Portugal, Greece, Egypt, Persia, Japan, China, Canada, Tibet and Cuba.

Name four Spanish explorers and state what induced them to come to America.

Name the thirteen colonies that declared their independence in 1776.

■

In 1994, a small midwestern district embarked on a strategic long-range planning effort that resulted in a statement of beliefs.[1] "We believe," the district declared, "that . . .

Everyone has individual needs.
Responsibility for education belongs to everybody.
Trust, care, and respect are needed for social harmony.
All learners have potential.
Everyone has intrinsic worth.
Individuals are responsible for the direction of their own lives.
Education is worth commitment.
Learning is life long.
Learning is essential.

Every individual makes contributions to society.
Change is inevitable.
Love is essential to human growth and development.
We are a part of the global community.
Self esteem is a critical part of human growth.
Joy and humor enhances [sic] the journey of life.
The spectrum of human emotions is an essential part of life."

While this is supposed to be a document of educational philosophy, eleven of the sixteen "beliefs" deal with feelings, emotions, social change, and the worth of individual students. Only five make any reference to "education" or "learning," and then only in the most nebulous way. Education, the district says, is "worth commitment," and is the responsibility of "everybody"; while learning "is life long," and "essential," and learners "have potential." The rest of the statement is a pastiche of therapeutic New Age banalities that could easily be transposed to a self-help seminar, a kindergarten, or a session of psychotherapy. "Trust, care, and respect are needed for social harmony," is a touching sentiment, as is the belief that "love is essential to human growth and development," and that "joy and humor enhances the journey of life." One forgets for the moment that this is a strategic planning document, not a script for an episode of *Barney*. It is a mantra of well-meaningness; a stew of good intentions.

Its educational significance is less clear.

What, for example, does the statement that "the spectrum of human emotions is an essential part of life" mean exactly for the development of the curriculum? The district's specific educational objectives do not shed much more light. "All students," they declare, "will participate in a foreign language experience prior to graduation."

The key words here are *participate* and *experience*. The objectives do not require students to *study* a foreign language or to achieve any level of proficiency in its grammar, vocabulary, or usage. They merely have to *participate* in an *experience* of a foreign language—perhaps through the folk dances of many lands or by pasting up collages of colorful multicultural characters, or by a class-wide South of the Border party, complete with *piñata* and foods referred to by their original *foreign language* names. Other goals include:

- "We will decrease the drop out rate to 0% by the 1996–97 school year."
  Perhaps potential dropouts will be convinced to stay in school because "Joy and humor enhances the journey of life." Educationists like to point to high graduation rates as a sign of success, when they often mean that the standards have been lowered to the point where no one could possibly fail to meet them. Dropout rates also can be lowered by making school even less demanding than leisure time.

- "By graduation all students will successfully demonstrate the practical application of current technology."

   This sounds somewhat more to the point, although it is unclear whether the objectives refer to the VCR, computers, or self-propelled lawn mowers. The district says it will implement this objective by hiring "a library/media technology specialist."
- "All students will demonstrate creative and critical thinking skills."

   Again the district's plan to implement this objective is to "Hire coordinator for critical thinking activities," no doubt a *specialist* in critical thinking. This objective, however, is more interesting for what it doesn't say. Of course, creativity and critical thinking skills are admirable objectives. But they are also notoriously difficult to define or measure. Would a drawing of the "spectrum of human emotions" fill the bill? A poster collage on the Journey of Life? Or a poem about "social harmony"?

   This is, of course, the attraction of vagueness. *You cannot fail if you can't measure or define the goal.* Whatever is produced under this regime can be declared a success, because the objectives don't tangibly address reading, writing, spelling, math, or scientific knowledge. Knowledge can be *measured*; "The spectrum of human emotions" cannot.
- "One hundred percent of children will start school ready to learn."

   Learn what? Amid the self-congratulatory rhetoric about its "mutual care and trust," the district managed in its belief statement, its mission, and its objectives to say nothing about the study or the mastery of any academic subject. It claims no responsibility for passing along any body of knowledge, or the mastery of any discipline. Joy, humor, self-esteem, intrinsic worth, needs, and emotions are covered; science, math, history, and writing warrant not a single word.

THE ATTACK ON EXCELLENCE

In 1993, the U.S. Department of Education issued a report charging that American schools were shortchanging their brightest pupils and that gifted students often sat bored and unchallenged in classrooms, where they endured the daily tedium of working on curricula far below their abilities and interests. (The study found that gifted elementary students probably had mastered as much as half of the curriculum in basic subjects even before they began the school year.) While major U.S. corporations were complaining that the shortage of high-achieving students in math and science was forcing them to fill jobs with students educated abroad, the department found that only two cents out of every $100 spent in education went to provide opportunities for academically gifted students. Although many school districts offered programs for talented students, they were often token efforts. But the indifference of American schools toward academic excellence is not merely reflected in the amount of money spent. Americans have long been ambivalent about "intellectuals," but seldom has it been more obvious that the culture of the nation's schools is suspicious of good students. "In America, we often make fun of our brightest students," Gregory Anrig, president of the Educational Testing Service, wrote in the report, "giving them such derogatory names as nerd, dweeb, or, in a former day, egghead."[1]

It wasn't just kids mocking kids. In American schools today, "elitism" is regarded with suspicion while "fairness" and "equity" are regarded with almost totemic awe. The result is that the stray youngster who isn't satisfied with self-esteem programs, rap sessions, and vaguely conceived "thinking" skills does not quite fit. Such nonconformists pose an embarrassing and awkward challenge to the educationist passion for cooperation, equality, "success for all," and the other buzzwords that constitute the dominant ideology of American schools in the 1990s.

Consider:

- In Fairfax County, Virginia, seven high schools have decided to dump class rankings, part of a national trend toward eliminating such distinctions and honors. Other schools have stopped naming their top student as valedictorian.[2] Many more schools are expected to drop both ranking and other honors as schools move ahead to replace traditional grades with "alternative assessments" that will blur the difference between average and above-average student performances.

- In the fall of 1993, the Los Angeles city schools implemented a new grading system that abolished the grade of "Outstanding," and replaced it with a system designed to make it easier for students to get the highest marks. Previously, the highest grades were reserved for students who performed advanced work, such as a fourth grader who was able to do fifth-grade level math. From now on, students will have to master only subjects at their own grade level. Under the change, the letter S, which used to stand for "satisfactory," or average work, became the highest grade, indicating "area of strength." Other grades include the letter G for "growth," and the letter N for "needs improvement." No grade denotes exceptional achievement.[3]

- The Illinois Junior Academy of Science, a private group dominated by teachers from schools across the state, voted to bar the Avery Coonley School, a private school in the Chicago suburbs, from competing for prizes in a statewide science fair after the school won its fourth straight team prize. The academy decided that Coonley's team should henceforth be banned from winning so the contest could be "more equitable."[4]

- Administrators from Minnesota's Apple Valley School District assured parents that gifted students would be given "enrichment exercises," while slower students worked to catch up in their outcome-based classes. A gifted student in Minnesota's Apple Valley School District describes his "enrichment" assignment: "We had to do a diorama this year on dinosaurs," he says. "We also did that in kindergarten. That was enrichment."[5]

- A student in Oklahoma writes to a state legislator, explaining his "enrichment" project: Eight high-achieving students, he says, "were sent to measure a room." While one kid took measurements, the rest of the exiles from the outcome-based classrooms sat around talking and goofing off.[6]

- Charles Willie, a professor of education at Harvard, declares that the goal of education should not be "excellence," because that is a matter of personal choice and requires sacrifice. Instead, schools should be concerned with "adequacy" and should weigh non-traditional types of intelligence, such as "singing" and "dancing" at least as heavily as "communication and calculation."[7]

- Peggy McIntosh, an influential educationist from Wellesley College, believes that "excellence" is a dangerous concept for schools and argues that schools need to stop giving out "gold stars" and other honors because they reflect an outmoded white male culture of "vertical thinking." McIntosh heads up a program known as Seeking Educational Equity and Diversity (SEED), which has already enrolled several thousand educators from thirty states for seminars on making schools more equitable and cooperative and freeing them from the "ideal of excellence." "She has a Pol Pot approach to education," says one critic. "She seems to be trying to make everybody equal by making sure that nobody knows anything."[8]

- While special programs proliferate for student needs, programs for gifted students are often targeted for budget cuts. In 1993, the Department of Education proposed to divert funds from the Jacob K. Javits Gifted and Talented Program to "schoolwide efforts to provide challenging curricula . . . to all students," and called for eliminating the National Research Center on Gifted and Talented Education, which has been a still small voice advocating for gifted students.[9] (Ironically, this was the same department that was almost simultaneously bemoaning the lack of resources for gifted students—proving once again that consistency is not a strong point of the education bureaucracy.)

- Both programs for gifted students and the practice of "tracking" students by ability have been attacked by critics who see them as "elitist." Under the banner of "fairness" and "inclusivity," educationists are moving bright students into classes with students of lesser abilities. In the same vein, advanced courses are under attack across the country as "racist" and "undemocratic." A top Justice Department official in the Clinton administration announced that tracking would be challenged in court on the grounds that it violated federal laws and court rulings outlawing illegal segregation.[10]

- In Alexandria, Virginia, the central administration decided to dismantle the district's honors courses in world civilization, planning to randomly mix ninth graders whose reading ability ranged from the second to the twelfth-grade level. The course was restored after politically influential parents protested. But the district's educationists added requirements that students in the honors class stay after school three days a week and attend four-hour Saturday sessions twice a month. Those requirements, some teachers complained, were intended to discourage kids from enrolling in the advanced courses. "It's all mean-spirited," a ninth-grade teacher in Alexandria said, "as if to say 'You white parents want an honors course; you think you're so smart; we'll show you.'"[11]

According to Patrick Welsh, an English teacher at Alexandria's T. C. Williams High, many of his students are youngsters "who cannot or will not do the work required to succeed in school . . ." while a smaller number "are so disruptive that they poison classes and make it impossible for other kids to learn." Both politics and the reigning educational ideology, however, dictate that high-achieving students are placed in the same classrooms and given the same course work. A student at Welsh's school told him about a class in junior high that had celebrated the richness of "inclusivity":

> By the middle of the second quarter the teacher practically gave up because of discipline problems. About four kids attempted to do any work. Kids were sleeping, talking and throwing stuff. When he would divide us into groups [the new panacea called cooperative learning] kids would say 'I'm not going to work. Shut up!' It was a lousy mix of rotten students. I learned absolutely nothing.[12]

There is probably no word used more frequently by educrats than *excellence*. They pledge it, commit to it, trumpet it, include it in mission statements, press releases, curriculum guides, and endless presentations to parents, school boards, and local businesses. To hear American educators talk, you'd imagine that they think about little else. Such is their faith in the word that educationists act as if the incantation of "excellence" somehow compensates for the ebbing of its substance. Throughout the 1980s and 1990s, the more they talked about it, the less they did to assure it. The more aggressive the assault on "excellence," the more strident the public relations campaigns insisted on the fealty and undying commitment of educators to preparing children for the global marketplace. Despite these protestations, however, educationist doctrine and practice is dominated by a voice of therapeutic egalitarianism that invokes terms like *equity*, *fairness*, and *cooperation*, but which is often hard to distinguish from the nagging, ancient voice of envy.

"My Kid Beat Up Your Honor Student"

A few years back bumper stickers began appearing on cars reading, MY CHILD IS AN HONOR STUDENT AT . . . Compared with the ruffles and flourishes— the parades and dinners and cheerleaders and newspaper articles—that celebrated the athletic achievements of various schools, the stickers were a modest expression of parental pride and recognition of academic achievement. They were also an endorsement of schools, presenting an unabashedly pro-education message. Unfortunately, it was *elitist*. Not everyone made the honor roll, which by definition excluded students who did not excel in academics. Thus the backlash.

In July 1994, *Education Week* devoted a full page to a commentary attacking the bumper stickers, and lauding parents who had responded with a bumper sticker declaring, MY KID BEAT UP YOUR HONOR STUDENT.[13] That slogan, wrote Mark Mlawer, the executive director of the Maryland Coalition for Inclusive Education, "helped clarify this issue" by expressing the "resentment at the unfairness of the honor roll and at those who flaunt their child's academic feats. . . ." Parents who carry the bumper sticker announcing that their child is an honor student, he claimed, "have turned their personal pride into a public event, and therefore are undoubtedly bragging." In general, educationists have few qualms about self-congratulation on a rather expansive basis. But Mlawer used the term *bragging* to signify any expression of pride of which he disapproves, a malediction that falls heavily on celebrations of educational success. As if he senses that his complaints might sound mean-spirited, Mlawer quickly adds that he is concerned with "moral issues."

"Both the educational practice of maintaining an honor roll and the parental practice of public proclamations of this status," he writes, "create and reinforce a certain specific of unfairness, one which *necessarily* causes resentment." [emphasis added] Thus he dresses up the green toad of jealousy as high principle and resentment as a passion for "fairness."

The honor roll, which singles out students who excel in school is, he says, "a tradition which reinforces some of the least attractive aspects of our culture, and for that reason should be eliminated or radically altered." Besides its elitist cast, Mlawer objects to the honor roll because it is so *academic.* It is a "dishonorable institution" because it does not take into account every child's "unique mix of abilities and talents, average capacities, and areas of incapacity and disability," by which he seems to mean that not everyone makes it. "If we wish to teach and transmit values like fairness," he says, "then we must award honor in a more individualized manner, one which takes into account a child's potential, efforts, and circumstances. . . ."

The passions aroused by the issue of academic honors are so fierce because the stakes are so small. For some students, the honor roll may be the only honor the world bestows on them during their adolescence. Even so, in the elaborate hierarchy of peer prestige, the honor roll is a relatively minor counterbalance to the honors handed out by nature and by peers. For the teenager who can't run the 100-meter dash in record time, looks unimpressive in basketball shorts, doesn't have naturally bouncy hair or a body destined for the swimsuit issue of *Sports Illustrated*; for kids who can't compete for status by owning the best cars, the latest video games, most expensive tennis shoes, or latest CD, the recognition of academic success is at best a minor consolation.

The sculptured blond quarterback and prom queen have been awarded accolades by nature that cannot easily be repealed. Try as they might, the legions of therapists, social workers, and educationists will not be able to level these advantages or soothe the wounded self-esteem of the dorky, the homely, and the flat-chested. So they focus instead on the academic achievers: the handful of students who have ability and have worked hard enough to excel in their school work.

Of course, they are not satisfied merely with leveling students academically. Distinctions of any kind annoy the genuine levelers. The executive director of the Van Cliburn International Piano Competition, for example, feels so guilty about being associated with something with *competition* in its name that he declares that "we must stamp out the concept of the better."[14] Obviously, educationists don't feel quite right about athletics (after all, it results in *winners* and *losers*). In the "new gym class," the *New York Times* reports, "competition is out and cooperation is in." Instead of playing basketball (and keeping score) students get to practice with a ball "that's the right size and weight for their skill." No one is made to feel inadequate by an aspiring Michael Jordan who can slam-dunk the ball. In the new class, everyone has a chance to dunk, or so it seems. The *Times* reports that the enlightened phys ed class provides kids with "a movable target that can be adjusted as their accuracy increases." But even then, "the goal is not so much to learn to score a basket as to develop body awareness. . . ." Games like dodgeball, which involve the elimination of players, are frowned upon, and kids no longer pick teams since it is traumatic to be chosen last.[15]

And of course it is. Recall that solemn ritual of the playground and gymnasium: The order you were chosen was a reliable barometer of popularity and status. To be chosen first was a sign that you were the most popular guy in the class; to be picked in the lower half was a sign of social failure; to be chosen last of all, of irremediable geekhood. But as bad as this was, choosing up sides was also a powerful incentive to be good at *something*. If not at football or volleyball, then at history or current events or English. To excel at something was not just a form of sweet revenge, it was a kind of modest salvation for kids who might not otherwise have fit in. No, it didn't compensate for the way burly guys drove Mustangs and got to date the best-looking girls, but it was a win nonetheless, to be cherished in private, with family and close friends. When the honor rolls are dropped, those victories disappear. The burly guys still get the girls and the fast cars.

Of course, not all honors students are social misfits; the stereotype is both unfair and inaccurate. But even if the honor student is also the quarterback, the academic honor is still distinctive precisely because it is an *adult* honor that provides the first tangible reward for the values and qualities students will need as grown-ups and what grown-ups regard as important. Honors say that the study of math or history or the well-crafted essay are worthy of admiration, a message adolescents are less likely to receive if the bestowal of honors is left to their peers alone.

There are also ideological consequences that inevitably arise from the practice of competing for and handing out honors. The attack on "elitism" and competition in the schools is at bottom not about education at all. It is about equality and ultimately about how much "fairness" we can expect from life. Educationists engage in endless and tedious debates about grades and the need to abolish failure, but at bottom many of them share the belief that there is something undemocratic not just about academic awards, but about competition in general. It's not just schools they want to make more fair; *they want life to be fair.* Prizes, scholarships, citations, laurels, and guerdons encourage competition, ratify success, and nurture a taste for being "better" than others. In other words, they prepare children for the real world. And some educationists are just sick about it.

The Cry of the Dodo

Alfie Kohn is one of American education's more successful entrepreneurs of antielitism. Kohn has been a featured speaker at state teachers union conventions and his books have sold briskly among educators across the country. Kohn's ideas are so popular that apparently he makes a living spreading his gospel: grades are bad, competition is evil, and rewards and punishments of every kind should be done away with. Kohn, whose books include *Punished by Rewards: The Trouble with Gold Stars, Incentive Plans, A's, Praise and Other Bribes,* waxes Dickensian when he contemplates the horrors of the marketplace and the complicity of schools in the degradation of innocent youth. "A treadmill appears under any student's feet when the first grade appears. . . ." Once a child graduates from school, he finds more competition, more rewards to be sought. "Now they must struggle for the next set of rewards, so they can snag the best residencies, the choicest clerkships, the fast-track positions in the corporate world. Then come the most prestigious appointments, partnerships, vice presidencies, and so on, working harder, nose stuck into the future, ever more frantic."[16] And to think it starts in first grade.

For Kohn, grades are the original sin and the root of the competitive evil. Not only do they "dilute the pleasure that a student experiences on successfully completing a task," Kohn claims, but they "encourage cheating, and strain the relationship between teacher and students. They reduce a student's sense of control over his own fate and can induce a blind conformity to others' wishes. . . . [17] Without rewards, incentives, and grades, Kohn insists that children will somehow come to develop an "intrinsic" interest in learning for its own sake. He advises teachers to scrap grades if they can; make them meaningless if they cannot: "Reduce the number of grades to two: A and Incomplete. The theory here is that any work that does not merit an A isn't finished yet." Never grade for effort. Never grade students while they are still learning something. No pop quizzes.[18]

Utopian ideas have long exerted a powerful and nearly irresistible attraction for educationists; but the appeal of Kohn's idea sheds light on the attitudes toward accountability and academic excellence among the educationists who are shaping the various reforms in American education—from Outcome Based Education to the ambitious agenda of Goals 2000, the federal legislation designed to establish uniform, national educational standards. Unions anxious to reduce measures of accountability wherever possible have a readily understandable attraction to any criticism of grading. But the assault on rewards also has a strong ideological pull for the educational levelers who are suspicious of any distinctions among students and who interpret equality as equality of achievement rather than equality of opportunity. For the levelers, every accomplishment must be deemed to be equal with any other. Prizes are given to everyone, lest anyone feel left out. Standards that might "exclude" anyone must be lowered or done away with altogether. If the movement had a slogan it would be the cry of the Dodo in *Alice in Wonderland*: "*Everyone* has won, and *all* must have prizes."

In fairness, Kohn is more honest about his agenda than many other critics of competition. While they concentrate on eliminating failure, Kohn admits his goal is to abolish success, or at least its trappings. Ultimately, however, there is not much difference between giving everyone prizes and giving prizes to no one. In either case, distinctions based on performance, effort, and ability are eliminated. Everyone has either won or lost; as long as everyone is in the same boat the levelers are satisfied with either result.

Despite Kohn's newfound celebrity, his ideas are hardly new. Over the last twenty years "absolute success for students has become the means *and* the end of education," according to University of Iowa education professor Margaret M. Clifford. "It has been given higher priority than learning and it has obstructed learning." Since the 1960s, educators have tested Kohn's ideas in thousands of schools where grades have been watered down or inflated, when they haven't been replaced altogether with more benign assessments. But instead of the "well-adjusted, enthusiastic, self-confident scholars" the child-worshippers of the 1960s imagined would emerge from the schools once competition was overthrown, Clifford noted, the efforts "to mass produce success in every educational situation" had created a cult of self-celebrating mediocrity, washed on every side by a tide of phony successes and inflated esteems.[19] Meanwhile, students who were gifted or who worked exceptionally hard were increasingly attacked or ignored by the people who were supposed to be educating them and encouraging "excellence."

Schools without Failure

In 1969, educationist William Glasser wrote *Schools Without Failure*, a veritable handbook for schools that would fail over the next two and half decades. He criticized objective tests, because they placed all their emphasis "on correct answers as opposed to reflecting upon important problems for which there are no right answers."[20] Indeed, Glasser objected to all closed-book examinations which, he said, were "based on *the fallacy that knowledge remembered is better than knowledge looked up.*"[21]

[emphasis in original] Glasser thus redefined knowledge as something that did not need to be known, a rather bold stroke even by the creative standards of educationism.

Glasser's critique of grades also was influential. Giving students grades, Glasser declared, was "probably the school practice that most produces failure in students." Grades were "an unpremeditated plot to destroy the students."[22] For the first six years of schooling, he insisted, no child should ever be failed, regardless of their efforts or their skills. After that, Glasser proposed replacing A's, B's, C's, D's and F's with S for superior work and P for passing. Lest the S be confused with an A, Glasser declared that no student be allowed to earn more than one S per semester. Even then, any student who wanted to get an S would have to agree "to devote some time each week to help those students who are not doing well." If students eventually did earn a passing grade, no mention of the earlier failure would appear in their transcript; it would be as if the failure had never happened. When a student left school, his records were destroyed.[23] Glasser seemed to think that the stigma of failure is removed simply by not writing it down. His policy, however, assures only that colleges, employers, and parents are not told of the failure; but it cannot be kept from the student himself. He knows. So Glasser does not succeed in abolishing failure, merely in obscuring the *recognition* of failure, which is not quite the same thing.

Eliminating grades, however, was just the beginning. Glasser also argued that there was something inherently unfair and undemocratic about homework. "Realizing that poor students rarely do homework," he complained, "teachers gear the assignments to the A and B students who do the homework, thus widening the gap between the successes and failures in school."[24] In other words, if good students do homework and poor students don't, should we dumb down the homework that is assigned? That was *exactly* what Glasser had in mind, and he was immensely influential in shaping education philosophy.

"Shorter and more relevant assignments might attract the poorer students," he wrote in 1969, "who could go at their own pace at home and might use home study to catch up instead of falling further and further behind as they do now. . . ." This means that all homework must be pegged at the level of the poorest of the students, lest they become discouraged or disheartened. "We must use homework in a way that reaches the poor students," Glasser insisted, "or at least not use it to their detriment while we are figuring out how to reach them." If this sounds like it is writing off bright students, Glasser was quick to point out that gifted students are also victimized by demanding homework assignments. "Excessive homework penalizes the bright, creative student," he explained, "because by doing it conscientiously, he has little time for other pursuits such as music, dancing, art, theater, science and crafts."[25]

Since he was writing in 1969, Glasser was apparently unfamiliar with hanging out at the shopping mall. He seems to have believed that youngsters would spend their free time attending Broadway productions and penning librettos if only they didn't have to write a geography paper.

But eliminating failure means more than simply not measuring students against one another. If they are measured against any objective standard, there is also a possibility students will fall short or even fail. So Glasser also proposed changing the standards and goals of education. He acknowledged that even in a system where students are only rated as "passing" P or "superior" S, "standards will have to be re-examined."[26]

Schools, Glasser said, should give up the attempt to keep academic standards high. "Our present attempt to keep standards high is ineffective," he wrote. "Teachers present too much material and hold students responsible for learning more than they can assimilate." Too many courses were too hard. "In courses such as chemistry, physics, advanced math, economics, or literature," Glasser complained, "a few able students keep up, but the rest fall behind and learn next to nothing."[27]

Under the no-failure regime, teachers would not be able to "maintain present unrealistic standards." They would have to teach less and to teach it more slowly. "We can continue to teach complex courses," Glasser allowed, "but we must cover less ground *and we must cover the material we do present more slowly and in greater depth.*"[28] [emphasis in original]

Another tactic Glasser recommended was redefining the goals of schooling. He suggested emphasizing "thinking skills," and a flexible schedule for students to meet their teacher's goals. "If one child takes a little longer than some others," he wrote, "it makes no difference."[29] Glasser's book is proof that ideas do, indeed, have consequences. Twenty-five years later, Glasser's ideas would be called Outcome Based Education.

Lowering the Hoop

Like Glasser, the architects of OBE envision a world in which no one fails, or at least in which no one fails in school. "For the most part," declares Albert Mammary, "we believe competition in the classroom is destructive."[30] Mammary has been superintendent of New York's Johnson City Central School District, where he developed an "Outcomes-Driven Development Model," which he describes as the "nation's first comprehensive school improvement model." The model is built on slogans along the line of "Success for All Students" and "Excellence for All." For Mammary, the first step to success begins with doing away with failure. "Outcome-based schools believe there should be no failure and that failure ought to be removed from our vocabulary and thoughts," he wrote in 1991. "Failure, or fear of failure, will cause students to give up."[31]

Former students may recall that, to the contrary, the fear of failure was an inducement to try harder, a spur that caused papers to be written and formulas memorized. But Mammary sees the threat of failure only as a barrier to enthusiastic learning. "When students don't have to worry about failure," he insists, "they will be more apt to want to learn."

Tests also are transformed in Mammary's vision. They are no longer trials of knowledge, but celebrations of success. "Testing should be creative," he insists, "aligned to learning outcomes, and only given when the students will do well." This is only the beginning of his redefinition of "success" and "excellence."

"Outcomes-based schools," he declares, "believe excellence is for every child and not just a few." They achieve this not by dragging the top kids down, he writes, but by bringing expectations for everyone up. He does this, however, by insisting that everyone be a winner. Mammary is explicit on this: "A no-cut philosophy is recommended. *Everyone trying out for the football team should make it; every girl or boy that wants to be a cheerleader should make it; everyone who comes to the program for the gifted and talented should make it.*" [32] [emphasis added]

There is a dreamy, utopian quality about all of this. Wouldn't it be nice if everyone was a prom queen; if everybody who dreamed of being quarterback could be one; if every aspiring pianist could star in a concert. The world, unfortunately, doesn't work that way. But that is precisely the point. Dreams have such power to fix our imaginations precisely because everyone cannot achieve them. Boys aspire to be the quarterback because of the level of accomplishment it represents. Not everyone can do it. If anyone could be quarterback, what is left to aspire to? There is also a practical concern here. A football team that must play anyone who wishes to be quarterback will quickly become a team in which no one will want to play any position. By abolishing failure (or at least the recognition and consequences of failure) and redefining excellence to mean whatever anyone wants it to mean, we deprive success of meaning. In the ideal OBE world, everyone would feel like a success, without necessarily having to do much of anything to justify their self-esteem.

In its goal statement, Milwaukee's suburban Whitnall district declared that "By 1996–97, *all* students will demonstrate 100% proficiency in the District's performance outcomes." Whitnall school board member Ted Mueller quotes one astute resident remarking, "If we require *all* students to be able to stuff a basketball to be able to graduate from high school, the only way you're going to be able to accomplish that is to lower the basketball hoop."[33]

Off with the Grades!

If Mammary appears a dreamer, there are practical applications of his philosophy. The most obvious is the hostility of OBE to traditional grades and measurements of achievement. The emphasis on abolishing grades and traditional tests is central to the philosophy of OBE advocates. "Grading lies at the core of how our current system operates," declares OBE guru William Spady, the director of the High Success Program on Outcome-Based Education.[34] Spady quotes conservative reformers such as Chester Finn in his writings, but he follows Mammary in calling for the leveling of distinctions based on ability, industry, or achievement. Grades, he writes, are gatekeepers, separating good students from others. "This, in turn, reinforces the system of inter-student comparison and competition created by class ranks. *Such a system, of course, gives a natural advantage to those with stronger academic backgrounds, higher aptitudes for given areas of learning, and more resources at home to support their learning.*"[35] [emphasis added] His objection appears to be based less on educational grounds than on his suspicion of inequality of any sort. Grades favor the smart and the studious. Spady wants to make up for the unfairness of it all. Grades are oppressive, Spady writes, because they "label students, control their opportunities, limit their choices, shape their identities, and define their rewards for learning and behaving in given ways." Grades pit students against one another, he complains, "implying that achievement and success are inherently comparative, competitive and relative" (which in fact they *are*, both in school and in life). Indeed, Spady sees the issue of grades in terms of class struggle. "The usual result: the rich get richer, the poor give up." Not necessarily. The student who gets D's can work to become a student who gets C's and the C student will strive to become a B or an A student. The A student may work harder so that he does not become a C student.

But Spady sees no link between grades and motivation to succeed or improve oneself. Instead, he focuses on the potential damage that poor grades might inflict on "young people struggling to define their identity and self-worth." He assumes here that identity and self-worth are independent of achievement. Like Mammary, Spady envisions a grading system with no failure, but also no bad grades at all. OBE, he explains, eliminates labeling and competitive grading and stresses "VALIDATING that a high level of performance is ultimately reached on those things that will directly impact on the student's success in the future. In other words, all we're really interested in is A-level performance, thank you, so we EXPECT it of all students, systematically teach for it, and validate it when it occurs."[36]

The OBE buzzword for its approved evaluation system is "authentic assessment." Assessment is authentic, apparently, only when it becomes impossible to rank one student's performance ahead of another. In this new system, Spady suggests that teachers will be able to "throw away their pens at evaluation and reporting time and replace them with pencils that have large erasers." Although he does not expand on the point, the abolition of "permanent records" has obvious advantages for educationists as well as students. The eraser takes both off the hook at the same time.

One form of accountability especially detested by the educational establishment creates measurements by which academic achievement can be readily compared among schools and among districts. Such comparisons are widely publicized and can have considerable influence on policymakers who determine how and where to distribute scarce tax dollars. Evaluations that are constantly in flux obviously cannot be compared in this way. At most, schools could report progress toward their educational "goals" which may turn out to be notoriously difficult to quantify. Those goals, however, will be a benchmark of sorts and educationists can be expected to point to them as authentic measures of their success. Indeed, success of one sort or another seems inevitable, since the goals often appear to be set to accommodate the lower common denominator.

The Attack on Ability Grouping

The most direct assault on programs for brighter students are denunciations of programs that group students by ability as both undemocratic and racist. "Classes for the gifted," Federal Judge Robert Carter said in a newspaper interview, "usually mean classes for whites and special education classes usually mean classes for black males."[37] The National Governor's Association released a study by UCLA professor Jeannie Oakes charging that "Conventional, if increasingly obsolete, conceptions of intelligence, as well as deep-seated racist and classist attitudes and prejudices, support tracking."[38]

The most common indictment of tracking is that it pins a negative label on children too early, thus becoming a self-fulfilling prophecy for children who find themselves stuck in a system of low expectations and limited opportunities. This is especially true of special education classes, many of which have indeed become dumping grounds for minority children. But the real evil of the tracking system is the way that it has been used to dumb down the classes for students who are most in need of academic help. Standards for children in the lower tracks are often scandalously low and thus *do* contribute to a widening gap between white and minority students and between students of varying abilities. A first grader who might have been half a grade below grade level and so is placed in a lower and dumbed down track might fall two or three grade levels behind by the time she gets to sixth grade.[39] But instead of focusing efforts on improving the curriculum or raising the standards and expectations of those classes, opponents have turned their fire on the overall system— including the practice of letting brighter students work at an accelerated pace in classes geared for students of advanced abilities. Instead of raising the floor, the trend is toward lowering the ceiling.

Struggles over tracking often pit middle-class families against the forces of equity, with huge stakes for the public schools. Parents who can afford to do so will often choose private or parochial schools based as much on the prospective student body as on the curriculum. But as English teacher

Patrick Welsh wrote in the *Washington Post*, ability groups may be the "last line of defense" for middle-class parents who either can't afford to escape or are genuinely committed to public education, but who want to "minimize their kids' classroom contact with troublemakers and laggards."[40]

In Alexandria, Virginia, where Welsh taught, the political pressures to create "inclusive" classrooms forced teachers to teach honors students at the same pace as students who were deficient "in even the most basic academic tasks." One of Welsh's colleagues recounted, "These kids feel that as long as they come to school, they are entitled to do exactly what they want to do. All they want is to get a D. If they get a C it is like they have wasted too much time working." Welsh has had similar experiences. "When I recently promised a student that if he finished an assigned novel I would give him a C for the quarter, he seemed offended. 'I don't want no C, man! I want a D,' he replied."[41]

Even where the class can operate at a reasonable level of efficiency, the one-size-fits-all classroom must still make compromises. "Some people will say that the top students are going to excel anyway," says eighth-grade teacher Richard O'Loughlin, whose Lowell, Massachusetts, school has abolished ability grouping. "Well that's not true. If they're not told a certain fact about history, they can't possibly know that. If they're not taught to think on an abstract level, they can't think on that level." In his mixed-group classes, he says, he must move much more slowly and often is unable to introduce activities like writing essays or drawing historical comparisons. "It's going to hurt the country to water it all down," he warns.[42]

As usual the educational merits of tracking are less clear than the politics. But the evidence suggests that no matter how politically incorrect they may be, enriched programs for brighter student do pay educational dividends.[43] Researcher Susan Demirsky Allan found that both meta-analyses (studies of other studies) and so-called "best-evidence" research agree that "some forms of grouping were found to improve the academic performance of gifted children, and it is likely that the real benefits were greater than could be shown by the method of measurement."[44] Likewise, James A. Kulik and Chen Lin Kulik, two of the most prominent researchers in the field, concluded that "academic benefits are striking and large in programs of acceleration for gifted students." The Kuliks also found that gifted students did much better in advanced classes than they did in mixed-group classes.[45] In fact, the overwhelming weight of the research evidence indicates that academically advanced students benefit greatly from programs that are geared to match their pace of learning. Although critics frequently claim that ability grouping might have damaging effects on the self-esteem of slower students, this also apparently is not the case. In 1985, Chen Lin Kulik found that slow learners actually had *higher* self-esteem in classes designed to work at their pace. (In contrast, programs for the gifted seem to have only a trivial effect on the self-image of bright students.)[46] Ability grouping allows slower students to experience the sort of success they are unlikely to enjoy in classes where they are mixed with fast-learning students. For gifted students, on the other hand, ability grouping may mean that bright students are faced with real competition for the first time in their academic careers.[47] Ultimately, however, the research findings may be beside the point since educational practice seems driven less by student needs than by establishment ideology. Lloyd Hastings, a principal from Texas, spoke for much of the educationist establishment when he said: "The ability grouping of students for educational opportunity in a democratic society is ethically unacceptable. *We need not justify this with research, for it is a statement of principle, not science.*"[48] [emphasis added]

The disdain of educationists for tracking and ability grouping is matched by their enthusiasm for "cooperative learning." Johns Hopkins University's Robert E. Slavin, who argues that ability grouping and tracking runs "against our democratic ideals" and "against our national ideology that all are created equal," enthusiastically endorses cooperative learning. Alfie Kohn sees cooperative learning as an antidote to competition, elitism, and is therefore "one of the most exciting developments in modern education."[49]

Supporters of cooperative learning often suggest that one of the real values of forcing students of various academic levels to work together is that gifted students will learn democratic values and humility in the process. Other educationists argue that gifted students will experience a "higher-level processing" of material that they have to explain to other, slower students in their groups, and will therefore improve their social skills and self-esteem along the way. Students often don't see it that way. When education professor Marian Mathews interviewed gifted sixth and eighth graders in cooperative learning groups she found:

- The brighter students couldn't understand why other students couldn't grasp material that they found to be easy. They resent having to explain material to students who don't listen.
- Gifted students resent the time taken away from their own studies.
- None of the students say they understand the material better after explaining it to others. Mostly, they were bored.
- They feel used.
- Because they are concerned about quality, many gifted students end up taking over the group and doing much of the work themselves. "I did a project last year," one student told Mathews, "and I spent half of my time explaining to the others in the group what to do and they sat there reading magazines in the library all the time. I did all the work and still got a D on it because they did absolutely nothing."

Rather than developing social skills, Mathews found, working in groups "appears to promote some arrogance, [and] a lack of trust in classmates (to do the work to the standards of excellence gifted students feel are necessary) . . ."[50]

Writing as a Team Sport

A variation of "cooperative learning" is the practice known as "collaborative writing," in which students are assigned to write a paper with other students, rather than conceive and craft an essay on their own. The process puts a premium on working together and consensus rather than individuality by having some students man the typewriter while others shout out orders. When one teacher announced a collaborative writing assignment in her class, one of the class's more talented writers shot back: "English isn't a team sport, Mrs. Brockman."[51]

But it is convenient, one teacher explains, because cooperative writing allows students to write about things they know nothing about. "Topic expertise," one teacher explains, "isn't necessarily a requirement for all group members. That's why three students—two of them tennis players and one not—could write a paper explaining why tennis is more stressful than any other sport, or why another group could write an essay providing survival tips for a science class, *even though two group members hadn't taken the course.*" [emphasis added] For the team writer ignorance is no longer an impediment.

If the alleged quality, insight, and creativity of the collaborative essays are not sufficient recommendations for the practice, there are other attractions for teachers. As one English teacher excitedly explained in the *English Journal*, "it seems important to note a not unpleasant side effect of collaborative writing. It drastically reduces teacher workload. If a teacher assigns a paper in a class of twenty-five, there will be twenty-five essays to take home and evaluate. If that same assignment were collaborative in nature, those numbers would change to roughly eight. That bears repeating. *Twenty five essays become roughly eight. Just think of the possibilities—and try to gloat quietly.*"[52] [emphasis added]

The Bright as "Role Models"

Naturally, advocates for cooperative learning do not emphasize the work-shirking aspects of the programs, however attractive they might be to the practitioners. Instead, they insist that they have substantial evidence that cooperative learning works as well as or better than other forms of grouping in raising academic standards and achievement.

Unfortunately, however, most of the studies they cite compare cooperative learning groups with traditionally taught control groups, but do not measure the performance of cooperative students against the performance of students in groups with different curricula and paces of instruction.

Based on the actual evidence, Durden and Mills write, "it is clear that the abandonment of all forms of ability grouping and the wholesale, uncritical acceptance of cooperative learning is at least premature, and most likely unwarranted."[53]

As serious as the doubts about its academic value might be, cooperative learning raises equally grave questions about its underlying morality. How appropriate is it to *use* bright students for the benefit of other students, at the expense of their own education?[54] "While there is nothing inherently wrong with serving as a positive role model on occasion," Susan Demirsky Allan remarks, "it is morally questionable for adults to view any student's primary function as that of role model to others."[55]

LEADERS AND FOLLOWERS

Mrs. Ramskugler,
    Stephanie needs to make sure and comprimise [sic] with her group. Each member likes to try and get his/her own way, which leads to arguments. The groups should be working towards everyone being equal and not towards leaders and followers.
    This is not a big problem—just something that can be improved with Stephanie and her group.
    Thanks [teacher]

The Ramskugler children are bright and high-achieving. They routinely brought home A's and B's on their report cards. One son received a congressional nomination to a military academy. But they waged a constant rearguard action against boredom and a school system clearly uncomfortable with having to deal with academically gifted children. Mrs. Ramskugler was hoping it would be different for her twin daughters, Melissa and Stephanie, who both were permitted to skip a grade and were enrolled in the sixth grade in Milwaukee's officially designated school for the gifted and talented.

It was there, however, that she was first confronted with the notion of "cooperative learning," where children worked in groups and a premium was placed on equality, getting along, and going along.

"I am painfully aware of this 'cooperative learning concept' which has become the new buzzword in education . . ." Mrs. Ramskugler later wrote. "I have a great deal of difficulty with this. While I fundamentally and philosophically agree that all are equal, it just isn't true." The letter from her daughter's teacher seemed to confirm many of her worst fears.

Her daughter Stephanie was in many ways a natural leader, a girl who participated actively in class and was a voracious reader who often found herself ahead of her peers. In a class where individual needs were paramount, Stephanie would have been the kind of student most teachers dream about. But in a class where "cooperative learning" was the dominant buzzword, students who might stand out or strive to be leaders were annoyances. Stephanie's curious and skeptical turn of mind and her eagerness to debate ideas were oddly out of place in a setting that valued "getting along," consensus, and "everyone being equal"—values that eclipsed notions of "excellence" even in a school theoretically set aside for gifted students.

"Arguing for arguing's sake is nonproductive," Mrs. Ramskugler later wrote. "But 'arguing' for discussion, expansion, and exchange of ideas would seem to me to be the desired result in this particular educational setting." But that implies individuality and a respect for students who aspire to rise above the norm, clearly not the goals her daughter's teacher had set.

Mrs. Ramskugler wondered: "Where does [her daughter's teacher] think the leaders of tomorrow come from? Test tubes? Think tanks? The leaders of tomorrow are the children of today. I resent the rampant and prevalent attitudes and techniques used to stifle bright and gifted children and the constant lowering of standards—both educational and moral."

CHAPTER 7

THE MAKING OF
AN EDUCATIONIST

Because thought is best expressed in language, the language employed by any writer or movement is a telling expression of the style and quality of their ideas. It follows that nothing is more revealing of the educationist mind than its attitude toward language and its use (and abuse) of words. Richard Mitchell, a connoisseur of the peculiar dialect of edspeak cites a (depressingly) typical piece of educationese:

> "These instructional approaches are perhaps best conceived on a systems model," the educrat writes, "where instructional variables (input factors) are mediated by factors of students' existing cognitive structure (organizational properties of the learner's immediately relevant concepts in the particular subject field); and by personal predispositions and tolerance toward the requirements of inference, abstraction, and impulse control, all prerequisite to achievement in the discovery or the hypothetical learning mode."

That expense of verbiage, Mitchell remarks, "may mean that what a student learns depends on what he already knows and whether or not he gives a damn."[1] Of such stuff are assistant superintendents made. Educationists are addicted to jargon precisely because it allows them to dress up the trivial and the obvious in the trappings of pseudo-profundity. Of course, this language does not exist in a vacuum—it is a product and echo of the home office of educationism: the colleges of teacher education. The schools that train teachers set the tone for the various educational enthusiasms that sweep across the field from time to time, but they also reflect the anxieties of the educationists themselves.

Unlike the more established disciplines of higher education, the position of education has always been shaky. Its pretensions to scholarship are, at best, questionable, and it is the one field that other academics are unanimous in regarding with disdain. "Course work in education deserves its ill repute," James Koerner wrote in the early 1960s. "It is most often puerile, repetitious, dull, and ambiguous—incontestably so."[2] Koerner found both the professors of educationism and the subject-field inadequate.

"Admission standards are low and sometimes non-existent," Koerner wrote, "course work is continuously atomized with little restraint; dissertations, when they are done at all, are frequently triumphs of trivia."[3] The result was that education was "one of the intellectually weakest, most nebulous, and generally unsatisfactory fields in higher education, although it is the biggest." Graduate programs, which were designed for administrators, were in Koerner's view even worse.[4]

Although more forgiving in his rhetoric, James B. Conant found many of the courses in the "foundations of education" to be stultifyingly dull and trivial. Most of them, he wrote, consisted of "scraps of history, philosophy, political theory, sociology, and pedagogical ideology" stirred into an indistinguishable mass by education professors who had no grounding in any of those disciplines, and whose teaching was "far too reminiscent of the less satisfactory high school classes" Conant had seen.[5] Professors of education were so notoriously mediocre that Koerner speculated that "intellectual drive is not the motive power of the field" as much as "a desire to get out of public school teaching or administering, an inability to do graduate work in other fields, and attraction to the amenities of academic life."[6] Koerner was hardly alone in his assault on the ed schools. Theodore Brameld, in *Cultural Foundations of Education*, described the typical teacher-training program as "littered with time-wasting, repetitious, and obvious courses in 'know-how,' many of which could be eliminated without loss except to the entrenched instructors of these courses."[7] In *Crisis in the Classroom*, Charles S. Silberman singled out basic education courses whose "intellectual puerility" was matched only by courses in educational psychology, history, philosophy, and sociology. But the "wasteland of teaching," Silberman said, were the courses in "methods of teaching," which had the distinction of being both "intellectually barren and professionally useless."[8]

These criticisms highlighted two separate but related problems in the teacher colleges: They were deficient both as a scholarly enterprises and as trainers of classroom teachers. In turn, those problems highlight the split personality of the schools: their desire to be regarded as genuine scholarly enterprises in constant tension with their bread-and-butter vocationalism. Educationists are painfully aware of their status in the academy; the soul of every educationist writhes under the scorn of counterparts in the liberal arts and in the *real* sciences. For despite the claim of educationists to be "scientists," there is no science of education; and despite the discipline's claim to equal standing with other schools and departments, its pedigree is virtually nonexistent. The educationist holds himself out (to children, parents, legislators, school board members) as an expert. But what is their *expertise?* "Most disciplines, certainly the basic ones, are built upon the sustained efforts of many generations of scholars working at the task of intellectual discovery and development, and at the task of perfecting the methodology of investigation that best fits the particular subject," Koerner wrote. "But education, like business administration, social work, and perhaps other fields, reversed the procedures and came into being *not because educationists had already developed a body of knowledge and research techniques, but simply because enough people thought that education ought to be a separate field*." [9] [emphasis added]

Like other academics wracked by scholar envy, the educationists have grasped at the trappings of academia, including its jargon. Lacking substance, they fall back upon obscurity. Educationists are bound as intensely to academia's Triple Imperative of Obscurantism as any scientific-wannabe in higher education. The reliance on obscure jargon, convoluted syntax, and the symbols and trappings of pseudoscience are essential for any academic because:

1. They can make even the most trivial subject sound impressive and the most commonplace observation immeasurably profound.
2. They make it much easier to avoid having to say anything directly or even anything at all. And, most important,
3. It is easier than real thought or originality.

These are corollaries to Stanislav Andreski's own law of "nebulous verbosity," which postulates that "Verbiage increases to the extent that ambition exceeds knowledge." Andreski's law perhaps explains the expense of labor that educationists lavish on the trivial, the obscure, and the pointless.[10]

That's "Dr." Educrat, to You

Consider, for example, these recently granted doctorates in education:[11]

"The use of goal-setting and positive self-modeling to enhance self-efficacy and performance for the basketball free-throw shot," for which the author was awarded a Ph.D. by the University of Maryland. At the University of North Carolina at Greensboro, a doctorate was awarded for "Selected clothing characteristics and educator credibility," in which an educationist scholar measured student reactions to three levels of garment color worn by teachers: (dark, pastel, bright), three levels of fabric design (stripe/solid/print or plaid), and concluded that teachers who dressed professionally were seen as more professional. (*Dress for Success* was right.)

Other doctoral dissertations by upwardly mobile educationists included: "The effect of the three-point rule change in college basketball," (which earned someone a doctor of education degree from Brigham Young University); "Teacher humor in middle school and educational criticism," worth a doctorate from the University of Oregon; "Benchmark evaluation of kitchen design specific computer-aided design software for conformance to 'Kitchen design . . . graphics and presentation standards'" which was worth an Ed.D. from the University of Nebraska, Lincoln; and "An ethnographic study of the use of puppetry with a children's group," which earned a doctorate from the University of North Texas.

One rising educrat won the right to put "Dr." on his mailbox by writing his dissertation on "An investigation into the personal meaning of golf."

A scholar at the University of Massachusetts was cagier. She realized that when you want to study something as mundane as what former football players do after they quit the game and whether they might benefit from career counseling programs, the important thing is to dress it up as aggressively as possible with impenetrable jargon. The product was a 226-page dissertation weighted down with the intimidating title: "Self-concept, andragogical orientation, and adaptation to transition in a group of retired professional football players, with implications for the design of a career transition program."

Likewise another candidate for a doctorate in phys ed left nothing to chance in his pursuit of absolute opacity. He was awarded a Ph.D. for a dissertation titled: "A three-level connectionist model for contextual interference effects in open-loop motor skills." As if that might be insufficiently dense, the candidate explained: "The purpose of this research was to create a connectionist model for simulating contextual interference effects in motor skills. The model was a multiple layer, heteroassociative, nonlinear, feedforward interpolative recall network trained by back-propagation of errors."

Because the proto-educationists must produce work that is deemed to be "original," they frequently explore questions that no one had ever asked before, perhaps because no one was interested in the answer. For example: A 132-page dissertation on "Weather conditions and productivity of junior high school students" investigated if weather affected the work of junior high students. It didn't. Similarly, a newly minted doctor of education won his academic spurs by researching "Effects of lunchtime instruction on student attitude toward science." Would teaching science during lunchtime (described as a "non-traditional time and setting for instruction" improve student attitudes?) The answer: No. Forget it. The future educrat, however, took eighty-eight pages to say this. A scholar at the University of Nevada at Reno probed "The effect of music on mathematics anxiety and achievement." Does playing music have any effect on math anxiety? she asked. No. Two other educationists won doctorates for investigating "Prepared-notes as events of instruction," and "The effects of listening skills instruction on students' academic performance." Do notes matter? Would students do better in school if they were given "listening" skills instructions? No, and no. A dissertation on "The relationship among roof problems and roof types on public school buildings in Georgia" takes 107 pages to conclude that there is, indeed, a relationship and somebody should do something about it. Kansas State University granted a doctorate in education for "Evaluation of the comfort property of selected lingerie fabrics," which found that indeed some lingerie was more comfortable.

Another educationist conducted "An investigation of the physical and psychological reasons given for membership non-renewal in a selected Community Wellness Center," and concluded that "decisions not to renew Wellness Center memberships were caused by a combination of personal, program, and other situational factors." Oh.

A doctorate was awarded for a 265-page discussion of "The contextual realties of being a lesbian physical educator: Living in two worlds." Short version: They are oppressed.

Other examples include: "Cognitive development and humor of young adolescents: A cognitive analysis of jokes," (worth an Ed.D. from the University of South Dakota) which spends 115 pages discovering that the verbal abilities of kids tend to be reflected in the kinds of jokes they tell. Ohio State granted a doctorate in 1989 for "The climbing patterns of four and six-year-old children on ladders with differing rung spacings."

A doctoral thesis at Bryn Mawr on "The relationship of teachers' uses of influence and children's responses: Level of conflict in the preschool classroom," found that "teachers used a high proportion of negative influence." [Translation: They told kids "no."] The doctoral candidate concluded in her dissertation that "while children initiated more conflicts than teachers, most of the children's conflict related behavior was a function of the teacher expecting them to conform to unrealistic classroom rules." Which seems to mean that when kindergarten kids act up, it is probably the teacher's fault.

A 367-page dissertation on "A case study analysis of thematic formations in nondirective play therapy" at the University of British Columbia uncovered the insight that "the arrays of play and verbal themes and patterns of transformation were highly individualized." Likewise, a dissertation that was deemed worthy of a doctorate in education by the University of Virginia in 1992 on "Secondary English students' responses to Classics Illustrated comic books" found, remarkably, that most students who read the comic book versions *had not* read the original book.

Training Teachers

Junk scholarship is not, however, the only consequence of the educationist passion to grow up to be a real academic. As educationists have emphasized "research" as the path to academic prestige, they have taken on the coloration of their ambitions, including academia's generalized contempt for teaching. Ironically, as they move toward respectability, educationist scholars have shown a marked desire to separate themselves from . . . education, or at least education in the classroom by teachers. The most prestigious ed schools—such as Harvard and Berkeley—have abandoned the training of elementary and secondary teachers. Their lead has been quickly followed by other top schools, which also have abjured any connection with the messy business of teaching teachers. Why bother, when there are academic riches to be won through research, grants, and consulting contracts? And when the long-sought Grail of Acceptance by *real academics* means getting as far away as possible from any connection to *teaching*.

Since the job of teaching teachers is a second-class activity even within schools supposedly devoted to teaching, much of the teacher training has devolved to the second- and third-tier teacher factories.[12] These schools are not distinguished by the ferment of their ideas or the vigor of their debate over the future of education. To the contrary, they are characterized by the remarkable conformity among both teachers and students about the nature and future of education.[13] Enthusiasm for cooperative learning, distrust of competition, a suspicion of grades and tests, and an aversion to traditional methods of teaching (including phonics) are almost universal in the schools of education. The beliefs that failure should be abolished and individualism de-emphasized are not merely embraced by the educationists-in-training, they are seldom even questioned in the classrooms in which the nation's future teachers are trained.

Such schools are caring environments, to be sure, peopled with earnest and sincere young pedagogues who may be unclear about the details of history, literature, or science, but who are committed to transforming society and curing the various ills of civilization and the pathologies from which they are sure their students will suffer. The schools of education have become priesthoods of good intentions and well-meaningness, where would-be teachers are taught how to cope with low self-esteems, dysfunctional families, and learning disorders: teachers as therapist, social worker, and Big Sister. The idea of education as the passing on of knowledge is a strangely alien notion to these idealists. As author Rita Kramer noted after visiting schools of education, "the main concern is not inspiring good students but protecting the average and poor ones." It is taken for granted in the education school classrooms that schools must be in the business of providing "a warm, caring environment. . . . They want everyone to end up with a passing grade—in school, in society, in life."[14] "Almost nowhere," writes Kramer, "did I find teachers whose emphasis was on the measurable learning of real knowledge."[15] When the self-esteem of students becomes the focus of the schools, she noted, it was no longer important what teachers actually taught or how well students actually performed. Thus, the emphasis in the teachers colleges is on "instructional strategies" to help teachers "cope" with disabled or slow students. Kramer also traces the uncritical embrace of multiculturalism by the teachers colleges as part of a larger attempt to find a substitute for measurable individual achievement, by emphasizing racial, ethnic, and gender identities—in hiring, in choosing books, in evaluating performance. As practiced by the educationists, multiculturalism has become a heavy club wielded against traditional curricula, reading lists, ability tracking, grades, standardized tests, discipline policies, and attempts to raise academic standards (which can be denounced as ethnocentric if they result in lesser rewards for any racial group).

Despite the huge stakes for American education, there is little debate in the schools themselves over the impact of such policies on low-income, minority, and gifted children. Actual research would, in any case, be beside the point. "The ed school establishment," Kramer concluded, "is more concerned with politics—both academic and ideological—than with learning."[16]

These schools produce virtually all of the men and women who will run the nation's schools—both public and private. Into their hands we commend our future. But given their orthodoxy, it is somewhat naive to imagine that private and parochial schools will somehow remain immune. It is even more naive to imagine that either the current or next generation of teachers and administrators will embrace reforms that reemphasize academic excellence and rigor.

"I WANTED TO BE A TEACHER"

wanted to be a teacher," a woman wrote me during my research for this book.[1]

"I didn't decide to teach because I couldn't think of anything else to do with my life. I didn't decide to teach because it was a "cushy" job. I wanted to be a teacher because I thought I could make a difference. Idealistic? Naive? Certainly. But I truly believed that I could be the kind of teacher that students remembered long after they had left my classroom. I believed that teaching was my destiny. Then I went to college.

"I remember looking at my schedule that fall and having a shadow of doubt cross my mind. To my untrained eye, the education classes appeared to be theoretical in nature, not practical: Reading, Visual Arts, Educational Psychology, Fundamentals of Education. Where were the 'roll-up-your-sleeves, dive-right-in' classes that would teach me how to be a teacher? I was looking for 'real life' preparation for the classroom. But instead, I learned about Piaget and the history of public education. I spent three hours a week for several months learning how to thread a projector and make laminated copies of phony lesson plans. The instructors wanted journals and projects and early morning meetings where we were all supposed to sit around and talk about how it 'felt' to be a teacher. We were sent to observe classrooms at the local high school, as if by watching these teachers at work, somehow we would know what to do when we stood up in front of thirty bored ninth graders. I had been watching and listening to teachers for almost sixteen years. I knew what they did. What most of them did *was* boring—especially to a twenty-one-year-old college senior. I didn't want to be that kind of teacher. I had my own ideas about how I would teach—how I would spark interest and creativity in the mind of reluctant junior high grammar students. I was dying to get out there and try it for myself.

"One afternoon, in a fit of frustration, I confided in an instructor who had appeared to me to be one of the few college instructors who really cared about teaching. I told him I was bored. Frustrated. That I was having trouble sitting through all these senseless classes, filled with their self-important gobbledy-gook. I told him I thought the education department at the college was not preparing me to teach—that I wanted to be shown the practicalities of teaching and be given the freedom to experiment with some of my own ideas.

"The instructor was furious. How could I understand something that I didn't have a degree in? Didn't I realize that the people I was criticizing had spent their lives studying these theories and knew more about education that 99.9 percent of the population? Creativity? Was I crazy or something? I had to be extremely naive to believe that a 'cocky, arrogant college senior' like me would be afforded the privilege of creativity. Who in the hell did I think I was, anyhow?

"And then it occurred to me—these so-called educators were not teachers. They had never taught a single day in any secondary classroom. They were not interested in showing me or any other student teacher how to be a 'good' teacher. For these instructors, with their doctorates in education, the primary goal was to indoctrinate all of us teacher wanna-bes into the subjective, mediocre ideologies of the professional educator. We were told to leave our creativity, uniqueness, and youthful enthusiasm outside of the college classroom and cheerfully conform to the bloated rhetoric of educators who designed their courses to be intimidating, complicated, and filled with senseless jargon that only sounded impressive.

"As a student teacher, I spent eight weeks watching and listening to a junior high English teacher who had become jaded and mean-spirited after too many years of clocking in and clocking out of a job she hated. She told me and anyone else in earshot how she despised the children she taught. She was not interested in her students or in her student teacher. She couldn't wait to dash out of the classroom at the end of the day. I did my best to ignore her zealous advice that I should be more intimidating—more threatening—and I found that the only reason the whole experience was tolerable was because of the wonderful support and encouragement I received from my students.

"Some of my innocence was lost that year. For my entire life, working hard and being myself were two things that had always led to success. But that semester of student teaching turned my world upside down. The things I valued most about myself—my creativity, my tenacity, my enthusiasm, my individualism, my intellect—were tossed aside and deemed inappropriate. In her evaluation, my supervising teacher concluded I wasn't cut out for the job.

"I often think that if I had been the kind of teacher she had wanted me to be, it all would have turned out differently. But I loved teaching. I loved the students and the moments where I knew that I was getting through to them. I had spent four years preparing to make teaching my life. I wanted to make a difference. I never taught again."

THE NEW ILLITERACY

Joan Wittig and Beverly Jankowski are not experts. They just didn't understand why their children weren't learning to write, spell, or read very well. They didn't understand why their children kept coming home with sloppy papers filled with spelling mistakes and bad grammar and why teachers never corrected them or demanded better work. Mrs. Wittig couldn't fathom why her child's teacher would write "Wow!" and award a check-plus (for above average work) to a paper that read:

> "I'm goin to has majik skates. Im goin to go to disenelan. Im goin to bin my mom and dad and brusr and sisd. We r go to se mickey mouse." [sic]

Mrs. Jankowski was similarly puzzled why a teacher would write, "I love your story, especially the spelling" on a story jammed with misspelled words. ("Once a pona time, I visted a tropical rian forist. It was very pretty. There were lots of trees and anamlas. My fifil anaml was a Jacwier. my ffifit insect was a wihite buterfly, my fifit riptil was a comilin. . . .")[1]

She was also appalled at the writing—again uncorrected—in her child's fourth-grade "journal." One entry read: "To day Dec. 9 1992 at 10:56 this was not planed to happen but it did a fire drill want off because in gym someone hit the fire dall and the glass borck. lot of fireman came to see wite happen. But they were vilinters fire man they smelled like smok but I get use to it the bell rann for a long time." [sic]

Another assignment asked children to discuss why, where, and how they would run away without their parents knowing it. The journal entry read:

> I would run awar because my mom and Dad don't love me. I would run away with my brother to the musan in mlewky. We will use are backpacks and put all are close in it. We will take a lot of mony with us so we can go on the bus to the musam. We will stay there for a long time so my mom and dad will know they did not love us." [sic]

Mrs. Jankowski was bothered by the assignment about running away but also by the level of skills that her child's school seemed to find acceptable. "If this is any indication of the skills my child demonstrated in grammar for the first semester of school," she said, "we are in big trouble."

While Joan Wittig did not have a degree in education, she did have some college-level credits in education and "a background of training others to perform accurately and competently in my numerous job positions, beginning in my high school years." That experience was enough for her to sense something was wrong. She was not easily brushed off by assurances that her children were being taught "whole language skills" and that there was therefore no cause to be concerned. Instead, she decided to find out what the school district was really doing.

Administrators and "specialists" assured the parents that their children would learn spelling and grammar eventually. Their children's teachers were not being sloppy, they were practitioners of what they called "invented spelling," a more *holistic* approach to language.

Invented Spelling

The two mothers should not really have been surprised by their children's papers, since many educationists in charge of teaching reading and writing no longer believe that it is necessary to teach or to correct spelling.

Educationists noticed that many children misspelled words and realized that it would take a great deal of time, effort, and commitment to fix the problem. Instead, they discovered "invented spelling." Children weren't getting the words wrong, they were acting as "independent spellers," and any attempt to correct them would not only stifle their freedom, but smother their tender young creativity aborning. Such ideas have been widely seized upon by educationists who see the natural, unconscious, and effortless approach to spelling not only as progressive and child-centered, but a lot less work as well.

"Learning to spell," The University of Nevada at Reno's Sandra Wilde insists, "should ultimately be as natural, unconscious, effortless, and pleasant as learning to speak."[2] The key words here are *natural, unconscious, effortless*, and *pleasant*. Wilde sees no difference between written and spoken language and ignores the necessary discipline that writing demands and speech does not.

Wilde and other theorists of "invented spelling" envision a new spelling curriculum that would shift from a "focus on error to a focus on creation." The idea is that kids should be free to misspell words—invent their own spelling—without having their spelling corrected or having the teacher tell them the correct spelling. This hands-off approach, we are assured, increases the writer's freedom and cuts down on frustration. This is far more enlightened, Wilde explains, than the "usual view of spelling as either right or wrong," an archaic conception that has been "replaced by a growing understanding of why children produced a particular spelling."

Under the new standards, children aren't expected to get it right, but merely to make "plausible representations of English words." For example, Wilde explains that a student might write JREK to stand for the word conventionally rendered as *drink*. The invented spelling, she says, "is the result of three phenomena: knowledge that *d* occurring before *r* sounds like a *j*, an accurate perception of the word's vowel as sounding like the letter named *e*, and omission of a nasal sound before a consonant because it is not very salient phonetically."

Though her explanation describes *why* a child might think that JREK might mean "drink," it's a long stretch to say that therefore JREK *should* be an acceptable and plausible alternative—or that the "usual" view of spelling as "right or wrong" should be scrapped. That is no more plausible that taking a common misunderstanding or error in arithmetic and making it the basis of "invented math." The confusion is as fundamental as mistaking a diagnosis for a prescription. Learning how a child makes a mistake might be helpful in recognizing the source of the error, as a way of helping children to avoid repeating it—but using that mistake as the basis of transforming the math curriculum would be, well, a mistake. (As we'll see later, educationists have, in fact, applied the same logic to math as well as spelling.)

But Wilde holds out great promise for the new regime: "If children are encouraged to invent their own spellings in this way from the very beginning," she promises, "they will be independent spellers from the start. . . ." And eventually, students will get around in their own way and their own time to spelling words correctly, although Wilde is rather vague about her timetable. All she says is that the "ability to produce a perfectly spelled piece of writing without a teacher's help . . . is certainly an appropriate goal for most students by the end of elementary school." In the meantime, the kids are on their own.

While the new apostles of invented spelling give lip service to making students "competent spellers," the emphasis of their literature is on the avoidance of the difficult, the reduction of stress, and on the creativity they insist will be unleashed if we just get over our hang-ups about *i* before *e* and *cat* instead of *kat*.

Wilde, for example, disdains spelling textbooks on the grounds that they are insufficiently humanistic and flexible, because they are so fixated on . . . spelling. "Spelling textbooks," she sniffs, "do not, for the most part, see students as individuals. . . ." Teachers, on the other hand, are supposed to keep out of the way. "Teachers should rarely tell students how to spell a word," writes Wilde. Kids are supposed to teach themselves: "As students sound out words, try different spellings to see how they look, discuss possible spellings with their peers, or check in reference books, they gain competence through acting independently. . . ." Wilde warns that teaching spelling can be actually harmful. "This creative intellectual process is short-circuited," she writes, "if the teacher provides spellings out of misplaced and premature concern for a correct final product."

There is, of course, considerable and growing evidence that all of this naturalistic self-teaching is not working out exactly as Wilde and her colleagues envision. Instead of embarking on a journey of self-discovery, children often pick up on the fact that since spelling is not counted, it must therefore be unimportant and irrelevant. The result is a generation of spellers who are undeniably independent in their approach to spelling, but seldom competent. A quick glance through student papers in high school and college is usually enough to disabuse all but the most committed educationist of the notion that spelling has improved. It is also enough to raise another question: Where is the creativity and stifled genius that should be breaking out all over now that the heavy hand of spelling has been lifted?

The fact is that American students are rotten spellers and their writing is often a grammatical embarrassment. While not admitting the role of educationism in the spread of this new illiteracy, Wilde does seem to acknowledge that the new curriculum is not going to create competent spellers after all. But the problem, she insists with educationist fervor, isn't with her curriculum—it's us. "For spelling curriculum and instruction to change in this country," Wilde exhorts the faithful, "beliefs and attitudes about spelling must change." Americans make way too much of good spelling. She complains that some people regard spelling words correctly as "almost a moral issue that is taken far more seriously than its educational importance warrants."

In fact, spelling words right is really only a "question of etiquette," Wilde argues. Employers and professors offended by bad spelling "feel this way not because they cannot understand what is being said or because the misspelling is a serious distraction but because they feel insulted by a writer who appears not to take the reader's sensibilities seriously enough. *Such constant vigilance about spelling, including a perfectionism that has filtered down even to the primary grades, must be relaxed if the students are to have enough breathing space to grow at their own pace in spelling.*" [emphasis added] Wilde obviously takes a rather expansive view of the breathing space people need if she is talking about college students and young adults who still haven't learned to spell. But her main point is that it is no big deal and neither the schools nor the poor spellers should be held accountable.

"Instead of one of the most important basics in education," Wilde argues, spelling "can really be better described as a detail." Her advice is that "everyone needs to relax a bit more about spelling." They are also relaxing a bit more about punctuation, grammar, and organization—all in the name of being *holistic.*

Holistic Literacy

The beauty of a holistic approach to writing is that it enables educators to change the rules of the game they have been losing. When the public began to notice the rapid decline in the reading and writing ability of American students, educationists responded with "holistic grading," which guaranteed that grades would rise without any improvement in writing. The National Council of Teachers of English was especially enthusiastic, offering workshops in holistic grading, which were aimed at getting rid of "trivia." "With this method," they declared, "the essay is read for a total impression of its quality rather than for such separate aspects of writing skill as *organization, punctuation, diction, or spelling.*"[3] [emphasis added]

"The method takes a positive approach to the rating of compositions by asking what the student has accomplished rather than on what the student has failed to do or has done badly." Textbook publishers quickly followed suit. A Macmillan/McGraw Hill *Performance Assessment Handbook Guide for Reading/Language Arts Teachers, Grade 2* described the new "modified holistic scoring" as a method that "does not consider grammar, mechanics, and usage to any real extent. . . ."

This attitude has also been reflected in some state "assessments" of literacy. In Virginia, all students were expected to pass the so-called "Literacy Passport" before entering high school. First given in sixth grade, students were able to take it in subsequent years until they passed all three sections. The writing section was evaluated in five areas—composition, style, usage, sentence formation, and mechanics—and students could get up to four points in each area. But they were not all weighed equally. State educationists insisted that the scores for "composition" be multiplied by three and the score for "style" by two. In contrast, scores for sentence formation, usage, and mechanics were only multiplied by one. As one former middle-school teacher wrote in a letter to the *Richmond Times-Dispatch,* the minimal weight attached to the mechanics of writing meant that "a student could receive a passing score without having to write complete sentences. Fragments and run-on sentences could dominate his sample. He would not need to concern himself with subject and verb agreement or with using words properly. His passing test could, in theory, contain no capitalization, punctuation, or proper spelling. Unbelievably, a student could receive a score of 1 (demonstrating little or no control) in the domains of Sentence Formation, Usage, and Mechanics, and still receive a passing grade. Together these domains make up only ⅜ths of the total score." She remarked: "Employers are not going to notice vivid vocabulary when the job applicant cannot spell or write complete sentences."[4]

Redefining Literacy

Another response of educationists to the decline of literacy has been to simply change the definition of literacy. A literate person is no longer someone who has mastered the grammar, usage, and diction of language. In the early 1980s, a Minnesota school district defined the literate person as "one who has developed a feeling of self-worth and importance; respect for and appreciation and understanding of other people and cultures; and a desire for learning. The literate person is one who continues to seek knowledge, to increase personal skills and the quality of relations with others, and to fulfill individual potential." As Richard Mitchell noted, this definition effectively leaves out Aristotle (didn't appreciate barbarians); Kakfa (not into self-worth and self-importance); T. S. Eliot (undemocratic); and Norman Mailer (poor quality of relations with others).[5]

The school district where Joan Wittig and Beverly Jankowski sent their children took a similar tack by relabeling reading and writing as "communication arts," which were designed to "provide students with opportunities to":

- Develop the *appreciation and enjoyment* of using language skillfully.
- Interrelate all language forms—reading, writing, listening, speaking— as a means of communication.
- Build life skills that will facilitate the fulfillment of career goals.
- Develop an understanding and competency in the use of technology (e.g. computers, *audio-visual equipment*, etc.) in communication arts.[6] [emphasis added]

From the emphasis on "appreciation" and "enjoyment" of communication arts to the emphasis on "life skills," the statement was a relatively pure statement of the most au courant educationist faith. For several decades now, educationists have emphasized "appreciation" rather than basic skills, perhaps because while spelling and grammar can be measured, "appreciation" and "enjoyment" cannot. The goal statement also carefully puts reading in its place. Rather than seeing it as the foundation of all learning, it is demoted to a communications skill on a par with "listening" and operating audio-visual equipment.

The goals statement's silence on grammar and spelling was not a casual omission. The specialists running the "communications arts" program had announced that they intended to phase out "traditional" spelling books over three years, as well as the "traditional use of grammar books." The specialists also had a distinctive attitude toward other sorts of books.

Henceforth, books chosen for the "communication arts" programs would have to meet the following criteria: They must "follow the genre emphasized in the curriculum," must be "age appropriate; fit the students' interests; develop human awareness [as opposed to what?]; and develop multicultural, world awareness." None of the criteria mentioned whether the books would be any good.

When the mothers pressed the school on their children's progress, the specialists assured them that they must be allowed to work at their own pace and that they would eventually pick up the necessary mechanics along the way. But Beverly Jankowski's son was already in ninth grade and she saw few signs that he had ever gotten around to picking up basic skills, as she had been promised. Instead, he was being assigned "cooperative writing projects," in which he and another student had to jointly produce an acceptable piece of writing.

In one assignment, her son and another high school freshman chose to write a letter of complaint. The first paragraph of the cooperative effort read:

Dear School Board:

We are writing in consern [sic] of an onfit [sic] phyical [sic] educational derictor [sic]. At New Berlin West High School we have landslids [sic] of problems, regarding [teacher's name]. The students and some faclty [sic] feel she unfit to teach a phy ed class. She contiuasly [sic] mock me, [student's name] and my assastare [student name]. etc.

The final draft, which "earned" the two students the above average grade of "B," read:

Dear School Board:

We are writing in concern of [sic] an unfit Physical Education Director. At New Berlin West High School we have landslides of problems regaurding [sic] [teacher's name]. The students and most of the faculty agree that [she] is unfit, ugly, unknolegable [sic], underqualified and uncoordinated. This just covers the Us, we could go on forever.

The teacher commented on this paragraph: "Powerful beginning." Neither the grammar nor the spelling was corrected.

In the second paragraph, the students wrote that "We have decided to tell you about one specific example that will prove how she mocks the students inteleigents [sic]." The teacher writes on the paper:

"Good idea to use a specific example."

In giving the paper a grade of "B," the teacher remarked: "Although the content is somewhat 'smart-aleckie' [sic] you demonstrated the ability to write a formal letter of complaint. Check spelling."

For two years, Joan Wittig agonized before transferring her children from the public school in her community to private schools. After only a semester at the private schools, her children were writing and reading at a markedly higher level. Their papers were neatly written, grammatical, and their spelling was systematically corrected. Impressed by the improvement, she decided to take her story to her local school board. She brought along copies of her children's work (before and after their transfer to private schools). Along with other parents, she questioned the district's enthusiasm for "whole language," a teaching philosophy where children, Wittig said, are "encouraged to write and spell any way they want and the teacher does not correct the spelling so that the child's creativity is not stifled."

"Is this to be considered teaching?" she asked. "Is effective learning taking place?" She also wondered about the schools' emphasis on "cooperative learning," in which children worked in groups. "I sent my child to school to be taught by a teacher," she said, "not by another student."

"Lazy, poor students rely on the good students to do all the work," she told the board. "Good students are reinforced that they must do everything if it is to be done right." A local newspaper story recounted the reaction to Wittig's presentation: "Superintendent James Benfield said such criticism could make school employees feel they are doing something wrong. 'We should not have employees criticized until we change the guidelines.'" If Wittig left the skirmish puzzled, she is not alone.

The Reading Wars

Given its importance, it is not surprising that the dispute over the teaching of reading is the site of some of the most intense and emotional battles in the school wars. Reading is at the heart of education, the basic skill upon which all others are built. History is full of examples of extraordinary educations based solely on the cultivation of language, through reading and through the mastery of words to express cogent and coherent thoughts. You'd hardly know this, though, from reading educationist theorizing about "communication arts skills" and "reading skills."

Typically, educationists contrast the ability to read and write coherently with what they call "higher-order thinking skills," which they insist are far more important for children to learn that any "rote" skills of the past. But there is another way of looking at reading. The "high-order thinking skills"—such as inquiry skills, inference, analogy analysis, and the like—are really only the building blocks for the genuinely higher order skills. "Much more worthy of being called 'higher-order skills',", argues Matthew Lipman, director of Institute for the Advancement of Philosophy for Children, "are reading, writing, and computation. The reasoning and inquiry skills are relatively simple and eminently teachable. One might think of them, together with mental acts, as fairly atomic, in contrast with which reading, writing and computation are enormously complex and molecular."[7] In other words, the so-called "higher-order thinking skills" are merely building blocks to the far more complex process of understanding required for reading, writing, and math. Reading a work of literature requires the integration of all such skills, as well as drawing upon knowledge, insight, and intuition. Mastering "inquiry" skills is to reading *Moby Dick* what the mastery of musical theory is to playing Bach's "Ave Maria." Important, yes; maybe even crucial. But not the highest order.

Reading is also the model for thinking precisely because it is an individual, solitary activity; one mind alone with another. A book is a single voice, expressing a singular point of view, and requires the individual attention and response of the reader. Of all of the activities of education, it is the most personal. Despite all of the hopeful therapeutic posturing about collective thinking in education, thought, like reading, is not a collective undertaking. All thinking, ultimately, is individual. Perhaps that is why it does not seem to fit into the modern school's emphasis on cooperative learning, consensus, sharing of feelings, and group orientations. "The acts that are at once the means and the ends of education, knowing, thinking, understanding, judging, are all committed in solitude," Mitchell writes. "It is only in a mind that the work of the mind can be done. . . ."[8]

That fact is not always recognized in the schools of the 1990s—where, Mitchell says, "the inane and unformed regurgitations of the ninth grade rap session on solar energy as a viable alternative to nuclear power are positive, creative, self-esteem-enhancing student behavioral outcomes; the child who sits alone at the turning of the staircase, reading, is a weirdo." In one of his most searing passages, Mitchell goes even further: "Educationists just don't *feel* right . . . about books. A book is the work of *a* mind, doing its work in the way that *a* mind deems best. That's dangerous. Is the work of some mere *individual* mind likely to serve the aims of collectively accepted compromises, which are known in the schools as 'standards'?

"Any mind that would audaciously put *itself* forth to work *all alone* is surely a bad example for the students, and probably, if not downright anti-social, at least a little off-center, self-indulgent, elitist."[9]

Why Johnny Can't Read

The most dramatic declines in the achievement levels of American students have been in their literacy. SAT verbal scores have reached historic lows, while national surveys have put the number of functionally illiterate Americans in the tens of millions. A 1994 report by the Educational Testing

Service found that half of the nation's college graduates could not read a bus schedule and that only 42 percent could summarize an argument presented in a newspaper article or contrast the views in two editorials about fuel efficiency.

A study that divided students into five levels of literacy found that only 11 percent of the graduates from four-year colleges and only 2 percent of graduates of two-year colleges reached the top level. Only 35 percent of the four-year college graduates were able consistently to write a brief letter about a billing error.[10] One study found that American business loses nearly $40 billion in revenue a year because of the low level of their employees' literacy and the added time required to train and retrain workers for new technologies. Recently the Stone Savannah River Pulp & Paper Corporation had to spend $200,000 to train workers to use computers after managers found that workers lacked the reading skills they needed to operate the equipment.[11]

Rudolf Flesch said something like this would happen.

In the mid-1950s, Flesch warned in the best-selling book *Why Johnny Can't Read* that American schools would produce a generation of illiterates if they continued to rely on faddish techniques for teaching reading. At the time Flesch wrote, American education was dominated by the "look-say" method of teaching. Instead of teaching children how to sound out words, the so-called phonetic method that had been used for generations, students were encouraged to look at and recognize the whole word. Flesch warned that the abandonment of phonics and other traditional approaches to reading was a "time bomb" primed to wreak educational havoc on the nation's schools.[12] Although his book drew widespread attention, he was generally either ignored or vilified by educationists. But nearly four decades of experience have vindicated his Cassandra-like warnings. While national test scores of reading and writing abilities are awful enough, the experience of California may be the most obvious test case of Flesch's theory.

In 1987, California radically changed its reading curriculum to de-emphasize what little phonetic instruction still remained. In ditching phonics, California embraced what educationists called a "literature-based" approach to reading that de-emphasized "skill-based" programs. Kids would be taught to read by having them experience the wonders of literature, rather than having to go through the dreary business of first learning the mechanics or rules of reading. It was, educationists insisted, "the natural way" to learn reading. One survey found that 87 percent of California's reading teachers embraced the new techniques and that fewer than one in ten heavily emphasized phonics. Many teachers said later that they thought the new curriculum required them to get rid of phonics altogether (a claim state educrats later denied for reasons that will soon be apparent). The result was a full-scale, statewide test of pro-phonics and anti-phonics theories.

In 1993, six years into the phonics-less curriculum, a national reading survey conducted by the Educational Testing Service found that California's fourth graders ranked forty-ninth—tied with students from Mississippi for dead last—in their reading abilities compared with students throughout the country. Even when California's nonimmigrant, white fourth graders were considered separately, they still finished in the bottom fifth of the fifty states in the test. "There's a lot of evidence that first-graders who do not get instruction in phonics fail to read adequately," said Robert E. Slavin, director of the elementary school program at Johns Hopkins University's Center for Research on Effective Schooling for Disadvantaged Students. "It's possible that the kids in the last several years were not taught word attack skills adequately. Today's fourth-graders were in the first grade three years ago."[13] State educrats, however, blamed the problem on a simple miscommunication. They insisted that they had never meant to totally eliminate phonics. But, inadvertently, they had provided stunning empirical confirmation of Flesch's worst fears.

How Kids Learn

For generations, children were taught to read by being first taught the mechanics of reading. They were taught that letters had sounds and that they could decode words by sounding them out. At the end of a couple of semesters, a child with the mastery of phonetics could read an estimated 24,000 words. Look-say requires children to memorize whole words, much like the Chinese learn individual ideograms. Thus, they learn by reading the same words over and over again. Instead of a potential vocabulary of thousands of words, children are able to read only a few hundred. The classic example of the repetition used to bolster the look-say method was the mind-numbingly inane Dick and Jane series of books. In 1930, the Dick and Jane pre-primer taught a total of 68 different words in 39 pages of text; by 1950, the pre-primer had grown to 172 pages, but the number of words had been cut to 58. By 1950, children were being soaked with the banality of readers that repeated the word *look* 110 times, the word *oh* 138 times, and the word *see* dragged gasping into the text 176 times. Eventually, children learned to recognize the words.

Flesch was merciless in ridiculing such approaches. "Learning to read," he wrote, "is like learning to drive a car. You take lessons and learn the mechanics and the rules of the road. After a few weeks you have learned how to drive, how to stop, how to shift gears, how to park, and how to signal. You have also learned to stop at a red light and understand road signs. When you are ready, you take a road test, and if you pass, you can drive. Phonics-first works the same way. The child learns the mechanics of reading, and when he's through, he can read. Look and say works differently. The child is taught to read before he has learned the mechanics—the sounds of the letters. It is like learning to drive by starting your car and driving ahead. . . . And the mechanics of driving? You would pick those up as you go along."[14]

Flesch predicted that such techniques would work no better for teaching reading than for producing competent drivers. By the mid-1980s, he had won the right to say that he had told us so.

As Flesch predicted, reading scores have dropped precipitously as schools dropped phonics and experimented with "look-say" methods or "language experience" or "whole language" programs. The intensity of the debate over the issue might suggest either that research data are mixed on the most effective reading methods or that we really don't know how children first learn to read. Neither is true. It's impossible to review here all of the salvos fired in the reading wars, but research support marshaled to support Flesch's position is formidable, to say the least.

- In a 1985 study titled *Becoming a Nation of Readers*, a commission of the National Institute of Education found that: "Classroom research shows that, on the average, children who are taught phonics get off to a better start in learning to read than children who are not taught phonics. The advantage is most apparent on tests of word identification, though children in programs in which phonics gets a heavy stress also do better on tests of sentence and story comprehension, particularly in the early grades."[15]
- In Harold Stevenson's international comparisons, he and his colleagues found that American students tended to be overrepresented among both the best and worst readers. The differences, they determined, could be explained by the presence or absence of phonics instruction. "Children who fail to catch on to this possibility tend to be poor readers; children who do learn to break down words by sound are able to read words of high complexity."[16]
- Studies that have identified the traits of effective schools—forceful administrators, high faculty expectations, an orderly school atmosphere—also found that successful schools shared similar approaches to reading including schoolwide concern about reading skills, the adroit use of reading specialists, and a phonics-based curriculum.[17]

Phonics advocates also point to trends in reading scores over the last few decades. If phonics really is effective, then reading test scores should go up when it is used more heavily and should decline when it is de-emphasized. In fact, it is possible to test such a hypothesis. Phonics made a temporary resurgence in the early 1970s, when beginning reading programs once again emphasized the mechanics of reading and sounding out words. By the 1980s, however, educationists had turned to "whole language" approaches and phonics once again fell into relative disuse. During that two-decade period, the National Assessment of Educational Progress conducted six national assessments of reading abilities. The NAEP found that during the 1970s, nine-year-olds showed a steady improvement in reading comprehension. But in the 1980s, the rise in reading scores stopped. Although reading scores in 1988 were higher than in 1971, the NAEP concluded, "this progress was made during the 1970s." Thus the reading scores of fourth graders rose during a decade when they had been exposed as first and second graders to basic phonics programs. As phonics programs were dropped, the improvements dropped off.[18]

The early start on phonics also appears to have long-term consequences. In 1988, the NAEP found that the reading scores of seventeen-year-olds— who had learned to read phonetically in the 1970s—showed improvement. The NAEP explained the relative success of those students as "due, at least, in part, to an early advantage" in their reading scores in the 1970s. While urging caution about drawing too sweeping a conclusion from such trends, Harvard Education professor Jeanne Chall noted that "there is considerable evidence that methods and materials and other school factors do make a difference in students' reading achievement . . . we may indeed find that the beginning reading programs in the 1980s—programs that put a greater emphasis on—'whole language'—may be related to the declines reported by NAEP in the scores of the nine-year-olds in the 1980s. We may also find that the beginning reading programs of the 1970s, which paid more attention to the phonological, to the alphabetic principle, to decoding, to phonics much maligned today may have contributed to the rising scores of the nine-year-olds in the 1980s and to the higher scores of the seventeen-year-olds in the 1980s . . ."[19]

Americans are not alone in experiencing drops in reading abilities. In Britain, educational psychologists first noted a drop in reading scores in 1990, and a government report confirmed the falling scores the next year. The exceptions were schools that employed intensive phonics programs. As a result of the ensuing outcry over the dropping reading scores, phonics instruction is once again being included in England's national curriculum.[20]

Perhaps the most powerful case for phonics was a landmark study by Marilyn Jager Adams, conducted for Center for the Study of Reading.[21] Adams put together what one critic called "an impressive, and often overwhelming, array of empirical research related to beginning reading."[22] Having reviewed "the experimental findings from every conceivable field" relating to the question of beginning reading, Adams concluded not only "that proficient reading depends on an automatic capacity to recognize frequent patterns and to *translate them phonetically*" but that the failure to learn such mechanics "may be the single most common source of reading difficulties." Learning to sound out words, she argued, helps children learn to identify frequent words and spelling patterns because children have to pay close attention to the sequence of letters. Children learn how words are spelled because the process of sounding out words helps lock correct spelling in their minds.[23]

Phonics is essential both for children who come to school with a solid background in reading preparation as well as for students who may come with little familiarity of letters, words, and stories. For students who are on the brink of reading, she found, "the basic phonics curriculum will generally consist less of new concepts and information than of review and clarification of things they already know." As a result, some teachers feel that an emphasis on basic phonics is inappropriate. "However," Adams's study found, "systematic phonics is no less important for these children" when it is used as a "support activity." Phonics is also opposed by some teachers of students who come to school with little background in reading. But Adams found that the problem of teaching low-achieving students to read is not the use of phonics, but the poor use of instructional materials. She found that schools with high proportions of students labeled at-risk "tend to spend not more, but less classroom time on reading instruction." Despite the need for more attention and time, schools with large numbers of students from low-income families actually schedule *less* time on reading than other schools—on average twenty minutes less a day.

While poorer students have a longer way to go to grasp the essentials of reading, they are being given less time to work on sounding out words, less time for "connected reading," and less time for writing. "And during the time they do read text," Adams found, "they cover less material and are less often challenged to think about its meaning or structure.

"In reaction to this situation, some may see phonics instruction as the problem with such programs for low achievers," Adams observed. "Yet the problem is not phonics instruction—all students, whether their preschool reading preparation is high, low or in-between, need to learn about spellings, sounds, and their relationships."

Phonics, wrote Adams, is so effective because "with experience, skillful readers tend to sound words out quite automatically. As a result, even the occasional, never-before-seen word may be read with little outward sign of difficulty. Just try it: *pentamerous, hypermetropical, hackmatack.*" Even more important, she argued, was the ability of phonetically fluent readers to sound out words whose meaning they know, but which they have not seen before on the printed page. This makes for more fluent reading, because children are not stopped as often by unfamiliar words.

Contrast that with the whole language approach in Joan Wittig's school district. Reading instruction begins with "pre-reading strategies" in which "Children predict what the story is about by looking at the title and the pictures. Background knowledge is activated to get the children thinking about the reading topic." Then they read the story. If a child does not recognize a word, they are told to "look for clues."

Specifically, the curriculum suggests that children: "Look at the pictures," ask "What would make sense?" "Look for patterns," "Look for clues," and "Skip the word and read ahead and then go back to the word." Finally, if all of this fails, parents/teachers are told, "Tell the child the word."[24]

Nowhere is the child told to "sound it out."

Oklahoma's educrats took a similar approach in setting out their reading "outcomes" for second graders. The statewide guidelines called on second graders to "use fix-it strategies in order to continue reading." What exactly did the educationists have in mind for kids who are unable to figure out a word? Their suggestions included: "ask a friend, skip the word, substitute another meaningful word."[25] (Ask a teacher? Sound it out? Apparently not.) A publication of the Wisconsin Public Department of Public Instruction warns parents explicitly not to tell their children to "sound out" unfamiliar words, "because sounding is only part of the game." ("Reading is not just 'sounding out words,'" the educrats explained with the usual mix of the obvious and the jargonesque. "Reading is the process of constructing meaning through the dynamic interaction between the reader, the book, and the reading/learning situation.")[26]

Look at the pictures. Skip the word. Ask a friend. Is this reading? Wittig and Jankowski found that in their children's schools, "repetitious and predictable" books were used in reading classes. "Children memorize the text as they 'read' the story over and over with the teacher." "It is our experience that they cannot read new books until the text has been memorized." But is memorization the same as reading?

When they pressed the teachers about this, the two mothers said, "We are told that reading should be a pleasant experience, not distressful."

Hole Langwidg

At first blush, the arguments for "whole language" seem self-evident, which accounts, in part, for their widespread acceptance. Advocates argue that teachers should emphasize comprehension and immerse children in high-quality literature. They insist they are teaching literacy by reading interesting and stimulating stories and undertaking projects that interest and involve children and reduce their anxieties about reading and writing. But in its purer forms, "whole language" is not merely an instructional technique, it is an overarching philosophy of education. Its advocates believe that children learn "naturally," that children learn best when "learning is kept whole, meaningful, interesting and functional," and that this is more likely to happen when children make their own choices as part of a "community of learners" in a noncompetitive environment. "Whole language" advocates describe "optimal literacy environments," which they say "promote risk taking and trust." These classrooms are "child-centered," and children learn at their own pace.

Not surprisingly, this is not a place where drills in phonics or an emphasis on the mechanics of reading is likely to be stressed. Nor is there much room for stressing that there are right and wrong ways of spelling or writing in this brave new world in which children monitor themselves, take chances, express their feelings, and look at pictures in books. Whole language, riffs one enthusiast, is "child-centered, experiential, reflective, authentic, holistic, social, collaborative, democratic, cognitive, developmental, constructivist, and challenging."[27] The more zealous advocates of this learner-centered, child-centered approach seem to believe that teaching basic skills is not only unnecessary, but could be positively harmful to the blooming creativity and self-esteem of young children. Putting too much pressure on children to learn the phonetic rules might get in the way of the child's enthusiasm, his wonder, exploration and his eagerness to sing beautiful songs from his unsullied soul. Rather than seeing such basic skills as providing children a key to unlock the secrets of literacy, they see such skills as anchors preventing children from continuing to trail clouds of glory.

Educationists, of course, insist that this romantic view of learning has a solid basis in "science." The history of this movement can, in part, be traced to the attempts of fledgling educationists to win some legitimacy for their field.

The March of Folly

In the late nineteenth century, a proto-educationist named James Cattell journeyed to Leipzig to study the psychology of learning. Cattell was later to found Columbia University's department of psychology and to train some of the most influential American educationists of the century. Most importantly, he provided a scientific gloss to the abandonment of traditional methods of teaching reading. Through a series of experiments, Cattell found that adults who knew how to read can recognize words without sounding out letters. From that, he drew the conclusion that words aren't sounded out, but are seen as "total word pictures." If competent readers did not need to sound out words, he declared, then there was little point in teaching such skills to children. "The result," wrote Lance J. Klass in *The Leipzig Connection*, "was the dropping of the phonic or alphabetic method of teaching reading, and its replacement by the sight-reading method in use throughout America."

As many of his successors would do, Cattell confused the "attributes" of readers (or in later edspeak, "the expected behaviors" or "outcomes") with the appropriate way of acquiring those attributes. Of course, skilled readers did not stop to sound out words; long practice had made that unnecessary. It was thus an "outcome" of learning to read; the mechanics of reading, including the ability to sound out words, enabled the reader to achieve that outcome. But since the actual process of sounding out words is not the desired "outcome," educationists decided that they could dispense with it.

The consequences of buying this argument included, as Richard Mitchell gibes, "not only the stupefaction of almost the whole of American culture but even the birth and colossal growth of a lucrative industry devoted first to assuring children won't be able to read and then to selling an endless succession of 'remedies' for that inability."[28]

Looking back at the growth of the "whole language movement," University of Illinois professor P. David Pearson remarked that during the past two and half decades, he had seen succeeding waves of "movement, fads and panaceas," from open classrooms to mastery learning. "But," he mused, "never have I witnessed anything like the rapid spread of the whole-language movement. Pick your metaphor—an epidemic, wildfire, manna from heaven—whole language has spread so rapidly throughout North America that it is a fact of life in literacy curriculum and research."[29] If Pearson is exaggerating, it is only insofar as he sees "whole language" as a relatively recent development. In fact, it is a reworking of ideas that have been fashionable for seven decades or more under a variety of names, titles, and sales pitches.

Yetta Goodman—who, along with her husband Kenneth, is a leading guru of "whole language"—acknowledges that it is an extension of child-centered and progressive educational ideas in vogue in John Dewey's time. She also acknowledges that "whole language" differs little in substance from what was known in the 1940s and 1950s as "language experience." She describes whole language as an educational philosophy that focuses "*not on the content of what is being learned,* but on the learner. . . . The teacher is viewed as a co-learner with the students. The environment is a democratic one . . ."[30] [emphasis added]

In "language experience," educators of the 1950s emphasized a holistic approach to teaching—what was then known as the "all around development of the child." Rather than simply *reading books,* the mavens of Life Adjustment and "language experience" involved students in group activities, excursions, discussions, storytelling, drama, music, and art. From all of these "experiences," children were supposed to produce "charts, lists, menus, plans, magazines, newsletters," and other "reading materials." Yetta Goodman acknowledges the obvious: "There is much in whole language that is similar to language experience and, indeed, many whole language educators, including me, were initially advocates of language experience." The architects of "language experience" believed that traditional divisions of subject matters into different disciplines were obsolete and advocated turning the schools into places in which children could be made "fully functional and self-actualizing individuals" through "collaborative group settings."[31]

In the late 1950s, "language experience" was discredited in the collapse of "life adjustment" education, but its impulses toward a more democratic, humanistic classroom have proven impervious to failure, rejection, and miserable test scores. Indeed, the movement that was a rollicking bust in the 1950s is reemerging as an educational innovation and "reform" in the 1990s. Moreover, it is spreading without any research or evidence to show that it works. Its foremost advocates take the lack of such research as a badge of honor. "So dynamic is the whole language movement," Kenneth Goodman crowed in 1989, "that innovative practice is leaping ahead of research and rapidly expanding and explicating the fine points of theory."[32] In other words, educationists are adopting whole language programs without waiting for any indication that they work and insist that the lack of research to support what they are doing is not a sign of recklessness or wishful thinking, but rather an indication of their *dynamism.*

What they lack in terms of evidence, whole language advocates make up for with their enthusiasm. Whole language, writes one devotee, is not merely a way of teaching kids to read, it is "a spirit, a philosophy, a movement . . ." with students "who have become eager and joyful readers and writers . . ."[33] How can mere literacy compete with *joyful* reading? Another describes whole language as "a way of thinking, a way of living and learning with children."[34] It involves "teachers who even outside their classrooms, are activists and advocates for children, for themselves, and for their curriculum."[35] So what if children can't spell, when they can experience the "great authenticity of life"?

Wrote one educationist: "To empower learners, whole language teachers do not select all the books to read . . . correct students' nonstandard forms at the point of production, spell on demand, or revise and edit for students."[36] Thus, the teacher's abdication of responsibility and the semiliterate, ungrammatical, misspelled, run-on sentences he or she tolerates are transmuted into "empowerment," as if a child is made stronger through uncorrected mediocrity. The resulting mass of junk writing is justified on the grounds that students should not be "bound to someone else's standards of perfection." A whole language devotee argues that the child needs to be liberated from "an uptight, must-be-right model of literacy." Thus far, the liberation has proceeded apace, with only pockets of resistance.

"Whole language" appears to have an iron lock on schools of teacher education, academic journals, and much of the education bureaucracy. Support for whole language is so uniform among professors of teacher education that many newly minted teachers have never been taught anything else. Critiques or negative reviews occasionally appear in educational journals, but they are rare and usually drowned out by a chorus of praise.

Professor Patrick Groff noted that over a recent five-year period, the journal *Reading Teacher* published 119 laudatory articles on whole language and only a single piece that referred to possible shortcomings. State education departments have been particularly susceptible to whole language programs and many have incorporated them into state guidelines—most dramatically in California. In addition, Groff noted, whole language "holds out the lure to teachers that they alone will become the judges of how well their pupils have learned to read. This totally unassailable exemption from accountability by teachers to parents and any other parties, is called 'teacher empowerment'" by advocates of whole language.[37]

Not surprisingly, whole language advocates are decidedly cool to the suggestions that student reading or writing should be measured through tests. "As scores become important," sniffs one whole languagist, "students become invisible." Given the results of such theories in actual practice, her attitude toward instruments of accountability and measurement is understandable. Whole language teachers, she says, prefer "alternative" methods of judging how well a child reads. Rather than "narrowly conceived tests," they much prefer portfolios of written work, along with "pictures, anecdotes, and tapes." All of which, undoubtedly, are wonderful. The point, of course, is that whole language advocates insist that there are no solid measurements of ability because there are no fast and firm standards.

So we get *pictures* and *tapes* instead.

The Attack on Phonics

While local superintendents and school principals are often at pains to assure concerned parents that their reading programs include some element of phonics, the leaders of the whole language movement make no secret of their contempt for phonics. Kenneth Goodman insisted that "direct instruction in phonics is neither necessary nor desirable to produce readers."[38] But their hostility runs much deeper. Critics who push for a phonic-based teaching are often derided as members of the Christian Right or educational simpletons.

Harvey Daniels, the director of the Center for City Schools, dismissed phonics as "the only approach to reading that removes meaning from reading."[39] Another advocate explained that "Phonics has to do with sound. Reading has to do with meaning."[40] The implication is that children who read phonetically may be able to decode and pronounce the words they read, but won't know what they mean—a charge that is frequently made by critics of phonics, who seldom bother to offer much evidence to support the contention. While deriding phonics as a form of dry, soulless "rote" learning, advocates of whole language claim that their approach differs from traditional practices because of its use of "authentic" literature in the classroom. Parents and school boards are often induced to buy into whole language approaches by the claim that the program will introduce children to literary works, in contrast to programs that rely on memorization and "drilling" in letter sounds. But the use of literature is hardly an innovation—literature has always been a part of reading instruction, except during those years when it was replaced by "age appropriate" readers dumbed down to the "See Dick Run" level of inanity. Both McGuffey's reader and Noah Webster's spelling book relied on literature to teach reading. Students in nineteenth century elementary classrooms could expect to read Lewis Carroll, Ralph Waldo Emerson, Daniel Webster, William Shakespeare, John Bunyan, George Washington, Sir Walter Scott, and Henry Thoreau, among others. As one critic noted, "Those children were not any smarter than the ones today. They just read better because they were taught properly."[41]

Reading without Tears

There is, in fact, nothing terribly new about either the techniques or the issues in the debates over reading in the nation's schools. Jeanne Chall, a professor at Harvard's Graduate School of Education, remarks that the current debates tend to echo similar arguments made in the 1920s. While the issues were similar, she found that the professional literature of the 1920s and 1930s was much more reasoned, even though there was "infinitely less research and theory on which to base the reasoning," than that in the 1990s. "In contrast," she wrote, "the reading literature of the 1980s and early 1990s uses stronger rhetoric and seems to base its positions more on ideology than on the available scientific and theoretical literature."[42]

The key to understanding what researchers have found is to recognize that grown-ups read differently than small children do. This should be painfully obvious; indeed, one needs to be a certified educationist not to see it. But Chall notes that whole language advocates continue to "view beginning and later reading as essentially the same." They have taken Cattell's error and turned it into practice. It has taken the accumulated research of nearly eighty years to establish that while "beginning reading may look the same as mature reading," it is, in fact, "quite different." Reading is always about understanding the meaning of words, Chall wrote, but beginning reading relies heavily on the ability to sound out words phonetically. "As reading develops, it has more to do with language and reasoning." Whole language advocates argue that learning how to read comes naturally and does not need to be taught. But, according to Chall, the evidence overwhelmingly suggests that "a beginning reading program that does not give children knowledge and skill in recognizing and decoding words will have poor results."

So what is the dispute all about? Why aren't the schools rushing to implement programs that demonstrably work and chucking out those schemes that have been so badly discredited? Why are educationists, who want so desperately to be thought of as *real* academics and scientists, so reluctant to base their methods on actual research? The answer, Chall said, lies in the "more powerful forces at work—values, ideologies, philosophies, and appealing rhetoric." Since the 1920s, when child-centered theories began to dominate the schools, the vision of education embodied in whole language has dominated educational thinking. "For a growing number," wrote Chall, "it means a philosophy of education and of life, not merely a method of teaching reading."

Chall defined it as a philosophy that emphasizes the "qualities and values of love, care, and concern for children." In the 1920s, reformers insisted that children should be taught to read for meaning from the very start, without rote learning; that they be liberated from the stultifyingly dull and dreary training in phonics and freed for a lifetime of creativity. The earlier child-centered advocates insisted that if they were given interesting stories, children would learn to read with greater comprehension, even if there was little or no teaching of the forms and sounds of letters and words. "Although the research of the past eighty years has refuted those claims," Chall noted, "they persist. If they are relinquished for a period, they return as new discoveries, under new labels."

Chall attributed the resiliency of such ideas to the desire of Americans to avoid pain, hard work, and discomfort, and to shield the tender sensibilities of the young from the rigors of a demanding curriculum. Learning basics can be hard and might entail both effort and disappointment. But basics also imply a set of standards outside of the child himself, a standard that is uncompromising and to which the child must accommodate himself. This, of course, is anathema to the democratic, child-centered classroom. Chall's analysis is worth quoting at some length:

"Why do these concepts of reading return again and again? Why are they so persistent?" the Harvard professor asked. "I propose that they are deep in our American culture and therefore difficult to change. These conceptions promise quick and easy solution to real learning—reading without tears, reading full of joy. They are the magic bullet that is offered as a solution to the serious reading problems of our times. Further, phonics requires knowledge, effort, and work. The whole or whole language way has always promised more joy, more fun, and less work for the child— and for the teacher."

Since the whole language movement claims that beginning reading is not conceptually different than any other kind of reading, "teachers are required to know less than for a developmental view of teaching." Underlying the whole language approach, Chall wrote, is the belief that "a good heart goes a long way, and the less teaching the better. It fears structure more than no learning. . . . It flees from the idea that there might be 'basics' to be learned first." Such an attitude is "imbued with love and hope," according to Chall. "But sadly, it has proven to be less effective than a developmental view, and least effective for those who tend to be at risk for learning to read—low-income, minority children and those at risk for learning disability."

WHY JOHNNY CAN'T ADD, SUBTRACT, MULTIPLY, OR DIVIDE (BUT STILL FEELS GOOD ABOUT HIMSELF)

I f the schools have embraced joyful reading, can joyful math be far behind? On the surface, it seems unlikely, since math ought to be relatively immune to the fuzzy approaches that emphasize feelings rather than substance. Mathematics, after all, is the great unequalizer; it has a way of separating those who can from those who cannot. While education- ists strain to reduce the stress and anxiety of learning, math is not pain- free and probably never will be. It has a penchant for accuracy and a rather uncompromising attitude toward self-esteem: If you can get the right answer you can feel good about yourself. But if you cannot, mathematics doesn't much care. The square root of 99 is still 9.9498743 no matter how a child *feels* about it.

Historically, of course, mathematics has not gone unscathed by the periodic fads that sweep across the nation's schools. The disaster of the New Math in the 1960s is still a fresh memory for many parents. But most Americans have a very clear idea of what kind of math they think the schools should teach their children. For most Americans, the teaching of arithmetic is a basic test of common sense. There is a nearly universal sense that $4 \times 8 = 32$—and that this is something that children ought to learn, even if some of them think it is hard or irrelevant, or insensitive to the needs of their inner selves.

But there is perhaps no other issue in the nation's schools where the gap between the public's expectations and the reigning ideology of the educationists is wider or more profound.

An overwhelming 86 percent of Americans think students should learn to do arithmetic "by hand," including memorizing the multiplication tables, before they start using calculators. The nonpartisan Public Agenda found that "the inability of some students to do simple arithmetic without a calculator was frequently offered as foolproof evidence of educational failure."[1]

But an equally overwhelming majority of "math educators" disagrees.

More than four out of five "math education professionals" believe that the "early u.. of calculators will improve children's problem-solving skills and not prevent the learning of arithmetic." Only 12 percent of the math educators share the public's fear that the use of calculators in the early grades might interfere with the development of the children's ability to do computation on their own.[2]

This de-emphasis of computational skills is reflected in national standards for teaching mathematics as well as in classrooms across the country which have embraced the new New Math. In the new classrooms, teachers no longer emphasize the importance of getting the right answers to problems, nor do they teach specific rules (or algorithms) for solving arithmetic problems. In a typical eighth-grade math class in California, for example, students work cooperatively, exhorted by their teacher to use their handheld calculators to solve even the simplest math problems. Many of them have used calculators since they were in kindergarten and many of them have never been required to solve a single multiplication or long division problem without using one. They are part of what one observer called the "biggest transformation of math teaching in three decades."[3]

In the new math class, the *Los Angeles Times* reports, "work sheets and drills at the chalkboard are out. So is an emphasis on complicated paper-and-pencil computations such as long division."[4] Indeed, the role of the teacher is very different in the new New Math classroom. Instead of being an expert who dispenses knowledge and provides corrective guidance, the teacher is more of a facilitator—careful not to reinforce right answers or correct wrong ones. This is important because the children are expected to invent their own solutions to problems—even in the first and second grades. "If the teacher were to judge the correctness of answers," three math teachers explained in the journal *Arithmetic Teacher*, "the children would come to depend on him or her to know whether an answer is correct."

Instead, teachers are encouraged to let the children debate solutions to elementary math problems among themselves. Instead of providing them with simple and easy-to-understand rules for adding, say 4 + 4, children are told to work it out on their own by agreeing or disagreeing among themselves until "agreement is reached." In one class, the authors of the *Arithmetic Teacher* article enthuse, children approached the problem of 74 divided by 5 by adding 5 + 5 + 5 + 5 + 5 + 5 "until the total comes close to 74."[5] The teachers seemed especially impressed by the creativity of the students who counted this out *on their fingers*.

Of course, if the students had the faintest familiarity with the multiplication table or the rudiments of long division, they would not have had to use their fingers in the first place. That is the point of teaching algorithms, or basic rules of computations. They were invented precisely so that people would *not* have to count their fingers and toes to solve each problem. But it is an article of faith among the new New Math educators that computations such as long division and long multiplication are obsolete and that memorizing or drilling students in such skills is both archaic and perhaps damaging to their fragile psyches. So the children are left to reinvent the wheel themselves.

But what happens if they fail to reinvent the wheel? What if counting on fingers doesn't work? What if no one in the class gets the correct answer? In that case, the *Arithmetic Teacher* advises, "the teacher would know that the problem was too hard for the class and would go on to something else."[6] Something, no doubt, *easier.*

Proponents of the new methods argue that they are encouraging children to "value" mathematics, and they are emphasizing *how* children learn, rather than *what* they learn. All of which, they insist, will make children more confident "problem solvers" who can "communicate mathematically" and "reason mathematically." The philosophy echoes the central tenets of "whole language," by insisting that children can move directly on to "doing math" without teaching basic, and often difficult, first steps. In whole language classes children are plunged into "reading" without learning how to sound out words. In the new New Math classes children dive straight into "real-life" problems without being taught the basic disciplines of how numbers are added, multiplied, or divided. The idea is that children will somehow learn the basic skills along the way—that the skills will somehow come to them "by doing" and do not therefore need to be taught first.

While the consequences of "whole language" and "invented spelling" are already painfully apparent, the full impact of the new New Math probably will not be felt for a decade or so, when the tsunami of mathematical illiteracy will hit higher education and the national economy full force.

Joyful, but Wrong

California, as usual, was one of the pioneers in the deconstruction of math education. In 1985, the state adopted new instructional standards in mathematics that foreshadowed the national standards that would be issued four years later. The California standards emphasized problem solving. For example, a typical eighth-grade student might be asked to "Write a set of directions for a younger student, explaining how to add $\frac{2}{5}$ and $\frac{1}{3}$. Then use a picture and write an explanation as to why you add fractions the way you do." The idea was to encourage children to *think and communicate mathematically*, a skill that was encouraged by having students write in journals and creating mathematical artwork. At least that was the theory. How well did it work?

In 1991 the National Assessment of Educational Progress rated the math skills of California students in the bottom third of the participating states. Despite the emphasis on problems such as adding $\frac{2}{5}$ to $\frac{1}{3}$, the NAEP found that *only one in 12* California eighth graders was capable of working the problem. Asked to explain the apparent failure of the state's new New Math, Francie Alexander, the state's associate superintendent, who had been the acting director of the state's Curriculum, Instruction and Assessment Division when the new standards were implemented, gave forth with the pathetic plaint that "We've all been led to believe we were above average."[7]

How did perceptions get so far away from reality? In part, educationists who were supposed to monitor the new New Math classes saw what they wanted to see, lavishing the new teaching style with educationism's usual effusive and uncritical praise. When the National Center for the Learning and Teaching of Elementary Subjects (NCLTES) observed how twenty-four California teachers implemented the math standards in their classrooms, an NCLTES author described one teacher's approach as filled with the spirit of "exploration and invention, conveying the idea that all students can learn, enjoy and use mathematics." The only problem was that the teacher's attitude of invention and exploration did not also include a firm grounding in basic math.

In one lesson, this practitioner of joyful math told students that they could find the perimeter by multiplying length times width. She also told the class to multiply *feet* times *yards* when calculating volume.[8] Another teacher was clearly versed in the new techniques, but "when she attempted to implement the standards she mistaught averages to her students." As two critics later noted, the authors of the NCLTES study "failed to record what, if anything the students they observed had learned."[9] But California's deconstruction of math was merely prologue to a wider attack on traditional mathematics.

The Standards

As researchers sift through the rubble of innumerate America, they will likely recognize 1989 as a turning point. In that year, the National Council of Teachers of Mathematics (NCTM) launched the new New Math revolution by issuing a comprehensive set of new standards for teaching math.[10] The new standards describe "a vision" for school mathematics that insists that the nation's schools embrace a curriculum for teaching mathematics "that capitalizes on children's intuitive insights and language" and that is guided not by the standards of a recognized discipline but by the "children's intellectual, social, and emotional development. . . ."

This means that from now on teachers should spend less time on "developmental work that emphasize symbol manipulation and computational rules, and that rely heavily on paper-and-pencil worksheets . . ." Such outdated approaches of teaching mathematical rules, the new standards sniffed, "do not fit the natural learning patterns of children and do not contribute to important aspects of children's mathematical development."

What's In, What's Out

In listing the areas that should receive increased attention, and those that will receive decreased attention in teaching math to K–4 students, the NCTM standards effectively codify the ideology of the new New Math. The standards call for teachers to devote *more* time and attention to:

Cooperative work
Discussion of mathematics
Questioning
Writing about mathematics
Content integration
Exploration of chance
Problem-solving strategies
Use of calculators and computers

The NCTM standards want teachers to give *decreased* attention to:

Early attention to reading, writing, and ordering numbers symbolically
Complex paper-and-pencil computations
Addition and subtraction without renaming
Isolated treatment of division facts
Long division
Long division without remainders
Paper-and-pencil fraction computation
Rote practice
Rote memorization of rules
One answer and one method
Written practice
Teaching by telling

For fifth through eighth graders, the NCTM standards proposed *de-emphasizing*:

Relying on outside authority (teacher or an answer key)
Memorizing rules and algorithms
Practicing *tedious* paper-and-pencil computations [emphasis added]
Finding exact forms of answers
Memorizing procedures, such as cross multiplication

In teaching algebra, the standards propose giving less attention to "manipulating symbols" and "memorizing procedures and drilling on equation solving." They also propose de-emphasizing learning formulas in statistics and probability and call for spending less time on teaching geometric vocabulary and "facts and relationships" in geometry.

Since children will no longer have to master paper-and-pencil computation, the NCTM's standards envision a dramatically expanded role for calculators—beginning no later than kindergarten. (The NCTM standards are unquestionably the single most influential driving factor behind the replacement of computational skills with calculators in the nation's classrooms.) "Calculators," the NCTM standards declare, "*must* be accepted at the K–4 level as valuable tools for learning mathematics." [emphasis added] The standards argue that calculators have made "computational proficiency" obsolete. And, since schools have failed in the past to teach students to master basic computational skills without their aid, the standards read, "we might argue that further efforts toward mastering computational skills are counterproductive."

In other words, the standards are a declaration of surrender.

Karaoke Math

The calculator, and the attitudes of educationists toward its use, are the most potent symbols of the deconstruction of teaching math. Zalman Usiskin, the founder and director of the University of Chicago School Mathematics Project is among the prominent educationists who argue that "calculators and computers render some content obsolete."

"I do not do long division or long multiplication anymore," declares Usiskin, who is marketing his own new New Math curriculum to schools. Usiskin explains that he has abandoned division and multiplication "not because I cannot do them or because I am poor at paper-and-pencil math; quite the contrary, I am very good at it.

"Rather, it is because I have the spirit of a mathematician—I am lazy and I always look for better [methods]. I have found one. It involves pushing a few buttons on my calculator." Calculators, he insists, "are here to stay." As a result, "long division, which in its present form first appeared in the late 1400s, is dying." Declares Usiskin: "If you want accuracy and speed, use your calculator. If it is not available, go to the next room and find it."[11] And if you don't need to be accurate, just estimate.

There is an eerie parallel here to the logic used by teachers of reading who try to justify abandoning the teaching of basic reading skills. Educationists noticed that adults do not wrestle phonetically with words as they decode the meaning of a sentence and leaped to the fallacious conclusion that since accomplished readers do not use such techniques, they did not need to teach sounding-out skills to children—forgetting that the child who is learning to read is very different from an adult who reads proficiently. By dropping phonics, educationists removed the very building blocks that made that proficiency possible. Math educators are making a similar leap of logic: Since skilled and advanced mathematicians can perform advanced calculations without pencil and paper, they argue that it is no longer necessary to teach children how to multiply or divide by themselves. But—as with learning how to read—there is a fundamental difference between the way children learn and how adults do math.

Usiskin uses the calculator as a tool, to *supplement* skills and knowledge he acquired as a child. In effect, educationists are now proposing *replacing* those skills with the calculator. While Usiskin probably learned the essentials of computation *before* turning to calculators, children taught under the standards will get the calculator without ever having learned to do such computations themselves. Thus, math educators are using the calculator not merely as a helpful shortcut but as a *substitute* for basic skills. That is a little like arguing that it is unnecessary to teaching spelling since we have computer spell-checkers. Why play the violin if you can buy a CD? Why learn to ride a bicycle if you can drive a car? Why learn to sight-read music if you can sing with a karaoke machine?

Admittedly, replacing computational knowledge with calculators does perhaps make some sense if mathematics is regarded as a strictly functional skill, where the only concern is an emphasis on finding the easiest, most painless method of solving a problem. But mathematics is more than merely function. It is a mental discipline that trains the mind for logical, ordered thinking that in turn provides students with the tools to move to higher and higher levels of reasoning and calculations. Ironically, experience shows that it is the well-trained mind that is more practical than the strictly functional approach. Instead of producing an independent and adaptable thinker, the "practical" new styles of teaching math guarantee that graduates will be totally dependent on technology. Without it, they will be lost—witness the look of stunned incomprehension in the eyes of the checkout clerk who is forced by cruel fate to make change without benefit of her cash register. While the clerk may be unable to perform simple acts of calculation because she is mathematically challenged, there is a growing possibility that she cannot add or subtract numbers because no one ever taught her how to do so.

"Think the Minuet in G"

None of this is to suggest that mathematics education could not use an occasional jump start. There is no moral imperative that mathematics be dull—the best math teachers have always found a way of infusing life into their classrooms. Nor should it be difficult to convince students of the relevance of mathematical knowledge to their lives, given its prominence in the new information age. A skilled teacher should have no problem pounding home the importance of mastering mathematics for students who want to make a living in the new economy.

Undoubtedly there are also ways of reducing anxiety and stress in math classes. But they can hardly be eliminated altogether. Genuine proficiency at mathematics requires knowledge of basic principles and systematic training and practice in their application. True, that might come more easily if a student felt good about himself as a "mathematical learner," but feeling good about oneself is not sufficient to master the discipline. One learns math by learning math and that takes hard work.

Eventually, of course, a student who is versed in the essentials of mathematics will learn to "think mathematically." But it is a rather fanciful notion that there is such a thing as "thinking mathematically" that does not include knowing how to add, subtract, multiply, and divide without the aid of a machine. You cannot "think" your way to the solution of an algebra problem without knowing algebra, however much math educators may enthuse over "mathematical thinking." Listening to the enthusiasm of the au courant educationists, one is reminded of nothing so much as *The Music Man* where Professor Harold Hill peddles his "think method" of teaching music. Band members are given no music and no practice— they are simply told to *think* the Minuet in G. It is in this same spirit that educationists insist that children do not have to learn long division, long multiplication, or how to do computations by hand as long as they *think* mathematically.

Of course, playing the Minuet in G requires musicians to "think musically," but it also requires them to have a clue about how to play their instruments. It is the same with math. Everyone wants children who "think mathematically" and are competent problem solvers. But proponents of the various fashionable think methods of teaching math insist we can get them without drilling students in the basic elements of solving problems. They do not, however, explain how any child is handicapped by learning basic skills and acquiring elementary knowledge.

These are, however, unavoidable questions. Is any child prevented from attaining higher-order math skills by knowing how to do long division without a machine? Does knowledge of the multiplication tables prevent anyone from becoming a proficient problem solver? And are graduates of programs that ignore basics and emphasize "thinking" any more likely to perform well at math than Professor Hill's band was to perform the Minuet in G?

A Kinder, Gentler Math

Unlike Professor Hill, however, the modern math educators are not conscious frauds. They are simply far more concerned with how children *feel* about math than what they actually know. Thus, one of the top priorities of the NCTM national standards is "Building beliefs about what mathematics is, about what it means to know and do mathematics, and about children's view of themselves as mathematical learners." That means, the standards declare, that "affective dimensions of learning play a significant role in, and must influence, curriculum and instruction."

The emotional traumas of fifth-, sixth-, and seventh-grade math students—described as "children in transition"—loom large in the standards that are ostensibly supposed to be about mathematics. Of their adolescent charges the math teachers say: "Self-consciousness is their hallmark and curiosity about such questions as Who am I? How do I fit in? What do I enjoy doing? What do I want to be? is both their motivation and their nemesis. From this turmoil emerges an individual, with patterns of thought taking shape."

Although math teachers of the past have been more interested in teaching square roots than curing adolescent angst and turmoil, the national math standards insist that math teachers have to make conscious efforts to be sensitive to their needs and should therefore make their math classes "interesting and relevant" and must encourage "a positive disposition toward mathematics." If teachers kept insisting on right and wrong answers and requiring students to master the rules and formulas of geometry and algebra, students might not be positively disposed and the NCTM couldn't stand for that.

Multicultural Math

As with changes in the way reading is taught, the new New Math is less about mathematics than it is about ideology. It is driven by the philosophy of teaching that puts a premium on child-centeredness rather than knowledge, and feeling good about oneself rather than intellectual training. But the debate over mathematics has also been clouded by more overtly political agendas, including the drive to make the nation's schools more multicultural. "Whenever possible," the National Council of Teachers of Mathematics standards insist, "students' cultural backgrounds should be integrated into the learning experience." Not missing a chance to patronize minority students, the standards note that "Black or Hispanic students, for example, may find the development of mathematical ideas in their cultures of great interest." It also means that math teachers must strive to create "caring environments" in which they are careful not to impose their knowledge of right and wrong approaches to mathematics on the students from differing backgrounds.

Such suggestions may explain why Jaime Escalante, the famed math teacher from Los Angeles, remarked that "whoever wrote [the standards] must be a physical education teacher."[12] Escalante, who gained international renown for his success in teaching calculus to students at Garfield High School in east Los Angeles, took a radically different approach to teaching mathematics than the standards. Instead of watering down the content of his classes or lowering his expectations, or emphasizing nebulous *mathematical communication skills*, Escalante drilled his largely Hispanic class in fundamentals of calculus, with notably successful results.

Despite Escalante's success, the educationist establishment has embraced the idea that students of different races and ethnic backgrounds have different "learning styles" that require adjustments in the content and the standards of subjects like mathematics. Among the more prominent diversity gurus to argue that black children learn differently is Peggy McIntosh, the director of Wellesley's SEED Project on Inclusive Curriculum (SEED stands for Seeking Educational Equity and Diversity), who claims that the emphasis on right/wrong answers is a culturally oppressive idea and unfair to minority children.

In presentations to teachers from across the country, McIntosh describes a young black girl from Roxbury working on a math work sheet, which requires her to add single digit numbers, such as 5 + 2 + 6. The child, however, did not grasp the mathematics involved and got all of the answers wrong. McIntosh explains that "She was trying to get these problems right. The alternative was to get them wrong. . . . So this is a situation within the win-lose world in which there's no way the child can feel good about the assignment." Multicultural educators need somehow to get beyond the win-lose world, McIntosh says, with its obsession with right and wrong answers. But, as author Richard Bernstein notes, "McIntosh never does solve the problem of teaching the little black girl how to do sums. She certainly never presents any empirical evidence that different children learn in different ways." And however you cut it, "the black child from Roxbury, after all, needs to know how to add, to get right answers, because when it comes to addition, there are right answers and wrong answers."[13] Maybe not.

Close Enough

As math educators have moved further away from the emphasis on right and wrong answers, they have developed new "holistic" tests that are adapted to the new fashions. Since students are no longer required to learn the basic rules or formulas of mathematics, they are also no longer required to get the exact answer on their math tests. Not surprisingly, this new approach has the added benefit of guaranteeing that test scores will go up, even as mathematical illiteracy spreads.

A case in point is a new mathematics test for junior high students that employs a sort of horseshoe "close-enough" philosophy. When the test was first offered in the New York City public schools, officials claimed that it marked an improvement over previous math tests (whose scores had been sagging) because the new test measured "higher order thinking skills," which apparently did not include actually getting the right answer to questions involving addition, subtraction, and division.

A sample question on the new test:

Sue has two cats, Bo and Rusty. She needs to buy a 60 day supply of cat food for them. Bo finishes three-quarters of a can of food each day. Rusty finishes half a can of food each day. Cat food costs $1 for three cans. What would be the cost of this supply of cat food for Bo and Rusty.[14]

Mark Sacerdote, a New York City math teacher, confessed in an op-ed piece in the *New York Times*: "The sad fact is that solving this problem is beyond the ability of most seventh graders. Ask any teacher."

But, he wrote, the scores on the new tests will likely be hailed as encouraging. The reason is that students would not have to know that the correct answer to the question was $25 for them to receive high marks. Under the new system, student answers were rated on a scale of 1 to 6 and a "competence" grade of low, medium, or high. That meant that a student who answered $40 could earn a score of 5 out of 6 and a competence rating of "high," if the panel of evaluators decided that the student committed only "minor computational errors." In fact, under the new guidelines, virtually any answer could win a score of 3 and a rating of "medium" competence if "enough of the calculation is shown to demonstrate some understanding of the process . . . but the work shown is confusing because of a major error."[15]

Such generous scoring seems certain to provide reassuring test scores, but as Sacerdote reported, New York's educationists were not content with the rejiggered tests. Seventh graders throughout the city, he wrote, had already studied the question on Bo and Rusty and "have been shown questions similar to those that will be on the test in order to familiarize them with the format." Another decision by New York's Board of Education also tended to inflate achievement test scores: The board routinely removed the test scores of more than 150,000 students with limited English proficiency and who are categorized as "emotionally handicapped" from its overall test scores. Moreover, it gave "modified tests" to students designated "academically at risk," a category that conveniently covered the students likely to score the lowest on any measure of achievement.[16] Wrote Sacerdote: "The Board of Education is doing what failed management traditionally does: fudging the figures and continuing business-as-usual. . . . We used to expect that our students would graduate from high school with at least basic proficiency in reading, writing and arithmetic. Today little is expected and less is required."[17]

Meltdown

Ironically, the new "reforms" may undo what little progress has thus far been made in teaching math since the 1980s. In any case, the full effects of the new New Math will be felt only when children exposed to the new fashions reach college and the workforce sometime over the next decade. When that happens, warns critic John Saxon, "the present disaster in science education will be drastically exacerbated." Saxon, the author of his own alternative mathematics series, describes the NCTM standards as "capricious at best and approach total irresponsibility at worst."[18]

While other critics focus on the downgrading of basic arithmetical computation in the new New Math classroom, Saxon points out that the NCTM standards make no mention of the need to prepare students for advanced science, such as chemistry, physics, or engineering, and appear to denigrate the idea that students need to be prepared for calculus. While noting that mathematics was needed for "business, economics, linguistics, biology, medicine, and sociology," the standards go on to say: "However, the fundamental mathematical ideas needed in these areas *are not necessarily those studied in the traditional algebra-geometry-precalculus-calculus sequence, a sequence designed with engineering and physical science in mind.*" [emphasis added] Thus, despite all of the educationist rhetoric about higher-level mathematical thinking and problem solving, the new New Math marks a sharp turn away from preparing students for the most competitive scientific and technical fields.

The educationist establishment, Saxon charges, has decided "with no advanced testing whatsoever to replace preparation for calculus, physics, chemistry and engineering with a watered-down mathematics curriculum" that will leave "American students bereft of the detailed knowledge of the parts that permit the whole to be comprehended." The new standards de-emphasize "the teaching of radical expressions, conic sections, paper-and-pencil solutions of trigonometric equations, and the solutions of the old-fashioned fundamental word problems that have been used historically to teach the concepts and skills necessary to solve all problems."

In contrast, Saxon's approach to math emphasizes the building blocks of mathematical knowledge and relies on drilling students in such skills until they become second nature. Although his curriculum is considered anathema to the educational establishment, Saxon's books are used in more than four thousand schools. His analysis of the nation's future needs is very different from the vision of the National Council of Teachers of Mathematics.

"We need to get as many students as we can through calculus in high school," Saxon writes. "We need students who are competent in the use of fractions, decimals, mixed numbers, percent and ratios. We need students who know trigonometry and analytic geometry. We need a work force that allows Americans to compete successfully in a technological world. We do not need guidelines that recommend leaving students ill-prepared for chemistry and physics and that ridicule preparation for calculus."

Like the enthusiastic embrace of the disastrous New Math of the 1960s, Saxon notes, the new New Math is being pushed by "experts" who are defying both the known research about how children learn and basic common sense. "Only in American mathematics education do people with a track record of abject failure arrogate the title of 'expert,' " Saxon writes. He predicts that as the effects of the dumbed-down math programs are felt, college math enrollment will drop and the number of Americans in physics and engineering will decline even further.

"And no one will be to blame. They will all say, 'It wasn't my fault.' I guess that is the advantage of being just a member of a committee of experts."[19]

DUMBING DOWN
THE TEXTS

"I doubt whether we are sufficiently attentive to the importance of elementary texts."

—C. S. Lewis in *The Abolition of Man*

Perhaps the most distinctive products of the educationist community are textbooks. Although they are created and marketed by private publishers, it is educrats who write the specifications, dictate the content, and determine the level at which they are written. Even more than the abstruse and unreadable cant of the educationist journals, the textbooks reflect educationist attitudes because they are used in the classrooms and often dictate the content of course work. Especially when used by teachers with little or no academic background in the subject being taught, the textbook often *is* the course. According to the American Textbook Council, a tiny number of texts control the nation's educational marketplace: two history series dominate the nation's elementary classrooms and somewhere between ten and fifteen history texts command pride of place in high school American and world history classes. Since studies have found that somewhere between 70 and 90 percent of history and civics courses are driven by textbooks, the council concluded, this near-monopoly amounts to a national curriculum.[1]

But textbooks also are important because they open a window onto the educationist mind. Textbooks are formed in the image of educationists, and reflect their values, priorities, and (most revealing of all) their attitudes toward books.

How Dumb Are the Textbooks?

In the 1830s, beginning readers would be assigned a lesson that began:"Come let us go into the thick shade, for it is noon-day, and the summer sun beats hot upon our heads. The shade is pleasant and cool; the branches meet above our heads and shut out the sun as with a green curtain. The grass is soft to our feet, and the clear brook washes the roots of the trees. . . ."[2]

A few years later, elementary school children might study a reader written at this level: "A little girl once came into the house and told her mother a story about something which seemed very improbable. The persons who were sitting in the room with her mother did not believe the little girl, for they did not know her character. But the mother replied at once, 'I have no doubt that it is true, for I never knew my daughter to tell a lie.' Is there not something noble in having such a character as this? Must not that little girl have felt happy in the consciousness of thus possessing her mother's entire confidence? Oh, how different must have been her feelings from those of the child whose word cannot be believed, and who is regarded by every one with suspicion."[3]

Few students in American schools today encounter readers of such sophistication. While SAT scores still remain below the level of the 1960s, the worst drops have occurred in the verbal skills of American students. Could the dumbing down of American textbooks have contributed to the de-verbalization of American students? Has the long-term dumbing down of the texts assigned to students had a cumulative effect in eroding not only their base of knowledge, but also their vocabulary and other reading skills?

In 1993, two researchers from Cornell University, Donald P. Hayes and Loreen T. Wolfer, set out to explore both questions.[4] Using a new measurement of the level of difficulty of schoolbooks—which they called LEX (for "lexical difficulty")—the two academics studied the content of 766 American and British schoolbooks, including primers, basal readers from the second half of first grade through the eighth grade and high school science, and English texts. The LEX measurement of reading difficulty rated the language used by the textbooks on a scale that works something like a thermometer, with a zero level and scores that range into the positive and negative areas. A score of zero means that a text had the reading level of the average newspaper. Any text with a score above zero meant that it was harder to read than a newspaper; any negative score meant that a text was simpler than a newspaper. The higher the positive score, the more difficult the text; the greater the negative score, the easier it was. Using LEX, they determined that *Time* magazine scored plus 6.8, while a difficult scientific article would score plus 58. At the other end of the scale, a farmer talking to his cow scored a minus 55.7

All of the basal readers published in this century, Hayes and Wolfer found, had a moderate to large negative score; every one of them was easier than the average newspaper. The most difficult texts were written before 1918, but they found that the reading materials used in American schools were dramatically simplified in the years after World War II. The "major simplifications" in American primers and readers in the elementary grades occurred in the late 1940s through the early 1960s. The books were simplified "not because the average American child had suddenly become dumber," Hayes and Wolfer remarked, "but because changes in educational philosophy prescribed it. Texts were simplified so as to increase children's 'success' in reading," even if this meant making the books less challenging.

Among their findings:

- The readers now used in sixth, seventh, and eighth grades are simpler than similar readers used in schools before World War II. "Even their sentences have been shortened—20 words per sentence before World War II, 14 words per sentence now," Hayes and Wolfer noted.
- Most baby boomers who attended school in the postwar years used texts with LEX scores between minus 53 to minus 65.
- Great Britain's schools did not simplify their readers after World War II, while American schools were using easier books.
- American first graders in the 1950s used readers with a LEX score 12 points easier than the readers used by the previous generation and 15 points easier than the books used by students in the same grade in Great Britain (even though they tended to be a year younger than American students.)
- The simplification of first-grade readers from the late 1940s to early 1960s "represents a nine percent reduction in the full range of natural text difficulty. *Put another way, post–World War II first grade basals were re-written to a level below that at which a farmer talks to his cow.*" [emphasis added]
- There is a "rippling effect" in simplifying texts. Where early reading materials are dumbed down, later materials tend to be dumbed down as well. In the post–World War II years, Hayes and Wolfer found that "simplification was pervasive." In every grade, baby boomers studied texts that were less demanding, less challenging, and written at a simpler level than the books studied by previous generations (which included large numbers of immigrants, many of whom did not speak English.)
- Since 1963, readers for first through third grades have been rewritten to pre–World War II levels, but readers for upper grades, including high school, "remain much simpler." In American high schools today, the average English text "is less difficult than the average eighth grade basal written before World War II."
- Readers that are now used in the fourth and fifth grades are written at a level below the mean LEX score for "funnies and comics."
- While many teachers no longer rely on basal readers and other texts exclusively in their classrooms, Hayes and Wolfer found no evidence that the supplementary or outside reading assignments were any more difficult. They found that the average book read outside of class by nine to twelve-year-olds had a LEX score of minus 32—which is below

the reading level of third-grade readers before World War II. Nor are readings drawn from literature that are assigned to high school students written at a more challenging level than the standard readers.

How has the simplification of the textbooks and readers affected SAT scores? Hayes and Wolfer noted that if there is a cause and effect relationship, there would be a lag between the time simplified textbooks would be published and when they would be widely disseminated throughout the nation's schoolrooms. Another lag would occur in the time that various age groups would spend in classes with dumbed-down texts. Students entering right after World War II would have largely escaped the impact of the simplified readers because their use would not have spread quickly enough to affect most students. Over time, the harder texts would be phased out and replaced by the easier readers; students would spend more of their time with the simplified books. Eventually, students would spend their entire twelve years in school using the simplified books. If the shift in books from harder to easier affected test scores, Hayes and Wolfer said, the decline in SAT scores should have been gradual, hitting a low point around 1977, when students who had spent their entire educational careers with the simplified books would be taking the SAT test for the first time.

In fact, that is exactly what has happened. Beginning in 1963, reading scores began to fall, and they continued to fall through the 1970s. Since educationists have not increased the reading levels of the texts they use in classrooms, Hayes and Wolfer predicted that scores will continue to be low. Their conclusion: "Long-term use of simplified texts produces a cumulating deficit in the breadth and depth of children's general knowledge and vocabulary. . . ."

But the textbooks are not merely dumb; they also are dull.

Mine Eyes Glaze Over

By virtually any measure, the textbooks used in American classes are unparalleled in their ability to leech the last drop of interest or life from the subject at hand. By and large, they are books without authors, who have been replaced by jobbed-out contract writers who are forced to scribble by formula, slaves to readability indexes, and mandated never to offend any conceivable special interest group.

The elimination of the author is not coincidental, since authors imply personality, a mind at work, and a distinctive eye and voice, with enthusiasms and interests that are reflected in the text. But the unassimilated, unpredictable voice of a single thinker does not quite fit in a culture that prefers "reading materials" to books. So authors are out, and with them any remnant of personality and narrative. Before educational progressives came to dominate American education and American textbooks, history texts were centered on character and events. Although often jingoistic and doctrinaire, many of them were also well written, memorable, and occasionally even moving. Progressives later would contrast their approach—based on making the material "interesting to the child"—with what they claimed was a traditional style of teaching dull facts through rote memorization. But the comparison of the powerful narratives and unforgettable characters of Francis Parkman and Samuel Eliot Morrison with the modern history textbook is hardly flattering to the latter. As it turns out, nothing is as dull as what educationists imagine is "interesting" to a child. It is a rather striking irony that a movement that so often invokes the "interest" of the child and the need for education to be "exciting" and "stimulating" has produced materials of such eye-glazing, brain-numbing tedium.

It was this characteristic that startled author Frances FitzGerald in the early 1970s. "A casual reader of American-history textbooks for elementary and secondary schools," she wrote in *America Revised*, "might be tempted to conclude that the signal quality of all of them is an astonishing dullness." But, as she noted, this was not always the case and was certainly not inevitable. History textbooks could be written honestly and accurately, while maintaining a storyline and holding the reader's interest. "American history texts are not, in other words, by their nature dull," she concluded. "They have achieved dullness. And, it must be said, they have maintained a fairly consistent level of dullness since the nineteen-thirties."[5]

In the hands of the textbook writer, even the most exciting stories achieve dullness. In one popular textbook, a battle between Indian tribes takes place, but it is told from the point of view of a little girl who goes inside her house to hide, rather than from the point of view of someone who actually saw any of the fighting. While a battle rages outside, the text meanders into a discussion of kachina dolls, as if fifth graders would find this "boring anthropological excursion" more interesting than reading about how the girl's older brother chased away the Navajo invaders. "Whoever chose this imagined anecdote," one critic observed, "seems to have little understanding of or stomach for fifth-grade tastes." A passage in the same book is described as "lifeless, monotonic, without feeling; accordingly a bus schedule and the Vikings are treated with equal passion."[6] The story of Paul Revere as retold in one textbook is so filled with irrelevancies that Columbia University's Robert Nisbet remarked, "The bright will merely yawn and keep searching for something in this book that elicits and evokes, stimulates and exhilarates. Their quest is hopeless."[7]

The educationist texts have little concern either with individuals or ideas, both of which are treated rudely. In a leading textbook, Thomas Jefferson's role as a political theorist and a political leader is ignored, except to say that the Declaration of Independence "shows to all how well he wrote." (As if the Declaration was an assignment in a program of "communication arts.") Brushing aside his philosophical and political significance, the text dwells on Jefferson's inventions, including a dumb-waiter and a swivel chair. In this version, the American Textbook Council remarked, "Jefferson comes across as a slightly cranky inventor who just happened to be a great national leader."[8]

Bereft of personality, the texts also sanitize the great debates and disputes of American history. A child reading a history text's description of the Civil War, FitzGerald wrote, "could not possibly infer from any text written since the thirties the passions that animated the war. Both Confederates and Unionists appear in the texts as perfectly reasonable people without strong prejudices. The conflict between the two economic and social systems is described in language so pallid that it does not begin to convey the meaning of the war for those who were involved." The treatment of more contemporary conflicts is hardly an improvement. "Reading [one text] one gets the impression that the Fascist dictatorships popped up in the thirties as mysteriously as toadstools after a rain."

The Textbook Industry

The modern textbook is the product of economics, politics, educational theory, and big business. Textbooks and other instructional materials now make up nearly a third of the nation's $13 billion domestic book market. About $2 billion a year is spent on elementary and high school texts and because many of the decisions for how that money will be spent are made at the state level, competition is intense and the payoffs can be large. Twenty-two states now have laws adopting textbooks at the state level. For the winner, the decision by a state (especially a state like Texas or California) to adopt their textbook means that the publisher will have a reliable cash cow for years. In California, where each grade level enrolls more than 400,000 students, the state selected a single history book for each grade. Those profits led publishers to invest millions of dollars in preparing a single text and $15 million or more for reading and math programs. The stakes for the publishers, the American Textbook Council says, result in "extreme sensitivity on the part of publishers to publicity and trends"[9] and virtually require a policy of studied inoffensiveness. Publishers are reluctant to stress any historical event or personality, lest someone be offended. Increasingly, they are whipsawed by pressure from interest groups ranging from evangelical Christians, to feminists, homosexuals, peace activists, environmentalists, and secular humanists to accommodate their agendas and priorities. "Publishers," Gilbert Sewall argued in 1987, "are increasingly in the business of appeasing willful interest groups."[10] In this environment, pandering to interest groups takes precedence over literary and even factual considerations.

The desire to be inoffensive and inclusive contributes directly to publishers' allergic reactions even to traces of a distinctive authorial voice. One of the nasty secrets of the textbook industry is that the authors sometimes listed on the cover have little or nothing to do with what appears between the covers. In 1994, the American Textbook Council noted, "Authorial content in textbook production is slight or non-existent."[11] An earlier study found that while publishers might approach a well-known historian, the big name may do little more than outline his or her ideas about the text and perhaps comment on the anonymously produced first draft of a history text. The actual writing, the council found, "is usually done by in-house writers, not historians, then revised by editors."[12] Even the practice of using in-house writers seems to be in decline, as more and more publishers turn to "development houses" and other outside sources. Historian Jean Karl described her own experience in a publishing company where text-books were fabricated: "Authors did not write books. Hired writers and people in the office did. The authors simply set the pattern for the material and read over what was done and made suggestions for change. I was editing material written by outside writers hired to do the writing of the social studies texts. The writing was very bad. Most of it needed to be rewritten entirely, but I was not allowed to do that much work on it, only to deal with the very worst of it."[13]

With no single author responsible and with the drafts of the textbooks moving from editor to editor, all the while being vetted for offensiveness and inclusivity, quality and accuracy are frequent casualties. Mistakes creep into the text and the editors who are supposed to be in charge are often more interested in marketing than getting the book right. A 1988 study by researchers from the Learning Development and Research Center of the University of Pittsburgh found that most elementary social studies textbooks were a mess. The researchers found the books filled with "unclear content goals, assumed background knowledge, inadequate explanations and . . . sloppy presentations." They found numerous examples of "bad writing, poor organization and muddled thinking." The problems were so pervasive that they could not be simply written off as editing problems. "Rather," the researchers concluded, "they show evidence of poorly developed ideas."[14]

Social studies textbooks are especially vulnerable to the depredations of marketing departments, selection committees, and semi-educated staff editors. Not only are many of the editors unversed in history, but the supervisory process has often been controlled by people who were either indifferent or even hostile to the past, which apparently is regarded as insufficiently enlightened, equitable, and multicultural. In some cases, the author-editor-revisers simply rewrote history to make it fit their guidelines. In the history textbook *The United States and Its Neighbors*, The American Textbook Council found: "Abraham Lincoln warrants two paragraphs, slightly more than Molly Pitcher, a minor heroine of the Revolutionary War. Valley Forge goes unmentioned. The production of potatoes, blueberries, and cranberries in New England receives approximately the same coverage as the history of the Progressive movement. World War II is covered in less than four pages, introduced with the subhead, 'Another War.'"

But that same book offered students a large four-color picture of a man who served as governor of New Mexico for four years in the 1980s. Why was Tony Anaya featured as prominently as Abraham Lincoln? "The evident, grim answer," the study of textbooks concluded, "is that Anaya is of Hispanic birth, thereby providing [the publisher] a chance to score some political points even if it shortchanges more significant individuals and events in the process distorting the content of history."

The report continued: "This willingness to distort in order to mention and appease various interest groups marks many of the history textbooks assessed in this study, much to the consternation of this assessment's reviewers, who repeatedly noted how crude and obvious, not to say meretricious, most of these efforts were."[15]

A few years ago, I was on a radio show and joked that Ted Turner, who was then planning to colorize many classic American films, had also decided to use the colorization process to make the films more culturally diverse. I suggested that Turner had instructed his minions to draw up guidelines ensuring that the characters in *Mutiny on the Bounty*, *Casablanca*, *Miracle on 34th Street*, and *It's a Wonderful Life* all be colorized so that they would "look like America." I called it "rewind multiculturalism," and said it would make watching American movie classics more inclusive and diverse, since there would no longer be so many white guys in leading roles. Of course I was making up all of this, but I was startled to discover how many people took me seriously. I suppose I really should not have been surprised, since a lot of them had witnessed the process of historical colorization going on in their children's textbooks. It is not unusual to find children who knew more about Crispus Attucks than Thomas Jefferson (that well-known slaveholder). Textbook publishers had learned years ago that they could ignore the Continental Congress with impunity, but would reap the whirlwind—and lose sales—should a single minority group feel excluded.

In their attempt to avoid controversy, the American Textbook Council found, "publishers have responded to the most restrictive of compliance regulations and the most aggressive of state requirements, thereby changing books for all purchasers."[16] The mindlessness of this process does not mean, however, that is it purposeless as well. At one time, American history textbooks emphasized an almost uncritical triumphalism, in which Americans were presented as innocent, noble champions of all that is good. While that picture needed revision, it has now been virtually turned on its head. Where Americans were once portrayed as champions of human freedom, they are now frequently portrayed as a nation of hypocrites, who routinely fell short of their ideals and mocked their pretensions with their racism, their rape of the land, and their colonialist ambitions. In this new vision, the story of America becomes a story of victims and victimizers, and history is rewritten, in part, to compensate the victims for their oppressors' wrongs and their neglect. An exercise in celebration thus becomes an exercise in self-contempt and skepticism.

Rewriting history in this way is justified by some educationists on the grounds that all such knowledge is merely a social construct in the first place. Adopting a sort of poor man's deconstructionism, they argue that there is no firm or fixed reality, no stable or fixed truths that can be objectively presented or understood. In this view—called "constructivism"—each individual has to "construct" his or her own meaning from literature or from history. In reading storybooks, language only means what students think it means; in history, events matter only to the degree that various groups (blacks, women, Hispanics) "construct" their own meanings. Taken literally, every single individual can construct his own meanings, each different from the others. Reality is not the same for men as for women, but it also is not the same from person to person. It is merely subjective and relative, and truth is ultimately unknowable. Since facts are neither fixed nor subjectively speaking "real," they can be manipulated almost at will. Historian Gertrude Himmelfarb notes that in literature, this attitude denies the "authority of the author over the interpretation," and the idea that some books are greater than others; while in history, "It is a denial of the fixity of the past, of the reality of the past apart from what the historian chooses to make of it, and thus of any objective truth about the past."[17] As applied in elementary and secondary schools, such ideas amount to a sort of deconstructionist "slumming," as ideas facilely manipulated by Jacques Derrida find their way into the hands of junior high teachers and assistant superintendents. While only a handful of educationists grasp anything but the broadest outlines of such postmodernist theory, it has provided a convenient conceptual gloss to their neglect and distortion of the past.

It has also contributed to the dullness of the texts. In the textbook *The United States*, the dramatic story of Captain Lawrence of *The Chesapeake* is edited out to accommodate a more inclusive, diverse, and politically correct agenda. Generations of students have been riveted by the retelling of how Lawrence, mortally wounded in combat with the British frigate *Shannon*, cried out "Don't give up the ship" as he was carried below decks. In the new texts, however, Lawrence falls victim to a sort of historical affirmative action. Instead of reading about his exploits, "we meet Maria Mitchell, a nineteenth-century astronomer; Susie King Taylor, a black Union army nurse during the Civil War; Martha Jane Cannary Burke (Calamity Jane); and Florence Kelley, founder of the National Consumer's League."[18] Of course, a case can be made that it's *important* to know the origin of the National Consumer's League and that earnest and committed activists deserve equal time with heroes and larger-than-life figures. It is much harder, however, to argue that this approach has not contributed to the MEGO (Mine Eyes Glaze Over) culture that hangs over the history classroom.

Writing by Color

History is not the only victim of the revisionist impulse. Literature is also subject to "reconstruction" at the hands of educationists, especially those who take literally the admonition that authors don't matter and that texts can mean whatever we want them to mean. Indeed, the American Textbook Council concluded that even in reading and literature classes "story selection now occurs almost exclusively on the basis of ethnic, gender, and other ascriptive coding by author and subject."[19] That would be a startling and outrageous charge, if there was not so much evidence to support it, including internal memoranda that have come to light in recent years documenting the extent to which publishers (and educationists) were willing to pander to special interest groups, even to the point of rewriting the actual content of stories. In one case, more than two thousand pages of internal memoranda from the Holt publishing company were subpoenaed as part of a federal court lawsuit involving textbooks in a southern school district. The documents show that when the company was revising the Holt Basic Reading Series in 1977, a staff editor decreed that at least half of all the characters in the stories be female. Detailed requirements were laid down for the portrayal of representatives of various groups. Men and women would always be portrayed as "sharing privileges, responsibility, and opportunity for personal growth"; black women should be shown as affluent, elderly characters should be spry and physically agile. Girls should sometimes be portrayed as "larger, heavier, and emotionally stronger and more aggressive than men," but never as "fearful, squeamish, passive, dependent, weepy, mechanically inept." Boys should "pay attention to personal appearance and hygiene," and read poetry. Blacks should never be shown as unemployed, on welfare, or in low-paying jobs; Indians should be shown in the "mainstream" of American life, and not on reservations; and all Asian Americans and Hispanics must be portrayed speaking English. The guidelines demanded stories that included single-parent households and specifically warned that Jews should never be depicted as "diamond cutters, doctors, dentists, lawyers, classical musicians, tailors or shopkeepers," since these were deemed to be "stereotypical."[20]

Editors were specifically directed to count the number of children, adults, and older people in the texts and in photos and illustrations and to keep track of the racial and ethnic makeup of every individual featured. One Holt memo proudly declared that the "in house count shows 146 female and 146 male characters, or a ratio of 1:1. Animal characters were not included in this count."[21] This proved to be a mistake. In 1980, Holt's series came under fire from feminist groups in Texas who argued that the 1:1 ratio of men to women concealed an insidious bias against women. When animals *were* included in the count, feminists insisted in testimony to the selection committee, male figures outnumbered females nearly two to one. Representatives from the National Organization for Women also complained that one story portrayed a boy with insufficiently enlightened attitudes toward a teacher he disliked. In this case, as in many others, author Stephen Bates notes, "Holt deferred to the views of outsiders."[22]

Holt was so anxious to acquiesce to such demands and achieve the perfect ethnic/gender/political blend in its readers that its editors went so far as to change the sex and race of the characters in some stories. Mrs. Jay in the story "Freddie in the Middle" is transformed into Mrs. Chang and the story itself becomes "Maggie in the Middle." Other stories by and about white males were systematically weeded out, edited, or replaced. One memo from the Holt files reveals the dilemma faced by the editors. "1. The body of Western literature . . . is made up primarily of works written by and often focused upon Caucasian males. 2. Many of the older works written by and about ethnic minorities and women which may be considered good literature reflect traditional prejudices and would tend to offend some people. . . . 3. The forthright language and candid subject matter in many of the best modern works by and about members of these groups makes them unacceptable in many high school classrooms. Attempts to have authors modify such works have rarely met with success."[23] That is, of course, the problem with literature; it tends to be forthright and candid; the characters do not fit politically predetermined models; its characters are not always admirable and the plots are occasionally disturbing. All of those characteristics seem to disqualify them from the modern reading text. But as the Holt files make clear, it was not always an easy matter to find replacements. Author Stephen Bates quotes Holt memos in which one editor confessed that he could not find any good stories with Asian-American female leads. Another editor noted that another story was "not great literature," but "we gain two points—a female leading character and characters with Spanish-American names." A third editor remarked: "I'm sorry, but I still do not see much merit in this story— aside from the ethnic aspect."[24]

What's Left Out

The domination of special interest lobbies in the process of confecting textbooks has also led to notable and embarrassing gaps in the texts, including the almost total absence of references to business or businessmen and a virtually complete aphasia concerning the role of religion in American life. A 1986 study of history textbooks found that no textbook for children in grades one through four included a single reference to any contemporary American who was religious or engaged in any act of faith. Reviewers found no references at all to any child who prayed, went to church, or temple.[25] A close study of textbooks for fifth and sixth graders found the same silence about religion, as well other traditional institutions. The words *marriage, wedding, husband,* and *wife,* Professor Paul Vitz found, "do not occur once in these books."[26] Children reading a typical fifth-grade U.S. history text would reasonably come to the conclusion that religion was either no longer practiced in this country or that it had long since ceased to have meaningful impact on its history, institutions, or social movements. The excision of religion was so thorough, Vitz found, that even a social studies text that devotes thirty pages to the Pilgrims includes not a single word or image about the Pilgrims' religion or the role that religion might have played in their decision to come to this country. Another text made mention of Joan of Arc but made "no reference to *any* religious aspect of her life." Vitz noted that this was "an obvious serious misrepresentation of her historical meaning," but concluded that Joan was apparently included in the book because "she was a woman of historical importance."[27]

Proving that not even the Nobel Prize was proof against the editors of elementary textbooks, one sixth-grade reader changed a story by Isaac Bashevis Singer to make it inoffensive. In Singer's original story, a boy not only prays "to God," but later says, "Thank God." In the educationist text, however, the editors removed the words "to God," and amended the phrase "Thank God" to the apparently less offensive "Thank Goodness."[28]

Since 1990, the historical role of religion seems to have gained more recognition in many textbooks. But the American Textbook Council concluded in 1994 that textbooks continue to neglect the contemporary aspects of religious life, including a remarkable reticence when it comes to any effect that religion might have either on public morality or the social movements of the 1950s or 1960s.[29] In contrast, the Council found that many texts take on a catechistic aura "with a faintly religious design" when they deal with environmental issues. The kinds of "fervor once reserved for a divine architect or saviour," the Council's 1994 report declares, "are now directed toward secular (or pantheistic) ends."[30]

The popular text *Environmental Science,* for example, attacks the "human-centered view" of "traditional Western teachings," which are characterized as encouraging "biological imperialism." It describes ecological issues as "a crisis of the human spirit" and calls for the creation of "a new ethical system based on sustainable ethics, the reductions of arms sales and global cooperation."[31]

Given the willingness of educationists to yield to special interest groups, it is perhaps not surprising that environmental education programs have become hothouses for pseudoscience and for ideological heavy-handed-ness. Some schools have taken to simply adopting materials designed by advocacy groups, such as Zero Population Growth (ZPG), and using them as part of the curriculum. Even textbooks from mainstream publishers take an activist rather than a scientific approach to environmentalism. Readers of Prentice-Hall's *Your Health* are urged to "Consider joining an environmental group" and "Become politically involved." The book lists Greenpeace, Zero Population Growth, Planned Parenthood, and Earth First! as environmental organizations students could contact. (Earth First! is the radical group of environmental terrorists manqué, best known for "spiking" trees to damage or injure logging machinery and personnel.) The same book urges students to lobby their elected officials "to provide financial support for nonpolluting transportation and energy-production technologies."[32] This is apparently not isolated. A review by the Arizona Institute for Public Policy Research of eighty-two textbooks, 179 environmental books for children, and eighty-four examples of curriculum materials provided to schools by environmental groups (and adopted uncritically for classroom instruction) found "that unbiased materials are a rare exception." The researchers concluded that "most materials present only one side of an issue, pick only worst-case examples, or simply omit information that challenges an apocalyptic outlook."[33] In one textbook, students are told that global warming will melt the polar ice caps, causing floods that will cover coastal cities. One junior high text shows the New York City skyline flooded and declares: "New York City would almost be covered with water. Only the tops of very tall buildings will be above the water."[34]

A storybook used in many classrooms describes the depredations of a bulldozer in the rainforest. Author Helen Cowcher describes in *Rainforest* how the forest triumphs over the evil predator when a rainstorm washes the bulldozer over a cliff, destroying both man and machine. The storybook, written for preschool children concludes: "The Machine was washed away! But the creatures of the rain forest were safe."[35] Presumably, this is intended as a happy ending.

**THE POLITICAL
CLASSROOM I**

J ade chose Harriett Tubman, while Lafayette picked Thomas Edison.
The girls had been assigned a research project on a famous American
"who had fought for justice" and had run printouts on their choices
from the school library's new CD-ROM encyclopedia. At first, their teacher,
Bob Peterson, was concerned that Lafayette had chosen a dead white
male like Edison. "My immediate reaction was to question how Lafayette
concluded that Thomas Edison fit the criteria of a famous person who
fought for justice," Peterson later wrote, "but she was determined to report
on him so I let it drop."[1] But Peterson also saw an opportunity to turn
the printouts into an occasion for a multiculturalist teaching moment.

The printout on Thomas Edison (a white male) was several inches
longer than the printout on Harriet Tubman (an African-American female).
Peterson asked the two girls to measure the printouts and to report to the
class "about their research." Edison's printout turned out to be ten inches
long—the Tubman printout was only two inches long.

In the hands of another teacher, the length of the printouts would have
been less important than their content, or they might have led the fifth
graders to try to learn more about the Civil War era and the growth of
modern technology, but Peterson was more interested in steering the class
toward the *real* issue: the racism and sexism of CD-ROM encyclopedias.
Peterson, who teaches at Milwaukee's Fratney School and who has written
extensively on what he calls "teaching for social justice," does not believe
that his teaching needs to be politically neutral; indeed, all decisions about
what to teach, he says, "are inherently political."[2]

Led by Peterson, some students in the class suggested that "maybe [the
editors of the CD-ROM encyclopedia] were racist, so first they put in white
inventors and then they added a little extra," while another student offered
that "Thomas Edison was a man and Harriet Tubman was a woman and
maybe it was men who did the CD-ROM." Other fifth graders argued that
the printouts were obviously unfair because "slavery was more important
than the light bulb" and because Tubman "had to risk her life and did
work that was more dangerous" than Edison's. (When it later turned out
that the school's own library had "three or four times" more books on

Tubman than Edison, no one suggested that this was a sign of unfairness, political bias, racism, or sexism.) "We ended our conversation," Peterson recounted, "by asking students how we might find out if the accusations of racism or sexism were accurate."

Peterson's class would spend several weeks on the interrogation of the CD-ROM. But he hastens to point out that his focus on racism and sexism— rather than history or science or economics—is part of the Milwaukee Public Schools' official "Learning Goals," whose number one goal is that "students will project anti-racist, anti-biased attitudes" and "analyze, critique and assess bias in all forms of communication."

In Peterson's class, that meant having his fifth graders get printouts on each of thirty different "famous people" Peterson had selected for the class to study and then *recording the length of the CD-ROM entries on large chart paper.* (Of the thirty "famous" people studied, the only white males were Lincoln, Washington, Edison, the Wright Brothers, General Custer, and John Brown.) The class spent the next two weeks classifying each person not by their historical role or accomplishment, but solely by their race, ethnicity, and gender—Puerto Rican females, Puerto Rican males, Mexican females, Native Americans, African-American females, African-American males, white females, white males, and measuring the length of each CD-ROM entry. Sure enough, white men, including Abraham Lincoln and George Washington, had the most inches devoted to them in the encyclopedia, while students, Peterson wrote, "were surprised to find that Felisa Rincon de Gautir, the first woman mayor of San Juan and a famous Puerto Rican leader, was not listed, nor were the nineteenth-century African-American journalist Ida B. Wells, Mexican-American farm workers organizer Delores Huerta, the first female chief of the Cherokee Nation, Wilma P. Mankiller. . . ."

The fifth graders concluded that "white males got the most information" and "Puerto Rican females got nothing." The fifth graders were appropriately indignant about this: "I hate it," declared one, "because it's not fair." Of course, the fifth graders might not have been in the ideal position to judge the relative importance of Abraham Lincoln and an obscure municipal official from San Juan—or to measure the relative significance of the first flight against the accomplishments of a union organizer. But they weren't being asked to judge the *content* of those accomplishments— merely to get a ruler and *measure them in inches.* George Washington was not discussed as the nation's first president: He was tallied as a "white male," and set side by side with Maria Cordero Hardy, a Puerto Rican scientist. Washington's printout was longer. Q.E.D.

Peterson's fifth-grade class (working cooperatively in groups) created large wall graphs using sticky tape to illustrate the disparities between the coverage of white males and other groups. The graphs showed the average *length* of the printouts by race, ethnicity, and gender—ranging from an average of twenty-eight inches for white males to zero inches for Puerto Rican females. (The printout for Abraham Lincoln, a white male, was quite a bit longer than the printout for Juana Inés de la Cruz.) Peterson proudly declared: "The vibrant colors of the sticky tape made the finished product show quite clearly the bias that we had discovered in the CD-ROM."

Peterson later admitted that "our statistical approach was far from accurate." Not only was the sampling limited, but the inclusion of Lincoln and Washington obviously heavily "weighted the statistics in favor of white men." But the fifth graders were in no position to know that their teacher had passed off this tendentious analysis as real "research." Peterson appears to be unconcerned at his manipulation of ten-year-olds into seeing racism, sexism, and bias all around them. He writes with evident pride that his "students gained experience in collecting data, manipulating it, and looking at it through the lens of race and gender . . ."

The fifth graders concluded their journey into bias detection by writing letters of complaint to the CD-ROM manufacturers, based on their "research" findings of racism and sexism. Peterson brags that his students "wrote from the heart." Warned one fifth grader: "My name is Alfonso and you made me and kids in my classroom mad. You discriminated against people that are ladies and non-whites."

Another student was more specific in his threat: "You better do something about it before I take you to court."

DUMBING DOWN
THE TESTS

John Jacob Cannell was blunt about his credentials: "I am neither a professional educator or a testing expert. I am a physician."[1]

As a general practitioner in West Virginia, Cannell saw a parade of teen pregnancy, depression, delinquency, and drug abuse. Often, those problems were evidence of deeper, underlying troubles and when they were, Cannell referred those patients to clinical psychologists. "The results of their evaluations," he later wrote, "were continually unsettling." Many of the troubled youngsters appeared to lag far beyond their peers in basic academic skills. Independent tests to determine the students' grade level and academic ability found that many of the students were "sitting in seventh grade general studies classrooms with third grade abilities."

But surprisingly, Cannell found, school officials often acted as if nothing was wrong. Schools often reported that these students "scored well on the school's 'standardized tests,' including reading." Cannell was finding that there was little if any relationship between the tests administered by the schools and those given by outside psychologists. Far from doing well, as their schools seemed to think, these students were floundering.

One case dramatically highlighted this pattern. Cannell treated a fifteen-year-old pregnant girl, who had a history of drug use and truancy. She read at only a fourth-grade level, while she had the math abilities of a third grader, despite an IQ of 112. She eventually dropped out of school, after giving birth at age sixteen. Cannell was curious about her schooling, so he asked for and was given her official school record.

"It indicated that Kim had never been offered remediation, never been required to attend summer school, and had never been retained," Cannell later recounted. "Her fourth grade teacher had considered and then rejected retention because the teacher didn't want [the girl's] 'self-esteem to be injured.' Her school had administered a standardized achievement test, the Comprehensive Test of Basic Skills (CTBS), in the third and sixth grades. It indicated Kim's 'total basic skills' were slightly '*above* the national norm.' "[2] [emphasis added]

The professional educators, counselors, administrators, and social workers at the girl's school may not have recognized that anything was amiss, but Cannell immediately saw that something was rotten with the entire system. His experience raised what was for Cannell an obvious question: "How could so many children test below average on independent testing but do well on their official school achievement test?" Despite the tens of millions of dollars spent on educational research and bureaucracy, no one, seemingly, had ever asked that question before. The U.S. Department of Education could offer Cannell no information or explanation.

But Cannell wondered: Could the educational self-deception he'd seen in the cases of his own patients be widespread? Could it, in fact, have become institutionalized? At about the same time he was treating the pregnant teenager, the states of West Virginia and Kentucky announced that their state test scores placed their students "above the national average" on the same CTBS achievement test. Education officials in West Virginia insisted that third graders in the state had scored at the sixty-fifth percentile and their sixth graders at the sixty-second percentile (the national norm being fifty). Kentucky claimed even more stellar scores: nearly 80 percent of Kentucky third graders were told they were "above average."[3]

The message from both states: All's well. The claims of academic success, however, raised several questions, which only John Jacob Cannell bothered to ask.

Despite the claims that its students were "above average," West Virginia had the lowest proportion of college graduates and the third lowest American College Test (ACT) college entrance scores of any state in the country. It ranked near the top in illiteracy, poverty, and near the bottom in the Armed Services Vocational Aptitude Battery scores. West Virginia's schools, moreover, were widely admitted to be a mess. So, Cannell wondered, "If West Virginia could be above average, what state is below average?" The same questions applied to Kentucky, a state with a lower graduation rate, per capita income, and lower college entrance scores than the nation as a whole.

He decided to investigate:

"I decided to present myself to a test publisher as a superintendent of schools from a small southern Virginia school district. I called a publisher and expressed interest in purchasing this company's standardized achievement test. . . . Almost immediately, I was talking to a saleswoman who implied that our district's scores would be 'above average' if we bought one of their 'older' tests! She further intimated that our scores would go up every year, as long as we 'didn't change tests.'"

What did she mean by "older tests?" How could she be so sure the poor rural district he claimed to represent would be above the national average?

To get some answers, Cannell embarked on one of the most ambitious and unusual educational research projects ever undertaken. Without any outside funding, Cannell, his nurse, lab technician, and X-ray technician contacted every state educational department, asking for their standardized test information.

His findings:

- Not a single one of the fifty states reported that its students scored below average at the elementary level on their total battery of scores. The California Achievement Test, the Stanford Achievement Test, the Metropolitan Achievement Test, the Science Research Associates Test, the CTBS, and the Iowa Test of Basic Skills allowed states to claim steady improvements that were not reflected in other objective measures.[4]
- More than two thirds of American students—70 percent—were being told that they were "above average" based on the test scores.[5]
- More than 90 percent of American school districts claimed to be performing above average. Cannell's study found "that some of the poorest, most desperate school districts in the nation are able to pacify the press, parents and school board by testing 'above the national norm' on one of these commercial 'Lake Wobegon' achievement tests. Among those claiming to be 'above average,' he found, were Trenton and East Orange, New Jersey, Boston, St. Louis, Kansas City, East St. Louis, and New York City—all districts notorious for the breakdown in their schools.[6] In many of those cities, years of misleading and Pollyanish claims of academic above-averageness had staved off critics, accountability, and reform, while many of the schools themselves went from wretched to hopeless.

Cannell found that states used various methods of reporting their scores; some used national percentile rank, some normal curve equivalent, some grade equivalent scores. Cannell's group simply reported the scores as they received them from the states. Whatever statistical method the state chose, however, it invariably showed the state was above the national average.

As might be expected, Cannell's report—and Cannell personally—were bitterly attacked by the educratic establishment, but his conclusions were ultimately upheld by the U.S. Department of Education, which concluded that "we generally concur with the central finding of Dr. Cannell's report."[7]

It turned out that many districts were using outdated averages, which made it theoretically possible that 100 percent of students could be above average, especially if the tests were old enough and schools were aggressive in teaching to the outdated tests. Cannell found that some testing companies did not adjust the "average" scores for eight to ten years and that some of the original norms might have been inaccurate. Such practices cast doubt on the entire testing system. As Cannell pointed out, "An above average score does not mean that the student or the district or the state is above the current year's average. It means only that the score achieved is better than the mean score achieved by the norm group in years past."[8] But this was a fact that few parents, legislators, or school board members could be expected to know and which few educrats bother to point out to them.

Another study prepared for the U.S. Office of Technology Assessment also acknowledged the "Lake Wobegon" Effect, attributing it to the "reuse of the same test from year to year." The study also concluded that the Lake Wobegon Effect "is largely the result of changes in the stakes that are attached to test results. Raising the stakes attached to the results for teachers and school administrators increased the incentives to get scores up. That changed the context of testing and, in many cases, led to inflated scores."[9] In other words: People were paying attention and were demanding some accountability from the schools. As sentiment for reform intensified, it became more urgent for educationists to appear successful and to mask their failures with "above average scores." Politically, it is difficult to overstate the value of test scores for pacifying or shooing off legislators and parents. Even the best prepared parent, armed with substandard work, is apt to be shaken when presented with colorful charts and statistics arrayed to validate and endorse the success of the educational status quo.

Given the high stakes, the pressures on schools to cheat on their testing may have proven irresistible to some. After Cannell published his study, he received letters from across the country detailing various testing ruses. "Some teachers openly admitted cheating," he wrote. "Others were concerned that if they didn't cheat, they would look bad compared to the teachers who did. All the teachers complained that cheating is encouraged by school administrators."

Cannell, however, goes even further in his indictment. Educationists are quick to blame their own failures on social problems, but Cannell argues that the schools themselves may have to take some responsibility for those same maladies. "I am convinced," he wrote, "that the current American epidemic of teenage pregnancy, depression, drug use, delinquency, and teen suicide is partially related to the low standards and the low expectations so evident in America's public schools. School officials blame these problems on single parent families, parental apathy, and permissive child-rearing. Undoubtedly, many of these present day realities do detrimentally affect children, but so do present day school policies."[10]

Redefining Mediocrity

Beyond the implications for standardized test reporting, Cannell's findings also shed light on an embarrassing aspect of the educationist culture—its apparent addiction to simply redefining failure as success and mediocrity as "above average" by simple diktat. Some educationists appear sincerely to believe that students' feelings are being hurt by low scores and that this should be corrected not by asking them to work harder, but by jiggering the scores. When too many students do poorly on tests or fail them outright, educationists respond not by redoubling their efforts to raise achievement levels, but rather by blaming the test.

That was the tactic selected by the Wisconsin Department of Public Instruction, when it found that too many test takers were failing the state's General Educational Development (GED) test—a test taken to obtain a high school equivalency diploma. Theoretically, the test is written so that seven out of ten high school seniors would pass. But a study found that only about 52 percent of Wisconsin's high school seniors could meet the minimum score of 250.

Now, there are several ways of looking at that result. If kids can't pass the test, the problem may be in what they are being taught or how hard they are working. The state's educrats could have undertaken a study of the state's curriculum and standards; or they could have exhorted aspirants to the GED to prepare more thoroughly—which might have had the effect of improving the GED's already somewhat shaky reputation. Instead, they decided to simply *lower* the passing score by 20 points—retroactively. Hundreds of applicants who had failed the test in previous years were now awarded diplomas. The state's superintendent of public instruction vehemently denied that he was "dumbing down" the test: he was merely *readjusting* the scores, he explained. The minimum score of 250 had been set in 1987 based on tests that showed that 70 percent of high school seniors should be able to score that high. (Most states still have a minimum score of only 225. Wisconsin's score was the highest in the country.) Thus, scores were being measured against standards that had been too high, too demanding.[11] The decision to lower the passing score sent a clear message: The problem isn't the schools. It isn't the students. *It's the test.* Students don't have to work any harder or do any better, but now they can pass the GED the new-fashioned way: by calling what used to be failure, success.

A representative of one of the state's teachers union explained that the issue was not about academic quality, but about "fairness." She was not referring to the unfairness of low academic achievement, but to the unfairness of tests that measure that achievement. Wisconsin's educrats seemed genuinely surprised when both employers and the holders of equivalency diplomas complained that their action had devalued the diploma—making it virtually worthless for finding qualified employees. This short-term "fairness" did not attempt to make more winners by teaching them more math or science or reading; rather, it was content with creating more winners simply by moving the finish line.

Fudging the SAT

Wisconsin's decision to "adjust" its GED score was simply a small-scale rehearsal for the decision by the College Board to make similar adjustments to the SAT—one of the two major college entrance exams used nation-wide. For three decades, the SAT has been at the epicenter of debates over the decline of American education. The precipitous fall in SAT scores in recent decades has been perhaps the most frequently cited evidence for the crisis in American education. Although the test has come under blistering attacks from anti-testing critics, it has been a constant source of irritation and embarrassment for educationists who are called upon to explain the drop in test scores.

Reflecting some of their anxiety, College Board officials have been tinkering with the test, although they deny that they are trying to artificially raise the sluggish scores. For the first time, they began permitting students to use handheld calculators for the math portion of the exam. Previously, students had been expected to know and perform the calculations them-selves. But in June 1994, the officials took the more dramatic step of simply raising the average test scores by fiat. As a result of the College Board's decision, the typical score on the math section will rise by about 20 points, while the typical verbal score will jump by 80 points *with no improvement in achievement in either area*. Under the new procedure, students will automatically be awarded more points for the same work—a student who would have gotten a score of 430 on the verbal section will now get a 510; a student who would have gotten a 730 score would now get a score of 800, the top of the scale.[12] (Another example of leveling from the top down: students who miss several questions will receive exactly the same score as students who score perfectly.)[13] As usual, the educationists behind the move tried to sell the new scoring system as a routine adjustment. "The question people will ask is, Aren't you making kids feel better by giving them higher scores?" a College Board official tried to explain. "The answer is absolutely, positively not. The performance that generates a 424 today will now generate a 500. The kid is no brighter, doesn't have any more bright answers, it's just the label is higher. Everybody will know."[14]

Of course that is precisely the point: everybody will *not* know. If everybody knew, why raise the scores for the same work? The College Board strained to justify its logic. Following a now-common path, it blamed out-of-date "norms" for the situation. When the SATs were begun in their modern form in 1941, the average score was 500. In the last five decades, the average scores have fallen to 424 in the verbal test and to 478 in the math test. Even though the 424 now represents the new average, the College Board explains, many observers "expect the average to be about 500," thus erroneously thinking that a 424 is a below average score. The new scoring system is designed to correct that misapprehension.

But outside of the College Board's own bureaucracy, no one ever thought of the 500 score as the average. Even if this was a cause of profound unease among students and parents, the Board could have simply announced that the new scores of 424 and 478 were "average" and that everybody should therefore feel better about them. This announcement, however, would have called attention again to the fact that what was now considered an "average" performance was far below the expectations of a few generations ago. It also would have permitted continuing easy-to-understand historical comparisons between SAT scores of the future with those of the past. So the College Board opted for inflating the scores so that mediocre scores were now relabeled as "average" and "above average." As one newspaper editorial explained, "So instead of being compared to their smarter grandparents, today's students will be compared to the Beavis down the street. Presto: higher scores. It is the Lake Wobegon approach to higher education, instantly elevating the clunk next door to above average status. Perhaps some day we can devise a test that will declare every kid to be above average. . . . Now if we can only get those pesky Japanese to go along."

The Fail-Proof Tests

Ironically, low expectations seem to have been institutionalized by some states that had set out with the intentions of actually raising standards. One of the popular reform efforts of the 1980s was the creation of so-called minimum competency tests or other exams that high school students were required to pass as a condition of graduating. Ohio's legislature, for example, hoped to hold the state's schools more accountable by creating an exit exam that all high school students in the state were required to pass. In practice, however, the exam's standards were anything but rigorous. Although the exam was required of high school graduates, the tests were set at an eighth-grade level.

On its face, the test was a ludicrous measure of accountability—it claimed to be setting standards for students leaving high school, but measured instead whether they had the minimum skills of an *eighth grader*. Passing the exam meant only that a student was prepared to *enter* high school, not *graduate* from high school. Students could pass the exit exam without having acquired a single piece of knowledge or skill over the four years since leaving the eighth grade. As absurdly lenient as those requirements were, however, the state might have faced the prospect of large numbers of students failing if those standards had been any higher— a result that appears to have been unacceptable to educationists and politicians alike. As it was, the vast majority of Ohio's students passed the tests easily. By 1 March 1994, for example, 99 percent of the state's high school seniors had passed the writing test and roughly the same percentage had passed the reading test. By 1 May 1994, fully 95 percent of white high school seniors and 90 percent of black high school seniors had passed all four required exit tests in reading, writing, math, and "citizenship."[15]

But that was not enough for the U.S. Department of Education's Office of Civil Rights (OCR), which launched an investigation into whether the exam violated the rights of minority students, because minorities failed the test at a higher rate than white students. As part of the investigation, the OCR announced that it would scrutinize the curricula of local school districts to determine whether they might have had a discriminatory effect.[16] "We are not challenging the test," an OCR official announced. "The issue is whether students are adequately prepared."[17] But the larger issue was whether students would ever be held accountable for their own performance and whether states would ever be permitted to set minimum standards—even ludicrously low ones—if those standards meant that *anybody at all* would not meet them. As the American Federation of Teachers' president Albert Shanker pointed out, students were given eight chances to take and pass the tests, beginning at the end of eighth grade, and they would be given a ninth chance before they were finally denied a diploma. Some students, however, made little effort to pass. Cleveland went as far as paying students to come in to take remedial sessions to help them pass the test, but many students failed to show up. On average, the students who had failed to pass the tests had been absent an average of thirty-two days—the equivalent of more than six weeks—during their junior year of high school. One fourth of them missed as much as nine weeks. "How many of them would have passed if they had made it to school regularly?" Shanker asked.[18] The federal investigation was later quietly dropped, but the fact that the state had faced the prospect of civil rights litigation hardly encouraged educrats to raise their standards or toughen their testing requirements.

"Authentic" Assessments

Another popular alternative to traditional measurements of academic achievement is the increasingly popular use of so-called "authentic" assessments—including "portfolio" assessments—to replace standardized tests and other exams. Alternative assessments are invariably a central aspect of outcome- or performance-based "reforms," since they claim to take a more "holistic" approach to evaluating student progress than do more traditional pencil and paper tests.

The idea of the portfolio is to gather together collections of student work over a semester or a school year—students essays, reports, math assignments, post-projects—to provide a more meaningful measurement of their progress and skills. Portfolios are popular in programs that claim to be outcome based or "performance based," because theoretically they demonstrate what students can *do*. As attractive as the idea might sound in theory, there is evidence that it does not work nearly as well in reality. In some classes a portfolio might consist of a handful of paragraphs; while in another it might consist of detailed essays that require extensive research. Such inconsistencies continue to plague so-called "authentic assessments." A detailed study of Vermont's use of "portfolio assessment," for example, found that teachers scored the portfolios inconsistently. An evaluation of the pioneering effort for the state's education department found the scoring of the portfolios "unreliable because in too many instances, two individual teachers graded the same collection of work differently."[19] The study found that the teachers' scores on student writing portfolios agreed with one another less than half the time. Even on portfolios of math work, the Vermont study found that teachers agreed on their scores less than 60 percent of the time. Such inconsistency would seem to suggest that judging the portfolios is so subjective as to be meaningless for purposes of comparison. One teacher's score of 90 might be another's score of 80, and another's 96. As a system of reliable measurement and accountability, portfolios are essentially useless in practice. Such assessments are, however, perfectly designed for a system in which there is no fixed or objective educational standard.

Although enthusiastically backed by educationists, the alternative assessments are also remarkably burdensome and time-consuming for teachers. Schools in Great Britain have experimented with "alternative" and "authentic" assessments that involve portfolios and other required "performances." Researchers there found that virtually every teacher surveyed "reported that major disruptions had occurred to normal classroom practice, and half of those surveyed felt that the [alternative assessments] were totally unmanageable." By one estimate, it took 82 to 90 hours "to plan for the assessments, collect needed materials for administration, do the assessments, mark them, and record the marks." Another estimate put the time allotted to the alternative assessments at two to five weeks out of the British schools' year. Such a huge investment of time translates into huge costs for the educational system. If similar assessments were employed in American schools, some experts have estimated, the costs could run into the billions of dollars.[20]

Like the Vermont study, British evaluations found that teacher scorings of the "authentic" assessments were suspect. Teachers "went to great lengths to protect their students from stress"—which, evaluators noted, raised questions about the comparability of the scores. In some cases, they found, "teachers could not overcome their natural inclination to give children direct help or to ask them questions that led to a correct response," while other schools "played it safe" by assessing the performance of student tasks that were so easy that success was guaranteed. Despite such experiences, American educationists continue to push for the rapid expansion of the use of alternative assessments throughout the nation's public schools.

THE POLITICAL CLASSROOM II

eter, Peter, Pumpkin Eater, the teacher explains to the first graders, conveys a dangerous message: that you have to put a wife in some sort of cage to keep her. In fact, the class is told, these apparently harmless nursery rhymes are rife with "stereotyped roles." (There are nursery rhymes that make utterly insupportable assumptions about what little boys and girls are made of: Little Miss Muffett—an obvious victim of gender stereotyping and outdated values; the insufferable *Georgy Porgy puddin and pie / Kissed the girls and made them cry*—a blatant case of sexual harassment; and the old woman in the shoe had so many children she didn't know what to do—an appalling case of child abuse and bad family planning.)

Having made the class aware "of the existence of sex-role stereotypes, sex bias, and sex discrimination" in the nursery rhymes, the teacher has the children rewrite the rhymes—as a group rather than as individual writers—to make them more gender-inclusive. The products of all of this—the nice, sanitized, and dull revised rhymes—neatly fit the lesson plan designed and written by the state's educational bureaucracy, the Wisconsin Department of Public Instruction (DPI), as part of the state's formal "sex equity" curriculum.[1]

Wisconsin's educrats have designed weeks' worth of classroom activities built around similar activities. Local school districts, for example, are encouraged to have elementary school students talk about sex-role stereotypes in their own families and to identify sex-biased toys. One suggested classroom activity would have children list the sexes and races of children depicted on the packages of various toys and encourages the children to become activists in fighting toy bias. "If you are in a store," a work sheet prepared by the state education bureaucracy reads, "talk with three people shopping there. Share your findings with each. Describe these people and their reactions." (One suspects that the reactions to the youth sexism cops *would* be educational.)

The state's educrats also recommend that older elementary students spend class time playing games based on television game shows (the educrats suggest that one game be called "Equity Feud") as a way to identify inappropriate attitudes toward gender issues. Teachers are urged to encourage children "to think about gender issues" and "to publicly affirm their beliefs" on such issues as whether "It is okay for boys to cry." (It is.)

In one activity suggested in the DPI's "Classroom Activities in Sex Equity for Developmental Guidance," elementary school students would spend as long as a week imagining "themselves as members of the opposite sex."

The crown jewel of this ambitious curriculum (which runs to more than 170 pages) is the recommendation by the state's educational bureaucracy that teachers have their middle and junior high students play a board game called "Opportunity Knocks," which is subtitled," A Game for Overcoming Stereotypes." Players compete for three kinds of cards, labeled respectively "Free from Stereotype Card," "Opportunity Knocks Card," and "Pressure Point Card." There are no winners and losers in this game, but there *are* right and wrong answers. The curriculum guide stresses the need to make sure students understand that "Traditional forces in society tend to reinforce sex-role stereotyping and reduce the ability of individuals to leave the sex-stereotyped role."

In this state-sanctioned classroom activity, students get points only for "correct" responses to the various questions they face. Some examples:

You have talked your parents into ordering a subscription to *Ms. Magazine*. Take one Free from Stereotype Card. (Share it with your family.)

You help your librarian organize a nonsexist book shelf in the school library. Take one Free from Stereotype Card.

You are a female. You are interested in women's liberation and do something about it. You decide to join the National Organization for Women (NOW). Take one Free from Stereotype Card.

You are male. Your parents tell you to stop crying and act like a man. Lose one Free from Stereotype Card.

You are a male. You would like to take a course in cooking, but don't because you're afraid the kids will laugh at you. Lose one Free from Stereotype Card.

You are a male. You've just watched the 'Lieutenant Fred Frisbee Police Hour.' Frisbee just went through six brutal murders—and never blinked. Frisbee is acting tough. He's a real male-role stereotype. Lose one Free from Stereotype Card.

You are a female. Your parents tell you to be neater and act more like a lady. Lose one Free from Stereotype Card.

You have just convinced your teacher to enroll in a Title IX workshop. Title IX is the law prohibiting sex discrimination in education. Take one Free from Stereotype Card.

Identify at least two ways that competition, which is part of the male sex-role stereotype, has a negative impact on individuals. Answer: Competition can lead to anxiety, a disregard for the rules in order to win, poor self-image for someone who is constantly a loser, a lack of cooperative spirit, insensitivity to the feelings of others. Value for correct answer: Two Free from Stereotype Cards.

At the dinner table, you share your ideas about the limitations of sex-role stereotyping with your family. Take one Free from Stereotype Card.

You write an article for your school newspaper entitled "Our Right to a Nonsexist Education." Take one Free from Stereotype Card.

You are male. You have just become the first boy on the school cheerleading squad. Congratulations. Take one Free from Stereotype Card.

The state education department also felt it necessary to provide an outline of sample activities in sex equity for parents and other community members. The official curriculum guide recommends, inter alia, that parents:

Support only those candidates for public office who support equal opportunity for girls and women.

Contribute time and money to office-seekers who support women's issues.

Support teenage pregnancy prevention initiatives.

Write your elected representatives in support of the Equal Rights Amendment.

MORAL DUMBING DOWN.

CHAPTER 12

THE "VALUES" WASTELAND

E ric Richardson was a seventeen-year-old member of the Spur Posse, a group of boys accused of raping girls as young as ten years old. After their arrests, the posse members reportedly returned to school as heroes, applauded for their exploits by their fellow students. In talk show appearances and media interviews, the boys were unrepentant. "They pass out condoms, teach sex education and pregnancy this and pregnancy that," Eric said after polishing off a Nacho Supreme and necking with his girlfriend in a booth at the Taco Bell. "But they don't teach us any rules."[1] His response was too glib and too convenient; it wasn't our fault, he was saying, you taught us to be like this. No school, however misguided, can ever be blamed for a piece of work like Eric Richardson. Even so, the evidence suggests that his ethical compass is not an isolated aberration.

A 1988 study of more than 2,000 Rhode Island students in grades six through nine found that two-thirds of the boys and half of the girls thought that "it was acceptable for a man to force sex on a woman" if they had been dating six months or more.[2] A write-in survey of 126,000 teenagers found that 25 to 40 percent of teens see nothing wrong with cheating on exams, stealing from employers, or keeping money that wasn't theirs. A seventeen-year-old high school senior explained: "A lot of it is a gray area. It's everybody doing their own thing."[3]

A 1992 survey by the Josephson Institute for Ethics of nearly 7,000 high school and college students, most of them from middle-and upper middle-class backgrounds, found the equivalent of a "hole in the moral ozone" among American's youth.

- A third of high school students and 16 percent of college students said they have shoplifted in the last year. Nearly the same number (33 percent of high school students and 11 percent of college students) said they have stolen from their parents or relatives at least once.[4]
- One in eight college students admitted to committing an act of fraud, including borrowing money they did not intend to repay, and lying on financial aid or insurance forms.

- A third of high school and college students said they would lie to get a job. One in six said they have already done so at least once.
- More than 60 percent of high school students said they had cheated at least once on an exam.
- Forty percent of the high school students who participated in this survey admitted that they "were not completely honest" on at least one or two questions—meaning that they may have lied on a survey about lying.[5]

"I think it's very easy to get through high school and college these days and hardly ever hear, 'That's wrong,'" commented Patrick McCarthy of Pasadena's Jefferson Center for Character Education. Michael Josephson, the president of the Josephson Institute of Ethics, describes a large and growing population as the "I-Deserve-Its," or IDIs. "Their IDI-ology is exceptionally and dangerously self-centered, preoccupied with personal needs, wants, don't-wants and rights." In pursuit of success, or comfort, or self-gratification, the IDIs are blithely willing to jettison traditional ethical restraints, and as a result "IDIs are more likely to lie, cheat and engage in irresponsible behavior when it suits their purposes. IDIs act as if they need whatever they want and deserve whatever they need. . . ."[6] American youth's culture of entitlement cannot, of course, be laid solely at the feet of the schools. If there has been an ethical meltdown among young Americans we need to look first to their parents, communities, the media, and even the churches for explanations. Society's shift from a culture of self-control to one of self-gratification, self-actualization, and self-realization and its changing norms regarding personal responsibility and character, was not restricted to the arena of public education. Even so, the ethical state of America's young people may, at least in part, have something to do with the way our schools teach them about right and wrong.

At one time, American students used to study historical role models like Benjamin Franklin, Florence Nightingale, Thomas Edison, Madam Curie, Abraham Lincoln, and George Washington—whose stories were used to provide object lessons in inventiveness, character, compassion, curiosity, and truthfulness. Following Aristotle, ethicists recognized that humanity does not become virtuous simply by precept, but by "nature, habit, rational principle." "We become just by the practice of just actions," Aristotle observed, "self-controlled by exercising self-control." This process was most effectively begun by placing examples of such virtues in front of young people for them to emulate. But while Asian children continue to read about stories of perseverance, hard work, loyalty, duty, prudence, heroism, and honesty, Harold Stevenson finds that "For the most part, such cultural models have been displaced in the United States today.""In its place, we provide children a jumbled smorgasbord of moral choices.

How Do You *Feel* about Cheating?

The course is officially about "citizenship," but the subject is values.[8] Specially prepared for students in the fourth to sixth grades, the class is designed to help students clarify and discover their own values on issues like lying and cheating. As a group or by secret ballot, the fourth, fifth, and sixth graders are asked: "How many of you . . .

> Think children should have to work for their allowances?
> Think most rules are dumb?
> Think that there are times when cheating is ok?
> Wish you didn't have grades in school?
> Think prizes should be awarded for everything?

The section on cheating asks students: "What are your attitudes toward cheating?" They are asked to complete the following statements:

> Tests are _____
> Grades are _____
> The bad thing about cheating is _____
> The good thing about cheating is _____
> If there were no such things as grades, would your attitude toward cheating change?
> Is school the only place cheating takes place? Where else does cheating take place?
> Is it ever OK to cheat? When?

It is not clear whether there are ever any right and wrong answers to these questions. The class takes a similar approach to lying. Students are asked, "Lying, What's Your View?"

The students are given a work sheet that tells them that "If most Americans reacted to lying the way Pinocchio did, they'd be constantly tripping over their noses." This is followed by an estimate from a psychologist that Americans tell two hundred lies per day. Given this information about the morality of their elders, the children are then asked to consider a series of questions:

> Do you think elected officials lie? On what do you base your conclusion?
> Do your parents think so?
> Do you agree with this statement, made by the Greek philosopher,

Plato, over 2,000 years ago, describing his ideal society. "The rulers of the State . . . may be allowed to lie for the good of the State."

Children in the class are then presented with a series of ethical problems. They are not asked to define right and wrong or moral or immoral. Instead, they are asked to say which actions are "acceptable to you, and in which are they unacceptable. Do any of the situations involve lying?"

A factory worker oversleeps and is late for work. He tells his supervisor that he was involved in a minor traffic accident.

Janine just can't face a big history exam for which she hasn't studied. She convinces her mother that she has a terrible sore throat and must stay home.

Bill runs into a friend he hasn't seen in months. The friend asks how he is. Bill smiles and answers "great!" even thought his dog just died, he's flunking English, and he just broke up with his girlfriend.

Far from being presented as role models or as "examples of virtue," adults are presented as casual, even chronic liars. Cheating is discussed not as something to be avoided, but as a decision that apparently has both a good and a bad side to it. Virtue is simply one option among many.

Students in other classes are also taught other ways of making ethical decisions through a program called PALS, which stands for "Peers Always Listen Sensitively," a "Curriculum for Teaching Peaceful Conflict Resolution."[9] The children are told to evaluate every situation in stages: first, they must identify the problem, then describe the possibilities, evaluate positive and negative consequences, act on the choices they've made, and finally learn from those choices. The fourth, fifth, and sixth graders are asked to apply those steps to a situation in which the child and his friends decide to buy a rowboat together. But the child is $10 short. He is asked to tend his father's store while he works in the stockroom. A rich man with failing eyesight gives him a $20 bill instead of a $10 bill. The work sheet tells the children: "You can keep the extra ten dollars and buy the boat you want. Mr. Kelly believes he is giving you ten dollars and your dad is not losing money." The work sheet asks children: "Do you keep the ten dollars? Shouldn't Mr. Kelly share his wealth, anyway? Does he have a right to so much when all you want is a little rowboat?"

The exercise concludes with the instructions that the children "Act out a plan. Learn for the future. What would you do differently if this happened again?" The curriculum says nothing about what plan they should follow or what lessons they should learn from it.

Such nonjudgmentalism is a feature of the approach known as "values clarification," in which, as William Kirk Kilpatrick writes, classroom discussions are turned into " 'bull sessions' where opinions go back and forth but conclusions are never reached." In such classes, the teacher resembles nothing so much as a talk show host, presiding over classes "where the merits of wife swapping, cannibalism, and teaching children to masturbate are recommended topics for debate." The approach dominates classes in human growth and development where sexuality is described in mechanical and functional terms and moral choices presented as morally neutral options and in "drug education programs in which drugs are scarcely mentioned except to say that taking them is a personal choice."[10]

Many of these classes seem to be based on the rather fantastic notion that since none of the civilizations anywhere in the world throughout the entire sweep of human history has been able to work out a moral code of conduct worthy of being passed on, we should therefore leave it to fourth graders to work out questions of right and wrong on their own.

The Values Clarifiers

The developers of Values Clarification and other nonjudgmental approaches to moral decision making often claimed to be value-free, but their agenda was quite specific. Their bête noir was "moralizing" in any form. "Moralizing," the authors of *Values Clarification: A Handbook of Practical Strategies for Teachers and Students*, wrote in 1978, "is the direct, although sometimes subtle inculcation of the adults' values upon the young."[11] For the authors of the new curriculum, this was not merely authoritarian and stifling, but also dangerous to the ethical health of children. By passing on a set of moral values, they argued, parents were hampering the ability of children to come up with their own values. "Young people brought up by moralizing adults are not prepared to make their own responsible choices," they warned.[12] In any case, moralizing was no longer practical. Children were bombarded with so many different sets of values and parents were only some of the many voices they heard. In the end, they argue, every child had to make his own choices. That, of course, is true—making choices is the essence of free will. But where values clarification departed from older moral philosophies was in its contention that children do not need to be grounded in value systems or provided with moral road maps before they are asked to make such choices. Values clarifiers also did not care what values the child chose to follow. Specifically, values clarification did not concern itself with inculcating values such as self-control, honesty, responsibility, loyalty, prudence, duty, or justice. In its purest form, values clarification did not even argue that these virtues were superior or preferable to their opposites and had little to say about concepts of right and wrong. The goal of values clarification was not to create a virtuous young person, or young adult with character or probity; its goal was empowering youngsters to make their own decisions, *whatever those decisions were*. The authors of the handbook explained that their curriculum "is based on the approach formulated by Louis Raths, who in turn built upon the thinking of John Dewey. Unlike other theoretical approaches to values, Raths is not concerned with the *content* of people's values, but the *process of valuing.* . . . Thus, the values-clarification approach does not aim to instill any particular set of values."[13] [emphasis in original]

The assumption behind such programs was that children had the capacity to develop character on their own; that students as young as third grade had the knowledge, insight, and cognitive abilities to wrestle through difficult dilemmas and thorny moral paradoxes without the benefit of a moral compass, either from parents or teachers. The Values Clarification handbook suggested that teachers help children develop their own values by asking such questions as "How do people get rich? Why are some people poor?" To answer such questions, it was apparently not necessary to study economics, nor was it necessary to study theories of justice or stories about the acquisition or loss of wealth. Students were also asked probing question about their family life. "Are you allowed to make a lot of your own decisions at home? About what?" "What would you do if you found some money in the street?" "Have you ever stolen anything?" "Are you ever alone in the house? How often? How do you feel?"[14]

Questions for older children included: "Have you ever signed a petition? For what?" "Are you curious about trying pot?" "Have you ever carried a picket sign?" "What do you think of the new morality?" "Do you get enough money for your allowance?" "Can you tell your parents your personal problems?" "Do you believe in burial, cremation, or what?" "Are there things you would not tell even best friends? What kinds of things?" "Do you feel satisfied with your life?" "Are you more or less religious now than you were three years ago?" "Is there an adult outside of school whom you dislike intensely? Why?" "Should your school give seniors full birth control information?" "What are you saving money for?"[15]

At the heart of the values clarification program was the effort to have students develop an individual identity. One exercise was "Are You Someone Who . . ." followed by a long list of options, including: "is likely to marry someone of another religion?"; "is likely to grow a beard?"; "would consider joining the John Birch Society?"; "is apt to go out of your way to have a black (white) neighbor?"; "will subscribe to *Playboy* magazine?"; "will change your religion?"; "will be likely to win a Nobel Peace Prize?"; "is apt to experiment with pot?"; "would get therapy on your own initiative?"; "will make a faithless husband? wife?"

The authors explain that such questions will cause students "to consider more thoughtfully what they value, what they want out of life and what type of persons they want to become."[16] But the questions send another message as well by treating the various options simply as different choices of apparently equal weight, like choices on a personality buffet line: Will you win the Nobel Prize or experiment with pot? Subscribe to *Playboy* or change your religion? There is no suggestion that growing a beard or cheating on your wife might be decisions that carry rather different moral weights.

Ultimately, the values clarification approach reduces moral choice to a matter of personal taste with no more basis in objective reality than a preference for a red car rather than a blue one. There is no right or wrong answer and no real ground to regard your own choice either as better or more valid than any other.

But is this really a process of working out moral values or is it simply a process of rationalization? Humans rationalize because it is convenient and it suits our interests. If we choose, we can shape morality to meet our inclinations and impulses, rather than try to shape our inclinations to accord with moral law. Moral reasoning, in contrast, involves asking whether an act is good, whether it is made with right intent, and examining the act's circumstances. To make such judgments requires an understanding of what the moral law might be, not simply how we feel about the act. But to take the subjective state of mind and make it the sole test of morality is to rationalize and call it moral reasoning. Checking one's inclinations is not the same as examining one's conscience, precisely because the conscience needs to be educated.

One would never get that idea from watching a values clarification "simulation" of a moral choice. In one popular exercise, students have to imagine that their class has been trapped in a cave-in. In the exercise, students are asked to imagine that they have to form a single line to work their way out of the cave. At any moment, another rock slide may close the way out. Those at the head of the line are therefore the most likely to survive. In the class exercise, each member of the class must give the reason he or she should be at the head of the line. The teacher tells them: "Your reasons can be of two kinds. You can tell us what you want to live for or what you have yet to get out of life that is important to you. Or you can talk about what you have to contribute to others in the world that would justify your being near the front of the line." After hearing all of the pleas, the class then decides the order in which they will file out of the cave.[17]

Like other values clarification chestnuts, youngsters are asked to make life-and-death decisions. But what are the practical implications? Do students emerge from the class more empathetic? More willing to sacrifice for others? Are they likely to treat their peers with more respect? Show more self-restraint in the presence of their parents? Or are they likely to have a keener sense of their own egos? From the perspective of clarifying values, it is perhaps not irrelevant to notice that a St. Francis of Assisi or Mother Theresa would not fit into the cave-in simulation, because it is unlikely that either would (a) argue for their right to push forward to the head of the line to save themselves at the expense of others, or (b) see this celebration of narcissism as an exercise in moral enlightenment. One might also wonder whether the discussion about the cave-in might have gone differently if students had been made to read the life of Gandhi before class.

Other exercises ask students to choose who should be allowed to stay in a fallout shelter (and who should be left to die) during a nuclear attack; to decide whether it is morally permissible for a poor man to steal a drug that his desperately ill wife needs; to work through the dilemma of trapped settlers who must decide whether to turn to cannibalism or starve to death; to put themselves in the place of a mother who must choose which of her two children she will save; and consider the ethical dilemma of a doctor who must decide to operate on an injured child despite the religious objections of the parents. "Like a roller-coaster ride," William Kilpatrick writes, "the dilemma approach can leave its passengers a bit breathless. That is one of its attractions. But like a roller-coaster ride, it may also leave them a bit disoriented—or more than a bit."[18] As entertaining as such problems may be, they are hardly a guide for developing a moral code; morality is more than solving a complex and perhaps even unsolvable puzzle. Take the case of the man whose wife is dying of an incurable illness and who needs a rare and expensive drug. Kilpatrick wonders whether youngsters who spend a diverting and lively class period debating whether stealing is right or wrong in this case would be less likely to steal themselves? Or lie? Or cheat? Or will they come to the conclusion that moral questions are inevitably so complicated, so fraught with doubt, that no one answer is necessarily ever any better than any other and that all moral questions come down in the end simply to a matter of opinion? Or will they get the idea that it is less important whether one steals or not than that one has developed a system of "valuing" with which one is comfortable?

One of the striking things about spending time with high school students is the near universality of this notion that values are something they work out on their own. One frequent speaker on ethical issues recounts his experience with high school students in which he presents them with a typical values clarification dilemma. They must imagine that they are on a lifeboat with another person and their family dog; the students can save only one, so they must choose either the human being, who is a complete stranger, or the beloved and cherished family dog. Typically, some of the students choose to save the dog and allow the man to die; most students choose to save the human being. But then the speaker asks them what they thought of their classmates who had opted for the dog over the man. Almost never, says the speaker, do students say that those choices were "wrong" or morally objectionable.[19] Even for those who made the correct moral choice, it was merely a matter of personal opinion, and they refuse to be judgmental toward those who put the dog's life ahead of the human being's. The concept that there might be universal and objective moral principles at stake is completely alien to these youngsters.

The Sexy Child

Discussions of "values" are not, of course, always abstract; students do not merely have to work out their opinions on honesty, on cheating, and on when it might be okay to steal or let someone else die. On a more immediate level, they have to decide how they are going to handle their hormones, e.g., since everybody else seems to be doing it, should they go ahead and have sex? By 1993, one out of five children aged thirteen to fifteen years old said they had had sexual intercourse; 55 percent of sixteen- and seventeen-year-olds said they were sexually experienced. Nearly a quarter of the students polled (23 percent) said they had lost their virginity before they turned fourteen; 47 percent before they were fifteen; and fully 72 percent of those teens who were sexually active said they had had intercourse before they were old enough to have a driver's license.[20]

Most American children now receive some form of sex education, but it is naive to assume that the classroom is where they get the most information about sex. In one poll, sixteen- and seventeen-year-olds ranked school last when asked where they have learned the most about sex—far behind friends (37 percent), parents (22 percent), and various entertainment outlets (18 percent). In contrast, only 15 percent said they had learned the most about sex in school.[21]

As unsurprising as that finding is, it probably deserves more attention than it has received. Educationist advocates of "comprehensive sex education" claim that their approach is "realistic" because it arms youngsters with the information they will need to survive in a sex-besotted world. But how realistic is it to imagine that they can predict precisely how the potpourri of sexual options they are offering will be filtered through the mind of an adolescent who has perhaps seen as many as 14,000 sexual encounters on television over the past year? Given this torrent of information and stimulation, the reactions of youngsters may be shaped as much by what they are *not* taught as by what is included in the curriculum. Famed child therapist Bruno Bettelheim remarks, "You don't learn about sex from parental nudity or by showering together. That's nonsense. How you feel about sex comes from watching how your parents live together, how they enjoy each other's company, the respect they have for each other. Not from what they do in bed to each other."[22] But a nineteen-year-old member of the predatory Spur Posse notes that "love and stuff like that really wasn't discussed" in his school's courses that dwelt nonjudgmentally (but graphically) on the plumbing and mechanics of sexuality.[23]

The Ideology of Sexualization

While the programs vary widely, the dominant ideology of the movement toward "comprehensive sex education" believes (1) that since children are sexual by nature, it is impossible to begin teaching them about sex too early, in fact, the younger the better, (2) that parents cannot be trusted to properly introduce children to their bodies and their sexuality because too many of them think sex is shameful or have their own hang-ups and outdated moral codes, (3) that it is more "realistic" to expose children to explicit information about a variety of sexual issues than to try to protect them from adult dilemmas, (4) that children can make intelligent and reasoned choices if honestly presented with a smorgasbord of sexual options, (5) that we can effectively separate sexuality from traditional codes of morality, and (6) that the solution to problems of teen pregnancy and disease lies in technology and education.

Groups as diverse as the American Medical Association and the National Education Association (NEA) now back sex education programs for children beginning in kindergarten and continuing step by step through high school. At each stage, children learn to shed their inhibitions and hesitancies; they are taught to be comfortable with words like *penis* and *vagina*, to be at ease with their bodies and their sexuality, and to understand the many acceptable alternatives from which they can choose. While many of the programs now include abstinence, sex restraint is often offered merely as one choice among many. Many of the programs teach teenagers that they can enjoy sexual pleasure short of intercourse and that there is nothing unusual or problematic about indulging in sexual fantasies about forbidden acts. Advocates also insist that children as young as elementary school be taught the mechanics of sexual intercourse and encourage candor about masturbation, regardless of how parents might feel about the subject. The textbook *Learning About Family Life*, which is widely used in "human growth and development" programs, tells teachers: "Masturbation is a topic that is viewed negatively in many families, based on long-standing cultural and religious teachings. Assure parents that your approach will be low-keyed and will stress privacy, *but also make it clear that you will not perpetuate myths that can mar children's healthy sexual development.*" Masturbation should also be presented in a gender-equitable manner, the book suggests, with girls allowed equal time for questions.[24] Surgeon General Joycelyn Elders was fired by President Clinton for suggesting that children be taught about masturbation. But her comments merely reflected the long-standing and highly orthodox view of the sex education establishment. The national "Guidelines for Comprehensive Sexuality Education," published by the Sex Information and Education Council of the U.S. (SIECUS), details both the information and the attitudes that should be conveyed to children from ages five to eighteen, including that "Masturbation is one way human beings express their sexuality."

The SIECUS guidelines propose that children between five and eight years old be taught that "Some boys and girls masturbate, others do not," and that "masturbation should be done in a private place." Children nine to twelve years old, SIECUS suggests, should be taught that "masturbation is often the first way a person experiences sexual pleasure" and that "masturbation does not cause physical or mental harm." By the time children reach early adolescence, the SIECUS curriculum becomes more explicit. Children twelve to fifteen should be taught that "How often a person masturbates varies for every individual," and that "Most people have masturbated at some time in their lives." Nor does SIECUS steer away from controversial aspects of the subject. It recommends that twelve- to fifteen-year-olds be taught that "Masturbation, either alone or with a partner, is one way a person can enjoy and express their sexuality without risking pregnancy or an STD/HIV," and also that there are "many negative myths about masturbation," and that "some religious groups oppose masturbation." The SIECUS guidelines also propose that high school students be taught that "Masturbation may be an important part of a couple's sexual relationship."

Other "developmental messages" recommended by SIECUS include:

(Early adolescence; ages twelve through fifteen): "Sexual feelings, fantasies, and desires are natural. Sexual feelings, fantasies, and desires occur in all stages of life."
(Adolescence; ages fifteen through eighteen): "Healthy sexuality enhances total well-being.
"Sexuality is an integral, joyful, and natural part of being human. . . ."
"Some common sexual behaviors shared by partners include kissing, touching, caressing, massage, sharing erotic literature or art, bathing/ showering together, and oral, vaginal, or anal sex."
(Middle childhood, ages five through eight): "Some men and women are homosexual, which means they will be attracted to and fall in love with someone of the same gender."
"Homosexuals are also known as gay men and lesbian women."
(Preadolescence, ages nine through twelve): "Homosexual love relationships can be as fulfilling as heterosexual relationships."
(Early adolescence, ages twelve through fifteen): "Many young people have brief sexual experiences (including fantasies and dreams) with the same gender, but they mainly feel attracted to the other gender."
"It is common for people to feel some attraction to men and women."
"People do not choose their sexual orientation."[25]

The trajectory of the comprehensive sex education movement seems to be toward ever more explicit discussions at increasingly younger ages with progressively diminishing judgmentalism. Thus *A Kid's First Book*

About Sex walks very young children step-by-step through a detailed exploration of their sexuality.[26]

"Go into a room that has a big mirror in it, and close the door," the book advises children. "Take off all your clothes and look at yourself in the mirror. . . ." This is followed by a discussion of nudity and the observation that in some families, "some or all of the people walk around a lot with no clothes on, especially if the weather is hot."[27]

A chapter on "Touching," asks children to consider touches such as rubbing, massaging, kissing, scratching, snuggling, stroking, and squeezing and asks them: "Do any of these kinds of touching feel sexy to you sometimes?" Sexiness is a concept of considerable importance to the authors of *A Kid's First Book About Sex.* "How does a sexy feeling feel to you?" it asks, offering children a number of possible answers, including "giggly," "excited," "happy," "weird," "warm," and "just different."[28]

"If you have feelings that are sexy," the book then asks, "where in your body do you feel them the most?" Perhaps realizing that small children might not have a firm grasp on the concept of "sexiness," the authors explain that a "sexy person is someone who: Enjoys touching; Really likes herself or himself and shows it; Likes her or his own body."[29] That could also be a definition of narcissism, but it does not strike a jarring note in a curriculum already likely to be structured around self-centered self-esteem.

A child is shown lying on a bed with his teddy bear. He is hugging himself, under the heading: "Feeling Sexy." The authors write: "feeling sexy is sometimes called feeling 'aroused,' or 'excited,' or 'turned on.' There a lots of things that make you feel turned on, like:

- Thinking special thoughts
- Seeing a special person
- Touching your own body
- Being touched by someone you like or love
- Touching someone you like or love."[30]

This is accompanied by descriptions of the physical reaction of the child's sexual organs to this arousal, including orgasm, which *A Kid's First Book About Sex* describes as a "a rush of excitement and then [feeling] relaxed and maybe a little tired." Using cartoons to illustrate their analogies, the authors go on to explain that an "orgasm is sort of like: Climbing up the ladder of a big slide and whooshing down. [A child is shown sliding down a slide.] Sneezing after your nose has been tickled. Peeing after you've had to wait a long time to pee."[31]

A Kid's First Book About Sex takes an especially expansive view of the possibilities of masturbation. A two-page spread is devoted to "pictures of different ways people masturbate." Children are asked, "Do you do it any of these ways?" Options—all of which are pictured in the book—include: "Squeeze a toy or pillow or blanket between my legs. Ride a horse or bicycle. Rub myself against the bed or table. Shinny up a pole or slide down a bannister. Pull my clothes tight around my sex parts. Touch with my hands or fingers." At the end a single child is shown with his arms crossed, saying "Not me! I never do it."[32] Whatever choice the children make, the book seems to say, is all right, because no one choice is preferable to any other. Listing things people do when they are by themselves, the authors mix the sexual with the banal:

Read
Burp
Sleep
Scratch
Pick their noses
Cry
Masturbate
Suck their thumbs
Work on projects
Sleep
Write or Draw Pictures[33]

Obviously, no choice is any more or less important than any other; it is simply an item on the smorgasbord. If the book has a single mood, it is casualness toward sexuality, a blithe indifference about what children choose to do, as long as they enjoy themselves. The book takes a similar attitude toward sexual intercourse. After introducing the basics along with definitions of homosexual, lesbian, and bisexual (illustrated with happy couples holding hands), children are asked what people of the same sex or opposite sex do when they are together. The list of options includes:

Play games
Sleep in the same bed
Eat snacks
Go to the movies
Make a baby
Go hiking
Have sexual intercourse
Watch TV
Listen to music
Go on vacation[34]

Getting married is not listed as one of the options.
Despite the high-profile controversies that flare up from time to time

over sex education programs, it would not be true to say that they have been implemented against the wishes of most parents. To the contrary, there are indications that comprehensive sex education enjoys quite wide support from parents who are willing to overlook the details. The appeal of such programs is not mysterious; parents want their children to have the information they need to survive in the 1990s. But beyond that, such programs are, perhaps in inequal measures, creations of confusion, fear, and that most ancient of human impulses, rationalization.

Confusion is readily explained. In the 1990s, sensuality balances precariously on a knife's edge of indulgence and anxiety; disease and abuse compete with desire and intimacy. Who isn't ambivalent? Nowhere, however, are those contradictions felt as sharply as in our attitudes toward sexually precocious children, because even "enlightened" parents who buy their children Madonna-wanna-be outfits and who regard talk about "innocence" as a reactionary fantasy, can't help but be uneasy at the implications of their children acting like or being seen as sexual objects or actors.

Parents who grew up in an age when sexual norms were in flux, and when traditional notions of morality were dismissed as priggish and judgmental, understandably have a hard time seeing their way back to the values they had derided. They cringe at the thought that they might be becoming their own mothers and fathers, those museum pieces of sexual repression and badgering. But they are also frightened by the specter of abuse, disease, and pregnancy. The spread of the AIDS virus provides an edge of nervous urgency that makes questions of morality, love, and marriage seem of less immediate concern than the overriding questions of life and death. Confusion easily translates into flight from a decisive stance. In the case of teenage sex, it has led to abdication of parental guidance to the schools. Child psychologist David Elkind notes that "many young people are exposed to programs and information that reflect adult anxieties about teenage sexuality much more than the very real concerns and anxieties experienced by the young people to whom the programs are directed."[35] By embracing the comprehensive sexuality curriculums, parents have turned to the "experts," who promise both a solution and absolution: a program that gets their child through high school without becoming pregnant or dying of AIDS, and lets parents off the hook.

Sex educators are helpful in rationalizing this abandonment, assuring parents that they are preparing children for the real world by treating them as knowledgeable and responsible quasi-adults who can discover their own values. If anyone wonders out loud about the wisdom of this practice, they are dismissed as "unrealistic" anachronisms who believe that parents should protect children, when it is clearly more "realistic" to turn the job over to the children themselves.

As Barbara Dafoe Whitehead observes, "This rhetoric is politically shrewd. It is smart to identify sex education with realism, honesty, and sexual freedom. (Its opponents are thereby unrealistic, hypocritical, and sexually unliberated.) Similarly it is advantageous to link the sex education campaign with the struggle against religious fundamentalism and, more generally, with opposition to religious argument in public life. When the issue is cast in Scopes-trial terms, it appears that an approach to sex education based in science will triumph over one rooted in blind faith."[36]

An extraordinary amount of effort appears to go into attempts to defend sex education programs by discrediting any critics as members of the religious right or as individuals who want to impose their sectarian morality on the schools.[37] Michigan's Senate Select Committee To Study the Michigan Model of Comprehensive School Health Legislation concluded that top state educrats "used taxpayer funds to hold training sessions around the state for local school officials on how to discredit Michigan Model opponents. . . . Any parent or teacher who got in the way of implementing the Michigan Model at a local school district was to be labeled as a right wing, fundamentalist Christian fanatic." The charges leveled against critics, the committee claimed, "would qualify as slander in any court of law."[38]

The treatment of parents with the temerity to object to sex education curricula also reflects a more general attitude toward the role of parents in public education today. "There is a pervasive attitude among many administrators and health educators," the Michigan Senate committee found, "that they know best what children need. They communicate to parents that they are the professionals and the parents are unschooled amateurs."[39] Too often, the committee found that parents were treated as if they were "an incidental biological appendage in the raising of their children. The attitude seems to be that serious work should be left for the experts."[40] The senate committee also concluded that parental and community involvement in determining what should be taught to children about sex was largely illusory. Although local administrators eagerly pointed to their inclusion of parents on advisory boards, the senate committee concluded that most of them were used to "rubber stamp" curriculum decisions already made by district administrators and "experts" in the field. "Advisory board members who do more than nod and reply 'yessir' to the school district's requests," the committee charged, "are often shunted aside and in some cases ridiculed or completely ignored."[41]

Such tactics are especially useful for the advocates of comprehensive sex education because they divert attention from two inconvenient facts: First, that despite their claims of expertise, the credentials of the sex educationists are often flimsy; and, second, that despite their claims of realism, their programs have been notable failures. As Whitehead noted, comprehensive sex education neither behaves like nor is treated like an academic discipline, which not incoincidentally explains why many of its central doctrines lack even a shred of documentary support. "Perhaps this is because comprehensive sex education is a policy crafted outside the precincts of the academy," Whitehead writes. "It is not rooted in a single discipline, or even a set of disciplines, *but can best be described as a jumble of popular therapies and philosophies, including self-help therapies, self-esteem and assertiveness training, sexology, and certain strands of feminism.*"[42] [emphasis added] In her study of New Jersey's experiment with mandated comprehensive sex education, Whitehead found that the leaders of the movement were "not researchers or policy analysts or child-development experts but public-sector entrepreneurs: advocates, independent consultants, family planners, free-lance curriculum writers, specialty publishers, and diversity educators." In any event, the lack of academic or research support for sex education programs may be besides the point, since, as Whitehead wrote, "the unifying core of comprehensive sex education is not intellectual but ideological."[43]

Karl Popper distinguished ideology from science by noting that science always subjects itself to rigorous challenges that seek to falsify its premises, but ideologies can never be proved wrong. In 1980, New Jersey became the first state in the country to mandate comprehensive sex education, even in the primary grades. But since its advent, the proportion of teenage births to unwed mothers in New Jersey has risen from 67.6 percent to 84 percent. "Arguably," Whitehead writes, "the percentage might be even higher" if New Jersey did not have mandatory sex education. "Nevertheless, it is hard for advocates to claim that the state with the nation's fourth highest percentage of unwed teenage births is a showcase for their approach."[44] But as Whitehead also noted, the lack of supporting data for their programs does not "discomfit or deter its advocates." Nor do studies showing that the increase in the number of teenage family-planning clients has been accompanied by rises both in teen pregnancy and abortion rates. (Although participation in the clinics did cut down on *live* teen birth rates.)[45] As one researcher observed: "Apparently these programs are more effective at convincing teens to avoid birth than to avoid pregnancy."[46]

As sex education programs have become more entrenched, the rate of sexual activity among teenagers has continued to explode. Of course, all of this cannot be blamed on comprehensive programs of sex education because family breakdowns, changing social norms, and the media certainly contribute. But advocates are unable to point to any compelling evidence that their efforts have resulted in greater responsibility or restraint among young people. As recently as 1982, 19 percent of fifteen-year-old girls reported that they were sexually active; by 1993, that had jumped to 27 percent. The number of sexually active teenage girls who report having multiple partners has risen from 38 percent in 1971 to 61 percent in 1993.[47]

The situation is not completely bleak. Some alternative sex education programs, most notably "Postponing Sexual Involvement," developed by researchers at Atlanta's Grady Memorial Hospital, have demonstrated that students who have taken a course that teaches them to abstain from sexual intercourse are much less likely to have sex than students who have not had that course. The Grady program was begun in the early 1980s, after a survey of more than a thousand teenage girls found that an overwhelming 84 percent of the girls wanted their schools to teach them how to say no "without hurting anyone's feelings."[48] Sex educationists, who simply refuse to believe that anything can induce teens to restrain themselves, largely ignored the implications of this result. But the researchers at the Grady Hospital took it seriously and decided to test whether the girls' responses were credible. They created a course that uses skits to rehearse ways of refusing demands for sex. The evidence suggests that the courses succeeded in changing both attitudes and behavior. One study found that students who had not taken the Grady course were five times more likely to have become sexually active before the end of eighth grade than students who took the course. By the end of ninth grade, only 24 percent of students who had taken the course had had sexual intercourse, compared with 39 percent of the students who had not been in the program.

Beyond the relative ineffectiveness of mainstream sex education, there is another irony that overshadows the debate over sex education. Obsessed with shielding children from the rude shocks of an unenlightened world, educationists are eager to guard children against the effects of competition and low self-esteem by creating a bubble of artificial success and affirmation. But when it comes to sexuality, the same educationists plunge very young children into a maelstrom of harrowing issues including abortion, homosexuality, divorce, and masturbation at the earliest possible age. The same educationists who insist that children must be protected from the traumatic and scarring influence of dodgeball blandly insist children can take HIV in stride. And all the while they are blasting away at the taboos, inhibitions, scruples, and hang-ups of the young, they insist that they are not violating childhood, but "empowering" children.

But the knowing child is not the same as a wise one. Nor is the (dis)illusioned youngster, for whom no mysteries exist, automatically equipped to make the best decisions, especially if his elders themselves seem so reluctant to provide him with a map of the wilderness into which they are so eagerly shoving him.

TELLING ON MOMMY AND DADDY

Kathleen Parker lost her temper, yelled, and threw a clock across a room. This, of course, did not make her a dysfunctional parent or an abusive mother. She had simply had a bad day. "As mothers like to say," she later recounted, "I'd been pushed to the limit." Afterward, she apologized for losing her temper and her child apologized for the whining and complaining that had set his mother off in the first place. The entire episode would have been quickly forgotten except for the epilogue. On the way to school the next day, Parker's son remarked, "I think maybe I'll talk to Mr. K.," the school's counselor. "He talks to the kids about their 'inner selves'," Parker explained. "Makes them feel good. Leads discussions about divorce and death." And apparently also discusses the shortcomings of parents with their children. The prospect that kindly, innocuous Mr. K. would be hearing "a one-sided and, I might add, inevitably dramatic rendition of events at our house," was not a pleasant one for Kathleen Parker. In her own mind there was a clear distinction between hitting and yelling; but in the 1990s they can be made to seem equally abusive. And how would Mr. K. interpret this particular lapse of clock throwing?

Mr. K. was, of course, only one of the growing cadres of helping professionals who serve as buffers for children in need. But as Parker later wrote: "We've also set up a dynamic in which children believe they need someone other than their parents to solve problems. We've relinquished the concept of family loyalty by encouraging children to talk openly about matters once considered private."[1]

This is especially true now that educationists have decided that they are on the front line in the fight against child abuse. The problem is undeniably a grave one. But the philosophy that permeates that the so-called "protective behavior" curricula is that *every* child needs to be warned about and prepared for the dangers of verbal, physical, and sexual abuse because *every* child is a potential victim. This is a responsibility that cannot be left to the family, because *every* child is a potential victim of his or her *own family*, a message reinforced for children with monotonous regularity.

I first became aware of the "protective behaviors" curriculum when a mother called me to tell her of an experience she had had with her daughter. Her child, an elementary schoolgirl, had come home in tears. When she saw that her mother was home and waiting for her, she rushed to her in relief. "I wasn't sure you'd be here," she told her mother. Her mother reassured her that she would always be there for her. In school that day, her daughter told her, her class had discussed "bad touching" including spanking. In the course of the discussion, children had been encouraged to share with the teachers and classmates whether they had ever been touched in that way and the girl had said that her mother had spanked her. The children were also told that people who engaged in "bad touching" would be taken away and put in jail. For the rest of the school day the girl was terrified that her mother—who had spanked her— would now be taken away and locked up for her "bad touching." Probably that was not the message that the teacher had intended to convey, but the child had put together the various elements of the discussion in her own way. Until that day, she had never imagined that her mother might be doing something wrong and it had never occurred to her that she might be put in jail. But the class had planted both disturbing ideas in the mind of the little girl.

Scaring Our Kids

The semirural Kettle Moraine School District in southeastern Wisconsin is an area noted for its conservatism and stable families, one of the last places that one would look for trendy or avant-garde educational practices. But in 1992, the school board adopted—with little or no discussion—a comprehensive 164-page program of "protective behaviors" for children in kindergarten through fifth grade.[2] It is a revealing—and ultimately quite troubling—document. Children are explicitly taught to fear sexual abuse from members of their own family and are coached in reporting any incidents to school officials. The curriculum is not isolated; a majority of American school children are now taught about the dangers of sexual abuse.

The "protective behaviors" curricula share many of the elements of courses in values, human interaction, and "drug awareness" including their use of the techniques of group therapy and encounter groups. They are distinctive, however, in encouraging children to be concerned about problems that had probably never before occurred to them. Third graders, for instance, are taught that "not all touching they experience is appropriate" touching, and that in trying to figure out what is a "good" touch and what is a "bad" "they should trust their own feelings about what types of touch are 'okay' for them."[3] A huge amount of class time is devoted to getting in touch with these feelings. In one class devoted to

"Identifying Body Signals," teachers are told to have the children close their eyes "and remember a time when they didn't feel safe."[4]

In another class session on "Sadness and Loss," teachers tell students to "close their eyes and put their heads down and think about the worst time in their life." Teachers ask the third graders "how they felt and behaved" regarding, among other things "their relationships." Children are also encouraged to "allow themselves" to be sad about something.[5] In the same unit, students fill out a chart listing things that "would cause your knees to wobble." An extraordinary amount of effort is spent encouraging children to get in touch with their anxieties. Third graders are asked to create a "worry bird" out of a small rock and whenever they are troubled about anything, they should "let the Worry Bird worry about it so they can stop worrying about it. . . ." Lest any child still be reluctant to share all of his feelings, the class also makes a "Boxed-up Feelings" box, into which each child can put letters expressing his "bad feelings toward others." If a student is mad at another student, he is encouraged to lay it all out in the letter, which can be unsigned. The teacher then reads each letter and gives it to the person targeted in the complaint.[6] This is supposed to illustrate the value of getting things off your chest.

A class devoted to "Coping with My Feelings" breaks the third graders up into four or five groups where the children discuss various emotions, including anger, sadness, fear, confusion, loneliness, worry, and embarrassment.[7] They are not asked to discuss happiness, hopefulness, love, or confidence.

As if real problems are not enough to achieve the desired results, teachers are also told to have the third graders imagine problems by thinking about a number of "What-If's," such as What If:

a. Nobody is at home when you get home from school.
b. The door is locked and nobody is at home when you get home.
c. You are trick or treating and somebody asks you to come into the house.
d. Someone tries to make you keep a secret that makes you feel mad, sad, or just not safe.
e. Someone showed you something you don't think you should see or tried to touch you where they shouldn't.[8]

In the curriculum, teachers are told to ask students to analyze several stories. In one scenario given to third graders, a little girl named Suzie is playing in her front yard when Mr. Jones, "a nice neighbor," comes by. Mr. Jones stops and begins to talk to Suzie "and while they were talking he said, 'Suzie, there's a spider on the front of your shirt.' Suzie got upset because she was afraid of spiders and Mr. Jones said, 'Hold still and I'll brush it off you.'

"When he was brushing the spider off, Suzie looked down and saw that there wasn't a spider at all. But Mr. Jones kept on touching her on the chest and pretending to brush the spider off." In the class session teachers ask the children, "How do you think Suzie felt? What should Suzie do? Should Suzie tell someone? Who could she tell?"[9]

This question of who children should tell when they feel uncomfortable is a major theme in the program. Students are asked to name "at least six trusted adults that they could talk to, if they didn't feel safe." The program is explicit that children should not be allowed to simply name members of their own family. The curriculum guide tells teachers to make sure that children include "resource people in their *community*, home and *school*." [emphasis added] To make sure that children are not left with the impression that it is enough to rely on their mothers and fathers, they are told to fill out a "Tree Trunk," with branches labelled "school," "home," and "community," and are told to write down the names of two "trusted adults" in *each* area in whom they could confide.[10]

In at least one respect, the "protective behaviors" programs appear to have an effect. Studies of students who have taken such courses have found that they are much more likely to claim that they have been victims of sexual abuse.[11]

Watch Out for Uncle Joe

The reason for the emphasis on nonfamily "experts" becomes obvious as the "protective behaviors" curriculum moves into later grades, where the examples of potential abuse turn from strangers and "friendly neighbors" to the possibility of abuse by family members, including parents and grandparents. In fifth grade, children are asked to discuss the dilemma supposedly created by this story: "Debbie really loves her dad. When he comes to visit they like to wrestle and play games. Debbie's father likes to tickle her and make her laugh. Usually it's fun, but sometimes he tickles her so hard it sort of starts to hurt." The children are asked to discuss how Debbie feels about such tickling and whether this is a good, bad, or "confusing" touch. They also discuss: "Is there anything Debbie can do about this?" and "Have you ever been tickled in a bad or mean way?"[12]

In a second story: "Barbara likes her Uncle Joe very much. When she visits him, she likes to sit on his lap and he tells her about when he was a boy growing up in Wyoming." The fifth graders are asked: "How does Barbara feel about sitting on his lap? What kind of touch is this?" Then they are asked: "Now pretend that Barbara doesn't like sitting on her Uncle's lap because he squeezes her too tight and puts his hand near her private parts." Other stories involve a grandfather who hugs and squeezes his granddaughter who then feels "nervous and ashamed."[13]

Fourth graders are presented this harrowing scenario: "Sandy has a problem. She thinks her father might hurt her, her mom, or her brother."

Fourth graders are then expected to describe how Sandy feels, and what Sandy should do. In a second story: "Jena doesn't know what to do. Her dad came home tonight and yelled at her for no reason. Jena can't think what she did to make her father angry. Jena is confused. She doesn't understand her dad's behavior." The fourth graders are then asked: "Who owns and is responsible for this feeling?"[14]

An unanswered and unaddressed question hangs over the course: The next time a relative asks them to sit on their lap, or a parent tickles a child, or a grandparent hugs a child tightly, how will that child react? What doubts and fears will be kindled? And in the process what will have been lost in the innocent joy a child feels when touched by a loved one?

The authors of the "protective behaviors" curriculum used in the Kettle Moraine School District argue that such courses are not merely desirable, but a necessity. To support their position, they cite decade-old statistics from the Department of Health and Human Services that 1.3 million children are abused badly enough every year that marks are left on their bodies. In addition, while they admit that there "seem to be no reliable statistics available of the incidence of *verbal* abuse," they go on to estimate that "at least one third of the population experiences this." Schools need to be involved, they argue, because "violence at home is a direct detriment to a child's school learning in that it interferes with ability to concentrate, decreases a child's ability and interest in risk taking involved in active learning and undermines 'sense of self' (self-concept)." Materials given to teachers describe critics as " 'back to basics' people, some conservative religious groups and other so-called 'pro-family' forces," but includes no research or warnings of possible negative consequences from such courses.[15]

As in other aspects of the debates over educational policies, the advocates of extensive courses on "bad touching" argue that they are realists while critics want to shield children from realities in their lives. That most children have never entertained the possibility that a parent might pose a malignant threat, advocates would argue, is a sign that they are not being empowered to protect themselves. Such reticence, they believe, reflects a misguided belief in childhood innocence and an unforgivable naiveté on the part of adults.

The Attack on Childhood

Adults once assumed that at least in the earliest years, there were some fears, problems, and doubts best kept from children because it was understood that they were the proper responsibility of the adults in their lives. But the advocates of the aggressive new anti-touching programs take it as a given that innocence is anachronistic and probably dangerous, a luxury that children of the 1990s can ill afford. So they argue that children need to face the ugly facts and be pushed into the front lines of the struggle against violence, perversion, and sexual exploitation. While they couch their advocacy of forced precocity in terms of empowering children, there is also an unmistakable undercurrent of rationalization at work here. What was once the absolute and unquestioned responsibility of adults is subtly transferred to five- and six-year-olds.

But can a flight from responsibility really be passed as realism? How realistic is it to expect children to handle the issues that haunt the anxieties of their parents? And how realistic is it to believe that a small child's *feelings* are always a reliable indicator of the appropriateness of adult behavior? How realistic is it to believe that such courses can genuinely empower children as young as five and six years old to protect themselves when adults are either absent or negligent? How realistic is it to imagine that such children can listen to stories about abusive uncles, parents, and grandparents, and strike a reasonable and reliable balance between fear and trust? And do such courses with their emphasis on "bad" tickling and lap sitting really help children learn to recognize serious sexual abuse? Or do they further complicate the issue by asking children to make delicate but crucial distinctions between the innocent touch of a parent and the "bad" touch of a stranger? Ultimately, how realistic it for educationists to imagine that they can interpose such wariness between child and parent without any lasting damage? Or that they can plant fears and anxieties in the child's imagination without unintended and potentially tragic consequences?

While most of the stories the children are compelled to confront may seem straightforward to the curriculum makers, they are likely to be highly confusing to a small child, who may never have thought to fear his parents. That confusion, of course, reinforces the need for the child to rely on outsiders, such as counselors, teachers, and therapists, and perhaps to test his own speculations about what might be appropriate and inappropriate behavior.

Afraid to Touch

At day care centers and schools across the country, teachers and aides are learning the new unwritten rule of contact with children. No matter how much they might crave affection, or need a hug or a pat, or simply want to sit on a grown-up's lap: Don't Touch. At many schools, the *Los Angeles Times* reports, the new edict is "Do not hug, kiss, lift, stroke, offer your lap, rub the back, tuck in the shirt, pat the hair, or be in any way physically responsive to their needs."[16] As accusations of sexual abuse and "bad" touching have risen sharply in recent years and teachers are often the target, the National Education Association, the nation's largest teachers union, now advises its members to "teach but don't touch." This advice distresses child development experts who argue that younger children need physical contact as much as mental stimulation. The younger the child, the more likely he or she is to need to be touched or held for comfort or reassurance. But, says Joy Sells, of Michigan City, Indiana, "As a teacher, I am fearful of touching a student on the shoulder and saying 'You're doing a great job. Keep up the good work.' I smile instead. . . . I don't touch my students. But the sad thing is that some of them desperately need that tactile response. Some beg for attention. . . . They want to tell the teacher about their fears, their joys and about what happened to them last night. They yearn for human contact. But as a veteran teacher, I've heard and seen too many horror stories about teachers' careers being ruined by a seemingly innocent gesture."[17]

Highly publicized cases like the McMartin Preschool case spread concern among professionals who work with children. "I call it the presumption of perversion," says Mark Poldner, a director of a children's shelter in Oak Park, Illinois. "There's so much emphasis on child abuse that almost any thinking man alone with a child is conscious that someone might think he is doing it for some perverse purpose." The McMartin case involved allegations of abuse involving as many as 250 children. But after the longest criminal case in U.S. history, the original seven defendants were trimmed to two, and both were eventually found not guilty. Critics have charged that overzealous professionals planted the allegations of abuse in the minds of children through unorthodox and manipulative techniques.

Considerable evidence indicates that young children are highly suggestible when it comes to remembering or imagining sexually abusive encounters. An article in the *Journal of the American Academy of Psychiatry* in 1986 found that more than one out of three allegations of sexual abuse were made by children involved in custody disputes.[18] Several studies using anatomically correct dolls have found some children willing to "remember" being touched in ways that never happened. In one study of girls aged five and seven who were examined by a doctor in the presence of a parent, researchers asked the children afterward if the doctor had touched them in their private parts. Three girls who had not been touched claimed that they had after being asked about it with the doll. One girl even claimed that "the doctor did it with a stick."[19]

Richard Gardner, a clinical professor of child psychiatry at Columbia University, likens the current fevered round of accusations of child abuse to a "modern witch hunt." Gardner, a highly respected expert on child abuse, calls the explosion of child abuse allegation a "third great wave of hysteria," similar to the Salem Witch Trials and the McCarthy Red hunts.[20] The hysteria has been orchestrated, Gardner charges, by what he called the "child abuse establishment," a network of social workers, psychiatrists, psychologists, law enforcement officers and bureaucrats in child protection services, and mental health facilities, which work closely together and have a vested interest in exaggerating the incidence of sexual abuse.

Members of this establishment tend to dominate and dictate the content of "protective behaviors" curricula taught in the schools.

Advocates of the "protective behaviors" courses cite well-publicized statistics that claim that 2.7 million children are abused every year—a rate of 42 per 1,000 children. But Douglas J. Besharov, a former director of the federal government's National Center on Child Abuse and Neglect calls the numbers "grossly misleading." Nationally 60 to 65 percent of all reports turned out to be unfounded and are dismissed after investigation, a rate that is up sharply since the mid-1970s, when only 35 percent of child abuse reports were determined to be unfounded. Based on his estimates that 30–35 percent of charges are substantiated, Besharov estimates that the legitimate complaints involve about 1 million children a year. Since the average family has 1.89 children, the number of families involved is about 525,000. When duplicated reports are factored in (about 20 percent are duplicated) the number of new substantiated cases comes to about 420,000 a year. But even then, not all of the cases involve sexual abuse. Nearly half of the allegations of child abuse involve neglect; 28 percent involve physical abuse, and 15 percent involve sexual abuse.[21] This is not a trivial number but it is also hardly evidence that *every* child is at risk.

Combined with the problems of false accusations, all of this would seem to argue for extreme caution in the "bad touching" courses being taught in elementary schools. But the curricula I examined included no discussions of problems caused by false accusations of abuse, nor do they even acknowledge the possibility that the courses themselves might frighten or confuse youngsters. To the contrary, teachers are admonished that it would be hypocritical if they failed to believe every charge made by a child. Despite such confidence, there is evidence that the early exposure to courses that warn children about abuse might have troubling consequences. One study of preschool children in Berkeley, for example, found that about half of the children who had attended sex abuse classes had become more likely to regard as "worrisome" such things as tickling and being given a bath.[22] Such results have led some critics, including Dr. Neal Gilbert, a professor of social welfare at the University of California at Berkeley to call the "protective behaviors" programs a "terrible mistake." He cites studies that found that up to 20 percent of the parents of young children see "immediate negative effects . . . after the children go through sex abuse education programs."[23] A study conducted at the University of Virginia concluded that up to half of the young children who go through such "touching" programs have increased worries about sexual abuse or fears of adults. Many of them have nightmares and become bed wetters.

University of Virginia Psychologist N. Dickon Repucci is one of a number of experts who question whether the courses offered in sex abuse have simply raised unnecessary fears in children. Despite their popularity among educationists, he says, there is no evidence that such programs do more good than harm and no study that shows that any of the "protective behaviors" programs have kept a single child from being abused.

But there is considerable evidence that children often received garbled messages from such classes. Repucci tells the story of a first grader who attended a class in which she was taught that she had the right to say "no" to any grown-up if they asked her to do something that made her feel uncomfortable. For several weeks after the class, he said, she insisted to her parents that she had the right to refuse to do anything they asked— including cleaning up her room—because that made "uncomfortable."[24]

CHAPTER 14

DOCTOR, DOCTOR

D ebbie Masnik knew her job description had just been radically changed when she learned that from now on, her sixth-grade class would include physically and emotionally disabled children—all part of the new movement in American education to "mainstream" the disabled into regular classrooms. But nothing prepared Masnik for the day an emotionally disturbed youngster defecated on his seat and set off a "near riot" among the class's twelve-year-olds. Other teachers in her school in Fairfax, Virginia, were told that they must be prepared to catheterize a paralyzed girl who has also been administratively mainstreamed.[1] In Eden Prairie, Minnesota, a seventh-grade social studies teacher must teach a class of thirty-two children that includes eight low-IQ children, a deaf child with cerebral palsy who can read at only a third grade level, and several gifted children. On paper, the class is an exercise in "full inclusion." In practice, she says, her class is a "three-ring circus." In Chicago, an eight-year-old boy named Michael, who is prone to sudden and violent mood swings, is included in regular classes, where his disruptions often make it impossible for any learning to go on. His principal explains: "It really means more stress for the teacher, less individual attention for Mike. It's the other kids who will feel the brunt of it." Regardless, 3,500 disabled students in Chicago were transferred into regular classrooms in 1992 and thousands more are transferred every year.[2]

In Charleston, West Virginia, a third-grade teacher struggles to maintain order and make it through lesson plans despite the occasional outbursts of a nine-year-old child who administrators insist must be taught in regular classrooms, even though he is unable to read or write and begins wailing and barking like a dog whenever he gets frustrated. "The whole class stops," the teacher says. "I feel like I'm watching a Ping-Pong game. The kids watch [the disturbed boy]. They watch me. Then, when I'm busy with him they act up."[3]

In Whittier, California, school officials have adopted a policy that will shift every ninth grader into regular classes, regardless of the severity of their mental, emotional, or physical disabilities. That means that autistic children and youngsters with Down's syndrome will now have to be taught in regular high school classes. When a reporter for the *Wall Street Journal* visited one of the freshman classes, the teacher asked the sixteen students in her algebra class to write down four things they had learned that day. While fourteen of them did so, two others sat by. One of them, named Joey, who was autistic, "repeatedly jingles a set of keys." The other, Phillip, who had Down's syndrome, "says he wants to eat and starts crying."[4]

Joey and Phillip are among the vanguard of the 1.6 million disabled students who have already been mainstreamed into regular classes as part of efforts to make schools more inclusive. The number is expected to rise rapidly, as more than 100,000 disabled students are shifted every year.[5] That estimate may be low because the policy of inclusion—bitterly opposed by many teachers and by some teachers unions—has been accelerated by federal dictates and court orders. Despite the lack of legislative action or local debate, the American Federation of Teachers' Albert Shanker calls mainstreaming the movement in American education that is "taking hold the fastest and is likely to have the profoundest—and most destructive—effect" on the nation's schools.

Inclusion is a movement driven by the belief that separate classes for emotionally and physically disabled students are akin to segregating students by race. Advocates of mainstreaming insist that including students with a wide range of disabilities in regular classrooms will help socialize both the able and disabled by teaching tolerance and an appreciation for differences. They tend to brush off concerns about potential disruption to the learning process, claiming that the end to the "segregation" of the disabled benefits all children, just as mixing students from different racial and ethnic backgrounds enriches the educational environment. Such views have been written into law by Congress and the courts and are being aggressively advocated by federal educational officials. In 1975, Congress passed the Disabilities Education Act, which required that disabled children be taught "to the maximum extent appropriate" with children who were not disabled. As one advocate for mainstreaming later explained, "Congress believed integration was vital in order to provide appropriate modeling for children with disabilities, in order to prepare them for living as adults in an integrated society, and in order to prevent discrimination against them."[6] From the beginning, social and political considerations were placed at the forefront, while concerns about the impact on classroom order and educational quality were shoved into the background. In the early 1980s court rulings expanded the rights of the disabled and restricted the options of the schools. In 1988, the Supreme Court barred schools from expelling or removing disruptive or violent emotionally disturbed students from classes without parental or court permission—even if the students posed a threat of physical violence.

In one of the more extreme applications of that doctrine, the state of Virginia found itself embroiled in a dispute with the U.S. Department of Education over its decision to expel a student who came to school with a homemade dynamite bomb. Because the student suffered from what was described as a "mild learning disability," the state risked the loss of $50 million in federal funding if it did not continue to provide free and continuing education to the boy.[7] The pressures to expand inclusion are expected to pick up momentum throughout the 1990s. In November 1993, the assistant secretary of education for special education bragged to Congress that a record number of disabled students were now in regular classes. "Historically," she said, "we have had two education systems, one for students with disabilities and one for everybody else. We are working to create one education system that values all students."[8]

The result of these policies and rulings is that mainstreaming has become the latest noneducational mandate laid on the schools; another expectation that the schools can be used as an instrument to undo the unfairness of life. But it is simplistic to see the schools merely as a victim of outside forces. Mainstreaming is a logical extension of the educationist conceit that schools could be socializing, egalitarian, and therapeutic enterprises— indeed that they could be all things to all people without compromising the ability of children to actually learn something.

Having embraced a therapeutic ethos that has teachers adjusting the personalities and self-concepts of youngsters, educationists now find themselves in a system in which teachers with little or no training must somehow handle classrooms with students still wearing diapers or fed through tubes. In some cases, math and English teachers have to be prepared to stop their lessons and suction mucus from a child's lungs or deal with a child who kicks, bites, and pummels other students.[9] High schools are forced to cope with students who may urinate on the floor and shred their clothes when frustrated. When schools resist moving children into regular classes, the federal courts are likely to order the transfer. In Huntington Beach, California, a six-year-old student who was prone to violent tantrums and unable to communicate verbally either with the teacher or classmates was ordered kept in regular classes after his father sued the district. After the ruling, the teacher who was expected to put up with the outbursts took a medical leave because she could no longer handle the strain and more than a third of the other children in the class were removed by their parents, who saw the boy's return as the end of any effective learning in the classroom.[10]

It is difficult to overestimate the problems such policies pose for even the most conscientious teacher. What teacher can maintain a lesson plan in a forty-minute period if there are even a handful of disruptions? And how realistic is it to expect that a child with a mental age of four can be successful in a classroom of ten-or eleven-year-olds? "It's like saying 'I want my five-foot-two-son to play varsity basketball," remarked Stanley Urban, a special education professor at Rowan College. In a few remarkable cases, of course, the five-foot-two son might flourish; it is more likely that he will be battered, bruised, and humiliated. A third alternative is that the rules of the game will be changed so that he gets to make as many baskets as anyone else, the hoop is lowered, the scoring made more equitable. Everyone becomes a winner. Only it's not basketball anymore. There are academic parallels, especially in classes where the standards and goals are modified to account for the vast range of abilities, interests, and levels of achievement among the students lumped together in the name of "inclusivity" and "fairness."

Despite the benign intentions of advocates, the nondisabled students are not the only ones to suffer from the rush to mainstream students with disabilities. Often the disabled themselves, who might have thrived on specialized attention from teachers trained to deal with their disorders, find themselves lost and bewildered in the unprotected environment of the regular classroom. Students who might have made steady progress in classes geared for their abilities can lag hopelessly behind their peers in the nonspecial classes. Deaf students are expected to learn in classrooms that may not be taught by teachers who know sign language, while students with milder cognitive disabilities may be placed in classes where little or no provision has been made for the way they learn. Advocates insist that they oppose this sort of "dumping," but their vision of an inclusive classroom fully equipped and geared for both students who are gifted and those who barely read at a second-grade level seldom translates into reality. Nor are they able to cite studies or research that support the kind of wholesale transformation of special education now underway. They can cite neither standardized tests nor any other data that record how well disabled students do in mainstreamed classrooms compared with how well they do in special classes. Nor do they have data indicating improvements in dropout rates, future educational attainments, or how well the disabled students do in later life in terms of getting and keeping jobs. Shanker complains that advocates brush aside such concerns by striking a pose of moral superiority. "Some full inclusionists talk as though they are in a battle pitting the forces of morality against the forces of immorality," he charged. "In reality, the battle pits ideologues who, without any evidence, would force destructive changes on our schools against people who believe that children's interest come first."[11]

Some critics of the mainstreaming movement detect a haunting echo of an earlier attempt to include the mentally disturbed in the wider society, with results that were somewhat less than successful. Dr. Larry Silver, a professor and director of training in child and adolescent psychiatry at Georgetown University's Medical School, sees a parallel between the impact of the deinstitutionalization of the mentally ill on the nation's cities and the current dumping of disabled students in the nation's schools. "My fear is that improperly mainstreamed children will be walking the hallways of our public schools like the new homeless," he says. "Much as it happened in our cities, the quality of life in the classroom will continue to deteriorate for the regular students, and we are actually destroying the chances that these children will integrate."[12]

The New Disabled

Despite that grim prognosis, we have discussed only half of the story of the role of "disability" in American education. Efforts to put genuinely disabled students into regular classrooms are being dwarfed by the equally concerted effort to relabel other students who may be experiencing academic or disciplinary problems—but who are otherwise normal—as "disabled." During the last few decades, the number of students classified as "learning disabled" has exploded as difficulties in reading or low achievement have been redefined into medical terms. More recently, educationists have embraced the practice of labeling rambunctious, overly talkative, or active children—mostly boys—as victims of "attention deficit disorder."

The medicalization of education fits well into a culture that is itself enamored of syndromes, complexes, addictions, and diseases to explain its own disappointments. Much in the same way that adults have grasped onto compulsive shopping syndrome, the injured inner child, and "chronic lateness syndrome" to explain (and explain away) failures, the schools have discovered the benefits of redefining academic failure as a "disorder"—thus shifting responsibility for failure away from both families and schools.

By the early 1990s, one in eight children in the New York City public schools was classified as "handicapped" in one way or another, double the number of only a decade earlier. One out of every four dollars spent on education in New York City was devoted to special education. Partly because of the generous funding of special education, the special education program became virtually a magnet for disability. Children who would have once been regarded simply as "slow" or as a discipline problem are now often shifted into "special education" programs by relabeling their behavior as a disability. Children who learn differently or at a different pace than other children, or who are unable to read at grade level, are all at risk of being classified as "learning disabled." Teachers and administrators have also learned that they could dispose of troublesome and annoying students without having to go through the rococo disciplinary processes by simply having the child diagnosed as in need of "special" education.

Economic and financial pressures also played a significant role: Even when regular classrooms were subjected to budget cuts, the special education programs were generally exempt. As class sizes for nondisabled students ballooned, the law required that special education classes have no more than twelve students per classroom; many of them had as few as six children in a class. By the early 1990s, New York was spending more than twice as much per student on special education children— $16,746 a year, compared with $7,107 per child in regular classes. That disparity also served as an inducement for educators to shift bodies from their own over-stressed budgets onto the fatter special education dime.[13] Unfortunately, the system also mislabeled thousands of children who were unlikely ever to return to regular classes. Fewer than one in five of the children labeled "handicapped" in New York City ever graduated from high school and many of them were, as critics of special education have long contended, dumped into a system of lower expectations, cramped opportunities, and stunted self-images.

The Learning Disabilities Movement

Considering its size and influence, it may come as a surprise that the field of learning disabilities did not really emerge until the mid-1960s. Today, somewhere between 7 and 15 percent of American school children are labeled as "learning disabled." In some districts—depending on the size of the LD bureaucracy and the fashionableness of the diagnosis—much larger portions of the student body have been classified as suffering from learning problems. Montgomery County, the richest school district in Maryland, now labels half of its special education students as "learning disabled."[14]

Typically, a student labeled as LD is a child with normal or high potential who has difficulty with the mechanics of reading or writing. But there is little agreement among psychologists or educators about what constitutes a "learning disability," how it should be diagnosed, or what educational program is best suited for an LD child. While there are some children who suffer from neurological impairments that hamper their ability to learn, the vast majority of children classified as LD have no physical symptoms or signs of neurological dysfunction. Indeed, as maverick psychiatrist Peter Breggin noted, "there are no known neurological deficits, no known genetic traits, no consistent clinical descriptions, no specific diagnostic testing, and no reliable techniques of treatment."[15] Robert Slavin of Johns Hopkins University remarks, "Whether the child actually has a learning disability or is a low achiever or slow to mature is a very fuzzy issue." Even so, millions of school children have been and continue to be classified as "learning disabled."[16]

This seeming paradox is explained by the roots of the LD movement, which was propelled less by research than by a burgeoning parents movement and the growing therapeutic superstructure of American education. Given the numbers of psychologists, therapists, social workers, and specialists employed by the schools, it should not be surprising that they have increasingly "discovered" new maladies and problems that require their ministrations. It should also not be surprising that the schools have embraced such explanations, rather than admit that their teaching methods, curricula, and priorities might be responsible for the rising tide of academic failure in general and poor reading skills in particular.

In his book *The Learning Mystique*, author Gerald Coles argues that learning disabilities are a product of a movement of parents and professionals looking for explanations for their children's lack of success in school. Especially among middle-class parents in the middle and late 1960s, expectations were high. Parents expected that their children would do well in school and continue their own path of upward mobility. As it became obvious that a substantial number of children from solid middle-class families, attending well-funded, state-of-the-art schools were unable to read or write very well, professionals and parents alike found their failures inexplicable. In some respects, the expectations themselves may have been unrealistic; success is never guaranteed and the possibility of failure had not been abolished either by prosperity or by the age of self-actualization. But while failure had long been accepted as part of life by previous generations, many parents in the 1960s not only came to expect that failure was obsolete, inappropriate, and unfair, but also bought into the increasingly popular educationist notion that learning could be a joyful process of self-expression and creativity. When their children came home functionally illiterate, something had to give.

Throughout the 1960s, educators had moved away from insisting that children master the mechanics of reading, including phonics. From 1963 on, SAT scores would begin to plummet, but there were other signs that children were not reading well, including children from affluent suburbs. The 1970–71 National Assessment of Educational Progress, for example, measured the reading rate and comprehension of nine-year-olds, thirteen-year-olds, and seventeen-year-olds. The test included five questions for each passage that students had to read, then ranked those who scored four or more correct and those who scored three or fewer correct. Nearly 16 percent of the nine-year-olds from "extremely affluent suburbs" scored correctly on three or fewer questions out of five; nearly one out of five of the nine-year-olds whose parents had post–high school educations also scored low. The picture was even worse for the older kids. More than 56 percent of the thirteen-year-olds from "extremely affluent suburbs" scored three or fewer correct answers.

For many of the parents of these children, accustomed as they were to success and acclimated to a pain-free educational scheme, these results seemed fluky. Since they felt themselves entitled to success, failure was an obvious aberration. Educators faced a similar problem: They could not blame the low test scores on racism or poverty or even lack of funding. Students from the most lavishly appointed schools in the nation were failing to make the grade.

The impetus for change came from the parents first. Middle-class parents, Coles recounts, began demanding that the schools do more for their children. These parents saw increased social spending targeted for "disadvantaged" youth and adult literacy programs and they demanded similar efforts for their children. This response was not inevitable. Parents could have blamed "systematic social influences on the schools" for the failures, or they "could have blamed principals and teachers for ineptly handling neurologically *normal* children." Or they might have decided that their children were "slow learners, ecologically disabled, or just bored to death by school." Instead, they gravitated toward the idea that their children suffered from "learning disabilities."[17] Throughout the 1950s and 1960s, small parents groups began agitating for changes, holding joint meetings with other parents, physicians, psychologists, and educators who increasingly had a vested interest in LD as a field and as an explanation. Inevitably, the professionals wielded considerable influence, but their audiences were also receptive to suggestions that there was a quasi-medical explanation for their children's difficulties. As the movement gathered support (and as test scores continued to decline), conferences were held, funds established, and lobbying groups deployed.

"Learning disabilities" appealed to many parents, Coles wrote, because "the term 'learning disabilities' extricated parents from 'blame,' as, for example, the classification 'emotionally disturbed' would not have done" and the term "did not carry the stigma of 'mildly retarded.'" But the scientific gloss of the LD movement provided it with credibility. "Another explanation for parents' misguided acceptance of the LD explanation was that they lacked the expertise for evaluating it," wrote Coles. "Credence in the scientific legitimacy of LD was no doubt enhanced by the genuinely valid information about the brain that appeared during the years in which it emerged. . . . The wealth of neurological discoveries created a context that could have suggested to some that LD was part of a new frontier in science."[18]

Despite the growing influence of the parent-professional advocates of "learning disabilities," Coles noted that the nation's schools did not have to enlist in the LD movement to the extent that they did. They had, after all, long been able to resist demands by community groups and parents and had a long history of making themselves inaccessible to special interests who did not share the fundamentals of the educationist creed. But the schools embraced learning disabilities with considerable enthusiasm. Faced with the prospect of explaining to Justin's and Jessica's yuppie parents why the children were unable to read, the explanation that they suffered from "learning disabilities" was the educationists equivalent of saying "Don't blame me."

It wasn't the way we teach.

It wasn't our abandonment of phonics.

It wasn't our low standards, or the time we spent on making children feel good about themselves.

It wasn't because we have stopped teaching children to acquire basic academic skills and figure they will pick them up on their own.

The creation of the learning disabilities industry got the schools and parents off the hook. The federal government's largesse guaranteed that the movement would grow exponentially. By providing funding for learning disabilities, Coles wrote, Congress "legitimated the category within the school and helped establish a set of professional and public assumptions. . . ."[19] Universities vied for a piece of the action and pumped up new credentialing programs in the field. In just three years, from 1969 to 1972, the number of students in postgraduate learning disabilities programs jumped from 538 to 2,148. "A profession was born," Coles later wrote, "but not out of scientific explanation, which was meager. Rather, as I have said, the explanation prospered because it was consonant with schools' other explanations of learning failure and reinforced rather than challenged fundamental assumptions about educational inequality."[20]

Studies have continued to show that even the latest diagnostic tools developed by the LD establishment have sharply limited validity. Detailed tests of children identified as LD often find few differences between the allegedly disabled children and those who are treated as regular students, except that the LD students score lower in reading and spelling. "In other words," Coles concluded, "LD was no more than 'a sophisticated term for underachievement.' "[21] But as the funding of LD programs increased, the number of students labeled LD rose in direct proportion. Johns Hopkins' Slavin quipped, "If there are 30 spots for learning disabilities, you will magically have 30 learning disability students. If there are 60, you will have 60."[22] Writing in the 1982 *Journal of School Psychiatry*, three researchers concluded that the label of learning disabled meant no more than that a child was performing below his or her potential, a remarkably plastic definition. "The fear," they concluded, "that LD may be anything the diagnostician wants it to be appears justified." Although that comment might sound unduly cynical, it appears to have some basis in fact.

Manhattan's Dalton School is one of the leading private schools in the country, but it was not immune to this aggressive therapeutic onslaught. The average IQ of kindergartners at Dalton is estimated at 132—and fully 40 percent of its graduates go on to Ivy League schools. Dalton is the school of choice for much of New York City's elite; there are more than

600 applications for the 95 places in beginning kindergarten. Among the celebrities to choose Dalton for their children are Yoko Ono, Diana Ross, Isaac Stern, Tom Brokaw, Dustin Hoffman, Robert Redford, and Supreme Court Justice Ruth Bader Ginsburg.[23]

But when it was offered a $2 million grant from a member of a wealthy New York family to identify and treat learning disabilities, Dalton embarked on a crash course. Although the elite school had never experienced any problems that might lead it to believe that some of its students might need such a program, Dalton used the money to hire 14 full- and part-time "learning specialists" for its K–3 school—a huge presence in a school with only 400 pupils and a regular staff of only 20 head teachers. The money also paid for a new screening test meant to diagnose the disabilities at a very early age. Within a few years, the zealous staff of remediationists "discovered" that an extraordinary number of the hitherto untroubled and apparently bright Dalton children suffered from various learning deficiencies. The specialists began flagging potential learning problems as early as the *second month* of kindergarten. In one three-year period, according to the *New York Times*, the specialists labeled 77 of the 215 five-year-olds at Dalton to be "at risk" after two months in the school's kindergarten class. If correct, that would mean that more than a third (36 percent) of Dalton's preternaturally bright kids were in fact closet LD cases. Diagnoses ranged from "sequencing ability defects" to "potential visual motor problems." Rather than challenge the diagnoses, the school continued to expand its remedial programs and the parents themselves insisted on getting even more therapy for their children. By the end of the 1980s, the LD bureaucracy had expanded at Dalton to include a full-time director and secretary, a special board to oversee the program and even an outside executive director to watch over the finances. Because the benefactor wanted Dalton's LD program to be a national model, she also brought in Columbia University's Teachers College to evaluate the program and publish research articles on it.

Overrun by specialists and increasingly driven by research demands, the program spun out of control. Teachers began to complain that their classes were inundated with "specialists" who would often declare that as many as half of the children in the class had learning problems. As one jaded Dalton teacher told the *Times*, "If you dig hard enough in any kid, you'll find a problem. If you want to have something to write down, you'll find something to write down." By 1992, fully half of the school's fourth graders had been referred for remediation of some sort. Finally, in 1992, the teachers revolted; many of the kindergarten teachers simply refused to use the LD screening test, which they felt was unreliable. A new principal moved quickly to shelve the LD study. Reported the *Times*: "Instantly, learning disabilities at Dalton plummeted." While as many as half of the students had been labeled learning disabled in the program's heyday, half a dozen kindergartners were receiving help from a specialist in 1994.

"That such a major shift could occur twice in one place in a decade," *Times* reporter Michael Winerip later remarked, "is stunning commentary on how subjective the identification of learning disabilities can be and how little is known about them."[24]

THE ATTACK ON LEARNING

CHAPTER 15

THE ATTACK
ON LEARNING

n 1947, one of the education establishment's most influential publications declared: "Far too many people in America, both in and out of
education, look upon the elementary school as a place to learn reading,
writing and arithmetic." That might have been acceptable for the frontier
days, but not, the educationist authors insisted, for a "highly industrialized
urban society."[1] The publication was the yearbook of the Association
for Supervision and Curriculum Development of the National Education
Association. *Organizing the Elementary School for Living and Learning*
represented an early high-water mark for the movement to remake schools
in a more progressive image and it was a forerunner of a movement that
was about to sweep the nation's schools. The educationist authors of the
yearbook called for refocusing the schools away from intellectual pursuits
to a new agenda of "life adjustment." In the new school, social values
were given far more weight than traditional subject matter. From now on,
the (NEA) yearbook declared, the school must put "human relationships
first" and must provide "a school environment where the satisfactory
adjustment of all pupils is of primary consideration. . . . This 'R' is of even
greater importance than the 3 'Rs' yet it has received little time or attention
in the school's organization."[2]

"Is it more important for Dick to excel everyone in his class and bring
home a report card of all A's," the yearbook asked, "or for Dick to learn
how to live with all the other boys and girls in his neighborhood?"

"Is it more important for Paula to learn that quarter note gets one count
or for Paula to learn the joy that comes from singing with her friends?"[3]
While the educationists do not explain why it's necessary to choose
between sight reading and singing with friends, the answers for them
were obvious: Academic achievement was far less important than "getting
along." Music meant singing with friends, not learning notes. The future
belonged not to individuals who excelled, but to groups who played and
worked well together. Schools should not be in the business of nurturing
future Beethovens, but members of the chorus.

Such well-adjusted children, the educationists insisted somewhat
immodestly, would transform the world. "Poverty, malnutrition, economic

injustice, intolerance, ignorance will all yield to a dynamic program of education in the hands of socially literate teachers."[4] The watchword: Change. And the educationists of the late 1940s saw faddishness not merely as a virtue, but almost as a moral imperative. "Change is a commonplace in certain areas of living. In such matters as communication, transportation, and recreation, the American people have come to expect and demand it. We demand a new model of automobile every year and look forward to a more frequent change in women's hats. In our social institutions, and in our schools particularly, we have failed to develop a comparable attitude towards change and development."[5] In obedience to that vision, educational fashions over the last half century have indeed been changed as often as hat and car styles. But the underlying impulse has remained the same.

The "new" curriculum of 1947 emphasized the child's emotional well-being, beliefs and attitudes, encouraged cooperative learning, and was characterized by a suspicion of grades and tests, the blurring of subject matter lines, and an approach to reading that sounded very much like what would be called "whole language" four decades later.

In the new schools, children were constantly assigned to work with groups that were not shaped according to ability. In the groups, "each learns from the other because all have a contribution to make to group living . . . A child's group is his fellows with all that this implies. And this implies that he functions in an interesting, wholesome fashion, and that he is emotionally and psychologically satisfied. A child's continuance in a group is based upon a consideration of successful human relationships."[6] In the 1990s, this innovation would be called "cooperative learning."

In the late 1940s, the Lafayette School in Washington, D.C. employed practices that would be described as "outcome based education" in the 1990s. "Teachers and children" at the school "no longer think in terms of promotions and failures. The end of the year is not a reckoning day. There can be no set time when any specific learning must occur for all children nor any support for school practices that 'fail' individuals for this reason."[7]

In 1947, the educrats declared that reading was to be taught not as a separate discipline, but "as a part of the whole school program of living." Children used their reading and writing skills not to master great works of literature, but to help them get along with others. "The challenging exhibits in the downstairs lobby . . . carry with them much interesting and explanatory reading material. A committee of older children, after consulting with the cafeteria manager, writes the menus for the day." In the new school, it is important for the child to feel good about himself and to belong to the group if he is to be creative. "To be really creative the child must feel that he is among friends, that he has status in his group."

Since belongingness was the priority, the new school rejected teaching children to learn phonetically. "Reading materials should be close to life and grow out of children's living," the yearbook advised. "They should be chosen for the younger child, not to give practice in word calling, but they should be used when they contribute genuinely to the enrichment of experience. *In the beginning stages it is not necessary for children to recognize words in order to participate in the reading process.*"[8] [emphasis added]

Why wasn't it necessary to "recognize words" as part of the process? The yearbook explains, "During this time the teacher is doing the greater part of the word calling but the children are participating in the meaning side."[9] That seemed to mean that the teachers *read* while the children *listened.* But was this reading? And was a student who participated in the "reading process" the same as a student who "read"?

Although educrats would later complain about all of the burdens laid at their door by society, the fact is that it was the school themselves that eagerly sought out many of the newer roles, including responsibility for the psychological health of children. "It is the responsibility of the schools to be alert to the symptoms of strong emotions," the 1947 yearbook averred, "to assist children in working out socially acceptable ways of expressing emotions and to be sympathetically tolerant of episodes in which children reveal their lack of success in handling them."[10] The Barnard School in Washington, D.C., was reported to have "become aware of the needs for being alert to symptoms of emotional instability. It was found that eighteen children showed symptoms of a highly nervous nature—short attention span, restlessness, lack of concentration, and inability to stick to a given task."[11]

They seem not to have considered the possibility that the kids were bored out of their skulls by all of this incessant compulsory good fellowship. The educrats who ran the school literally decided that if kids were not engrossed by this orgy of belongingness, they must be sick and thus in need of medical attention. In the 1990s, educators would call this "attention deficit disorder."

The transformation of the schools was presented as a radical innovation, as the same ideas would be four decades later. "In the caravan of civilization," the educrats declared in 1947, "we have constantly to cast aside those things which become useless. . . ." This included much of what had been the traditional business of the school. Standardized tests, for example, had to be tossed from the rapidly moving caravan, the yearbook insisted, because tests took up too much time and interfered with the teacher's ability to help children become socially literate and well adjusted. Spending excessive time on spelling, math, science, and history meant that the teacher "has no time to go out on the playground with her youngsters to find out, if she can, why Sally has been so ill kempt during the last few weeks, or what makes John want to hit every boy he passes."[12] In other words, academic concerns were interfering with the teacher's ability to take on the roles of mother, social worker, and psychologist. "We are going to have to change our ideas about the things we expect of teachers," the yearbook said in something of an understatement.

In the Life Adjustment curriculum, the teacher was not an authority figure, certainly not seen as someone with the wisdom or knowledge she was charged with passing on to children in her classrooms. It was not her role to open doors of adulthood to children; indeed, it would go too far even to suggest that she was supposed to be a role model of any kind. In modern terms, she was expected to be what we might today call a "facilitator" and an extremely modest one at that. "She will help the child to understand why he's going to school. She will *talk over* with the group the things that they may do together and will *help* the group to find projects for which they are going to be *jointly responsible*. She will *help* the children learn how to *work together* so that each is *happy* in the working. . . .

"She will *listen* to each child *as he reveals his real self to her, and she will help find what he needs in order to grow*. . . . She will give each a chance to grow in his own way, to make decisions for himself, to initiate and carry out projects *dear to his heart*."[13] [emphasis added]

Teaching knowledge and mastering the disciplines of reading, writing, and math were obviously low on the list of priorities. Teachers were supposed "to hold the way the child *acts* and what he *believes* as important as what he knows, and because the teacher believes that habit patterns and attitudes are important, *so will the child*."[14] [emphasis added] The yearbook does not say what would happen if a child chose not to agree with the teacher or share her attitudes toward knowledge, beliefs, and feelings. Presumably, this would have been rare, since the obvious outcome of such schools would be children trained in collective and group thinking rather than individual thinking. "The school should be sympathetically tolerant of classroom and playground efforts of children to win group belonging," the yearbook advised.[15]

But what about the loner? Or the child who prefers to read by himself or the child whose ambition was something more robust than "belongingness"? The yearbook is not concerned with nonconformists. Life Adjustment placed a far higher premium on usefulness than independence of any sort. Teachers in the new regime would "cease thinking of marking children and will start thinking how much the child is growing day after day, week after week, how much progress he's making toward the kind of boy or girl which our town, our America, and our world finds useful."[16] Not iconoclastic or original, but "useful."

The authors of the yearbook wrote all of this in a tone of assurance that reflected the consensus in educational circles that schools should concern themselves with developing functional outcomes rather than liberal education. The authors did not bother to argue their premises; they were simply assumed. This reflected the fact that progressive ideas about education were not merely dominant; by 1947, they had been in the ascendancy for decades. There were some stray dissidents. Columbia's Jacques Barzun, among them, charged that educationists had inverted the whole purpose of schooling by assuming in each pupil "the supremely gifted mind, which must not be tampered with, and the defective personality which the school must remodel."[17] But the life adjusters had the powerful organizational support of the educational bureaucracies of the time, including the U.S. Office of Education, the schools of teacher education, as well as the National School Board Association, the National Congress of Parents and Teachers, and the National Association of Secondary School Principals. By the 1940s, scarcely a single educational publication was not awash with the jargon of educational progressivism. Phrases like "personality development," "the whole child," "creative self-expression," "the needs of learners," "intrinsic motivation," "teaching children, not subjects," "staff planning," and "real life experiences" filled the books, speeches, reports, and conferences of educationists. They were, Lawrence Cremin later noted, "a cant, to be sure, the peculiar jargon of the pedagogues," but they reflected how thoroughly America's educators had bought into the new philosophy and how complete had been the victory of the progressives.[18]

Romantics and Radicals

Very little that would later appear in the works of educational reformers and radicals could not be found in some form in the works of Jean-Jacques Rousseau, the original philosopher of child-centered education and chief popularizer of the romantic view of childhood innocence. It was Rousseau who gave to the movement not merely its idealistic posture, but also its style, especially what one critic calls the penchant for sweeping overstatement and tendency to "substitute metaphor for argument."[19]

In *Emile*, Rousseau outlined a plan for tearing down traditional notions of education and replacing them with a theory for creating a new man and a new society. The title character, Emile, is presented as a model. Given a tutor at birth, he is raised (if that is the proper word) by means of a "natural education," in which he learns from "experience." Author Robin Barrow describes *Emile* as a blueprint that "challenged no less the presumption that [children] should be fed a body of information and socially hallowed maxims, that they should be veneered with knowledge, and that they needed moulding, shaping and directing if they were to be responsible adults."[20]

The purpose of Rousseau's natural education was to liberate the child from the shackles of custom and tradition. Rousseau judges education not by whether it succeeds or fails to pass on knowledge or skills, but on whether or not it produces a person who is a fit citizen for the perfect society envisioned in his treatises.

In Emile's education, there is no emphasis on vocabulary; and he is kept safely away from any prescribed rules of conduct, since he will be able to develop those himself. Rousseau's lack of interest in using education to inculcate morality was closely related to his attitudes toward literacy. Children should not learn moral lessons from books. "Not just because Rousseau distrusted moralistic writings," notes Barrow, "but because he claimed to be suspicious of books altogether."[21] For Rousseau it did not matter if Emile did not even know what a book was until he was in his teens. He dismissed the usual academic curriculum, which he described contemptuously as "heraldry, geography, chronology and language" as useless.

Proving his intellectual patrimony to the educationists of the twentieth century, Rousseau argued that it was unimportant for students to know how to find Beijing on a map. Instead, they would spend their time acquiring "useful knowledge." Most of the attainments of the schools of his time were irrelevant, he argued. "I would rather have him a shoemaker than a poet," he wrote, "I would rather he paved streets than painted flowers on china."[22] In Rousseau's cult of child worship, students studied only what they wanted to study.

Rousseau's teacher does not teach in the usual sense of the word. "It is not your business to teach him the various sciences, but to give him a taste for them and methods of learning them when his taste is more mature." And whenever possible, all teaching should be done in the form of "doing" rather than reading or listening.[23]

Although Rousseau presents all of this as a picture of "natural education," it is only natural to the extent that Rousseau and his tutor represent "nature." The laissez-faire posture of Rousseau's tutor turns out to be illusory. Barrow describes Rousseau's tutor as a "detached and manipulative figure" who "guides, controls and manipulates."[24] Far from liberating the child from adult influences, the new teacher is far more despotic than the allegedly more autocratic teacher because he aims to shape the *whole* person, rather than just his mind.

Dewey and His Disciples

Even before John Dewey came on the scene to give the progressive impulse in education its philosophy and intellectual framework, reformers were moving to transform America's schools. Horace Mann, whose efforts contributed so much to the rise of public schools in this country, had "a boundless faith in the perfectibility of human life and institutions," as one historian noted. They could be weapons against evil as well as the "great equalizer" and "the balance wheel of the social machinery."

Historian Lawrence Cremin describes the powerful lure of Mann's vision. "Poverty would most assuredly disappear, and with it the rancorous discord between the 'haves' and 'have-nots' that had marred all of human history. Crime would diminish; sickness would abate; and life for the common man would be longer, better, and happier. . . . Little wonder that it fired the optimism of the American Republic."[25]

By the late 1800s, various groups were actively pressing the schools to move away from their "narrow" focus on academics and begin to concern themselves with the "whole boy." Progressives like Jane Addams saw schools as the centerpiece in efforts to create new communities in the nation's cities. In 1920, she complained, "We are impatient with the schools which lay all stress on reading and writing, suspecting them to rest upon the assumption that all knowledge and interest must be brought to the children through the medium of books. Such an assumption fails to give the child any clew to the life about him, or any power to usefully or intelligently connect himself with it." In particular, she thought modern man needed to be trained and educated in collective, group activities, which she invoked as the spirit "of team work." If they approached their jobs in the right-thinking spirit of teamwork, she thought, dozens of workers in a coat-making factory could make "the entire process as much more exhilarating than the work of a solitary old tailor, as playing in a baseball nine gives more pleasure to a boy than afforded by a solitary game of handball on the side of a barn."[26]

Schools were also enlisted in the task of Americanizing the children of immigrants. Reformers, Cremin writes, wanted to "turn schoolhouses into neighborhood centers for every sort and variety of community activity; the school would be meeting place, public forum, recreation house, civic center, home of all formal and informal education."[27] In short, schools should begin to take on roles traditionally left to families, churches, and communities. Although he did not set these movements in motion, it was Dewey who gave them their intellectual shape.

Dewey blamed the disruptions of industrialism for uprooting communities and families and he argued that the schools would now have to step in to fill the gaps left by the weaknesses of the older and now displaced institutions. To meet the need of the new era a "complete transformation" of education was needed. Dewey condemned the isolation of the schools from the rest of society, but also the passivity of their methods of teaching and their curricula. Dewey argued that education for too long had been focused on "the teacher, the textbook, anywhere and everywhere you please except in the immediate instincts and activities of the child himself." Henceforth, the child would be the center of education. His work echoed *Emile* and he was widely compared to Rousseau.[28] Like Rousseau, Dewey argued, "I would have a child say not, 'I know,' but, 'I have experienced.'"

Along with other leading figures of the movement, including Francis

W. Parker and William Heard Kilpatrick, the reformers set about to change the style and content of American schooling. As a supporter later enthused: "These rebels ruthlessly proposed to discard the current schemes of subjects, textbooks, recitations, large classes, fixed furniture and, to carry out their proposals, inaugurated three decades of revolutionary experimentation."[29]

In place of academic subjects and textbooks, the reformers insisted that the new standards must be the child's immediate interest and sense of relevance. On the subject of teaching history, Dewey wrote: "A knowledge of the past and its heritage is of great significance when it enters into the present, but not otherwise. And the mistake of making the records and remains of the past the main material of education is that it cuts the vital connection of present and past, and tends to make the past a rival of the present and the present a more or less futile imitation of the past. Under such circumstances, culture becomes an ornament and solace; a refuge and an asylum."

It is unlikely that Dewey envisioned a complete evisceration of the study of history. But as Frances FitzGerald would later note, whatever Dewey meant, "the NEA educationists chose to take the narrowest possible view of it. While the bohemian progressives rejected historical training as but another way to repress the glorious clouds of imagination that children were born trailing, the NEA committee members rejected history as trivia— as games or ornaments of the elites. Under the noble standards of usefulness, they turned American history into civics and civics into propaganda for their version of the social good."[30] But this was to be a nagging and persistent problem for the Deweyites, and in part the responsibility lies with Dewey himself. He inaugurated the tradition of vagueness that has succeeded him through the decades. What exactly was "essential" and must be taught? What could be scrapped? As Cremin later noted, Dewey didn't provide much help to those who followed him. His own criterion "is so vague as to be little aid in judging curricular proposals." During the next several decades, the price for this vagueness would become more obvious. "For simple as it is to discard traditional curricula in response to cries for reform," Cremin noted, "it is even simpler to substitute for them a succession of chaotic activities that not only fail to facilitate growth but actually end up miseducative in quality and character."[31]

Some early critics also noticed that Dewey's ideas seemed suffused with an emphasis on conformity. As early as 1916, one careful observer noted, "In the Deweyan social system there is no room for any individual who wishes to lead his own life in the privacy of reflective self-consciousness. Privacy is to be regarded as a sinful luxury. Individuals are to remember that, after all, they are only 'agencies for revising and transforming previously accepted beliefs.' In sum, one is driven to the belief that, in spite of Mr. Dewey's fine defense of individualism, his moral ideal is really that of the 'good mixer.'"[32] Such dissent had little impact on the growing educationist movement.

The Cardinal Principles

Dewey's vision of the new American school was embraced by the proto-educationists of the time, who gathered together (as is their wont) in the usual collection of committees, conferences, and declarations. The rising tide of progressivism can be traced in two crucial documents setting out divergent ideas of the purposes and ends of education.

In 1893, the Commission of Ten, headed by Harvard's Charles Eliot, laid out the traditionalist credo, with a firm emphasis on the pursuit of knowledge and the central place of the disciplines of liberal education. "As studies in language and in the natural sciences are best adapted to cultivate the habits of observation; as mathematics are the traditional training of the reasoning faculties," the Eliot report declared, "so history and its allied branches are better adapted than any other studies to promote the invaluable mental power which we call judgment."

Twenty-five years later, that point of view would be repudiated by a commission formed by the National Education Association and dominated by the new breed of progressive educationists. The "Cardinal Principles," issued in 1918 by the Commission on the Reorganization of Secondary Education, remains to this day the ur-document of American educationism in the twentieth century. Eight decades of "reform"—from the dismantling of the traditional curriculum and educationism's suspicion of intellectualism to the child-centered classroom, whole-child education, affective learning, and the bloated missions of the modern school—can be read in the principles set out during the presidency of Woodrow Wilson. Henceforth, schools would concern themselves less with academic matters than with the "preparation for effective living." The Cardinal Principles dismissed the Eliot report's emphasis on liberal education as elitist and argued that it would be more "democratic" to provide training in practical homemaking and the manual arts to the majority of students. It did not seem to occur to the NEA, either then or later, that the practical effect of such "democratic" policies was to close the doors of liberal education to those groups who were even then showing their first interest in expanding their intellectual horizons.

The Cardinal Principles, which are voluble to the point of tedium on every aspect of schooling, dismissed scholarship with a single sentence: "Provisions should be made also for those having distinctly academic interests." And that's it; the commission offered no further comment, suggestions, or guidelines. (Thus creating another tradition of "goals," "outcomes," and "strategic planning" documents that would manage to say little or nothing about the teaching of any academic subject.)

The seven "cardinal" principles began with: Health. The NEA Commission declared: "Health needs cannot be neglected during the period of secondary education without serious danger to the individual and the race." (As Richard Mitchell notes, "How true. You can't make effective livers out of dead children. And think of the race! Suppose they *all* die!"[33]) The Cardinal Principles called for teachers who would inculcate in the entire student body "a love for clean sport." The second principle was "Command of Fundamental Processes," by which the commission apparently meant basic skills.

Worthy Home-membership was the third goal. "In the education of every high-school girl, the household arts should have a prominent place because of their importance to the girl herself and to others whose welfare will be directly in her keeping." This would include an understanding of "the essentials of food values, of sanitation, and of household budgets." In the new schema, literature would not be neglected, but it would be subordinated to the "worthy home-membership" goal. The commission's attitude toward books was strictly functional. "Literature," it declared, "should interpret and idealize the human elements that go to make the home." Which presumably leaves out *Madam Bovary.*

The fourth principle: Vocation. The goal of the schools should be to "equip the individual to secure a livelihood for himself and those dependent on him," including the ability to "maintain the right relationships toward his fellow workers and society." Students would also be taught to "develop an appreciation of the significance" of vocations and have "a clear conception of right relations between the members of the chosen vocation, between different vocational groups, between employer and employee, and between producer and consumer."

Perhaps the most radical "principle" concerned Civics Education, which was designed to replace history. The proto-educationists and bureaucrats who staffed the NEA commission had little interest in the past, except where it accorded with their own notions of what was relevant and interesting to children in the immediate present. "Too frequently, however," the principles declared, "does *mere information,* conventional in value and *remote in bearing* make up the content of the social studies." [emphasis added] The educationists who wrote the Cardinal Principles were especially uninterested in the U.S. Constitution and the ideas of the Founding Fathers. "Civics should concern itself less with constitutional questions and remote governmental functions," the commission declared, "and should direct attention to social agencies close at hand and to the informal activities of daily life that regard and seek the common good. Such agencies as child-welfare organizations and consumers' leagues afford specific opportunities for the expression of civic qualities by the older pupils."

The commission specifically encouraged "the assignment of projects and problems to groups of pupils for cooperative solution and the socialized recitation whereby the class as a whole develops a sense of collective responsibility. Both of these devices give training in collective thinking." As Richard Mitchell notes: "Here we see the theoretical foundations of the rap session, the encounter group, the values clarification module, and the typical course in education, but also something far worse."[34]

Implicit in the cardinal principles was a distrust of the individual mind. Students who were expected to engage in "socialized recitations" would presumably not discuss the principles of separation of powers or the need to protect the minority from the majority, or the fierce nonconformity of the individuals who crafted the Declaration of Independence, the Constitution, or the Federalist Papers—these were "mere information" that are "remote in bearing" from the immediate interests of school children. The colonization of America, the search for religious liberty, the Bill of Rights, moral issues of Civil War, Reconstruction, the Industrial Era, the titanic struggles with Fascism and Nazism, would all be subsumed under the heading of "mere information," or "remote government functions," which educationists found far less interesting than studying the activities of "social agencies close at hand."

Sixth among the "cardinal principles" was Worthy Use of Leisure. The commission found that "Heretofore the high school has given little conscious attention to this objective." At one time, it was actually assumed that people were capable of deciding how to relax without the intervention of the schools. The NEA was determined to correct such misapprehensions. The school, it declared, had "so exclusively sought intellectual discipline that it has seldom treated literature, art, and music so as to evoke *right emotional response* and produce positive enjoyment. Its presentations of science should aim, in part, *to arouse a genuine appreciation of nature.*" Many artists might find it odd that the commission would regard "intellectual discipline" as being somehow incompatible with "right emotional response." As Richard Mitchell remarks: "A pack of manual arts teachers, educationists and bureaucrats can tell us what a right emotional response would be, presumably. They can clarify for us, without any tedious attention to inorganic chemistry or the laws of motion, not only an appreciation of nature but a *genuine* appreciation of nature."[35] Mitchell detected the same bland self-assurance in the commission's seventh principle, "Ethical Character," which the NEA declared to be "paramount" in a democratic society, "as if Plato, Epictetus, St. Augustine, Voltaire, Kant, Spinoza, and so on . . . had somehow missed the point now perfectly clear to certain manual arts teachers and associate superintendents."[36]

The real measure of the educational revolution was not in the statements of principle, but in the experience of the classroom. From the beginning, the results were mixed. In the hands of brilliant and inspired teachers, some of the progressive schools were notably successful. They were lively, innovative, and managed to strike a balance between the subjects taught at the interests of the students. As he afterward insisted, this was what Dewey had in mind all along. The key was in maintaining a balance between educational content and the needs of the child. As quickly became apparent, however, not every teacher could keep that equilibrium.

Dewey had urged schools to adopt a variety of innovations in teaching subject matter. They did not need to rely solely on books or recitations to teach science, but could take children on field trips to farms, for instance, to learn principles of biology, chemistry, and physics. But Dewey recognized a problem that was overlooked by many of his disciples: Not every teacher could manage the new program. He wondered, for example, whether a trip to a cow barn would be useful in teaching chemistry if the teacher didn't know chemistry. It might be a good idea to teach mathematics by playing store; but how effective would it be if the teacher was shaky on the basic elements of arithmetic? The only way that real life experience could be used to effectively educate children was for the teacher to be master both of the techniques of stimulation and the purpose for which the students were being stimulated.

It was all too easy, as Dewey was to recognize, to emphasize the technique and neglect the substance. "Dewey sought to substitute for the older curriculum he so roundly criticized a new program that was better planned, better designed, better organized . . . " historian Lawrence Cremin observed. "He was destined for disappointment; and a quarter-century later he pronounced progressive education a failure, a movement that had destroyed well but too soon abandoned the more difficult task of building something better to replace what had been done away with."[37]

One of Dewey's most influential followers was William Heard Kilpatrick, who presided over the education of a generation or more of educationists from his perch at Columbia's Teachers College. Kilpatrick devised what was to be known as "the project method," which he described as a way for children to participate in a "wholehearted purposeful activity in a social environment" and which meant that children would learn by doing. If the subject was agriculture, teachers would have children plant corn. But it would be up to the child to work out how to plant; the teacher would let him "experience" the process, rather than teach him the rules or techniques for planting.

While this sounded much like Dewey, with its emphasis on "experience," Kilpatrick differed from Dewey in fundamental ways. He was not interested in striking a balance between subject matter and child; indeed, Kilpatrick opposed defining subject matter in advance lest it hinder the child's creativity. Where Dewey had wanted to develop a new curriculum—"a new body of subject matter better ordered and better designed"— Kilpatrick emphasized the rapidity of change, the unknowability of the future, and thus the futility of developing any fixed curriculum at all. As Cremin noted, Kilpatrick's "unrelenting attack on subject matter 'fixed-in-advance' ultimately discredits the organized subjects and hence inevitably shifts the balance of Dewey's pedagogical paradigm toward the child." Kilpatrick took Dewey's idea that a child learns by doing and transformed that into an educational philosophy in which the child came before the subject matter. Ultimately, that philosophy came to dominate progressive education. Cremin estimated that Kilpatrick taught some 35,000 students from every state at Teachers College, at a time when most articulate leaders of education were being trained there.

Anyone who held the senior chair of philosophy in education would have been immensely influential. But as Cremin noted, "In the hands of the dedicated, compelling Kilpatrick, the chair became an extraordinarily strategic rostrum for the dissemination of a particular version of progressive education that still remains the dominant version of the movement within the American teaching profession."[38]

Although it was scarcely a protozoon compared to the Blob it would become, the educational bureaucracy played a critical role in spreading these trendy ideas throughout the nation's schools. Despite being limited by federal law to simply disseminating information and statistics, the U.S. Office of Education became "a prime propagator of progressivism" and used its growing volume of publications to expand upon the wonders of the new philosophies. Equally influential was the National Education Association, which saw its membership grow from 10,000 members in 1918 to 210,000 in 1941. The NEA kept up a constant tattoo of support for progressive ideas in its journals, which reached far into the educational hinterlands.[39] By 1937, progressivism was no longer an insurgent movement; it had become the educationist mainstream.

For some, the essence of progressivism was the revolt against Puritanism and the celebration of self-expression, freedom, and creativity. Others saw it in political terms, as a battering ram against capitalism. Over time, it was the bohemian, avant-garde pedagogues who became dominant and defined progressivism in their own image. In the name of child-centered education, schools championed the self-expression of children in hopes of unleashing joyous waves of creative energy. Again, the reality did not always accord with the hopes. "Taken up as a fad, it elicited not only first-rate art, but every manner of shoddiness and self-deception as well," Cremin later recounted. "In too many classrooms license began to pass for liberty, planlessness for spontaneity, recalcitrance for individuality, obfuscation for art, and chaos for education—all justified in the rhetoric of expressionism. And thus was born at least one of the several caricatures of progressive education in which humorists reveled—quite understandably—for at least a generation."[40]

Scenes from the Front **1928**

H ere is a group of six and seven year olds. They dance; they sing; they play house and build villages; they keep store and take care of pets; they model in clay and sand; they draw and paint, read and write, make up stories and dramatize them; they work in the garden; they churn, and weave, and cook.

"A group is inventing dances. . . . In a darkened room films are being shown. . . . A primary class is getting ready for an excursion on the morrow to a bakery. Another has just returned from a trip to a woolen mill. . . . A breathless group is stocking a new aquarium to be sent to the third grade. . . .

"What a contrast between this picture of happy, purposeful living and that of the old school!" In the old classroom, "behind every classroom door lurked a deceptive Pandora's box of fears, restraints, and long weary hours of suppression." Students were sentenced to "memorize, recite, pay attention," and ground down by the "the grindstone of an educational discipline."[1] In such antediluvian schools, "the program of the child's education is organized about school subjects. Not so in the new schools.

"What a difference! The logically arranged subjects of the past—reading, writing, arithmetic, spelling, geography, history—are replaced by projects, units of work, creative work periods, industrial arts, creative music, story hours, informal group conferences, and other vastly intriguing enterprises."[2] Activities include such vastly intriguing projects as caring for a flock of chickens, a study of boats, and a study of wool.[3]

In describing the child-centered school of the 1920s, Harold Rugg and Ann Shumaker painted a portrait of an institution that celebrated "creative self-expression, the confident affirmation of the importance of self in place of that of conformity and inferiority. . . ." In the new school, children would "share in their own government, in the planning of the program, in the administering of the curriculum, in conducting the life of the school."[4]

Traditionalists favored "discipline, logical thinking, power of sustained intellectual effort, the retention of classified knowledge. They coveted better scholarship, logic, grasp of the continuity of racial development." In contrast, the architects of the new child-centered classroom were "proponents of freedom in education" who emphasized the "continuous growth of the child, freedom, initiative, spontaneity, vivid self-expression."[5] The child-centered school was determined to make sure that "the whole child is to be educated." This meant that the focus of the school is not merely intellectual, but also "physical, rhythmic, emotional" and concerned with developing "a child's total personality." In fact, the two great goals of the new school were "drawing out of the child's inner capacities for self-expression" and "tolerant understanding."[6]

Rugg and Shumaker acknowledged their debt to Rousseau. The child-centered schools of the 1920s "for the first time in history, are actually working out in practice, something which Rousseau perceived and only vaguely described to his contemporaries. . . ."[7]

Rather than academic subjects, the social aspects of the child's life were not the center of the new school. "The old school . . . left the child entirely unaided in coping with social situations. . . . The new school, on the other hand, encourages the child to be a distinct personality, an individualist . . . but, of course *not to an unjustifiable degree.* It sets up situations which provide constant practice in cooperative learning. It encourages activities in which he can make a personal contribution to group enterprises; in which he has social experiences. . . ."[8] (emphasis added)

Much of the school day is consumed by programs of group dance, committees, clubs, and assemblies of various kinds. In art, as in much of the rest of the school's program, there is no standard higher than the child himself. "Art in the new schools is naive, neo-primitive. The child is permitted to set his own standards as he works. The 'masters' are not set out to be worshipped respectfully. . . ."[9] Finger painting was sufficient as long as it was a purposeful act of self-expression.

The students sit in a semicircle while the teacher introduces an exciting new subject, "something that means a great deal to all of us"—food. Food, she explains, is important to everyone and we can all help increase our awareness of its importance. The class is broken into committees to study different aspects of food.

Describing the new curriculum, author John Keats noted that the children's report cards would make no mention of the study of food. The children would receive grades in reading, writing, social studies, music, math, etc. But they wouldn't be dealt with as separate subjects, but rather "through the device of the overall group enterprise." Instead of arithmetic, the children play grocery store and elect a cashier and clerk. The spelling words also share the food theme: eat, grow, help, etc. "In language arts the children will read: 'Food helps us grow. Food grows on farms.'"

Neither history nor geography will be studied per se, but through their study of food, the children will be led to discover that many different foods in the local supermarket came from strange lands where the soils and weather are different and where people talk and dress differently and prepare food differently. The lesson they will learn is that we all have in common the fact that "we all eat food." The student groups present reports and create murals and posters on food.[1]

The philosophy in the class is that the children will somehow pick up the basic skills through the study of food, "by a kind of painless osmosis." Keats reported that for the teacher of this classroom, "Far more important than any specific achievement by any individual in any of the fundamentals . . . is that all the children learned to find happiness in tackling a job together."[2]

It is a nurturing environment in which everyone succeeds because the teacher thinks that competition "can be a source of acute social sickness." So in her class, "instead of being asked to come up to some arbitrary standard of accomplishment in which some would excel and some would fail, everyone succeeded, or at least grew. Everyone realized his best self." The teacher insists that this "is just like real life."[3]

Group behavior rather than individual achievement is the order of the day. "Everywhere, the emphasis is on the group; the password is cooperation. . . . Group learning, group responsibility, group guilt, preoccupation with the group lies behind all the educational pragmatist's practice."[4] "The teacher does not mean that it is one of the jobs to make children work and play with others," Keats wrote. "She believes that it is *the* task."[5]

The teacher also embraces the new philosophies for teaching reading. Her mentors have taught her that there is really no such thing as "reading," but merely "reading skills," because it takes one kind of skill to read a menu, another sort to read a bus schedule or a comic book. "Hence," Keats noted, the teacher's approach to reading and other subjects "tends to be formulistic; she does not teach children to read, but she teaches them several reading How Tos." In her class, children read from a book called *At Play*, a level-one primer, "written by eight teacher-college females all working together." No casual reader would be tempted to confuse *At Play* with a work of literature. But it is a masterpiece of repetition: in 121 pages, children are confronted with only 81 new words. On 72 of its pages, there are no new words at all. Keats noted that the story content is "nonexistent." There is a great deal of Oh, oh, ohing and Look, look, looking.[6]

This does not bother the teacher, because she is "not much interested in quality, and she is also less interested in whether a child can read at a certain grade level than she is in discovering whether the child is 'growing' in his ability to read."[7]

In the same school, Keats said, you might easily "find foreign-language students involved in baking foreign goods, sewing costumes, collecting travel photographs from magazines and comparing travel articles and engaged in sundry other activities that have nothing to do with learning the language." When asked whether this was really the best way to teach students to speak or understand a foreign language, the teacher would explain that the key is not how well a student speaks a language, "but how he *behaves* toward his fellow man of a different nationality, political faith, creed and race."[8]

Although he was not then, nor ever intended to be, a professional educator, Keats nonetheless asked searching questions. The kids in the classes were undoubtedly happy; they were clearly having a good time. But were they *learning anything?* Did the emphasis on groupthink place too high a premium on conformity? Did some groups serve as cloaks for a "lack of personal effort?"

He wondered, did they really learn math while playing store? Or geography by discussing the foods of any lands? And—why food? If the point was to interest or inspire the children, why choose a subject so mundane and limited? Why food rather than fairy tales? Or literature above the Oh, Oh, Look, look level?

An Endangered Species

Keats also found more traditional teachers. The traditional teacher did not ask the class "where its several childish interests lie. Instead she outlines the work she expects all to attempt, explains it and assigns it to the class as a whole, and then expects each child to do his own work to the best of his ability." In those classes, children are expected to work and think individually. She discourages whispering and passing notes.[9]

The traditional teacher also tries to capture the class's interest, "But she is not in the least interested in whether everybody is having a good time, or *wants* to learn what she is there to profess. Her point is that work is *required* and that all students are expected to compete against an objective standard of achievement." She regards competition as a virtue, not a social disease; and so hands out stars and grades for performance. The rewards reflect standards that are not set by kids, but by the teacher herself, based on her presumption of society's standards. She does everything she can to help out slow children, but she does not neglect the more gifted students. She has no intention of compromising her standards to make anyone feel good.[10]

In her class, Keats wrote, books were chosen for their literary merit. Even first graders are expected to read real stories—stories with a beginning, middle, and end. While her counterpart's class is using words like food, eat, help, and farm, the traditional teacher assigns *Peter Rabbit*, which includes words like *implore, exert,* and *scuttered.* She believes in teaching phonics systematically, because she knows that is the only way for children to achieve word mastery. She believes that English is a discipline with rules of its own "and she is unwilling to excuse mistakes in grammar no matter how poignantly they may reveal a developing social conscience."[11]

Keats detected in the two classrooms a fundamental philosophical difference as to "the nature of learning, the nature of things learned, and most important, as to the true role of the individual in society. . . ." While the first teacher "conducts her class from the point of view that the individual has only a functional significance in society," the traditionalist "is dedicated to the proposition that society is merely a function of individuals."[12]

In 1958, the traditionalist was already considered out-of-date and out of step. The future belonged to "food."

CHAPTER 16

EDUCATIONAL WASTELANDS

The Life Adjustment movement that would sweep American education in the late 1940s and early 1950s began, appropriately enough, in the bowels of the educational bureaucracy. In 1944, the U.S. Department of Education launched a study of vocational education, setting off a round of committee meetings and conferences that culminated in a 1945 conference, which unanimously endorsed a resolution that envisioned a new mission for secondary schools. Henceforth high schools would be expected to prepare only 20 percent of students for college; another 20 percent for "desirable skilled occupations," while the remaining 60 percent "will receive the life adjustment training they need and to which they are entitled as American citizens. . . ." Between April and November 1946, no fewer than five regional conferences were held and there was little dissent from the conclusion that schools were "failing to provide adequately and properly for the life adjustment" of American children. The whole weight of the educational establishment was mobilized for the new "reform," which insisted that the schools replace the anachronistic idea of training minds with the modern notion of "preparing children for future living" by recognizing the "importance of personal satisfaction and achievements for each individual within the limits of his abilities."

There were scattered criticisms of the new fashions, but they tended to come from outside the education establishment. John Keats, the author of *Schools Without Scholars*, was an unabashed nonexpert. Of his own qualifications, he admitted, "They are largely nonexistent. I am not now, nor have I ever been, nor do I expect to be a professional educator. I am simply a parent of three school children. Together with several million other parents, I have wondered why our public schools teach what they do." None of that dissuaded him from labeling Life Adjustment "so much fatuous diaperism."[1]

The new educational philosophy of American public schools, he wrote, was "compounded of the pragmatic thoughts of the late John Dewey plus a dollop of sentimentality and a generous helping of the oversensitive conscience of the social worker whose life is chiefly spent among those who do not seem able to help themselves."[2]

Along with Keats, the most influential critic of the public schools in the 1950s was Arthur Bestor, the author of *Educational Wastelands*, which he subtitled *The Retreat from Learning in Our Public Schools*. Although his immediate target was Life Adjustment, Bestor recognized that the underlying issue was the basic question of the ends of education. A product of progressive education himself, Bestor spanned the era of progressivism's rise, its dominance, and its decline into anti-intellectual palaver (a degeneration that would continue long after Life Adjustment faded from the scene). A ruthless debunker of educationist pretensions, Bestor's critique is worth considering not merely because of its historical influence, but for the light it sheds on current disputes. His apologia for liberal education and the necessity for schools to concentrate on "rigorous intellectual training" is as relevant to the educational debates of the 1990s as it was to the debates over Life Adjustment in the 1950s and child-centered schooling in the 1920s and 1930s.

To read Bestor's send-up of the charlantism of his day is to be reminded of the remarkable persistence of pedagogical quackery. In the school wars, Bestor wrote, "The issue is drawn between those who believe that good teaching should be directed to sound intellectual ends, and those who are content to dethrone intellectual values and cultivate the techniques of teaching for their own sake, in a intellectual and cultural vacuum."[3] He could easily have been describing the educational "goals" and "outcomes" of hundreds of districts in the 1990s, when he noted that "High sounding objectives, such as teaching children 'to help solve economic, social and political problems'—are being offered today as the preambles to educational proposals of the utmost vagueness. Their vagueness is one of their principal dangers, for all the established guideposts vanish into the mist. The public is supposed to take everything on trust."[4]

Bestor argued, inter alia, that:

- *The one indispensable function of the school was to emphasize rigorous intellectual training.* "Our civilization requires of every man and woman a variety of complex skills," Bestor wrote, "which rest upon the ability to read, write, and calculate, and upon sound knowledge of science, history, economics, philosophy, and other fundamental disciplines." Such knowledge was not necessary just for advanced study, but in its own right. If schools did not concern themselves with health, he noted, "the nation will not go uncared for." But if "schools and colleges do not emphasize rigorous intellectual training, there will be none."[5]
- *Rigorous intellectual training, far from being impractical, was the only practical education for the modern world.* Children can be taught to design methods of planting corn or how to build a boat. But unless

they are given more powerful intellectual tools, they won't be able to go beyond that point. "One does not need higher mathematics to build a workable waterwheel or an oxcart, but one does need it to build a dynamo or a jet plane." (Bestor's jibe would resonate in late 1950s after Soviets launched Soyuz—at a time when Americans children were still adjusting themselves to life.) Bestor argued that intellectual training was highly practical for a society that demanded the ability to perform complex tasks and that such knowledge "becomes more practical because it becomes more powerful."[6]

- *The claim by educationists that traditional education concerned itself with "mere facts" was both untrue and a sign of their abysmal ignorance of what liberal learning entailed.* "No misconception is so prevalent and so deceptive as the notion that liberal education is merely the communicating of factual information," Bestor charged. "The liberal disciplines are not chunks of frozen fact. They are not facts at all. They are powerful tools and engines by which a man discovers and handles facts." The educationist tendency to caricature traditional education as the rote memorization of facts, Bestor wrote, reflected "an outsider's view of intellectual life. No one who knows at first hand what goes into the training of a mathematician or a biologist or an historian could ever imagine that the process follows any such absurd pattern as this."[7]
- *The academic disciplines were not arbitrary "subject-matter areas," but were instruments for finding truth and training the mind to think.* They "represent the various ways which man has discovered for achieving intellectual mastery and hence practical power over the various problems that confront him."[8] Linguistic disciplines were cultivated because wisdom can be found in many languages; the present is shaped by the past, so scholars cultivated historical techniques to understand it; the sciences have enabled man to understand the universe. Man created physics and chemistry, not as a collection of facts, but as tools to help him master and subdue matter. None of the traditional disciplines were arbitrary; and thus none should be arbitrarily discarded or boiled down into an indistinguishable stew.
- *It was absurd to regard the extension of liberal learning to large numbers of students as "anti-democratic."* "Liberal education," Bestor argued, "means deliberate cultivation of the power to think."[9] So why would educationists want to close such doors? Millions of Americans now enjoyed the quality of housing, diet, and the freedom of travel that were once the exclusive domain of the aristocracy. But if the extension of those benefits to the masses was applauded as democracy in action, why should intellectual values be the exception? The popular notion that only a small minority of students needed liberal education, Bestor argued, amounted to a form of "regressive education."[10]
- *Concentrating on student "interest" was all well and good, but once*

you have their attention, you ought to have something worthwhile to teach them. "Motivation is important, but it may be likened to a fuse. It burns to no purpose unless at last it touches off something more powerful than itself. If its far end is embedded in nothing, it will sputter and glow through its entire length, and then die out, leaving only a trail of ashes behind."[11]

It was true that children will not learn if they are not interested, but the fact that they are interested and happy is not therefore evidence that learning is taking place. "A preoccupation with arousing interest may—and frequently does—lead to the introduction into the schoolroom of projects totally without educational value. . . . And programs of the utmost triviality are defended time after time on the meretricious ground that they interest the student." Bestor reminded his readers that "school is no mere entertainment hall; it arouses interest for a purpose. The test of a school, after all, is how much students learn."[12]

- *Educationists were utterly unqualified to determine what should be taught in the schools.* The insistence that professors of education and the products of courses in the *techniques* of teaching should also have control over the intellectual *content* of those courses, Bestor argued, was based on the acceptance of "unfounded pretensions" of the educationists. "We have permitted the content of public school instruction to be determined by a narrow group of specialists in pedagogy, well-intentioned men and women, no doubt, but utterly devoid of the qualifications necessary for the task they have undertaken." The result was that intellectual training, which was "once the unquestioned focus of every educational effort has been pushed out to the periphery" of American education by "the 'experts' from state departments and colleges of education: the curriculum doctors, the integrators, the life-adjusters—the specialists in know-how rather than knowledge."[13]

Much of the problem was that most educationists—then and later—were trained in techniques of elementary thinking, but knew very little about how the child moves to more complex knowledge. "Professors of pedagogy doubtless know a great deal about the way in which a child passes from the stage of counting his toes to the stage of doing arithmetical sums in a notebook," Bestor wrote. "They know next to nothing of the process by which a man moves from analytic geometry to differential calculus." Unfortunately, educationists did not know what they did not know. It was true, he said, that small children learn best from the use of concrete objects rather than from abstractions. But it was a fatuous mistake to continue to use the same techniques as a child grew older and his mind matured. It was true that the local fire department was more real to a small child than the "remote functions" of government in general. It was also true that the local railroad was more compelling than discussions of economics. But sooner or later, he would have to move on. "Let the first grader, then, find out all he can about the local fire department and the choo-choo," Bestor suggested. "But this process is not to be repeated indefinitely. In the end the child can learn to think clearly and effectively only by learning to analyze into their elements the problems connected with these matters, and by thereafter studying such elements systematically, *according to the recognized and appropriate categories of mature thought.*"[14] [emphasis added]

Perhaps Bestor's most valuable contribution was a lucid definition of the requirements of what he called "effective thinking." Forty years later, it still poses a powerful challenge to the nebulous maunderings about "higher order thinking skills" that still dominate educationism. Bestor defined four requirements for the educated mind:

First, it must have a thorough command of "the essential intellectual tools," the most important of which was the ability to read. For Bestor that would include the knowledge of more than one language. Almost equally important was an ability "to put complex ideas into intelligible prose and to handle the niceties of syntax with the assurance born of grammatical analysis." The essential intellectual tools would also include mathematical abilities.

Second, "effective thinking depends upon a store of reliable information, which the mind can draw upon." Educationists (then and now) claimed that children do not need information, because they can look it up in reference books. But, as Bestor noted, even looking something up requires a good deal of information since facts relate to other facts. The reader must bring to the reference book "a fund of ready knowledge sufficient to make it intelligible." A child might be able to follow a chain of cross-references, "but eventually he must trace a connection to something he already knows, else the pursuit is an utterly meaningless one."

Third, the educated mind must be practiced in "the systematic ways of thinking developed within the various fields of scholarly and scientific investigation." This meant knowing not just the facts of history, but also problems of historical causation (which, in turn, could be understood only if the events of history were known).

"Finally, but only finally, comes the culminating act of applying this aggregate of intellectual powers to the solution of a problem." In modern educationist jargon, this would be the "outcome," but it presupposes all of the other steps. If any of the steps are neglected—if students are not given the basic intellectual tools or the information or the practice of systematically applying their minds—it was naive to think they can simply leap to the "outcome" of effective thinking. But this notion, Bestor wrote in 1953, was "characteristic of regressive education" whose practitioners imagined they could neglect the teaching of reading or the basics of mathematics in their obsession with the liberated and creative mind.[15]

Bestor also argued that traditional liberal education was the only education suitable for a society that valued the individual before the group. "Liberal education is designed to produce self-reliance," he offered. "It expects a man or woman to use his general intelligence to solve particular problems."

"One can search history and biography in vain for evidence that men or women have ever accomplished anything original, creative, or significant by virtue of narrowly conceived vocational training or of educational programs that aimed merely at 'life adjustment'," Bestor wrote. "The West was not settled by men and women who had taken courses in 'How to be a pioneer.' . . . A citizen today needs an *education*, not a headful of helpful hints."[16]

Failed Reform

On the surface, the late 1950s was a period of immense turmoil in education, as reformers reacted against child-centered and life adjusting educational schemes. Alarmed by evidence of educational decline and by the Soviet Union's scientific advances, the country committed itself to a return to academic rigor. Historian Lawrence Cremin wrote what was in effect an obituary for the movement in 1962. "The life adjustment movement quickly disappeared, as much the victim of its own ill-chosen name as of the deeper attacks on its principles and practices."[17] But Cremin's obituary was premature. Life adjustment did not disappear; it merely went underground.

The back-to-basics movement of the late 1950s largely evaporated when the nation's attention turned to the question of equity in the 1960s. The Civil Rights movement shifted the focus of attention to the relationship between schools and poverty, inequality, and segregation. The Elementary and Secondary Education Act of 1965 (ESEA) deployed the considerable weight of the federal government behind the movement to place schools in the vanguard of the movement toward social, economic, and political equality. It was sweet music to the educationists of the old school to hear their decades-old faith reinvigorated by Lyndon Johnson's declaration: "The answer for all our national problems comes down to a single word. That word is education."

ESEA's stated purpose was to "compensate" low-income youths by directing millions of federal dollars for remedial programs in schools with a large number of poor students. Known as Title I (later Chapter I), it was the forerunner and model of what would become a procession of "categorical" education programs, aimed at specially targeted populations in the public schools.

While the amount of money involved was relatively modest, the federal government played a critical role in encouraging the nation's schools to dramatically expand their roles, setting off the process of mission bloat that would expand over the next three decades. It also guaranteed the ascendancy of special interests in a new and increasingly Balkanized educational system. The most obvious consequence of the new priorities was the inrush of noneducational "specialists" into the schools to ply their trades. Throughout every level of education, school districts began to hire diagnosticians, social workers, psychologists, aides, and specialists in various fields of the social sciences. The courts and an activist federal government were increasingly intrusive into the business of the schools, creating mandates, and demanding new priorities. In 1974, the Supreme Court in *Lau* v. *Nichols* required local school districts to make special allowances for students who did not speak English, a decision that led to the rapid growth of bilingual education programs, which were, in turn zealously enforced by the U.S. Office for Civil Rights. In 1975, Congress passed the Rehabilitation Act and Education for All Handicapped Children, which required schools to provide free and appropriate education to all children deemed to be disabled. The courts also drastically expanded student rights at the expense of the schools' ability to maintain discipline. In the 1969 case, *Tinker* v. *Desmoies*, the Supreme Court declared: "students [do not] shed their constitutional rights at the classroom door," a phrase that proved to be, as Gilbert Sewall later noted, "as powerful— and potentially destructive—as a lightning bolt." The ruling not only undermined the authority of the school and the ability of adults to keep order, but also "stimulated an adversarial relationship between apprehensive adults and empowered children." Most dramatically of all, the courts turned many urban schools into instruments for desegregation, ordering massive busing programs, which often generated heated opposition and led in some cases to virtual takeovers of some districts by federal judges.

Throughout the 1960s and 1970s, waves of successive fads would sweep over the classroom, from the New Math to the Open School. As authority weakened, grades inflated and requirements were scaled back. Even so, the schools came under fire from educational radicals, who did not think the fads went far enough and who now found an enthusiastic audience for their critiques. A. S. Neill's *Summerhill* became a huge best-seller, even though its description of the English "child-centered" school that had operated since 1924 contained little that was either original or fresh in the way of theory. In the 1960s its decidedly moldy Rousseauism was hailed as a revolutionary tract. Neill's book was required reading in at least 600 university courses by decade's end, and was selling at the pace of 200,000 copies a year. Critics like Gilbert Sewall attributed the book's popularity to its success in restating "in readable and self-righteous prose the old case that baby-knows-best." Neill believed that "all childhood activity should be voluntary," an idea that "fitted cozily with current cries for absolute freedom from swelling numbers of rebellious youth."[18]

But as the first glow of rehashed educationist idealism dimmed, many of the bold experiments—the new "relevant" curricula, the faculties who prided themselves on being "in-touch" with their students, the rap-sessions-as-teaching—turned out to be embarrassing busts. In *Crisis in the Classroom* Charles E. Silberman had described what he thought was the success story of Portland's John Adams High. When it opened in 1969, Adams was a sixties-style, state-of-the-art school. It was racially integrated, well funded, and featured the latest in "peer counseling," interdisciplinary courses, pass-fail grading, work experience programs, with a curriculum organized around problem solving. Silberman noted that the curriculum for the first week of classes was built around discussions of racial incidents that occurred on the opening day of school.

The experiment failed. By the mid-1970s, Sewall reported, Adams was "a laughingstock of trendy methods, besieged by violence and white flight." In 1980 Adams was closed because of falling enrollments. The principal reportedly moved on to high-level positions in the federal educational bureaucracy.[19] Unfortunately, the experience at Adams was not isolated. The 1970s witnessed an almost unprecedented decline in American education. Achievement in abstract problem solving and reasoning "plunged dramatically." While the ability to compute did not decline after 1973, the ability of students to think through problems dropped. Despite the renewed emphasis on "appreciation" and "comprehension," the ability of Americans to understand what they read was also declining. Analyses of the National Assessment of Educational Progress from 1970 to 1984 found that declines in basic abilities began to show up in the fifth and sixth grades, and continued through high school. In particular, the tests found that students' knowledge of the structure and function of government fell sharply; there was a steady decline in science achievement among seventeen-year-olds. Between 1969 and 1974, student writing deteriorated badly. There was also evidence that students were spending less time on their studies. By 1978, more than two thirds of high school seniors spent less than five hours a week doing homework; only six percent did more than ten hours a week.[20]

The gains of the earlier back-to-basics movement had been wiped out, but by the early 1980s the failures of the revived progressivism were so glaring that they were about to set off another round of reform and retrenchment. It too would fail.

MOLD

The scene is a school board meeting of a semirural midwestern community. Parents have mobilized opposition to the new Outcome Based Education curriculum in the district and a junior high teacher has been designated to reassure them. She is neither shrill nor doctrinaire. In fact, she is every good teacher you ever had.

She assures the parents how much she cares about their children, and obviously means it. But she wants to set the record straight: She wants to teach her students more, not less, and all this talk about "dumbing down" the curriculum misses the point. Her goal, she says, is to try to teach "what is important for kids to know." That means ditching much of the traditional—useless—science curriculum, such as teaching "the names of the nine planets and how far they are from the sun," which she calls "facts that are not applied; facts that are not used."[1]

She explains that she and other junior high science teachers have diligently tried to determine what exactly is scientifically "important." To determine this, she says proudly, they consulted experts. In this case *high school science teachers.*

The real change, she says enthusiastically, is that from now on she and other teachers will approach science from a "whole learning" perspective. By this she means she will integrate other subjects into science. For example, teachers now "incorporate writing and reading into science." She appears to genuinely believe that is a remarkable innovation. (The work of Ptolemy, Descartes, and William James apparently doesn't count. They are, needless to say, also not part of her curriculum.)

"Education practices," she insists, "have to meet where we are going." The lights dim and she begins a slide presentation on where, apparently, we are going. She wants to show the parents children "doing things." Despite what they may have heard, the children aren't doing anything "kinky or weird."

Just dull and trivial.

She doesn't see it that way. She insists that the new hands-on science is exciting, enriched, packed with higher-order thinking skills. No longer do kids sit neatly in rows and have rote facts jammed into their heads; in her classrooms, the *children are doing science themselves.*

They grow mold.

In poster-board presentation after poster-board presentation students demonstrate: How We Grew Mold.

There was, teacher says, "a lot of communication and a lot of observation. We really emphasized the higher order thinking skills." What she meant, of course, was that they talked about mold, looked at mold, and compared mold. This is no mere rote mold. Not simply information about mold. This is *higher order* mold.

Of course, mold does have its illustrious place in the annals of science. But the teacher makes no mention of penicillin or the story of its remarkable discovery through mold. The emphasis here is on relevance. Reads one poster board: MOLDY PIZZA AND MOLD.

"We know how to grow it," she tells the parents. "We know how to avoid it." This, no doubt, is an example of how higher-order thinking skills can be applied in, say, the refrigerators of college dorms. For the teacher this "usefulness" is in obvious contrast to the frivolous and unnecessary study of—and this is her example—the solar system, the knowledge of which cannot be applied or *lived* as conveniently as the mastery of the properties of mold.

Contemporary educators are convinced, as were their fathers and grandfathers in progressive education, that the driving force behind education must be the interest of the child. It is an article of faith that kids can only be engaged in the study of science or history if it is made directly relevant and immediate to their own lives. But the same folks who talk so much about making learning "interesting" also imagine that mold is more likely to fire a child's imagination than space.

Outside of the classroom, youngsters are devoted fans of *Star Trek* and *Star Wars*; they understand the difference between impulse power and warp speed; they devour science fiction novels; video games beyond number presuppose intergalactic travel. There are no popular video games based on mold.

REFORM AND COUNTER-REFORM

CHAPTER 17

THE BLOB

During the last four decades, periodic efforts to reform American education have repeatedly fallen short or failed even when they have had overwhelming political and public support. To understand why, it is necessary to recognize the role of "The Blob," former Education Secretary William Bennett's term for the education establishment. When Arthur Bestor was describing the wasteland of American education in the early 1950s, he attributed the impetus for dumbing down the schools to an "interlocking directorate" of schools of education, local school administrators, and the cadres of officials, "experts," and bureaucrats who populated the state departments of public instruction and what was then the federal Office of Education.[1] Despite their different functions, they tended to be mutually supporting; the bureaucrats set certification requirements that guaranteed full classes for the professors of education, who in turn provided the staffs for local superintendents and principals. This helped explain the remarkable unanimity of opinion within educational circles. Celebration, rather than skepticism, seemed to be the norm among educationists.

To Bestor, this "monolithic resistance to criticism reveals the existence and influence of what can only be described as an educational partyline. . . . " But Bestor's "interlocking directorate" was a mere simulacrum of what The Blob would become over the next few decades. It is particularly notable that he did not include the National Education Association, which would become the chief enforcer of the party line and eventually would transform not merely the politics of education, but politics itself.

Rise of the Interests

Throughout the 1970s, the power of special interest groups in education grew far beyond anything Bestor might have imagined. As the power of local school officials was increasingly constrained by state and federal initiatives, groups like the NAACP Legal Defense and Education Fund, the Council for Exceptional Children, the National Association for Career Education, and the American Council on Sex Educators, Counselors and Therapists gained effective control over educational policy making in their own fields. Having found that legislators and educational bureaucrats at the state and federal levels were more agreeable than local elected officials, the various interest groups actively lobbied to shift more power to the more amenable government agencies. They also lobbied incessantly for ever-wider expansions of the missions of schools. Their success was reflected in the expanding bureaucracies of public education.

In 1960, classroom teachers made up nearly two-thirds of the full-time staff of American schools. By 1991, classroom teachers barely made up half of the full-time employees of American education; nonteaching staff had risen from 25.2 percent of the total to 46.7 percent in three decades. Between 1960 and 1984, local school districts increased their spending on administration and other nonteaching functions by 107 percent after inflation—a rate almost twice the increase in per pupil instructional expenses. During the same period, the proportion of money spent on teachers' salaries in elementary and secondary education fell from more than 56 percent to less than 41 percent.[2]

Bloating the bureaucracy of the schools skews the budgetary priorities of some districts in bizarre ways. In 1990, New York's troubled school system spent less than one dollar in three on classroom instruction. At the same time, the city's Board of Education had a staff of 4,000, which filled eight buildings. (In 1994, Chancellor Ramon Cortines admitted that the Board of Education had routinely understated the number of employees in its central office staff and suggested that the real number might have been double the 3,500 reported in past years.)[3] Translated into real terms, those numbers meant that a remarkable number of people were being added to the payrolls of public education, none of whom had anything to do with teaching children in the regular classroom. They were the guidance counselors, curriculum specialists, psychologists, deputy superintendents, assistant superintendents, assistant deputy superintendents, affirmative action officers, Chapter 1 coordinators, in-service trainers, facilitators, lobbyists, human growth specialists, and special education administrators, among a cast of tens of thousands. In Washington, D.C., the staff of the central administration more than doubled (up 103 percent) between 1979 and 1992, at a time when the number of students actually fell by 29 percent. Nor was the flight of dollars from the classroom limited to big cities. In Wisconsin, a 1989 study of 110 elementary schools found that only 33.5 percent of the spending reached the classroom.[4] A study by the Wisconsin Policy Research Institute found, for instance, that the Milwaukee Public Schools allotted each central office administrator $157 for books and magazines—in contrast to the $68 allocated per elementary pupil for supplies, materials, books, furniture, and equipment. In 1990, the value of the central office's furniture and equipment equalled the total combined value of the equipment and furniture in twenty-six elementary schools in the city.[5]

Despite all of this, educational bureaucrats have continued to relentlessly push for increases in the missions of the schools—expansions that would result in further escalation of noninstructional hiring and spending. In 1993, for example, Wisconsin's superintendent of public instruction, Herbert Grover, called for broadening "the definition of education to include a child's continuing intellectual, physical, emotional, and social development and well-being." His proposed budget called for putting elementary schools in the business of "full-time preschool child care, before- and after-school child care, parent training and family involvement in education, early childhood education programs and health, mental health and social services." In other documents, Grover fleshed out his vision. Henceforth, schools would offer "home visits to new parents," information services and referrals related to child health and nutrition," and "activities and materials designed to encourage self-esteem, skills and behavior that prevent sexual and other interpersonal violence."

As if they did not have enough on their plate, Grover wanted middle and high schools to enter into cooperative agreements to offer "health, mental health and social services, employment services, summer and part-time job development, drug and alcohol abuse counseling, human growth and development instruction and community education. . . . "[6] Why not also sell lottery tickets? Do windows? Shampoo rugs? Take passport photos? Feed my goldfish? Or talk to my plants? But I digress—which, I suppose is the point. Grover's agenda reflects the digressive sprawl in the role of the schools. The multiplying roles of American schools bred bureaucracies, which bred more bureaucracies, which in turn created new and highly motivated constituencies, which pressed for increases in staffing and spending. No organization, however, exerts as much raw clout over America's schools as the NEA.

Clout

The National Education Association occupies what may well be a unique place in society. It is at the same time a professional organization, a trade union, and a political powerhouse. The NEA is both educationism's chief ideologist and its bouncer. A measure of its unchallenged power within the educational establishment is that the NEA can be both critic and defender of the system at the same time. A prime architect of and apologist for the status quo, the NEA often claims a leading role in educational "reform" efforts. It can deny the existence of any educational crisis in nearly the same voice it insists on the urgent need for more money; it postures as defender of children, but can also demand that its members refuse to write letters of recommendation for high school seniors and can shut down whole districts in contract disputes. While occasionally assuming an adversarial posture to local school boards, it often controls those boards. Frequently, its positions are indistinguishable from those of state and federal departments of education.

In some states, the teachers union has become the functional equivalent of a political party, assuming many of the roles—candidate recruitment, fund-raising, phone-banks, polling, get-out-the-vote efforts—that were once handled by traditional party organizations. The result in many states is that the legislatures, no less than the educational bureaucracies, function as wholly owned subsidiaries of the teachers union.

The influence of the NEA extends back to the early years of the century, but until the 1960s, when it turned sharply toward activism, it remained remote from politics. In 1961, President John F. Kennedy opened the way for public employee unions by approving federal public sector unions; by 1965, closed union shops for teachers were becoming widespread; shortly thereafter, the NEA officially endorsed strikes by teachers. Despite its new militancy, the NEA has remained a uniquely privileged organization. It remains a "federally chartered corporation," a holdover from its days as a professional organization, which means that it is exempted from property taxes. No other union enjoys such status. The growth of the teachers union bucked the national trend toward de-unionization. In 1958, 35 percent of American workers in the private sector were unionized; by 1992, that had fallen to a mere 11 percent. The opposite, however, was true of public employee unionization, which grew from 12 percent of the public sector workforce in 1958 to 37 percent in 1992. By then, the NEA had 2.1 million members.[7]

Economist Leo Troy points out that the public employee unions differ fundamentally from their traditional private sector counterparts. Private sector unions primarily are concerned with economic issues, while public sector unions are concerned with political power and their ability to reallocate income toward their employers, the government. Unlike their declining private counterparts, the public employee unions were also in position to insulate themselves from competition. As critics Peter Brimelow and Leslie Spencer note, the NEA was in an exceptional position in that it was a "near-monopoly supplier to a government-enforced monopoly consumer."[8] And they were determined to keep it that way.

In 1972, NEA President Catherine Barrett was able to boast: "We are the biggest potential striking force in this country and we are determined to control the direction of education." NEA Executive Director Terry Herndon was even more ambitious when he declared six years later that: "We want leaders and staff with sufficient clout that they may roam the halls of Congress and collect votes to reorder the priorities of the United States of America." The NEA's biggest political score was the election of Jimmy Carter as president in 1976, with their active and enthusiastic support. In return, the NEA wanted Carter to give them a new federal Department of Education, which they assumed they would dominate. Even though one survey found that only about a third of teachers in the country thought a new department would "have a positive impact on public school quality," Congress deferred to the clout of the teachers' union. By a narrow 215 to 201 vote, the House approved the Carter/NEA legislation. The night before Carter signed the bill creating the new department, a leading NEA officials offered a toast: "Here's to the only union that owns its own Cabinet Department." Critic Gilbert Sewall remarked later that "By then the NEA's power brokerage had become a study in greed and hubris."[9]

With members in every congressional district in the country, the NEA emerged as a political force that no politician could afford to ignore. It evolved from a professional organization primarily concerned with educational issues into a political action organization with a sweeping brief to transform American society. In recent decades, the NEA has taken positions that assailed standardized tests as being "similar to narcotics" for "maiming" children, and endorsed a nuclear freeze, gay rights, statehood for Washington, D.C., the Equal Rights Amendment, and every Democratic presidential candidate since Carter. The NEA has denounced U.S. militarism as the "primary source of juvenile alienation and violence," and has come out squarely against conservative nominees for the Supreme Court and against efforts to hold schools and teachers more accountable for their performance.

As an organization, the NEA encourages the kind of ideological conformity usually associated with the political correctness of the higher reaches of the academy. In 1991, the NEA convention passed a resolution calling for more vigilance in protecting First Amendment rights while at the same meeting forbidding some delegates from displaying pro-life materials and barring the Boy Scouts from the convention's exhibit hall. All free speech, the NEA declared, should be protected; but some should be less protected than others.

But the NEA's passions are stirred most deeply by threats to its monopoly status. With militant consistency, the NEA opposes measures to shift power and responsibility over education to parents. *The Chronicle of Higher Education*, for example, reported that the NEA "has attacked parents' moves to gain more control, saying that they have gone overboard and that teachers cannot be effective under parental veto power." For the NEA, school choice poses a mortal threat to its power base. In 1993, the California Teacher's Association imposed a special $63 per teacher levy on its 225,000 members so it could wage an all-out fight against a school choice referendum on the ballot in the state. The year before, supporters of the choice measure charged that teachers union with actively sabotaging efforts to obtain pro-school-choice signatures by signing faked names and by offering cash to professional signature-gathering firms to refuse to assist the effort.[10] (Under the choice plan, parents would have been offered vouchers worth $2,600, which they could use at any private school they chose.) When the measure finally found its way on the ballot, the teachers union waged a well-financed and bitterly vitriolic campaign that succeeded in defeating the measure. The *Los Angeles Times* estimated that the teachers union spent more than $10 million to defeat the measure. In the city of Los Angeles union leaders rallied teachers to "fight this battle as if our lives depend upon it, because our livelihoods do." In a stem-winding speech to more than 700 union stewards, the union's president, Helen Bernstein, warned: "We must act as if we had only forty-six days to live. This is Armageddon. . . . Your schools must become a hotbed of [anti-referendum] activity. . . . The bottom line is you must get to the soul of every [teachers union] member."[11] That appears to have included a campaign against the measure during class time. Supporters of the choice measure charged that the union used school equipment to photocopy and distribute union attacks on school choice.[12]

The president of the California teachers union justified the questionable tactics used to derail the referendum by declaring: "There are some proposals that are so evil that they should never be presented to the voters. We do not believe, for example, that we should hold an election on 'empowering' the Ku Klux Klan. And we would not think it's 'undemocratic' to oppose voting on legalizing child prostitution." In their critique of the NEA in *Forbes*, Brimelow and Spencer remarked: "It takes a real zealot to compare those who oppose raises for schoolteachers with promoters of child prostitution. But that's what the NEA thinks about allowing you to choose your children's schools."[13]

Fear of Success

In Jersey City, New Jersey, the school district spent more than $9,200 a year per student, but still failed to provide anything remotely resembling a quality education. Only 40 percent of the city's high school students graduated, many of them with minimal skills. The schools were so awful that the state took control in 1989. With the existing bureaucracy of the system intact, the state was unable to make much improvement. But when the city elected an advocate of school choice as mayor in 1993—with the overwhelming support of the city's minority community—the state's teachers union put the fight against choice at the top of its list of "Battles to Come" and asked teachers to authorize additional payroll deductions to campaign against pro-choice legislative candidates. Jersey City's Mayor Bret Schundler was not dissuaded. "The teachers unions aren't afraid we'll fail," he said. "They're afraid we'll succeed and show that empowering parents instead of bureaucrats is the key to improving schools and weeding out poor teachers."[14]

It is important to note that the NEA does not always speak for its own members and the behavior of the teachers union should not be confused with the attitudes of individual teachers. Despite the union's adamant opposition to vouchers in Jersey City, for instance, the head of the city's organization of school principals reported that teachers who actually lived in the city itself supported the choice initiative. Indeed, despite the NEA's adamant opposition to merit pay for teachers, surveys have found that as many as 69 percent of public school teachers think that "paying teachers based on job performance in addition to seniority and level of education" would actually strengthen the teaching profession. Other studies found that a majority of teachers belonging to the NEA voted for Ronald Reagan in both 1980 and 1984, despite the NEA's endorsement of Democratic candidates.[15]

But as Brimelow and Spencer reported, the NEA is not set up simply to reflect the ideas and interests of its members. Because it is so "critically dependent on legal privileges and favorable public policy," the union has evolved into a "weird institutional mutant: part labor union, part insurance conglomerate (of all things), part self-perpetuating staff oligarchy," and part political party. Although there are 13,000 local affiliates, the NEA is a remarkably centralized organization; all of the members of the local affiliates automatically join and pay dues to the state union and the NEA. A 1993 estimate in *Forbes* placed the total annual take from members' dues to be $750 million.[16] In addition, the NEA apparently rakes in an additional $10 million a year from insurance premiums which its teacher-members pay for the union-marketed life insurance plan. On top of that, the NEA has entered into a tangled web of murky alliances with various other insurance carriers and vendors. In Michigan, for instance, the Michigan Education Special Services Association (MESSA) is a subsidiary of the Michigan Education Association (MEA). MESSA markets Blue Cross & Blue Shield health insurance to local school districts at a cost of $1,000 more per person that the state's own employee health plan. In 1993, the union subsidiary had a staff of more than 200 and $370 million in revenues.[17]

As the home base of many of the NEA's top officials, the Michigan union is a model for the exercise of political clout by the teachers union. An analysis of political campaign spending by the *Detroit Free Press* in 1993 found that "when it comes to spending—some would argue buying—power, one special interest, the Michigan Education Association, owns a sugar factory." The paper labeled the union "the unelected behemoth of Michigan politics." So powerful was the MEA in state politics that the *Free Press* concluded, "if the MEA doesn't own legislative votes, it isn't because the union hasn't tried to buy the election of the lawmakers who cast them." Most of the money went to Democratic candidates—in fact, in 1991–92, nearly a quarter of all the special interest money spent on Democratic candidates came from the teachers union. No other political action committee even came close to the MEA totals, including the onetime powerhouses of the United Auto Workers and the AFL-CIO. "While the other unions talk big," a Democratic insider told the paper, "the MEA backs it up with the dollars. In many respects they are the Democratic Party" in the legislature.

The MEA's executive director modestly tried to downplay the union's raw clout. "We're aware that we've become a major player," Beverly Wolkow told reporters. "We elect legislators that have philosophies similar to ours. . . . But we don't ask for absolute control."[18]

In Michigan, the union has used what control it does have to oppose charter schools, privatization of school functions, limits on tenure, and proposals to reform the state's draconian certification requirements. A 1992 study of more than 600 tenure cases in Michigan found that many districts in the state spent more than $100,000 to fire a single teacher and that the process usually dragged on for four years or more. In one case, a local district spent fourteen years trying to fire an incompetent teacher.[19] Although the union later joined in supporting reforms in the system, tenure remains a formidable barrier to accountability in Michigan.

Betraying the Teachers

Although all of this is done ostensibly to protect and benefit teachers, there are some former members who argue that the teachers union's success has come in some measure at the expense of the teachers themselves. Even though the Milwaukee teachers union professional staff made triple the salary of a teacher with seven years of experience, former teacher Michael Fischer charges that the union provided few services for the classroom teachers. "While the union was inept at helping create working conditions favorable to successful student achievement," Fischer later wrote, "there *was* an area where the union exhibited great strength: no teacher could be fired from the Milwaukee Public Schools, regardless of how incompetent." In the early 1990s, one study found that no teacher had been fired for incompetence in the last five years and every teacher who was eligible was granted tenure. Out of 2,000 teachers evaluated each year, only two or three in the entire city had received unsatisfactory evaluation. But throughout those years, working conditions had deteriorated and teacher pay had stagnated (even though overall spending had skyrocketed). When the public became disillusioned with the results the schools were producing for their tax dollars, blame focused not on the unions or administration, but on the teachers themselves, who had enjoyed relatively little of the largesse. "The union," Fischer charges, "has been instrumental in creating an environment where the following occurs: teachers receive little respect or professional regard, have miserable working conditions—conditions that clearly contribute to student failure—and receive a salary incapable of supporting a family, but cannot be fired. Are these not the conditions we would create if we *intentionally wanted* ineffective institutions?"[20]

In some districts, the combination of aggressive unionism and arcane tenure rules has made it virtually impossible to fire teachers short of their commission of a felony. In some cities, even a felony conviction isn't enough for a school district to get rid of a teacher. In New York City, a special education teacher who was arrested, convicted and sent to prison for trying to sell $7,000 worth of cocaine to undercover police officers in 1989 was not only able to keep his job, but continued to receive his full salary while he was in prison. Even after five years—and $185,000 spent on disciplinary hearings—New York's schools were unable to fire the convicted drug dealer, Jay Dubner, who was protected by tenure and the teachers union. The board's failed attempt to fire Dubner dramatically illustrated the Byzantine disciplinary process required to remove teachers—even those who were accused of the most extreme misconduct. In eight hearings spread out over ten months, Dubner's lawyer argued that his client had been unfairly dismissed and explained that Dubner was forced to sell drugs to support his own $300-a-day habit. In mid-1994, now out of prison, Dubner still had his job.

Despite the cost, complexity, and futility of the effort to fire Dubner, his case was not really all that unusual. In New York State, school districts spend an average of $194,520 to fully prosecute each case of teacher misconduct, a process that takes 476 days.[21] Not surprisingly, many districts simply choose to look the other way rather than descend into the Kafkaesque maze of tenure protections, litigation, and union agitation.

The NEA as Ideologist

As senior member of the educational establishment, the NEA also serves as its chief propagandist. Through hundreds of briefing papers, leaflets, publications, and newsletters, the union maintains a steady drumbeat of denial about the problems of public education, opposition to choice and accountability measures, and support for child-centered education "reforms." Often, it must execute an intricate balancing act: demanding more money and sweeping "restructuring" of schools while also insisting that reports of their problems are grossly exaggerated. In 1991, Gerald Bracey, a research analyst for the NEA, labeled reports of the decline of educational quality "the Big Lie" and attempted to debunk reports of declining test scores. Bracey reflected the NEA's general attitude toward school reform when he characterized the 1983 *Nation at Risk* report, which warned against the rising tide of educational mediocrity, as "a xenophobic screed."[22] As recently as 1994, the Wisconsin Education Association Council provided its members with an issue paper detailing ways to combat the "myths of public school failure."[23] The same union provided its members with detailed talking points to help them discredit studies that question the link between spending and achievement and encourage members to shift the blame for poor academic performance onto families and communities.

While it does not always endorse specific programs, the teachers union has tended to be among the most enthusiastic supporters of Outcome Based Education and its various manifestations. The Division for Professional Development and Training of Wisconsin's teachers union, for example, enthusiastically advances the idea that educators should adopt "constructivist" approaches to learning. In one flyer distributed to state teachers, the union pushes the idea that "The central theme of constructivism is that each human being must inevitably develop or construct meaning. Learning is not a matter of merely reading, listening and repeating what others say is true. Each of us must 'make meaning' or make sense of our own world." In effect, this is a low-budget form of the deconstructionism so popular in higher education. With those various post-structuralist theories, "constructivism" shares the belief that knowledge is "problematic, emergent," and probably unknowable. As advanced by the teachers union, the new theories dictate that "understanding rather than coverage is a central principle" in the new regime, which demands new forms of "authentic assessment"—not surprisingly, such assessments do not include objective or standardized tests that might hold students and teachers alike accountable for their performance. In fact, the Wisconsin union insists that "schools must encourage teacher experimentation by suspending threatening evaluative processes (for teachers and students) over the short term."[24] In other words, let us experiment, but don't hold us responsible for whether or not it works. Interestingly, no matter what the theory of the moment might be, educationists almost invariably end up with the demand that they be relieved of "threatening evaluative processes" and, indeed, of accountability of any sort.

The NEA also maintains a tight hold on American schools by controlling the portals of admission. The union works closely (some would say incestuously) with teacher's colleges to maintain a professional monopoly on entrance to the teaching profession. What Bestor called the "interlocking directorate" is dramatically illustrated by the National Council for Accreditation of Teacher Education (NCATE), the body that accredits about 500 of the nation's 1,200 schools of education. Although state governments certify individual teachers, they tend to mirror the standards handed down by NCATE. The accrediting body was officially formed in 1954, when the American Association of Colleges for Teacher Education joined with the National Education Association, the National School Boards Association, the Council of Chief State School Officers, and the National Association of State Directors of Teacher Education and Certification to form NCATE.[25] The NEA has always loomed large in this gathering of educrats. In 1992, NCATE's board chairman was Keith Geiger, the president of the NEA.

In a detailed critique of teacher education in the United States, Donna H. Kerr, of Princeton's Institute for Advanced Study, described the accrediting organization as a model of the educational Blob as a whole. She concluded that, given its makeup, "NCATE and its standards can hardly help but function as a vehicle for special interest groups to register officially their concerns and to institutionalize their claims." This was because the agency itself had "evolved as a compromise of special interests." Because those interests were specifically guaranteed input into the process of formulating standards, the teacher education programs crafted in NCATE's image "can hardly help but emerge as patchwork rather than integral wholes from anyone's point of view, especially not a student's."[26] Given its vested interest in the status quo, the groups represented in NCATE together represented the strongest opposition to efforts to reform teacher education.

The relationship among the teachers union, teachers' colleges, and bureaucracies is symbiotic. Union officials push for additional salary and benefits for teachers who do course work beyond their bachelor's degrees, assuring the schools of education of a continuing supply of warm, tuition-paying bodies. In turn, the educationists in the ed schools tend to be loyal supporters of the NEA agenda, while state educational bureaucrats maintain tight restrictions on requirements for teachers that make sure that educated specialists without degrees from teachers' colleges or union cards are not permitted to teach in public school classrooms.

Reform and Counterreform

As evidence mounted during the 1970s and early 1980s that the performance of American students was falling, the educational establishment formed a solid phalanx against the burgeoning back-to-basics movement and other reform efforts. The various components of the bloc bitterly opposed state legislation that demanded greater accountability for student performance and turned a cold eye on suggestions that the priorities of the schools needed to be re-evaluated. Even as test scores slumped, educationists lashed out at critics, questioning their intelligence, morals, and sound judgment. Throughout the decline of the 1970s, Gilbert Sewall later wrote, the education establishment "acted as though its innovations and activities should be regarded as doctrine beyond debate. It has conducted public *auto-da-fé* (at convention and conferences) in which heretics feared for their careers." Faced with unrest among parents, taxpayers, and legislators, the educrats "snubbed grassroots sentiment with astonishing arrogance. . . . In the face of electoral criticism it has reacted with petulance and contempt."[27]

A revealing episode occurred in April 1977, when forty prominent educationists—bureaucrats, curriculum specialists, university professors, and assorted establishment figures—gathered to consider the state of American education and the condition of the "basics." But after meeting for three days, the educrats concluded their conference by flatly denying that they had *ever* abandoned basic academics, and as proof, they restated their support for the Cardinal Principles of 1918. The basic job of the schools, they declared with insouciant arrogance, was teaching health and physical fitness, social and civic responsibility, creativity, use of leisure, humaneness, and positive self-concept.

"This was an astonishing end run around the issue at hand," Sewall later wrote. "According to the ... participants, *what the schools were already doing was the very essence of the basics.* Here there was no affirmation of scholarship, no case for standards for excellence, no admission of wrong directions, no desire to streamline school operations. There was no celebration of cognition, ratiocination, thinking. There were, instead, the same tired bromides, more whitewash, more self-deception, more evidence of programmatic bankruptcy in education's reigning elites."[28]

By 1983, however, the establishment's stonewalling was no longer sufficient to distract the public from the increasingly obvious signs of educational decay. Achievement tests had fallen steadily for two decades and were lower than when Sputnik was launched in the late 1950s; national assessments showed that nearly 40 percent of seventeen-year-olds could not draw inferences from written materials; four fifths were unable to write a persuasive essay; two thirds were unable to solve mathematical problems with multiple steps. There was widespread evidence that the curriculum of elementary and secondary education had fallen apart. Many schools were offering as much credit for courses in drivers education as in history or biology. Less than a third of high school graduates took courses in intermediate algebra; only 6 percent of students completed calculus. Only a third of the nation's high schools offered physics classes taught by qualified instructors. In the brief five-year period between 1975 and 1980, public four-year colleges were forced to increase their courses in remedial mathematics by 72 percent. By the early 1980s, despite dramatic inflation in grades, two thirds of high school seniors reported they spent less than an hour a night on homework.[29]

Even so, few observers expected that much of anything would result from the sixty-five-page report of the eighteen-member National Commission on Excellence in Education. But its stark language, warning of "a rising tide of mediocrity that threatens our very future as a nation and as a people," launched a massive reform effort that touched virtually every district in the country. The states were especially active: Thirty-nine states created some form of teacher evaluation, while forty-seven states beefed up their testing of students. Forty-two states toughened their high school graduation requirements. Teachers' salaries were dramatically increased—in the next ten years, the average teacher's pay rose 22 percent faster than the cost of living. Spending per student rose by more than 90 percent—more than double the rate of inflation. The reforms of the 1980s had some notable successes; they slowed (at least for a time) the decline in SAT scores. By the early 1990s, more students were taking tougher courses,

CHAPTER 18

OUTCOME BASED EDUCATION

Diane Spoehr wanted to be a supportive parent. She was involved in her children's education and even worked as a volunteer at Eastside Elementary School in her community of Sun Prairie, Wisconsin. Using slogans such as "All Students Can Learn" (an idea that Diane Spoehr liked), Eastside had implemented a new philosophy of education called Outcome Based Education—which insists that students be given as much time as they need (or want) to learn the subject matter. In her daughter's fourth-grade class, Spoehr found that every time a project or a report came due in language, math, social studies, or science, half to two thirds of the class did not have the work done. Even so, there was no penalty or loss of credit for the late assignments.

In Outcome Based Education, she was told, no student ever fails. Every student must be given as much time as needed to meet the outcome goals. That also meant that if sloppy, incomplete, or poorly done assignments were handed in, students were not graded down, because they could *always* be redone. In practice, that meant that the only thing students had to do was keep up with the lowest achiever in the class, because outcome based classrooms did not move on until *all* students met the goal. The students, not the teacher, set the pace.

Spoehr found that half of the fourth graders at Eastside could not tell time or count change. But there was no sense of urgency in correcting the situation. Students were allowed to take tests over and over again until they got a passing grade. As a result, students as Eastside were three and a half months behind students in the same grade at private schools in the area. If her children's school seemed uninterested in academic achievement, Diane Spoehr found the school remarkably interested in her children's attitudes and *feelings*.

First graders, for example, were told that "getting the correct answer in math is not as important as explaining how you solve the problem," but were constantly writing papers with titles like "How Do You Feel About Work in (insert subject)."

Fourth-grade students spent an entire unit (four to five weeks) studying Wisconsin's Indians. But at the end, there was no test. The teacher explained, "There was too much material to test and, anyway, the main reason for this unit is to be sure the students develop the proper attitudes toward Indians." The new philosophy also was reflected in the school's new grading system. Starting with first graders, students no longer receive As, Bs, and Cs on their report cards. Instead, they are given "C," "S," or "N."

"C" stands for "consistently," "S" for "sometimes," "N" for "Not Yet."

"These grades," Mrs. Spoehr pointed out, "could not be more ambiguous. They mean nothing. Does 'sometimes' mean twice a day, once a week, three times a month? Is 'not yet' implying that this is an expected goal this quarter, or have we not been introduced to this, or is the teacher frustrated beyond reason with a child's refusal to try and 'not yet' doing anything? 'Not yet' could mean any of these things. These 'report cards' did not report anything." The lessons the children were learning, she concluded, were "procrastination, the ability to do any quality work without consequences, lack of responsibility, and the acceptance of mediocrity."[1]

■

Cheri Yecke was the 1988 Stafford County (Virginia) Teacher of the Year and in 1991 she was a finalist for the Agnes Meyer Outstanding Teacher Award sponsored by the *Washington Post*. After her family relocated, her daughter, Tiffany, was enrolled in schools that had begun implementing Outcome Based Education. A seventh grader, Tiffany had been an eager student, but shortly after she started at her new school, she began to beg to stay home.

"The work was far too easy," Cheri Yecke recalls, "but what was worse was that any display of intelligence was ridiculed in a cruel and demeaning way by many of the other students. Hard work and self-discipline are looked down upon, and status is often achieved by non-performance. The prevailing attitude among many students is 'Why study? They can't fail me so who cares?' What sort of work ethic is this producing in these children? No one fails, regardless of how little they do. Instead, they receive 'incompletes,' which can be made up at any time. The kids have the system figured out. When there is a football game or show on TV the night before a test, a common comment is: 'Why study? I'll just take the test and fail it. I can always take the retest later.'

"A natural consequence of such a system is that well-meaning and hard-working teachers have been forced to spend considerable amounts of class time reteaching material and giving retests. Obviously, this approach slows the pace of instruction, and as a result, some teachers have had to lower their standards and expectations in order to avoid having an overabundance of incompletes." But Yecke also noted that "good teachers have always practiced the most basic tenet of OBE, that all children can learn, although it was never called OBE at the time. Class time was used for instructional purposes, so that a challenging pace of instruction could be maintained and more material could be covered in depth." Students who needed help could get it after school.[2]

■

Oklahoma's superintendent of public schools assures an interviewer that the state is committed to excellence in education.[3] The new Outcome Based Education standards, she insists, are the most rigorous the state has ever had. But a public school teacher whose ten-year-old fifth grader is in a pilot program of the state's new Outcome Based Education explains to a television reporter that his son has done fifteen book reports in the last nine months, but that only one of them was written. The rest involved cutting out pictures and pasting them on cardboard. In math, the only new skill he learned in his entire year in fifth grade was "estimating decimals."[4]

In 1990, Oklahoma's state legislature, hoping to beef up its standards, passed a bill requiring that all teachers be trained in Outcome Based Education. The state's educational bureaucracy then developed several volumes of "learner outcomes," which included no fewer than 7,000 objectives.

For first graders, one objective was: "The student plans and monitors own reading progress." First graders are, of course, legendary for their planning abilities, which are second only to their notorious skills in "monitoring." The new "rigorous" outcomes also made short work of useless mathematical knowledge, like the multiplication tables. The goals for grades six to eight declare: "Many of the (computational) skills to which so much time has been devoted are obsolete skills which no one needs today." No one.

Another document handed down by bureaucratic enthusiasts of the new rigorous outcome based curricula was titled Priority Academic Student Skills (PASS). Designed for students in the fifth, eighth, and eleventh grades, it described what every Oklahoma student should know by the end of the year. State education officials wax rhapsodic about the new curriculum's commitment to excellence. But a high school history teacher says: "Looking at this outline, teaching strictly this outline, you could probably cover this in one month. To say this is all you need to know . . . is rather ridiculous."

A high school math teacher says: "The material is just not difficult enough for a bright or average child. You'll graduate kids with a minimal education." A veteran algebra teacher says that the state's PASS test requirements are two to three grades below what high school juniors should know. "This would in no way help show that a high school student is competent in math," he says bluntly, "because it doesn't really get into whether they can add, subtract, multiply, and divide." (These are, presumably, among the outdated skills they no longer need). His students, he says, would be "humiliated to the point of anger" if they were given a dumbed-down test of the sort outlined by the state educrats.[5]

But the harshest critics are the students themselves. In Minnesota's Apple Valley School District, high school students put out an underground newspaper opposing OBE. "It's not teaching real life," complains one student. "Granted, we are in high school. But we have to start dealing with reality. In the real world, you're not going to have the same situation twice." Another critic is high school senior Marisa Meisters, who wrote to a local newspaper that: "As a senior, at Arrowhead [High School, Wis.], I have seen the results of OBE firsthand. The bottom line is that it does not work.

"The main goal of OBE is to teach students how to work in groups. The students in each group who understand the concept are supposed to teach the others in the group. Instead of moving on to more challenging concepts, the faster students have to wait for the entire group to understand the concept before they move on. Another OBE goal is to allow students to master subjects by retaking any test until the student can pass. The result is that students do not study. Why should they when they can keep retaking the test? Eventually the student is bound to guess right."[6]

■

By the mid-1990s, no buzzword was more potent or controversial than Outcome Based Education, an idea touted by educators as a way to raise academic standards and make schools more accountable. Opponents were equally fervent in denouncing the same reforms as evidence of dumbing down American education and expanding the role of schools into the areas of student values and attitudes at the expense of learning. The two sides could not describe OBE more differently; indeed, the debates—in states such as Pennsylvania, Virginia, Washington, Colorado, Wisconsin, Minnesota, Kentucky, and Connecticut—often seem to take place across an abyss of mutual misunderstanding.[7]

The politics of OBE are anything but simple. OBE programs are bitterly opposed by some conservative parent groups, but have been widely embraced by moderate and conservative business leaders. On the other hand, OBE (under a variety of different names) is championed by the education establishment (and is de rigueur at teachers colleges), but it is opposed by one of the nation's largest teachers unions, the American Federation of Teachers. (Perhaps reflecting the confusion, Pennsylvania's AFT chapter began one letter opposing the state's OBE plan by declaring: "We are not now, and never have been, right wing kooks.")[8] In Connecticut, opposition to OBE took educationists by surprise because it came primarily not from fundamentalists, but from the state's affluent suburbs. In its account of the dispute, the *New York Times* described Outcome

Based Education as "a movement to improve the public schools that has gained a rare consensus among Presidents, governors, business leaders and educators. . . ." The paper quoted a prominent educator who sniffed that OBE was a movement "led by all the relevant forces in the country. . . ." and marveled at the temerity of parents who would seek to thwart such an impressive display of unanimity. Critics, however, saw the issue very differently. One member of the Greenwich, Connecticut, PTA complained that "It's not a program that improves education; it's a program that rounds out education with all sorts of social goals. And it hurts a lot of children it's designed to help."[9]

Among the more unconventional (and scathing) critics of the new educational fashions was British comedienne and actress Tracey Ullman, who cited OBE as one of the reasons she chose to move her family back to England. "Mabel, my seven-year-old daughter, really needed to get some old fashioned British schooling. Some discipline. Some intolerance and indifference from her teachers," she explained to an interviewer. She was unimpressed with the educational establishment's enthusiasm for the new approach. "In California everything is s-o-o-o touchy feeling. They are into this silly outcome based education where it doesn't matter if she knew HOW to spell her name as long as she knew WHO she was. And it didn't matter if she KNEW that two plus two was four as long as she had enough self-confidence to ASK how to get 'to the conclusion of the problem.' What a crock! She was going to end up as dumb as a mudflap. Had to get her out."[10]

Part of the problem is that different people mean different things when they talk about Outcome Based Education. Adding to the confusion, some districts apparently have adopted OBE techniques but deny having done so when parents and/or reporters make inquiries. School administrators who are understandably reluctant to venture into such treacherous waters often downplay, deny, or evade the philosophical underpinnings of the reforms they advocate. In some communities where OBE has encountered strong opposition, educationists have adopted the strategy of simply renaming it (as, for example, Performance Based Education)—a ruse that has done little to enhance their own credibility or build trust among parents. Outcome Based Education is "a chameleon," one parent-activist in Minnesota says. "It's so elusive, it's hard to sink one's teeth into." Even those who agree that education should be judged by student outcomes differ on what outcomes should be measured and how they should be measured. But lost in the fog of jargon that surrounds OBE are radical differences over the role of schools in society.

A Semantic Hijacking

Ironically, "outcomes" were first raised to prominence by leaders of the conservative educational reform movement of the 1980s. Championed by

Chester E. Finn Jr. among others, reformers argued that the obsession with inputs (dollars spent, books bought, staff hired) focused on the wrong end of the educational pipeline. Reformers insisted that schools could be made more effective and accountable by shifting emphasis to outcomes (what children actually learned). Finn's emphasis on outcomes was designed explicitly to make schools more accountable by creating specific and verifiable educational objectives in subjects like math, science, history, geography, and English. In retrospect, the intellectual debate over accountability was won by the conservatives. Indeed, conservatives were so successful in advancing their case that the term "outcomes" has become a virtually irresistible sales tool for academic reform.

The irony is that, in practice, the educational philosophies known as Outcome Based Education have little if anything in common with those original goals. To the contrary, OBE—with its hostility to competition, traditional measures of progress, and to academic disciplines in general—can more accurately be described as part of a counterreformation, a reaction against those attempts to make schools more accountable and effective. The OBE being sold to schools represents, in effect, a semantic hijacking.

"The conservative education reform of the 1980s wanted to focus on outcomes (i.e., knowledge gained) instead of inputs (i.e., dollars spent)," notes former Education Secretary William Bennett. "The aim was to ensure greater accountability. *What the education establishment has done is to appropriate the term but change the intent.*" (emphasis added) Central to this semantic hijacking is OBE's shift of outcomes from cognitive knowledge to goals centering on values, beliefs, attitudes, and feelings. As an example of a rigorous cognitive outcome (the sort the original reformers had in mind), Bennett cites the Advanced Placement Examinations, which give students credits for courses based on their knowledge and proficiency in a subject area, rather than on their accumulated "seat-time" in a classroom.

In contrast, OBE programs are less interested in whether students know the origins of the Civil War or the author of *The Tempest* than whether students have met such outcomes as "establishing priorities to balance multiple life roles" (a goal in Pennsylvania) or "positive self-concept" (a goal in Kentucky). Where the original reformers aimed at accountability, OBE makes it difficult if not impossible to objectively measure and compare educational progress. In large part, this is because instead of clearly stated, verifiable outcomes, OBE goals are often diffuse, fuzzy, and ill-defined—loaded with educationist jargon like "holistic learning," "whole-child development," and "interpersonal competencies."

Where original reformers emphasized schools that work, OBE is experimental. Despite the enthusiasm of educationists and policymakers for OBE, researchers from the University of Minnesota concluded that "research documenting its effects is fairly rare." At the state level, it was difficult to find any documentation of whether OBE worked or not and the information that was available was largely subjective.[11] Professor Jean King of the University of Minnesota's College of Education describes support for the implementation of OBE as being "almost like a religion— that you believe in this and if you believe in it hard enough, it will be true." And finally, where the original reformers saw an emphasis on outcomes as a way to return to educational basics, OBE has become, in Bennett's words, "a Trojan Horse for social engineering, an elementary and secondary school version of the kind of 'politically correct' thinking that has infected our colleges and universities."

Goals from Hell

By definition, Outcome Based Education is about outcomes. Almost invariably, however, those outcomes are nebulous and framed in the obscure jargon that seems endemic to OBE. One of Minnesota's original outcome goals called for the "Integration of physical, emotional, and spiritual wellness." Kentucky's state educational goals include such "valued outcomes" as "Listening," which officials defined as "students construct meaning from messages communicated in a variety of ways for a variety of purposes through listening." This was distinguished from "Observing," which they defined as "students construct meanings from messages communicated in a variety of ways for a variety of purposes through observing."

Other goals included: "Interpersonal Relationships," in which "Students observe, analyze, and interpret human behaviors to acquire a better understanding of self, others, and human relationships;" "Consumerism": "Students demonstrate effective decision-making and evaluate consumer skills"; "Mental and Emotional Wellness": "Students demonstrate positive strategies for achieving and maintaining mental and emotional wellness;" "Positive self-concept": "Students demonstrate positive growth in self-concept through appropriate tasks or projects"; "Adaptability and Flexibility": "Students demonstrate the ability to be adaptable and flexible though appropriate task or projects"; "Multicultural and World View": "Students demonstrate an understanding of, appreciation of, and sensitivity to a multicultural and world view"; and "Ethical view": "Students demonstrate the ability to make decisions based on ethical values."[12]

Obvious questions remain unanswered here: Whose ethical values will be used to establish the acceptable outcomes? Will any size fit? How will they be measured? How will schools determine whether a student has met its goals for "Interpersonal skills," or "Consistent, Responsive and Caring Behavior," or "Open Mind to Alternative Perspectives." And what will they do if students fall short of these mandated "outcomes"?

In developing "outcomes," academic areas are not neglected but they often bear only a passing resemblance to traditional fields of study. Geography is transformed into "Relationship of Geography to Human Activity," in which "Students recognize the geographic interaction between people and their surroundings in order to make decisions and take actions that reflect responsibility for the environment." (Note that this does not actually include knowing something so mundane as what countries border the United States.) Similarly, the "aesthetic" goal, in which "Students appreciate creativity and the value of the arts and the humanities," could conceivably be achieved without students having read a classic work of literature or seeing a masterpiece of art.

Pennsylvania was something of a trailblazer in the area of establishing "goals" for outcome based educational programs. Officials there were so enthusiastic that they embraced fifty-one separate "learning outcomes," of which the vast majority concerned values, feelings, or attitudes. One "outcome" defined as a base goal in the Pennsylvania curriculum was that "all students understand and appreciate their worth as unique and capable individuals and exhibit self-esteem." It did not describe how self-esteem would be exhibited or measured. Other learning outcomes included:

- All students develop interpersonal communication, decision making, coping, and evaluation skills and apply them to personal, family and community living.
- All students relate in writing, speech or other media, the history and nature of various forms of prejudice to current problems facing communities and nations, including the United States.
- All students make environmentally sound decisions in their personal and civic lives.[13]

Once again, it was not clear how the schools would keep tabs on environmental decisions made in students' private lives or how they would remediate environmentally incorrect behaviors.

In Milwaukee, where the average grade point average of high school students hovers around a D, the district's Department of Curriculum and Instruction developed ten "goals and performance indicators" for students. The number one "goal and indicator" for the Milwaukee Public Schools (MPS) did not deal with math, reading, or even with a readiness to work. Instead, Goal One read: "Students will project anti-racist, anti-biased attitudes through their participation in a multi-lingual, multi-ethnic, culturally diverse curriculum." (Note: students *will* project the requisite attitudes. Not *study*, or *understand*, or even *learn about*. They will *project* the mandated attitudes. What happens if they don't?)

The second goal related to the arts. The third goal insisted that: "Students will demonstrate positive attitudes towards life, living, and learning through an understanding and respect of self and others." (We can think of this as the Don't Worry, Be Happy Goal.) It is not until Goal Seven that anything as mundane as math is suggested and not until the eighth goal that the MPS bureaucrats get around to teaching youngsters to write. This is how the MPS educrats put it: "Students will communicate knowledge, ideas, thoughts, feeling, concepts, opinions, and needs effectively and creatively using varied modes of expression." And presumably use as many words as possible in doing so. Other goals include: "Students will learn strategies to cope with the challenges of daily living and will establish practices which promote health, fitness and safety"; and "Students will set short and long-term goals, will develop an awareness of career opportunities, and will be motivated to actualize their potential."[14]

The suspicions that OBE might be a stalking-horse for politically correct social engineering are fueled by its penchant for setting "outcomes" that relate to social, cultural, and political issues. This is not to suggest that all OBE programs have a hidden political agenda. But its authors do seem to have a far more expansive view of the role of schools than more traditional educators ever envisioned. Albert Mammary, for example, writes: "We believe that if students don't get love at home, they should get it in schools. If they don't get caring at home, they should get it in schools. If they don't belong and aren't connected at home, they should get it in schools. If they don't get food and clothing at home, they should also get that in schools."[15] This would seem to suggest that schools not only become centers of social work and welfare, but also substitute families. Defenders of OBE scoff at charges that the new curricula involve social engineering; and they are right to the extent that many programs bear little resemblance to the grandiose visions set out by Messrs. Mammary and William Spady, the director of the highly influential High Success Program on Outcome Based Education. But given the vagueness of the jargon-laden "outcomes" it is difficult for parents to know in advance what their students will learn and equally hard to measure success after the fact. Such confusion provides ample opportunity for abuse. Even so, the result is less likely to be indoctrination than a pervasive mediocrity.

Criticism of OBE's abstract academic goals is not limited to conservatives. Albert Shanker, president of the American Federation of Teachers, has joined the chorus of OBE critics who question its academic priorities. "OBE standards include academic outcomes," he notes, "but they are very few and so vague that they would be satisfied by almost any level of achievement, from top-notch to minimal; in other words, they are improvement over what we have now. Pennsylvania's writing outcome, for example, called for "All students [to] write for a variety of purposes including to narrate, inform, and persuade, in all subject areas." Remarked Shanker: "In an excellent school, this could mean a portfolio of short stories, several one-hundred-word essays, and numerous shorter ones. In a poor school, it could mean three short paragraphs loaded with misspellings.

"Vaguely worded outcomes like this will not send a message to students, teachers and parents about what is required of youngsters. Nor will they help bridge the enormous gap between schools where students are expected to achieve . . . and schools where anything goes." The very number of "learning outcomes" is significant. As Shanker notes, the large number of outcomes "sounds demanding, but it's the opposite." That is because teachers are already spread thin and will therefore have to pick and choose among the dozens of mandated "outcomes." It is not hard to predict what sort of choices they will make. Remarks Shanker, "It's a lot easier to schmooze with kids about 'life roles' than to make sure they can do geometry theorems or read *Macbeth*. In an educational version of Gresham's law, the fluffy will drive out the solid and worthwhile."[16]

Mastery Learning

While Outcome Based Education has a long and checkered ancestry, its immediate predecessor was "Mastery Learning," Benajmin Bloom's theory that some of the lessons of successful one-on-one tutoring could be transferred to education as a whole. Bloom argued (as OBE advocates do) that under the right conditions, all children can learn. They simply had to be given the time and attention. In Mastery Learning, students were tested and retested until they reached "mastery" of the goal, whatever it was. If they failed the test, they received remediation, often from the students who had already passed the test. On paper, Bloom's theory seemed unobjectionable. Richard Mitchell characterized Bloom's "discovery" this way: "First teach someone something—some 'material,' maybe. Next give him a test. If he passed, good; go on to something else. If he flunks, start over. Keep at it. Stunning. What's next?"[17]

In practice, it wasn't so simple. The emphasis on tutoring worked well if a student and teacher worked one-on-one. But in a class of thirty, it was more complicated, especially if students in the class had widely varying abilities. In theory, every child moved at his or her own pace, but in reality, the average teacher was faced with the task of teaching at a dozen or more different levels simultaneously. Bright students could not simply be allowed to be moved on until the slower students had mastered the subject, so they had to be recruited as "peer tutors" for students who needed help. Those that were not tutoring were supposed to be given "enrichment activities." But there was no set time limit for the class as a whole to move on. In theory, Mastery Learning abolished the clock and the calendar. Limiting the time for a given unit of material would discriminate against slow students, advocates argued, because it would keep slow students from learning thoroughly.

In fairness to Bloom, there are some indications that Mastery Learning did help some slower students by giving them more time and attention. But the system also created a "Robin Hood Effect," by taking from the brighter students to give to the slower.[18] Mastery Learning classrooms did not, however, turn out to be the egalitarian paradise of cooperative and mutual support that its advocates had hoped. Inevitably, students were grouped and classified by whether and when they had "mastered" the goal—and everyone in the classroom knew who was learning quickly and who was holding up the show. As more and more students passed the tests and retests, the number of students who were being remediated got smaller and smaller and their status as the class laggards become more and more obvious. Educationists imagined that this environment would teach valuable lessons in interpersonal communication, cooperation, and tolerance. As one proponent gushed, brighter students who were pressed into service as tutors were being given an opportunity to "gain personal interaction experiences which are not usually available in more strictly individualized programs."[19]

Somehow, the bright students failed to appreciate the opportunity as much as the educationists had hoped. Mastery Learning failed to produce the improvements Bloom had claimed and it was ultimately discarded. In practice it had been unworkable because it had expected far too much of both teacher and students. Teachers were unable to individualize instruction in large classes and students did not respond to the elimination of grades and the use of group learning to motivate themselves or teach themselves. But the flaw of Mastery Learning was more fundamental: By focusing all of the efforts of the classroom on the slowest students, Mastery Learning inevitably moved toward lowest common denominator standards. In practice, the doctrine that every child must succeed meant that success had to be defined and redefined lower and lower lest the teacher and the system burn themselves out. A teacher who set goals too high, but who was required to make sure all students succeeded, faced the prospect of an eternity spent on a single subject. It turned out to be much easier to set standards that all children *would* meet in reasonably short period of time. High expectations were the first casualty; standards quickly followed.

From Mastery to OBE

At first blush, Outcome Based Education bears an uncanny resemblance to Mastery Learning. This is hardly surprising, since some of the early architects of OBE worked closely with Bloom and were heavily influenced by his ideas. But when William Spady, the director of the High Success Program on Outcome-Based Education and the godfather of the OBE movement, convened a meeting of forty-two educationists in January 1980 to form the "Network for Outcome-Based Schools" he "pleaded" (his word) with the group not to use the words "mastery learning" in the group's name. His aversion to the terminology was not, however, a matter of substantive disagreement; in fact, Spady saw nothing wrong at all with the underlying philosophy of Mastery Learning. It was simply a matter of public relations. As he later explained, "the word 'mastery' had been destroyed through poor implementation."[20] Spady never acknowledged that Mastery Learning failed precisely *because* the theory did not translate into the reality of the classroom.

But critics who see OBE merely as a repackaged version of the discredited Mastery Learning also miss the point somewhat. As it has emerged over the last decade and half, OBE is less a program than it is a grab bag of ideas long fashionable in educationist circles—from its emphasis on personality and value adjustment, its resurrection of the "child-centered" classroom of the 1920s, the "project method" of the 1930s, to its tendency to resist measures of accountability. At least in the beginning, however, it was a rhetorical tour de force. Governors and legislators who embraced "outcomes" often imagined they were talking about test scores of academic content, measurements of how much math, science, and history students had learned. Spady, however, meant no such thing.

Indeed, he is quite clear on this point: Asked to define "outcomes," Spady is at pains to disabuse anyone of the impression that he is talking about curriculum content, i.e., what will kids know? or what can they be tested on? "But," he explains, "outcomes are not content, they're performances."[21]

The educational system Spady envisions is "grounded on future-driven exit outcomes that will directly impact the lives of students in the future, *not on lesson and unit and course objectives. This means that content details will have to give way to the larger cognitive, technical, and interpersonal competencies needed in our complex, changing world.*" [emphasis added]

Exactly how "exit outcomes" will be divorced from "content details" is unclear. But it seems to mean that details of history (such as who won World War II) might be sacrificed in favor of material that will "directly impact" the lives of young people. Teaching "things," or specific knowledge, is thus downgraded in the service of what Spady vaguely describes as "larger . . . competencies." This appears to be educationese for saying that one need not know where England is as long as one has mastered "spatial" competencies; one need not know history as long as one has attained an interpersonally competent exit outcome.

Of course, Spady doesn't expect this to come all at once. He acknowledges that schools will have to muddle through for the time being with existing curriculum content, or what is left of it. Spady envisions a three-part process of transformation.

In the first stage, existing subject areas (science, math, history, English) "are taken as givens and are used to frame and define outcomes." In its infancy, OBE will be content to define outcomes in terms of math abilities, knowledge of history, etc. These are the terms on which OBE is usually sold to parents and school boards. This is, however, only the beginning as far as Spady is concerned.

In the second stage, which Spady calls "Transitional OBE," educrats create "a vehicle for separating curriculum content from intended outcomes *and for placing primacy on the latter.*" [emphasis added] In this stage, traditional curricular content is replaced by outcomes emphasizing Spady's "higher order competencies and orientations." As if to emphasize how separate these competencies are from the traditional content of the curriculum, Spady stresses that "these broad competencies are almost always *content neutral.*" [emphasis added] Indeed, he goes so far as to declare that: "Content simply becomes a vehicle through which [higher-order competencies] are developed and demonstrated."

By the third and final stage—what Spady calls "Transformational OBE"—the divorce between course content and the "exit outcomes" is complete and irreversible. Traditional curricular content has faded away altogether. In "Transformational OBE," Spady writes, "curriculum content is no longer the grounding and defining elements of outcomes."[22] Actual knowledge—the ability to write a coherent letter, add a column of numbers, know the century in which the Civil War took place—should not be allowed to crimp the style of the higher-order competencies. Predictably (and also conveniently), these competencies cannot be measured by tests or other verifiable, comparative measures. Indeed, Spady describes the student of the future as a sort of performance art—a work in progress.

Offering an example of what he has in mind, Spady told one interviewer that students might be required to design a bridge in lieu of being tested on math, English, and civics. Working in groups, the students would design strategies for the project. For English, they would write a report about the bridge. For math, they would calculate the measurements of the bridge. For civics, they would conduct an Environmental Impact Study. The end product, or "demonstration," would meet all of Spady's educational goals.[23]

But does it meet society's educational goals? It would, of course, if our goal was to create a society of bridge builders. But what if we want students who can not only build bridges, but also houses, and information highways, who can design jet engines, and probe the mysteries of DNA? The kids who design the bridges (or demonstrate their ability to design bridges, which may not quite be the same thing) may be able to do those things as well. But those more complex tasks require more than the bridge-demonstration—they require knowledge, the full grasp of the disciplines of higher mathematics, physics, and the properties of matter. It is that *knowledge* that provides them the power to extend their demonstrations to higher and higher and more complex levels. The student who can build a boat or plant trees knows how to build a boat and plant trees. He may know something about math, physics, and botany, but the demonstration does not tell us whether he also knows enough about mathematics to make the calculations required for making the next generation of boats, or enough knowledge of natural science to understand the complexities of a changing ecosystem.

Spady insists that it not important what the student knows, only what he can do. But what a student can *do* is a direct product of what he *knows*; it is the knowledge that provides him with the power, not the artificial demonstration. Students, for example, may demonstrate folk dances of many lands, but do they understand anything about world history? They may dress up as Indians, but they do know anything about the history, culture, religion, and language of Indians? Do students who tattoo numbers on their arms really demonstrate meaningful knowledge of the Holocaust?

Rapidly changing technology and an ever-growing knowledge base are often cited as reasons to emphasize "thinking skills" rather than knowledge, since current knowledge shortly will be obsolete. The obsolescence of that knowledge means that a premium needs to be placed on intellectual adaptability. That is both a plausible and a persuasive argument, but it begs the question of just how best to go about ensuring adaptability. As is often the case, the best way of answering the question of what we will need in the future is to look to the past.

The last fifty years have seen perhaps the most rapid change in human history; the world of the late 1930s has been swept away by a tsunami of social, political, economic, and technological change. But let's imagine ourselves back in 1941, faced with designing a curriculum to prepare students for that future (our past). The first question to ask is whether students who were trained fifty years ago in the rigorous study of mathematics, science, literature, and history—as known and understood in the 1940s—were significantly disadvantaged or ill-prepared. Would they have been better off if they had instead been asked to "demonstrate" their knowledge of bridge building circa 1941? Were the students drilled in calculus, biology, and (the comparatively primitive, but still complex) physics of the time hindered from growing and adapting to technological change? Did required courses that emphasized the knowledge of history and literature impede their participation in, or understanding of, the social upheavals of the civil rights movement? If so, how do we account for Dr. Martin Luther King Jr.? Did an education in the fundamentals of economics prove to be irrelevant, or did it provide a basis to understand and adapt to changing economic conditions? Would students of the 1940s have been better off "demonstrating" that they knew how to run the school store? Or would they have been better prepared for the changing world by being grounded in the basic economic principles of supply and demand?

While Spady downplays such "knowledge," it is, in fact, precisely such knowledge that provides adaptability; it is only the knowledgeable who learn how to be more knowledgeable. Rapid changes in knowledge don't change that. Mastery of higher mathematics makes it possible to move to even higher levels; a grasp of the fundamentals of matter lays the groundwork for the next step forward. Understanding the past shines a spotlight on the present and the future.

Both science and society likely will undergo dramatic transformations in the next half century and educators are right to stress the need to place a premium on the ability to learn how to learn. What they forget is that the best way of learning how to learn . . . is learning *something*, such as a discipline, by mastering its content and its protocols. It is impossible to learn how to learn about math without learning math. The same is true with history: It is futile to learn to "think historically" without knowing what happened.

Lip-Synching

There is also an element of intellectual fraud in the suggestion that actual knowledge can be replaced with requirements that students behave "as if" they had such knowledge. By emphasizing "demonstrations" and "behaviors," educationists insist that it is enough for students to do what scientists, historians, and other scholars do without actually having to have all of their knowledge, discipline, or skills. Educationists notice that scientists conduct experiments and demonstrate the product of their research. Of course, scientists bring to bear math, physics, and a knowledge the properties of matter, but since that knowledge is not the "outcome," educationists are willing to relegate the specific disciplines of math, physics, and the properties of matter to the back benches as long as the kids can *act like* scientists and conduct an experiment. Seen this way, the emphasis on demonstrating "behaviors" rather than knowledge is the educationist version of lip-synching—as long as it looks good it'll pass muster, but no real talent is required.

Consider, for example, the difference between educating a man for democracy on the one hand and educating a man for "democratic behaviors" on the other. The educationist might notice that men steeped in the knowledge of law and statesmanship behave in a certain way. But the educationist believes that we can skip the knowledge, the history, the statesmanship, and just focus on the way they behave and make *that* the outcome—which is then expected of *every student*. Educationists, for instance, might look on members of the Constitutional Convention and note that they worked together in conventions and congresses. Rather than requiring students to study the philosophical, economic, and historical background of the Founding, the educationist instead might have students engage in class projects in which they can exercise "collective thinking," a concept that would have been appalling to a Benjamin Franklin or a

George Mason. The students would probably not recognize this, since they have not been burdened with the "mere information" and remote facts of the actual Founding.[24]

Besides the element of make-believe at work here, there is also a healthy dose of farce. As Richard Mitchell notes, the difference between actually knowing a discipline and "acting as if" one knew it is the difference between being trained to play "Lady of Spain" on bicycle horns and actually knowing something about music. (Musicians, after all, have been known to play "Lady of Spain." Therefore, that is an expected behavior. Right? Or have we missed something?) The difference, of course, is the difference between the knowledge of something from the inside versus knowledge of something from the outside. Since most educationists have only the dimmest notions of what scientists or statesmen actually do, they are hardly in a good position to see what it is they might be missing. People who don't know physics are unlikely to appreciate the role of such knowledge in the experiment; they see only the product. Similarly, a person ignorant of the history and philosophies of democratic man can dismiss that history as "mere information" and insist that exercises in "collective thinking" are just as useful.

What's Wrong with Outcomes

All of this raises some troubling questions about the use of "outcomes" in education. Conservatives who championed outcomes in the 1980s now insist that Outcome Based Education represents a distortion of an idea that is still fundamentally sound. They argue that it is still preferable to judge schools on their educational outcomes rather than "inputs"—as long as those outcomes are rigorous and cognitive. Of course, all education is about outcomes at one level or another. But educational reformers at both ends of the spectrum seem to believe that it is possible to define education on the bases of enumerated goals and outcomes that become, in effect, the curriculum itself. But the hijacking of the term "outcomes" by the educationists represents more than simply a political coup, and conservatives are naive if they fail to see this or to recognize the fundamental and perhaps fatal flaw that is inherent in the focus on outcomes. Ultimately, it is an act of educational hubris, whether it is undertaken by the educationists or their conservative antagonists.

When schools define what they offer to students, they are being realistic about their capacities and their limits. When they define "outcomes," they are neither realistic nor cognizant of those limits. In a stunning display of hubris, the educationists claim to be able to define and prescribe the beliefs, values, attitudes, and behaviors of the educated man or woman. Not surprisingly, their vision is banality incarnate.

In sharp contrast, liberal education has always recognized that there are incalculable differences between individuals in capacity, interest, and talents, and that it is therefore necessary to approach the mystery of the human intellect with humility. The liberal arts assume that there will be as many "outcomes" from reading great literature, or history, or wrestling with science as there are students. If ten students read *Hamlet*, there are likely to be ten (or more) different responses at radically different levels of understanding, insight, and intuition, not all of them easily foreseeable, much less defineable. While it is possible to teach the play, it is beyond the reach of even the most gifted teacher to try to list all of the possible responses and unconscionably arrogant to try to master the mystery of the human mind's reaction by codifying them as acceptable "outcomes."

By trying to reduce this explosion of unpredictability, individuality, and idiosyncrasy to a list of designated outcomes, educationists often end up with a standard as trivial as "the appreciation of gender roles in Elizabethan plays." This is the unresolvable paradox of attempts to capture and define the necessary "outcomes" of a quality education. As many "goals" as they draw up, educationists fall far short of the countless possibilities. They end up producing endless lists and innumerable goals because they are chasing a will-o'-the-wisp.

However they are drawn up, the emphasis on student outcomes reverses the focus—and ultimately the responsibilities—of education. At one time, the role of the school was to provide students with the tools they would need later in life. It was up to the students to decide what use they would make of those tools. Educators were given the responsibility of providing children with the phonetic and grammatical tools they would need to be competent readers. Schools were charged with training students in mathematical proficiency, teaching them the basic principles of multiplication, division, algebra, and calculus. It was the function of liberal education to expose the young to the best that was written and thought, but it was left to the student to decide what he would make of those thoughts. His school may have provided the raw material in the form of great literature, but it was left to the student to work out what values, attitudes, and behaviors he would make out of it. The liberally educated man or woman was not asked to "project" or "demonstrate" certain behaviors—he or she was merely expected to *think*. Although the term is out of favor these days, these could all be characterized as educational "inputs," and they were the essential business of education.

Schools were expected to pass on certain elements of the culture to the young, including extending their historical memory; they were expected to ground the students firmly in the personalities, issues, and events of American history. In measuring the "outcome" of such lessons, it was considered sufficient if students had absorbed and could think about those events. But it was also pretty much left up to the student what he would think about those events. The school's job was not to shape those opinions, merely to provide the knowledge and intellectual skills. Having done that, its job was over. Some students, grounded in solid reading and writing skills, would go on to write annual reports, while others would write librettos. Those were all acceptable "outcomes," but they were also, ultimately, the students' responsibilities, not the schools'. The school had done its job when it had graduated students with well-stocked minds, who were culturally literate and well versed in the essential knowledge of the time, and equipped with the rhetorical, mathematical, scientific, and historical skills needed to be an educated citizen. In other words, teaching children "the basics" *was* the outcome.

This is what makes the entire debate about outcomes so slippery; by definition, all education is about outcomes. But the educationist focus on "outcomes" upends the meaning of education by substituting artificially created "goals" for the *means* to attain those goals. By definition, the "outcomes" become more important than the crucial issues of what shall be taught and how it shall be taught. One can read dozens of educationist "goal" statements without coming across a single reference to specific academic disciplines, much less the basic building blocks of "higher-order thinking skills" such as phonics, the memorization of the multiplication table, a solid grounding in scientific principles, or detailed historical knowledge. In practice, Outcome Based Education gives educationists permission to shirk what had been their responsibility—to pass on such knowledge—and to usurp the responsibilities and freedoms that once belonged to the student. Any reform movement that fails to ground itself firmly on what students need to be taught and refuses to define what educational inputs schools will provide is almost certainly doomed to fail.

OBE Reality Check

While many of the new state "goals" for improving education make impressive-sounding promises of increased rigor and accountability, they often fail to live up to their promising jargon. For example, in Missouri, state guidelines list goals and activities that might fulfill them. In one exercise, children would ostensibly "demonstrate" their mastery of the following outcomes: They would "Plan effective verbal and non-verbal communications for a variety of purposes and audiences, anticipating the impact of the message (Goal 2, Standard 1). Present ideas, opinions, and arguments in an organized and convincing way (Goal 2, Standard 4). Make decisions that are informed, reasoned and responsible (Goal 4, Standard 1)." And finally, the students would "Identify, analyze and evaluate events, issues and human actions, considering their effect upon individuals, society, and the environment throughout time (Goal 4, Standard 4)."

They would do this by conducting a trial of the wolf in the story "The Three Little Pigs."

Students are presented with two different versions of the "Three Little Pigs" story. "After reading the stories themselves, listening to them read, or hearing the tapes" (it apparently doesn't matter whether they can read the story, even though this is a language arts class), they then discuss the plot and the "feelings and viewpoints of the characters." The guidelines recommend that "the students through brainstorming and/or research" [N.B.: The research is optional] plan and produce the trial.

In the trial, children would take various roles (judge, jury, pig, wolf, policeman, etc.) and present evidence from both sides of the issue. The guidelines call for them to present arguments—orally or in writing (again, for the educrats, it doesn't seem to matter which)—as well as "creative punishments as an alternative to jail for the guilty party." Recommended activities—keep in mind this is a language arts class—include making masks and costumes, building houses with blocks or art materials, playing the game of pigs and wolf, and cooking "wolf" stew and/or tasting various pork products. They could also "research real facts about pigs and wolves" and read books about lawyers.

The standards don't say why, if the children can read books about real lawyers and learn real facts about pigs and wolves, they need to be playing with blocks? Or playing house with pork products? The answer is that the standards regard both reading the story and researching the facts as "optional." This casualness toward educational content runs throughout the guidelines. The educrats' standards say that students will need "Limited knowledge of what a 'trial' is and some knowledge of the appropriate vocabulary." *Limited.*

The point of the exercise is not to teach children the rules about the legal process, but only to give them enough information to give them the impression they are engaging in a trial. In other words, lip-synching.

The same guidelines recommend a project in which children fill out voter registration cards, vote in a mock election, and write letters of thanks to the county clerk. For such a modest undertaking, the educrats make decidedly immodest claims. Filling out the card, voting, and writing a single letter, Missouri's educrats claimed, would once again show that students knew how to "Identify, analyze and evaluate events, issues and human actions, considering their effect upon individuals, society, and the environment throughout time (Goal 4, Standard 4). Understand and apply the principles expressed in fundamental documents shaping the United States' constitutional democracy." This project would also demonstrate their ability to "Revise and adjust written oral, and non-verbal language use, style, tone, and structure to communicate with different people and within different situations (Goal 2, Standard 3)."

Missouri high school students also can demonstrate that they can "Make decisions that are informed, reasoned and responsible (Goal 4, Standard 1)." "Identify and analyze potential risks in daily living, and apply appropriate health and safety measures, procedures and practices (Goal 4, Standard 10)." And they can "Evaluate information, ideas, arguments, and products to determine patterns, relationships, perspectives, credibility, and cause and effect. Verify whether or not a solution addresses the problem to which it is applied (Goal 3, Standard 8)."

What do students actually do to achieve these goals? The Missouri guidelines call for them to "complete a personal stress assessment instrument" and perform biofeedback experiments by wearing biodots, observing the dots' color and monitoring their "mental and physical health at the time." The students compare their moods with the color on the biodot and keep a journal.[25]

GOALS 2000 AND THE COUNTERREFORMATION

Goals 2000, which seeks to create national educational "goals," is essentially a continuation of the educationist counterrevolution. The legislation, which was adopted and signed into law in 1994, creates new layers of educationist bureaucracy and power, including the nineteen-member National Education Standards and Improvement Council (NESIC), a National Education Goals Panel, the National Skill Standards Board, the National Educational Research Policy and Priorities Board, the National Library of Education, the National Occupational Information Coordination Committee, and the National Education Dissemination System.

Functioning as a sort of faux-national school board, the National Education Standards and Improvement Council will certify new "voluntary" national standards. The NESIC is explicitly set up to be dominated by establishment interests; the legislation requires that its membership include five professional educators, five education "experts," five representatives of advocacy groups, and five representatives of business, industry, and higher education. Although unelected—and dominated by the very people upon whom it is supposed to impose some accountability—the board will have sweeping powers over the nation's schools.

Even though the legislation is portrayed by educationists as focusing on highly publicized "goals," the law's most important element may be the creation of new national standards for spending levels, teacher salaries, and other so-called "inputs"—which are now euphemistically called "opportunity to learn standards." As one critic notes, those standards will be drawn up by educationists chosen by the secretary of education with the advice of NESIC and "will determine what financial, physical, and human resources must be available at every school in the nation."[1] Goals 2000 describes the new national standards as voluntary, but states are likely to abide by the new rules because they will be tied to federal education dollars. Beyond the direct regulation of local spending policies, the new guidelines also seem likely to encourage litigation to force states and localities to equalize their spending. At a meeting discussing the pending legislation, attorney Jonathan Wilson warned: "You can say that it's voluntary, but it won't be. I'm a lawyer . . . all I need from you to get me into court that I don't have now is [opportunity to learn] standards. Because I have got a state law that constitutionally says that you have got to provide an adequate education, and the thing that keeps me from going to court is I don't have a measure for what that is. You give it to me, and I'll get things required—not voluntary."[2] Warming to the prospects of the new federal standards, Wilson declared: "I see this as the lawyer's civil relief act of 1992. Just keep coming!"

Perhaps the greatest triumph of the educationists was their success in stymieing moves toward tougher measurements of a student's actual knowledge and performance. NESIC will have the power to certify state assessment programs. But the legislation specifically forbids states from using those tests as graduation requirements, as standards for promotions, or virtually anything else for at least five years. Where assessments of student performance exist, Goals 2000 guarantees they will be toothless. The legislation explicitly forbids states from testing student achievement until they can satisfy federal educrats that they have equalized their "opportunities to learn"—such as per pupil spending and teacher salaries. Unless states want to forego future federal aid, this provision effectively reverses the movement toward measuring student performance and holding educationists accountable.

Goal Bloat

Goals 2000 embraces many of the flaws of educationism and raises them to the level of national policy. Even at the local level, curricula designed by committees are notorious for their lack of focus and coherence. Usually, what emerges is a cobbled-together compromise among competing interest groups that have made sure that their own hobbyhorse is included in the "goals," without regard to whether it is consistent with the other goals, whether it makes any sense in the context in which it is placed, or whether the students will be able to make heads or tails of it. Goals 2000 takes the same process and writes it large.

In 1994, a thirty-eight-member panel of artists, educationists, and token business representatives who were charged with developing national standards for the arts came up with no fewer than eighty-two separate "goals" that they proposed to inflict on the schools. As *Education Week* noted, some educators were growing concerned that the standard-setting effort was creating so many goals "that schools will be unable to implement all of them." The panel's "achievement standards" for students in grades kindergarten through fourth grade included the requirement that the children: "With competence and confidence perform folk dances from various cultures." Students in grades five to eight would be expected to "Competently perform folk and/or classical dances from various cultures" and would also have to "describe similarities and differences in steps and movement styles." (*We're sorry, Mrs. van Gogh, but Vincent just doesn't seem to have a knack for dancing well with others.*) Other goals included having students "accurately describe the role of dance in at least two different cultures or time periods." Students in grades nine through twelve would be required to "Analyze how dance and dancers are portrayed in contemporary media." And so on, for more than six dozen separate measures of arts achievement.[3]

The Education Department also ran into problems in establishing standards for English and language arts. In March 1994 the department pulled its funding from the group that was supposed to develop the English standards because the group's proposed standards were so woolly that even the hardened educrats of the federal bureaucracy were offended. The first attempt at defining what every American student should learn in English, the department said, completely failed to "define what students should know and be able to do in the domains of language, literacy, and literature." Instead of specific measurements of literacy, the proposed goals were "vague and often read as opinions and platitudes." They were, in short, typical of many of the educationist efforts to define "outcomes."[4]

Even when standards were successfully developed, they raised questions about their realism. "I can call spirits from the vasty deep," Glendower boasted. "Why, so can I, or so can any man," came Hotspur's retort, "But will they come when you do call for them?" The same question seems appropriate for the ambitious and voluminous standards proposed for history. The proposed standards for world history, for example, ran to 313 pages. Even if the guidelines were flawless, the notion that they could be effectively implemented on a nationwide basis seems fanciful. As one University of Chicago professor noted, "It's an impossibly ambitious and rich curriculum they're putting before high school teachers and students." He did not have to mention that many of those teachers will not have degrees in history at all. What will they make of the dozens and dozens of standards on eras and cultures of which they are stone-cold ignorant? The standards for elementary school were scarcely more realistic—they took up 77 pages, a length and level of detail hardly suited for the typical elementary teacher.[5]

Beyond the sheer volume of the overstuffed goals was a process that illustrated the folly of attempting to craft anything like a one-size-fits-all "national" goal. Imagine every awful curriculum-cobbling process—squared. Not only were 6,000 "teachers, administrators, scholars, parents and business leaders" given a say in the history goals, but thirty-five special interest groups ranging from the American Association of School Librarians to the Missouri Synod of the Lutheran Church consulted as "advisors." The standards themselves were written by "battalions of classroom teachers" and then reviewed by a gauntlet of nine different "focus groups" that represented more educationist interest groups. At each stage the standards were revised and made more "inclusive" or acceptable to the sprawling constituencies. Because "consensus" was the byword only the most outlandish demands could be ignored, and even then not easily. As one defender of the process conceded: "The new standards are sprawling, both too little and too much—just like the process that produced them."[6]

Inevitably, the national standards for U.S. history became bloated with special interest pleadings. The proposed National Standards for United States History tried to divide American history into ten eras, with two to four "standards" of what children should learn about the period, for a total of thirty-one separate standards. Lynne Cheney, the former head of the National Endowment for the Humanities, charged that the result was a monument to historical revisionism that deleted all references to Paul Revere, Robert E. Lee, Thomas Edison, the Wright Brothers, Alexander Graham Bell, Albert Einstein, and Jonas Salk. Ulysses S. Grant gets a single mention, as does Lincoln's "Gettysburg Address." In contrast, Cheney noted, Harriet Tubman, an African-American woman active in the rescue of slaves—a contemporary of Grant and Lee—got six mentions. One theme that runs through the standards is the division of history into victims (virtuous, pure, inspirational) and oppressors (white, wealthy, powerful). The first meeting of the U.S. Congress goes unnoticed, she charged, while the standards mentioned the Seneca Falls "Declaration of Sentiments" nine times and required that students study the founding of the Sierra Club and the National Organization for Women. The authors of the standards were also anxious to emphasize the various evils of American society: They include seventeen references to the Ku Klux Klan, and nineteen references to Red-hunting Senator Joseph McCarthy and McCarthyism.[7]

Not surprisingly, the process that culminated in the thirty-one history standards was shadowed by political agendas as various interest groups demanded that material be included in the guidelines. Few of the participants dared argue against the movement toward ethnic, racial, and ideological inclusiveness, and as Cheney later remarked, "what got left out was traditional history."[8]

Under heavy pressure from the American Historical Association (AHA)—a bastion of political and multicultural orthodoxy in the academy—the standards for world history were also ideologically tinged. The AHA reportedly threatened to withdraw support for the goal-setting proceedings if the standards gave any special emphasis to Western Civilization. Cheney was told by one member of the goal-setting council that the AHA effectively "hijacked the standards-setting." While some historians bitterly objected to the heavy-handed agenda being inserted into the national standards, he told her, the critics "were all iced-out."[9] The guidelines are heavy on victimology, feminism, critiques of imperialism and colonialism, and the celebration of non-Western cultures. They also bear the unmistakable mark of the educationist mind. The "standards" proposed that students "discuss social oppression" during the Renaissance and suggested that students stage a television talk show on Renaissance gender roles.[10] (Next on *Oprah*: Eating disorders in the Elizabethan Age!) By the time the standards for world history were released, the champions of inclusiveness scarcely bothered to conceal their contempt either for their critics or for Western culture itself. Historian Peter N. Stearns of Carnegie-Mellon University derided traditionalists as "those who think there are some special marvelous features about the Western tradition that students should be exposed to—indoctrinated in—as a way to realize their own values are privileged. . . . "[11] This is, of course, the standard multiculturalist rhetoric of the academy, but the context here is not unimportant. Debates that once involved a handful of academics and resulted in politically correct reading lists in handfuls of college history courses were now being played out in bureaucracies that hold the whip hand over every school in the country.

Official Knowledge

That dramatically raises the stakes, because the definition of the national educational "goals" comes perilously close to defining what some critics call "official knowledge." Stephen Arons, a professor of legal studies at the University of Massachusetts, Amherst, and author of *Compelling Belief: The Culture of American Schooling*, calls Goals 2000 "a top-down, authoritarian and systematized model of schooling." By seeking to create a national curriculum to reach its various goals, "the government will be provoking a storm of conflict which it can neither resolve nor control." This is the legislation's fatal flaw, suggests Arons. Battles at the state and local level over Outcome Based Education may be mere rehearsals of the struggle over the national "outcomes." This will not only severely damage the schools, he argues, but the sweeping new powers of the federal government also raise significant questions in and of themselves.

A basic constitutional principle, Arons insists, is that political majorities should never be empowered to regulate or manipulate the content of communication or the freedom of individuals to form or express opinions. The problem is not who will win the cultural and political fight to control the curriculum; it is that "the more we submit these matters of intellect and conscience to political determinations, the less respect for intellectual freedom, cultural diversity, and critical thinking we should expect our children to learn."

Because the national "goals" come so close to the establishment of an official ideology, they challenge fundamental constitutional protections. "The creation of a national curriculum would be as contrary to the fundamental freedoms of intellect and belief protected by the First Amendment as would the establishment of a national religion or the approval of a national catechism," charges Arons. Educrats may argue that the national curriculum would be inoffensive because it would "value-neutral." But such a claim, Arons writes, "ignores a fundamental reality of learning and teaching."

"Government technocrats would be as convincing as if they claimed that an established religion would be constitutionally acceptable as long as it were based on monotheism. In a pluralistic society, value-neutral schooling is a contradiction in terms."[12] Arons is not arguing a novel theory. The U.S. Supreme Court addressed the problem in its 1943 decision, *West Virginia* v. *Barnette*, when it declared: "Probably no deeper division of our people could proceed from any provocation than from finding it necessary to choose what doctrine and whose program public educational officials shall compel youth to unite in embracing. . . . If it [public education] is to impose any ideological discipline, however, each party or denomination must seek control, or failing that, to weaken the influence of the educational system." That case involved rules that required school children to salute the flag, but it seems equally applicable to any attempt to impose an official ideology—including the ideology of multiculturalism—on the curriculum, or to attempts by the federal government to define a coda of "official knowledge" for all of the nation's schools.

Avoiding Reform

Even if we did not have the particulars of how Goals 2000 was being implemented, we could be confident in predicting its ultimate failure. The flaw in Goals 2000 is fundamental: It avoids fixing what needs to be fixed, leaving intact the educational establishment's throttlehold on the school. It ignores the pattern of reform and counterreform that has rendered past efforts so unsuccessful and perpetuates many of the failed ideas that have scuttled its predecessors. The legislation radically centralizes decision making when decentralization is urgently needed, and relies on the same vague notions of outcomes that have already crippled Outcome Based Education programs across the country. Goals 2000 does little to encourage innovation or accountability; it does not advance merit pay for teachers, school choice, nor does it address the problem of bureaucratic bloat. In fact, it creates elaborate new bureaucracies certain to be dominated by the very same interests that created the status quo they are supposed now to reform.

By now, the pattern is clear enough: No matter how well intended, attempts by the federal government to reform the schools are by definition intensively bureaucratic. Federal reforms require elaborate systems of measurement and accountability and that requires new layers of administration, which also become barriers to innovation and flexibility. Beyond that, however, the federal bureaucracy has long been both stronghold and lodestar for the educationist establishment. Any measures that shift more power to the bureaucracy automatically shift power to The Blob, since the centralization of curriculum writing and goal setting guarantees the dominance of the educationist elites. The elites have been pressing for just such a consolidation for decades, recognizing that centralized "reform" bureaucracies are likely to be more amenable to educationist doctrine and pliant to special interest lobbying than either legislatures or local school boards with their notoriously unmanageable electorates.

At the heart of the problem is the question of priorities. If the goal is to create a system of effective schools that listen to and serve the diverse interests of communities and students across the country, then we would create a diversity of systems, recognizing that no one-size-fits-all program could possibly work in every part of the country and for every group of students in the same way at the same time. If, however, the goal is to insulate educationists from the messiness of such diversity, then standardization makes perfect sense. It is easier to create one standard than many different standards; it is also easier to control.

By federalizing educational policy, educationists have turned the focus of accountability upward toward the bureaucracies rather than downward toward students and their parents. Instead of requiring schools to satisfy their primary customers, schools will be required to follow standards set in Washington, D.C. Instead of crafting programs that meet the needs of the parents and taxpayers of their own communities, schools become accountable primarily to their constituencies in the educationist establishment. Since the educationist establishment is responsible for the educational status quo—it has, after all, formulated, advocated, and protected the failed policies of American education—entrusting reform to its tender mercies guarantees its failure.

AN
ENDANGERED
SPECIES II

When a Madison newspaper, the *Wisconsin State Journal*, asked its readers to nominate their favorite "tough" teacher, the paper got only a handful of responses. "Tough" is not nearly as popular as "caring," or "compassionate," or "empathetic." But all the letters mentioned the same teacher: Jack Reynoldson.

"He didn't terrorize us and he didn't deprecate us," a former state assistant attorney general wrote. "He did motivate us. He understood the relationship between discipline and focus—and the relationship between focus and learning."[1]

He is also the kind of teacher the Madison Public Schools can't wait to get rid of.

Reynoldson is an obvious throwback. He conducts his classes with boot camp order and his students are drilled in diagramming sentences, memorizing lists of vocabulary words and important dates in history, and learning the Latin roots and suffixes of words. While other Madison classrooms are emphasizing "cooperative learning," Reynoldson stresses competition, often dividing his class into "squadrons," each run by students with proven leadership abilities. A reporter who visited his class recounts Reynoldson's military-style approach to learning:

> "On your feet!" barks the Korean War veteran to his classroom of eighth-graders.
>
> With military precision, the teenagers jump to attention.
>
> "What's wrong with this sentence?" asks Jack Reynoldson, a teacher at Whitehorse Middle School. He uses his pointer to draw attention to the Blooper of the Day written on the chalkboard: "Of the two girls, Suzy is the most agreeable."
>
> Students quietly raise their hands. He calls on one.
>
> "It should be, Of the two girls, Suzy is the *more* agreeable." "Correct," says Reynoldson, then addressing the class: "Be seated."
>
> A pause, then he barks, "Face west!"
>
> The students shift their desks in unison, and then, sitting starched

straight, they prepare for what has become a morning ritual: diagramming sentences.

This sort of thing gives au courant educationists the willies; the display of authority, the insistence on order, the absence of caring and sharing, the specter of rote learning and *right* and *wrong* answers. At sixty-four, Reynoldson has been teaching since 1955, but he has resisted pressures to retire, in part because he seems to enjoy shocking the educationist elites around him. He refers to them as "psychobabbling mavens," who want him to "teach 'human adjustment'. . . . It's touchy-feely stuff." But, insists Reynoldson: "Encourage academic achievement, and with that will come self-esteem."

As a teacher, Reynoldson's record is impressive, both for high-achieving and low-achieving students, including minority students in his classes. Despite the drill-sergeant manner, Reynoldson is known for working with students closely, especially those who need extra attention. He corrects papers one-on-one and gives students extra chances to pass tests if they fail. Students say that although he is tough, he is fair in administering discipline and they admire his insistence on academic results.

To the principal of Whitehorse Middle School, Reynoldson is a hopeless anachronism. "What we find, unfortunately, is that it isn't an inclusive classroom," Principal Robert Pellegrino told a reporter. Pellegrino is also concerned that Reynoldson's style does not sufficiently nurture his student's creativity. "My observation," he sniffs, "is his students are trained instead of taught." Some parents occasionally also object to Reynoldson's style and standards. One mother pulled her daughter out of Reynoldson's class because she claimed that it was "emotionally unsafe." Other students flatly disagree. "He's my favorite teacher ever," one fourteen-year-old told *State Journal* reporter Debbie Stone. "You can talk to him and he helps you with stuff."

Reynoldson himself has no intention of changing or conforming. For the last forty years he has resisted every fad and fashion and he doesn't see any reason to change now. "I will not conform to stupidity," he insists. "I think in education today we have lost a sense of mission and we have substituted politically correct clap-trap." Reynoldson's mission: "To teach kids a lot of stuff."

But educrats like Pellegrino seem intent on forcing Reynoldson out of the school. Several years ago, the principal filed a sexual harassment charge against Reynoldson on the grounds that he used a (fully clothed) female mannequin in class. The mannequin (named Alice) was used to post notes and assignments for students. The controversy dragged on for two years, costing the parties more than $18,000. In the end, Reynoldson was cleared of the charges—the district couldn't convince the arbitrator that Alice was an act of sexist insensitivity. In fact the arbitrator found that the environment in Reynoldson's class was generally free of sex bias, but nevertheless told Reynoldson to get rid of Alice.[2]

Reynoldson replaced her with a male mannequin named Riley.

SCHOOLS THAT WORK

S o what is the answer?

If there is an antidote to the dumbing down of our children it is to be found in the many schools that work. In virtually every community in the country, there are schools that break the mold of educational mediocrity, succeeding—often against great odds—in producing literate, confident, capable students. Some of these schools are found in affluent suburbs, some in impoverished inner city neighborhoods; some are private, while others are public schools; some are predominantly white, while others have largely minority student bodies. These educational success stories are not distinguished by their funding, their status, or their religious affiliations, but rather by certain qualities and commitments they share in common.

The goal of educational reform, simply put, is to make more schools effective and to get more children into those schools.

In contrast to the weak or nonexistent research that supports educationist fads and pseudoreforms, we know a great deal about what makes schools effective; the research into successful schools is, moreover, remarkably consistent. Effective schools are not characterized by small class sizes, exceptional teachers, the ethnic makeup of the faculty, or by the quality or age of the physical plant. They do, however, all have forceful administrators, high expectations among the faculty for student achievement, involved parents, and an orderly school atmosphere. Successful schools, according to Gilbert Sewall, all tend to give absolute precedence to academic achievement by emphasizing cognitive learning. They emphasize "pupil mastery of low-level skills," which leads to "unrelenting attention to the progress of all students in the essentials of reading, writing, and computation." The objective, to which all of the schools' efforts are aimed, is higher cognitive development and more advanced knowledge.

Successful schools also maintain high standards and expectations: Students who fall below the minimum standards will be failed. But such schools do not write off any child as ineducable or unable to master basic, fundamental skills. In good schools, principals and department heads "act as fierce guardians of instructional quality. . . . They tend not to be permissive, informal in their staff relationships, or overly interested in public relations. . . . " Good schools are also intent on constantly monitoring and evaluating student progress. Most important of all, perhaps, effective schools recognize that pupil progress is not wholly dependent on home, parents, or other outside factors and that the schools themselves must take some responsibility. In outstanding schools, Sewall notes, "school staffs are not hostile to the concept of accountability and accept responsibility for educating their students. They do not reject the validity of test scores, even when results are disappointing. Rather, they use test outcomes to decide what is and what is not working in the curriculum. In such an atmosphere teachers do not feel that they are or should be beyond evaluation."[1]

Research into effective schools has been consistent in confirming that general outline. In the early 1970s, George Weber, an analyst for the Council for Basic Education, studied four schools—two in New York, one in Kansas City, one in Los Angeles—whose third-grade classes had reading achievement scores far above those of other urban schools. Each of the third-grade classes he looked at had scores equal to or above the national norm and a very low percentage of nonreaders. What accounted for this superior performance? All four schools had strong and determined leadership, teachers committed to educational excellence, and strict policies related to discipline and order. Weber also found that each of the four schools shared similar approaches to reading. All four schools had:

- A schoolwide concern about reading skills
- Adroit use of reading specialists
- A phonics-based curriculum
- Close attention to individual student reading interests
- Careful evaluation of pupil progress[2]

Weber's research was echoed by studies of British students by researcher Michael Rutter, who exhaustively traced the progress of 2,700 students in London schools from the end of their elementary education through secondary school. The students in Rutter's survey attended twelve different schools—all of them nonselective and all with a substantial percentage of low-income, minority children. Rutter and his team found wide variations among the schools and the levels of achievement of the students. At the most successful schools, Rutter found, students who could be classified as "low-ability" achieved at the level of "high-ability" students at the least effective schools. While the family background and social class of the students clearly made a difference, so did the schools.

Rutter and his associates were able to identify the common traits of the best schools. They were run by teachers and administrators who "take school seriously"; they had clearly defined and carefully monitored standards for their teachers, who in turn took their responsibilities to be role models seriously. Teachers tended to be highly organized, prepared, and punctual; the schools also had high expectations for the students and set demanding workloads. Teachers in the successful schools assigned a lot of homework, but also rewarded diligence.[3]

Even more provocative were the findings of another British researcher who set out explicitly to compare the effectiveness of different styles of teaching. Neville Bennett wanted to pit traditional approaches to education against more fashionable, "progressive" styles, and to determine which method resulted in higher levels of student performance. Bennett made no secret of the biases he brought to the study: He was inclined to support the trend toward more informal or "open" classrooms then in vogue among educationists. But as a genuine scholar, he was bothered by the wholesale rush to implement faddish new ideas and programs "not on research evidence, but on faith."

"On both sides of the Atlantic," he warned, "innovation is being urged without research. This of course is not new in education, the common response being that educational decisions cannot afford to wait for years while careful trials are instituted and evaluated. Yet it is a strange logic which dictates that we *can* afford to implement changes in organization and teaching which have unknown, and possibly deleterious, effects on the education of the nation's young."[4]

Bennett contrasted the "progressive" and "traditional" approaches to education. In the progressive classroom, the teacher was a "guide to educational experience." In the traditional classroom, the teacher was a "distributor of knowledge." Progressive schools regarded external rewards and punishments as unnecessary, while traditional classes still emphasized external rewards, such as grades; progressive classrooms were "not too concerned with conventional academic standards"; progressive classes had little testing, while traditional classes had regular testing; progressive classes put the accent on cooperative group work, while traditionalists emphasized competition; and so on.

Bennett, frankly, expected the students liberated by the progressive style to excel in comparison with students who were still expected to memorize, practice, and learn facts by rote. To the contrary, his study of thousands of third- and fourth-grade students in 750 English schools found that the students in the traditional classes out-tested the progressive students by every measure—even in creative self-expression. Sewall later noted that "pupils in progressive classrooms that emphasized self-expression *did not* evince greater imagination or creativity than their formally instructed counterparts."[5] Students in traditional classrooms did better in math and reading and appeared to have lost nothing by not having their self-esteems massaged, their personalities adjusted, or their self-expressiveness nurtured. The key element behind the success of the traditional classrooms turned out to be rather mundane: Bennett found that students in traditional schools spent more time actually working on the subject matter they were being taught than their counterparts. In classes where the focus was squarely on academic achievement, students were required to spend more "time-on-task," which in turn translated into higher levels of achievement. Ironically, Bennett found, not only did brighter children fare less well in "progressive" classes, but so did shy and insecure children, who tended to thrive more easily in the highly structured (and therefore less threatening) environment of the traditional classroom.[6]

Although it is relatively easy to identify what makes school effective, it is far less easy to say how to go about *making* schools effective. The barriers, as we have already discussed, are formidable. Federal and state mandates and diktats that trickle down the bureaucratic hierarchies often make it impossible for schools to emphasize academic achievement. Top-down management undermines strong local leadership and waters down attempts at discipline and accountability. This is the paradox of school governance. While every school has a designated leader, they are still essentially leaderless institutions; they are staffed by professionals who are given the discretion of janitors; they claim to be accountable, but are insulated by elaborate layers of contracts, rules, laws, and regulations from any consequence of failure. The monopoly enjoyed by public education eliminates much of the incentive for change and precludes the sort of competition that might foster innovation. Not surprisingly, then, the move toward more effective schooling is more likely to flourish in the market-place rather than inside the monopoly itself.

ike many of Baltimore's schools, Barclay is predominantly African-American and poor. More than two thirds of the students who attend the inner-city Baltimore school qualify for free lunches. Most of them come from the city's Greenmount district, a neighborhood distinguished by its high crime rate and the aggressiveness of its drug dealers, who work the same streets as Barclay's students walk to and from school. Throughout the 1970s, Barclay—like other schools in city—spiralled into decline. As truancy rates rose and test scores sagged, the city's bloated school bureaucracy handed down discredited fad after fad, which succeeded only in further depressing academic achievement. While the city's top educrats managed to spend $14 million on their own renovated central-office headquarters, teachers at Barclay were forced to scavenge pieces of used textbooks and paste them together, since there wasn't enough money to buy intact books.[1]

Barclay's story could easily have been another dreary recitation of failure, dysfunction, violence, and excuses. Instead, it became one of Baltimore's—and urban education's—most unexpected success stories. As usual, the story of Barclay's turnaround centers on a single figure: a tiny, unprepossessing, but committed woman named Gertrude Williams, who became principal of Barclay in 1978. Forging a powerful alliance with parents from the neighborhood, Williams waged a lengthy and bitter fight against the city's education bureaucracy, its school board, and two former superintendents. In the end, her tenacity paid off, providing a case study in both the difficulties and the rewards of fighting back against The Blob.

By the time Williams became principal, there was no longer any question that Barclay was failing, although not because of any lack of effort. Williams confronted drug dealers who were hassling her students, went out into the streets to round up truants, and pushed her teachers to do the best they could. But her efforts only highlighted the apparent futility of the attempt to save the school. The central administration's response was more rules, regulations, and special programs.

The bureaucracy lacked the sense of urgency that Williams brought to her job. One of eight children, Williams had been steeled with the idea that the only way for a young black girl, or anyone else, to be free and independent was through education. Her own experience—her hard work in high school that led to a scholarship and college—made her an evangelist on the subject. Now that she was a principal, however, she saw students falling back into poverty, dependency, and despair. The system seemed to be willing to live with the mediocrity of the urban schools. She, however, had not become a teacher to preside over the failure of the students entrusted to her.

Searching for alternatives, Williams was willing to stray from the educationist path and in 1980 she visited one of Baltimore's best-known private academies—the Calvert School, a school as prestigious as it was successful. A nonsectarian school founded in 1897, Calvert prided itself on producing students with solid academic skills. Its graduates were so successful that its unabashedly traditional and highly structured curriculum was packed into all-inclusive boxes—including instructional materials, books, even paper and pencils—and distributed throughout much of the English-speaking world through Calvert's Home Instruction Department. If the Calvert boxes were good enough for missionaries in Ghana, aborigines in Australia, and home schoolers in Vermont, Gertrude Williams wondered, why couldn't she use them at Barclay? If they worked so well for other children, why wouldn't they work for Barclay's students? Of course, it represented a radical departure from the culture of public education, but philosophically, she was attracted to the priorities of the Calvert curriculum. Calvert's statement of Philosophy and Objectives made no reference to self-esteem, environmental stewardship, interpersonal relationships, emotional and spiritual wellness, or multiculturalism. Instead, they were refreshingly straightforward:

- The essence of a Calvert education is a solid grounding in reading, writing, and arithmetic.
- The reading program uses materials of superior literary quality and stresses comprehension and analysis skills. Under close supervision, students learn to write with style and discipline.
- The principles of English grammar reinforce proper written and oral expression.
- Basic mathematical skills are mastered so they become a useful tool in solving quantitative problems.
- Science, geography, and history are integral parts of the curriculum and stimulate interest in our world and our heritage.
- Music, French, art, and art history are offered to broaden artistic and cultural horizons and to encourage creativity.

Calvert's curriculum does not include rap sessions in "the spectrum of human emotions," but offers "an education characterized by a sense of enthusiasm, responsibility, and self-discipline." The language of the therapeutic culture—the cant of social workers, psychotherapists, and guidance counselors, which dominates the usual public school statement of philosophy—is completely absent from Calvert's declaration of mission. It does not encourage one to develop an inflated sense of their entitlement; Calvert's goals do not mention self-esteem at all; the school does, however, aim at instilling *confidence* as something to be *won* and *achieved*. "The tasks that each Calvert student accomplished engender a greater sense of self-confidence, poise, and presence." It offers no courses in "values clarification," but "places a significant emphasis on character development and understanding of the fundamental principles of good citizenship."[2]

Another distinctive aspect of the Calvert curriculum is its attention to detail. From first grade on students begin writing in the characteristic script lettering with block capitals known as "Calvert cursive." Neatness counts and so does correct spelling. In the Calvert program, teachers correct every mistake—there is no invented spelling or "emergent" grammar. As one journalist has remarked: "The motto . . . seems to be: 'It's not finished until it's perfect.' Students receive praise not for acceptable work but for wholly correct work."[3]

After sharing the Calvert curriculum with her teachers and with some of the parents of children at her school, Williams became convinced that its back-to-basics approach was exactly what Barclay needed. "We sought a curriculum that would work," Williams later explained, "that would enable our children to go anywhere and be knowledgeable, to speak intelligently, and to read, write, and compute." The Calvert curriculum offered "the kind of high expectancies that we have not had in years in public schools."[4]

But there was no way to pay for it until 1988, when the Abell Foundation, which was run by a former president of the Baltimore School Board, offered to pay for Williams to bring the Calvert program to her inner-city school. Williams now had the curriculum, the support of the faculty and parents, and the money to pay for a program with a proven track record of success. But in Baltimore's heavily centralized system, that was not enough.

Her proposal to incorporate the Calvert curriculum at Barclay was greeted with a combination of overt hostility and indifference by the central administration. The superintendent of schools simply refused to take any action on Williams's idea. Her successor, a thoroughgoing educrat named Richard Hunter, flatly rejected the idea, jibing that the Calvert program was "a rich man's curriculum." In a perverse way, the superintendent was saying that it would somehow be "elitist" to provide poor, black children access to a successful curriculum. He regarded a program of high expectations that focused on academic achievement as inappropriate for poor, minority children.

But Williams knew what a poor man's curriculum looked like; Barclay had one. And it wasn't good enough anymore. Learning the basic skills of reading and writing and math wasn't the elitist privilege of the wealthy, Williams argued, it was the key to liberation for the poor.[5]

For the educationists who ran Baltimore's schools, the failure of black children was acceptable, or at least tolerable, but innovation was not. Williams's proposal was a threat because it challenged the complacency of the status quo, breaking lockstep with other schools that had made their peace with failure. Faced with apparently immovable opposition, Williams mobilized grassroots support in the community for her plan; petitions were hand-delivered to Superintendent Hunter asking him to step out of the way and let Barclay try something new. He refused. Williams learned that the central bureaucracy had killed her idea when she read about it in a local paper. That should have been the end of it, but it wasn't. Barclay's parents loudly protested Hunter's decision and their fight against the central bureaucracy drew local media attention.

But the decisive blow in Williams's fight against the central educracy was struck by Baltimore's new mayor. Kurt Schmoke was the city's first black mayor; more importantly, a Rhodes scholar himself, he shared Williams's attitude toward education. At a public meeting in June 1989, Williams made an eloquent plea to the mayor for her idea. When he asked her, "Why aren't our children learning?" Williams answered: "Because the system is failing. How can a child learn if the curriculum is always changing? We need to try some proven strategies. . . . " When a mayoral aide tried to cut her off, Mayor Schmoke intervened: "Miss Williams and I are talking," he said. "Let her continue."[6]

The mayor ordered Superintendent Hunter to work with Williams, which he did reluctantly and with obvious distaste. He eventually approved the plan to incorporate the Calvert curriculum into Barclay in early 1990 and it was implemented the following fall. (Superintendent Hunter's contract was not renewed in December.)[7]

Three years later, Barclay had been transformed into a national model. An evaluation by researchers from Johns Hopkins University found that the program "has produced significant changes in the ethos of the K–3 classes and the entire elementary floor of Barclay School. The classes and halls are more orderly; the students seem more focused on academics. Students attendance was up and achievement, as measured both by the district's standardized tests and the Calvert-administered Educational Records Bureau (ERB) test were also up significantly. The Johns Hopkins evaluation singled out student writing, where they found improvements to be "particularly striking."[8] On reading tests, the mean scores of first and third graders in 1993 were more than twenty percentage points above the *national* mean. In the second and third grades, Barclay students scored above the sixtieth percentile on the ERB writing skills tests. Before the Calvert program had been introduced, none of the same-grade groups at

Barclay had scored above the forty-seventh percentile. Math scores were also up at Barclay.[9]

There are other measures of success as well: In April 1994, *Education Week* reported that twenty children at Barclay who had been designated as "severe" under the Chapter 1 compensatory education program had made so much progress that they were now classified as "gifted and talented."[10]

"By any reasonable measure," the Johns Hopkins evaluation said, "the first three years of the Barclay/Calvert experiment have been a success."[11] Under Williams's leadership, the Calvert curriculum has not been watered down to accommodate Barclay's students; the students have risen to the challenge of the demanding curriculum. Barclay's first graders work with geometry and fractions, adding and subtracting two-digit numbers, measuring lines, liquid, and weight; they are drilled in phonics and reading comprehension. First graders learn about vowels, blends, consonants, clusters, endings; they study possessives, abbreviations, contractions, compounds, and antonyms and synonyms. Third graders read and memorize poetry, study the biographies of famous men and women, and dip into myths and legends. They are provided with the foundation for the study of history and literature; but they also continue to build basic reading skills. Third graders study the concept of alphabetical order, how to use a dictionary, long and short sounds, prefixes, suffixes, diphthongs, word division and accent, and compound and base words. In math, third graders are drilled daily on facts and problem solving, and continue their study (begun in second grade) of multiplication and division. They work on rounding numbers, fractions, decimals, measurements, geometry (curves, two-dimensional shapes, three-dimensional shapes, perimeter and area, grids, symmetry, and volume), and begin to make their own picture and bar graphs.[12]

A writer for *Education Week* could not conceal her admiration for the transformation of Barclay. Using the stylish "Calvert cursive," Barclay's students write every day, "whether it's about their most recent . . . reading assignment, a class field trip, or their own lives. . . .

"On a recent Friday, students down the hall in Patricia Bennett's second-grade class learned about the connection between the number of syllables and vowel sounds in a word. In the dinosaur-decorated classroom, students punched the air with their fists each time they heard a syllable in a word Bennett called out. 'Sidewalk' earned two energetic punches.

"In another room, third graders combined reading and geography skills as they deciphered a map of a fictional country. Fourth graders, meanwhile, were choosing a topic for a composition, finishing a geography unit on the Amazon jungle, or starting a geometry lesson in parallel lines."[13]

Nowhere did the life at Barclay ever remotely resemble the crude caricatures educationists use to characterize "traditional" education. The halls and the classrooms buzzed with the excitement of *achievement.*

THE COMING EDUCATIONAL REVOLUTION

Why do institutions change? What causes reformations and revolutions? Just in the past decade, we've seen the collapse or radical transformation of massive institutions that once seemed monolithic, invulnerable, and impervious to change. This list of shattered giants ranged from the Soviet Empire to American automakers, corporate giants like IBM, and even the Democratic House of Representatives. Each institution shared an inability to acknowledge the need to change or adjust to a changing world, fluid markets, or a shifting public mood.

In each case, the original inspiration—whether it was idealistic or entrepreneurial—had degenerated over decades of power and unchallenged dominance into bureaucracy and arrogance as each institution grew increasingly remote from its constituencies and its customers. For years they were insulated by their monopoly on information or the lack of meaningful competition, or by simple inertia which they mistook for permanency.

Instead of devoting their energies to reforming themselves or adapting themselves to new realities, they devoted their efforts to fending off threats from the outside. Dominated by an encrusted nomenklatura, who had become enamored of their own perquisites, they became increasingly hostile to change, relying on their power to crush opposition rather than new ideas to insure their hold on power. But when their failures became too obvious and the consequences too great to deny or ignore, they fell.

In Eastern Europe, the loss of the monopoly on information and communications enjoyed by the Communist Party may have precipitated the final collapse of the dying regimes. With the advent of something as seemingly trivial as the fax machine, the state could no longer control either information or the terms of the public debate—a fatal development for totalitarian regimes that thrived on ignorance. Global communications had made their regimes obsolete.

Similarly, corporations that had produced low-quality and overpriced products found they could no longer control a marketplace in which they were challenged by competitors who gave consumers what they wanted at a reasonable price. The global marketplace had made their corporate cultures obsolete.

But the rise of competition and the advent of the information age has a similar effect on all closed systems, including public education. Educationists no longer are the only source of curricula for elementary and secondary studies. On the most basic level the proliferation of home computers and the increasing ease of access to alternative courses of studies make decentralization increasingly easy and inexpensive. Entrepreneurs, parents, nonpublic schools, and innovators within public education can create alternative schools or even schools-within-schools with an ease that would have been unimaginable only a decade ago. Not surprisingly, the growing popularity of charter schools, for-profit schools, home schooling, private tutoring, and the challenge posed by school choice are already transforming the educational landscape.

At the same time, it is becoming harder to disguise the gap between the claims of public education and its realities. No other institution could survive such a record of mediocrity and failure unless it was insulated by the traditional protections of a monopoly—a guaranteed source of funding and layers of regulations, mandates, and bureaucratic insulation from accountability. But a closed system requires protection from competition and a monopoly on information if it is to survive. Both are breaking down.

Global competition has permanently raised the stakes for American schools. At one time, it may have been possible to have minimal literacy skills and still get a job that guaranteed stability and a shot at middle-class status. Not anymore. While many parents may still be in a state of denial about the dumbing down of the schools, Americans are about to receive a rude reality check. Increasingly, students, communities, businesses, and society as a whole will pay a staggering price for the decline in educational standards. When Americans realize that they are not immune to the consequences of educational failure, the educational establishment will be forced to defend its own exemptions from reality.

When that happens, the educationists will be unable to respond. The establishment has become ossified in its structure and its ideas, increasingly unable to respond to challenges except by vilifying critics and demanding more money. The establishment's lack of internal debate may seem a sign of its monolithic power but it is also the source of its radical instability. Because the educational establishment seldom bothers to talk to their critics (they are content to label them as "fanatics," "zealots," or members of the "Christian Right") educationists have become tone-deaf to the concerns of parents and society on whom the schools rely for funding and support. As a result, public education is on the brink of what may be the most sweeping reform in its history.

Redefining Public Education

If the goal of educational reform is to make more schools effective and to get more children into those schools, the first step of meaningful reform is to recognize that saving our children is not the same as saving the public school system. That means changing our definition of "public" education, by seeing it as a commitment to provide all children with a quality education rather than as the perpetuation of a specific system of funding and bureaucratic organization. Ultimately this is where the battle will be joined: The defenders of the status quo want to pretend as if the future of American education is identical to the future of America's current government monopoly of public education, as if protecting the *system*— the interlocking directorates of the education establishment, the bureaucratic infrastructure, and funding mechanisms that support them—was the key to the future of American education.

The nomenklatura of the status quo have become so inward-looking that they often behave as if the fate of America's schools depends on guaranteeing their own status, privileges, and powers, regardless of the consequences of the nation's children. Their attacks on school choice, for example, are not based on the fear that private or parochial schools will fail to educate their students, but rather that they will *succeed.* It is the fear of success that drives the educationist argument that competition from the private schools might somehow weaken the public schools by drawing off either students or public dollars. This is not an argument about quality education, but about institutional privilege and it carries weight only if the preservation of the institution is more important than the expansion of educational opportunities. Among educationists, this is often simply taken for granted, but if the question is how to get children into effective schools, it becomes apparent that *the system is merely a means to that end; it is not the end in and of itself.*

Focusing on the future of public education in terms of the existing public school system is like discussing the eradication of poverty by declaring that the top priority must be the preservation of the Department of Health and Human Services, or discussing the future of America's farmers in terms of whether or not policies will strengthen the Department of Agriculture. It is one thing to oppose a policy that will cost workers their jobs; it is quite something else to oppose job-creation efforts because they might result in budget cuts for the Department of Commerce. Only the most hidebound bureaucrat thinks in such terms; but it is a measure of the level of the educational debate that the educrats have been able to frame the debate on effective schools in such nakedly bureaucrat-o-centric terms.

Also at issue is our attitude toward monopolies and competition. Imagine for a moment a system in which the government would insist on using only computers designed and built by government employees under rules banning the purchase of any nongovernmental computer software or hardware. Imagine a food stamp program that required the poor to shop only at government-run stores where they could buy only government-produced food. Or a social security system that provided money that could be spent only at state stores or at government monopoly resorts (and imagine for a moment the quality of those facilities and the level of service they would offer). If anyone suggested that such a system was wasteful and inefficient and that it might be improved by permitting some competition, their proposal would be met by fierce opposition from the beneficiaries of the status quo—the operators and manufacturers of the state-run computer system, the bureaucracy and unions representing employees of the state-run food stores, and so on. They would insist that any move to permit freedom of choice or competition would destroy the government monopoly operations. In short, they would make arguments *identical* to those being made by opponents of school choice.

Other critics of choice insist that choice will hurt public education because it will spark a flight of public dollars away from the public schools and they express concern over students who might be "left behind." Such fears reflect the educationists' lack of confidence in their ability to compete with private schools. In effect, they are admitting that many students and parents would take advantage of an opportunity to get out from under the monopoly system if they were given the option. But ultimately, the educationist's concern is disingenuous. The claim that poor children would be left behind in the public schools ignores the fact that it is precisely such low-income children who have borne the heaviest brunt of the educationists' failed policies. A system of vouchers would provide low-income students the same opportunities that middle- and upper-class children already enjoy, while depriving the educational monopoly of the last of its captive audience.

Rather than struggling to adapt to the changing marketplace by making their schools more attractive and more effective, educationists have chosen to stake their political all on maintaining their exclusive grasp on public financing. But a system of effective schools would not be exclusively a system of *public* schools. If Americans want to provide as many students as possible access to an effective education, they will draw on a diverse mix that will include private, parochial, and even home schools. This does not necessarily mean that the nation will spend less on education, but it does mean a fundamental change in who controls how educational dollars are spent and how they will be distributed.

Education researchers Terry Moe and John Chubb have argued that traditional notions of public education—in which public dollars go only to schools run by public entities—has worked to create bureaucracies, stifle autonomy and innovation, and make effective schools unlikely. Public sector politics, they argue, is "essentially coercive" because "the winners get to use public authority to impose their policies on the losers." But effective schools thrive best in an environment that is decentralized and freed from the controls that are inevitable in a government-run system.

A market-based system allows innovation and flexibility because it permits the people who run the schools to decide what will be taught and who will teach. There is no attempt to impose uniformity or "official" versions of acceptable educational policy. Because the private schools have no power to coerce either attendance or financial support, they rely on their constituencies for sustenance. Public sector schools also rely on their constituencies—but in the public sector, "parents and students are but a small part of this constituency" and whatever influence they have tends to be heavily outweighed by the mutually supporting special interest groups of the educational establishment, including the teachers unions and professional organizations.[1]

The relative impotence of parents in running the schools is not merely a sign of their political weakness, Moe and Chubb argue, but is the very nature of the system, because ". . . even in a perfectly functioning democratic system, the public schools are *not meant* to be theirs to control and are literally *not supposed* to provide them with the kind of education they might want. The schools are agencies of society as a whole and everyone has a right to participate in their governance. Parents and students have a right to participate too. But they have no right to win. In the end, they have to take what society gives them."[2]

Thus the radical nature of school choice: "Under a system of democratic control, the public schools are governed by an enormous, far-flung constituency in which the interests of parents and students carry no special status or weight. When markets prevail, parents and students are thrust onto center stage."[3]

The worst mistake to which policymakers are prone is to imagine that they can fix the schools by means of the same blunt instruments that have created the present crisis. Rather, they can save public education only by eliminating the monopoly status of public schools. When Congress passed the GI Bill, it attached dollars not to institutions, but to individuals who could use the money to attend any institution of higher education they chose, including private and religious colleges. State universities were not destroyed.

Even in a market-based school system, those schools that remain public can be strengthened to make them more competitive. The judicious use of charter schools can help give public education options for innovation and experimentation by letting local communities, businesses, or even the teachers themselves the option of running local schools. Where possible, legislators should cut back on or eliminate altogether state and federal mandates that stifle creativity in the schools and do away altogether with any nonacademic requirements larded onto the schools in recent decades. This requires a fundamental change in the way we think about schools. For much of this century, we have asked them to be all things to all people and it has not worked. By pushing society's most complicated and intractable problems into the classroom, we have guaranteed that the schools will flounder. By overloading them, we've ensured the schools' inability to succeed academically; but we have also forced them to carry a crushing political burden. Perhaps its is time to recognize that we did American public education no favor when we turned it into a lightning rod for our most emotional and divisive social issues by asking the schools to somehow resolve the questions that the rest of society has found to be unresolvable.

Meaningful reform means recognizing that the effective schools of the future will do less, but they will do it better. They will focus as exclusively as possible on *learning*.

Not to put too fine a point on it, meaningful reform means breaking the stranglehold of the educational bureaucracy and the educationist establishment on the nation's schools. Any systematic effort to improve the schools that fails to wrest them from the "interlocking directorate" of the special interests will run aground—as previous attempts have done when they left intact the very institutions that nurtured, sustained, and fed off of educational mediocrity. In addition to school choice, policymakers in the public sector should:

- Abolish the Department of Education and all fifty state education departments.
- In state universities, abolish undergraduate schools of education. Repeal laws that artificially pump up the remaining schools of education by requiring or rewarding meaningless coursework or degrees.
- There are thousands of well-educated, eager, committed would-be teachers artificially barred from the nation's classrooms by restrictive rules designed to protect mediocre but credentialed teachers. Policymakers should break the educationists' closed guild by allowing for alternative forms of teacher certification. Better yet, they could scrap state teacher certification altogether, opening up the teaching profession to noneducationists.
- Pay good teachers more, lousy teachers less. In return, treat teachers as professionals.
- Make it easier for districts to close failing schools; fire lousy teachers; expel disruptive students. Eliminate tenure.
- Help restore rewards for successful students by allowing employers to use tests to screen employees.
- Remove the mandates. Schools should be free from requirements that they solve society's social, environmental, economic, and sexual problems and be permitted to get back to the business of teaching children to read and write.

While such measures would clear away much of the deadwood of educationism, the genuine reform of education will take place at the grassroots level, through a combination of developments that will include innovative and charter schools, new technologies, and school choice.

Innovative Schools

While educationists continue to devise elaborate "multicultural" curricula for inner-city public schools and argue that minority children need to be protected from unfairly demanding "rich man's" curricula, a handful of innovative schools are drawing attention precisely for their rigorous programs and traditionalist approach to learning. In Chattanooga, Tennessee, six schools operate programs designed around Mortimer Adler's "Paideia" curriculum—a self-consciously traditional approach with no provisions for electives, no self-esteem courses, and high standards for every student. "By all accounts," columnist William Raspberry wrote, "it works. Parents of rich children and poor, black and white camp out as long as a week in advance of registration to secure a place in these new schools. The children are expected to achieve honor-student results, and they do." Standardized test scores are among the highest in the state; nearly 98 percent of the Paideia graduates go on to college.[4]

An even more striking success story is the Mohegan Elementary School in the South Bronx, a public school located in one of the worst neighborhoods in the nation. Mohegan is one of several dozen schools to throw out the educationist model and adopt a curriculum known as the "Core Knowledge" plan, developed by E. D. Hirsch Jr., the author of *Cultural Literacy*. Hirsch's curriculum is a highly structured program designed to ensure that every student is taught basic knowledge of history, literature, science, mathematics, and the arts. Every student is taught the same curriculum because, as Hirsch argues, "If you're going to be a working member of society, you have to have the same background knowledge."[5] In contrast to the vaguely worded "goals" that focus on "learning skills," Hirsch's curriculum emphasizes the content of learning. Instead of learning "map skills," or learning "about plants," students in the "Core Knowledge" curriculum will "identify the seven continents" and "learn the difference between evergreen and deciduous trees."

"Yes," Hirsch argues, "problem-solving skills are necessary. But they depend on a wealth of relevant information." Children who have to survive daily life in the South Bronx, he noted, already demonstrate they have "high-order thinking skills." They lack academic knowledge, which is the focus of "Core Knowledge."[6] What is striking about Hirsch's curriculum is its lack of condescension; it makes no concessions to allegedly different styles of learning or the arguments that poor, minority students need to be given a less challenging course of study. First graders in the Mohegan School, for example, read "The Legend of Sleepy Hollow" and "Narrative of the Life of Frederick Douglass"; they study Lincoln's "Gettysburg Address," the Tang dynasty, and Shakespeare. The first-grade curriculum also includes study of the solar system, fundamental principles of music, and some elementary algebraic concepts.[7]

Educationists critics indignantly charge that Hirsch's emphasis on "cultural literacy" means a Eurocentric curriculum heavily weighted toward books by and about dead white men. But Hirsch's curriculum clearly does not exclude what they would call the multiculturalist perspective; the difference, however, is that the "Core Knowledge" program does not subordinate every other consideration to a head-counting, color-coded agenda. The result is a program that has already established a proven track record of success among poor, minority students—the very groups that white educationists claim that they are defending against Hirsch's allegedly discriminatory curriculum.

At the South Bronx's Mohegan Elementary School, reading test scores were up 13.5 percent in 1992, the year after Hirsch's program was first implemented. Discipline problems were also down and journalists who visited the school found the children enthusiastic about their classes, even about their homework."What we are doing here," the school's principal Jeffrey Litt told reporters, "is creating an educated child."[8]

Private and Parochial

The most widespread challenge to the failure of public education is the parallel system of private and parochial schools that exists—often side by side—in virtually every community. There is nothing experimental about the success of private and parochial schools. While only 23 percent of public school eighth graders reached the "proficient" level in mathematics in the 1992 National Assessment of Educational Progress exam, 32 percent of children in Catholic schools and 43 percent in other private schools scored at the proficient level. Once again, the differences are often the most pronounced in inner-city schools. Even though they often spend far less than their public-sector counterparts, inner-city Catholic schools consistently succeed where public schools fail.

Between 1987 and 1993, Milwaukee's public schools increased their per-pupil expenditures by nearly a third (32 percent); during the same period, the predominantly black Messmer High School, an independent Catholic school, saw its per-pupil spending fall by 14 percent. Although it spends only $4,622 per student (less than any public high school in the city), Messmer has a 98 percent graduation rate. Although 60 percent of Messmer's students come from single-parent households, 78 percent of its graduates go on to college.[9]

Like other Catholic schools, Messmer tends to focus its limited resources on core academic courses. But it also shares an ethos common to successful Catholic schools, an "inspirational theology," that gives the schools a strong sense of purpose and moral authority. Such schools are "communal organizations" with shared values and activities that encourage close contact between students and teachers, who see themselves as moral and intellectual role models. This common vision stresses "ideals of human dignity and caring and the belief that human reason can discern ethical truth."[10] For many of the parents who choose religious schools, those values are as important as any academic advantage their children might gain. Yale Law School Professor Stephen L. Carter describes the attraction of the religious schools:

> Parents who seek a religious education for their children are often more interested in the inculcation of strong values—and, in particular, the school's reinforcement of the values they teach at home—than they are in the religious aspects. Their image of public schools, accurate or not, is of a place where values are destroyed instead of reinforced. The battles over such issues as sex education and condom distribution provide examples of just what many parents fear most about schools: that they will, because experts distrusted by the parents say so, shoulder aside values that the parents cherish most.[11]

At Milwaukee's Messmer High, this emphasis on values translates into demanding expectations both for academic work and behavior. "We set expectations and expect them to follow through," the school's vice principal explains. If a student isn't able to comply, Messmer's not the school for them." Explains another administrator: "We don't have standards for which we make excuses, like 'I came from a single-parent family.'" In practice, that means an attention to the smallest details of discipline, including issues that would be regarded as absurdly minor by public school administrators. Messmer's rules include a set of "non-negotiables" for both parents and students, including: No weapons, or threats of any kind; no drugs; no caps or hats of any kind; no talking back to any adults in the building; and mandatory parent-teacher conferences.

Home Schooling

There are no hard and fast numbers, but the Home School Legal Defense Association estimates that there are about 630,000 children in home schooling families; of which 474,000 are of school age. "We may be small," the group says, "but we are not insignificant."[12] Home schooling is no longer the slightly exotic and exclusively church-related phenomenon it was only a decade ago. As the numbers of parents disillusioned by public education grows, the ranks of stay-at-home schools have swollen. Wider access to computers and on-line tutorial programs has encouraged a new wave of home schoolers to desert the public schools; the *Wall Street Journal* reported in a front-page story, "not for religious reasons, or to thumb their noses at the establishment, but simply because they think they can do a better job teaching the children themselves." The information superhighway now lets home schoolers have instant access to sophisticated databases as well as curricula specifically designed for their use. Networks of families who opt to educate their children at home are now forming their own athletic leagues, newsletters, and electronic bulletin boards for sharing and evaluating computer software, as well as their own support groups and lobbying organizations that can be mobilized with impressive consequences. When Congress was considering expanding the government's regulatory power into home schools, the movement galvanized an avalanche of calls, letters, faxes, and telegrams that successfully derailed the power grab.

As their numbers and sophistication grow, home schoolers are also receiving respect for their academic effectiveness. In Oregon, more than two thirds of the children educated in home schools who took national achievement tests scored at or above the national average for public school children. Home schoolers in Washington State also scored in the upper third of students nationally—once again, above the level of the state's public school children. The movement received a prestige boost when the *Wall Street Journal* profiled three home school graduates from the same family who had all been admitted to Harvard, which says it takes up to ten applicants each year who have had some home schooling. A senior admissions officer at Harvard reported that applications from home schoolers were "definitely increasing," and that "In general, those kids do just fine."[13]

Tutoring

As the deficiencies of the public schools become more obvious, some parents are turning to the use of private tutors to make up for the gaps in their children's education. The popularity of tutors is especially evident in affluent areas, where parents may pay $35 an hour or more for teachers to make house calls. The status of the tutor is a mark of the shifting priorities of American education. Once stigmatized as a sign of underachievement, tutors are now often hired for high-achieving students who are not academically challenged in their regular schools.[14] Ironically, the private tutors have become a status symbol at precisely the same time as public education has moved away from providing distinctive programs and honors for gifted students, in the name of eliminating competition. As more schools move away from ability grouping and/or water down their programs for bright students, tutors who can provide students with a personalized, advanced, and challenging curriculum will continue to gain in popularity.

The Teachers

There is a central role to be played by teachers in the reform of American education. If teachers want to win back public confidence, they have to be more than the organized special interest group that opposes every reform and always pushes for more money and less accountability.

How about this for a start:

1. Break ranks with the bureaucrats. Why have teachers been so willing to cover up for bloated bureaucracies? Why haven't they made a better case that teachers' salaries and jobs are not responsible for all increases in school spending?

2. Try honesty. The public expects too much from teachers because educationists have led it to believe teachers could be substitute parents, psychotherapists, cops, social workers, dieticians, nursemaids, babysitters, and nose wipers and still do a decent job teaching kids to read, write, and do math. Instead of saying no, educationists have added courses in environmental education, death education, personal hygiene, self-esteem, driver's ed, job readiness, sexual harassment, radon studies, yoga, yogurt awareness, and god-knows-what-else.

   Now teachers are the ones left holding the bag when it turns out that less than half the day is spent on academics. Teachers should make a preemptive strike. They can put it this way: "You want kids who can read and write, fine. If you want us to be teachers, don't give us your dirty laundry."

3. Dumbing down is going to backfire. The best job guarantee for educators is still quality. The teachers unions have had some success in painting critics as right-wing zealots. But the public's not dumb and businesses aren't going to keep accepting recruits stuffed with self-esteem who can't add a column of numbers. Raising (not lowering) academic standards is just good politics. In return, teachers might reasonably ask that teachers be put in charge of their classrooms again. The most common complaint among rank-and-file teachers is discipline in the classroom. They can't teach if they have to be cops. But when they kick kids out, the administration doesn't back them up, and the courts have created elaborate legal hurdles. This leads some educationists to complain bitterly that private schools do a better job because they can get rid of troublemakers. Instead of always saying how unfair that is, why not ask for a level playing field by raising your own standards? What a teacher says goes. If a teacher says a kid is gone the kid is gone. The public will buy it.

4. Let's raise teacher pay by rewarding excellence. Teachers unions hate merit pay, but if teachers want to win back public confidence, they should be open to the idea of paying better teachers more money. The most gifted teachers would not be overpaid at $70,000 a year. The flip

side is that it should be easier to get rid of deadwood. Protecting the burned-out and incompetent is no longer an issue of job security; it has become a credibility test for the entire profession.

5. Competition may not be such a dirty word after all. If there really was a market for good teachers, members of the profession (the better ones) could actually get *more* leverage.

In short, teachers interested in improving their schools could find common ground with educational critics: ditch the bureaucracies, slim down the curriculum, trade accountability for more authority, build political support with higher standards, and boost pay for their most effective colleagues.

The "Broken Windows Theory of Schools"

Alongside teachers, the key players in the reform of American education will be the parents. Frequently, I am asked how parents can tell whether their child's school is good. And how can they go about making it better? The bad news is that there is no easy answer because no handy checklist of indices of good schools exists; even if it did exist, it would be of uncertain value because the information provided by the schools would be uneven and often of questionable validity. Since John Jacob Cannell published his study of the "Lake Wobegon" syndrome in test scores, it has been clear that standardized test scores need to be approached with caution and skepticism; schools remain adept at reporting positive results and putting the best possible face on mediocre ones. When 90 percent of the nation's school districts are claiming to be "above average," however, it is clear that these results need to be seen as public relations tools rather than as hard and fast measures of academic quality. The same caveat applies to grades, which have been inflated far beyond the point where they were a reliable indicator either of effort or achievement. Merely because a child comes home with papers and tests festooned with gold stars and enthusiastic affirmations does not mean that all is well.

This obviously is the first problem that parents face: the lack of reliable information from the schools. The same lack of feedback that has contributed so much to the nation's continuing state of denial about its educational collapse makes it hard for parents to play their own proper role in turning the schools around. Understandably, schools want to put themselves in the best possible light, but given the incendiary nature of the school wars, many educators have also developed a practiced reticence when it comes to telling parents what is actually going on in the classroom. Parents, for example, who are concerned about a school's policy on reading are likely to ask administrators whether or not their child will be taught phonics. Even if the school is committed completely to a "whole language" approach to reading, the parent is likely to be told that, yes, of course, phonics is taught "as a component" of the reading program, or that the curriculum is a blend of whole language and phonics instruction. In many cases, this is true and the results are good; but in many other cases, it is misleading and intended to be misleading.

In her book *Ed School Follies,* author Rita Kramer recounts an exchange among student teachers at a major teachers college. The students ask a senior educationist, " 'What do you do when parents complain that their kids aren't learning phonics?' Her answer to that one brought down the house. 'Don't *tell* them you don't teach phonics,' she said. Then added, 'You do.' They all smiled and nodded, as though they understood quite well what she meant."[15] Unfortunately, the attitude that parents need to be deflected rather than enlisted as partners is not limited to the teachers colleges.

As we have seen, statements of educational "outcomes" are seldom helpful or illuminating. The vast majority of schools will insist on their absolute and unwavering commitment to excellence and to academic rigor, but merely saying so doesn't mean its true. Likewise, lists of required courses, which can be impressive at first glance, seldom provide much insight into the content or the standards of those courses. Charming and caring teachers may be reassuring, but they are not a reliable indicator or whether Johnny will be able to read, spell, or do sums. Nor can parents be sure their child's school is effective merely because it is modern or equipped with the very latest in technology. District after district has proved that well-appointed facilities are in no way incompatible with educational mediocrity. Parents are well advised to approach all of these issues with some agnosticism.

Having said all of this, I should hasten to say that there are indeed ways of evaluating a school; it is possible for parents to get a sense of any school's fundamental values and the likelihood that it will provide its students with a sound education. The technique I propose is borrowed from political scientist James Q. Wilson and could be called the "Broken Windows Theory of Schools."

Wilson's theory originally was developed to deal with the problem of crime and neighborhood safety, not education. But the same principles that track the spread of disorder in the streets can also be applied to the breakdown of academic order in the schools. "Social psychologists and police," wrote Wilson and coauthor George Kelling, "tend to agree that if a window in a building is broken and is left unrepaired, the rest of the windows will soon be broken. This is as true in nice neighborhoods as in run-down ones." A car left unattended and obviously abandoned will likely be vandalized or stripped within hours in some neighborhoods. Even in affluent areas, a car that is battered and dented is likely to be fair game. The reason for the rapid spread of broken windows through a neighborhood and the trashing of the abandoned cars is the same: "one unrepaired window is a signal that no one cares, and so breaking more windows costs nothing."

If people believe that private property—whether a car or a home—is well taken care of and watched over, they are less likely to vandalize it because such behavior is more likely to be dangerous and costly. But Wilson and Kelling noted, "vandalism *can occur anywhere once communal barriers—the sense of mutual regard and the obligations of civility—are lowered by actions that seem to signal that no one cares.*"[16] [emphasis in original]

Effective schools also rely on communal values and barriers, which is why the theory of broken windows can be applied to academic standards. When evaluating schools, *look for the big picture in the details.*

If you want to find out what is really important to a school, don't ask the principal, *look to see if spelling and grammar are corrected on a child's paper.* If it is not, it is the equivalent of a broken window: a sign that no one cares about whether children acquire basic academic skills. If a child brings home a paper that is sloppy and filled with misspellings, it is a signal that no one cares whether they get it right. To the educationists, this may seem a minor detail, but it says a great deal about the educational neighborhood and where it is headed. If teachers are unconcerned about poor writing, how likely is it they will provide children the "essential intellectual tools" or the fund of knowledge they will need? How seriously will they take their obligation to train children in the "systematic ways of thinking developed within the various fields of scholarly and scientific investigation"? And, ultimately, how serious are they about setting and maintaining demanding standards for academic achievement?

Consultants and educationists might leaf through the minutes of school board meetings and read reports by strategic planning task forces to determine the ethos of a particular school, but there are other reliable indices as well: How long does it take for graffiti to be cleaned up? How does the school react to student insolence to teachers? Are parents regarded as distractions or annoyances? Educationists will dismiss this as simplistic, but effective schools all understand that their ethos is expressed through just such details. They recognize that standards are maintained by insisting on high expectations in *every* aspect of school life. They also recognize that confidence grows from mastering the elementary skills and from the small victories.

At Baltimore's Barclay School, "The motto ... seems to be: 'It's not finished until it's perfect.' Students receive praise not for acceptable work but for wholly correct work." Neatness is not just emphasized, it is required. So it is not an accident or afterthought that a special cursive handwriting is introduced as early as first grade, reinforcing the message: this is important, it needs to be done well, *but you can do it.* At Milwaukee's

Messmer High School, the culture of the school is founded on the nonnegotiables: no caps or hats, no lipping off to grown-ups.

Could Barclay and Messmer be successful without such stringent attention to the smallest details of school life? Perhaps. But the details are part of the fabric of success and are all the more important because that fabric is so fragile in their communities where the schools are located.

The broken windows theory of education can be applied to other areas as well.

- Do the school's goals or mission statement make any mention of specific disciplines? The failure to say a single word about math, writing, reading, history, or science is an educational broken window, a red flag that the people who run the schools have, at best, a vague notion of what they are teaching. Compare the goals or mission statement with the goals of Baltimore's Calvert Academy. Are they written in the language of character, citizenship, and academic achievement? Or the therapeutic jargon of educationism?
- What proportion of an average school day is spent on core academic subjects (reading, math, science, social studies)? If it is less than two-thirds, the school's priorities are questionable.
- Do student receive letter grades? The mere presence of A's and B's on a report card says little in and of itself. But if grades have been abolished or replaced with vague or confusing new measurements, parents should be concerned. They should also be concerned if their children are being awarded A's for work that is substandard or sloppy.
- How much of the day is spent working "cooperatively"? Are gifted students working up to their level? Or are they being used as peer tutors? Although it does not apply to every student, the way a school treats its brightest students is an important indicator of its attitude toward achievement in general. Decisions to cut back on programs for the gifted and talented or any diminution of honors awarded to the best students are dangerous warning signs that the leveling impulse is stronger than the commitment to excellence.
- How dumb are the textbooks? If parents find out that the school uses textbooks with the reading level of a farmer talking to his cow, they have a clear picture of the intellectual level of their child's classes.
- Ideas have consequences. Do students discuss values, ethical dilemmas, and sexuality as questions without answers? Do school officials talk about "self-esteem," or instilling confidence? Do they know the difference?
- Does the school teach reading through systematic phonics? Are teachers candid about their answer? Defensive? Misleading?
- Who runs the classroom? The teacher or the kids? Do teachers see themselves as authority figures or merely as "facilitators"? How do the

students see them? Do the teachers regard themselves and are they regarded as role models?

- How orderly is the school? The best schools would never be mistaken for a Trappist monastery, but chaos is never the sign of an effective school, no matter how much educationists gush about spontaneity.
- Does the school see students as individuals or as members of groups? Does the school aim to educate independent individualists or group-thinkers? Equally as important: Does the school encourage students to think of themselves as individuals or as members of an ethnic, racial, or gender subgroup?
- Is the principal a wimp? This may seem flippant, but effective schools have strong leaders who project their vision throughout the school. A weak and indecisive administrator is a sign that no one is in charge or that the leadership is weak, confused, and vague. Strong, committed, vibrant schools are not run by Milquetoasts.

Reforming the Parents

Parents are, of course, part of any solution. But if we are honest, we also need to acknowledge that they are also part of the problem. While much of this book has been devoted to the inadequacies of American schools, the dumbing down of American kids is also very much a family affair, often abetted and even encouraged by parents. Our dilemma would be considerably eased if parents were clamoring for higher standards, more homework, and more rigorous grades. But this is hardly the case—teachers often have to adjust their expectations and standards downward because they cannot count on support from home for more demanding requirements.

Apologists for public education are quick to seize upon changes in family demographics—including the rise of single-parent households—as a social problem that is beyond their control, but which contributes to academic declines. Their arguments cannot be dismissed, because it is true that the schools can no longer count on the backing of a two-parent household in every case. But the family background of students is hardly an argument for weaker academic standards. A child from a dysfunctional family already faces formidable social and economic barriers, without having educational failure added to his burdens. And it is naive to assume that schools can offer an array of social programs without abandoning their own primary responsibilities, or that they can succeed where the rest of society has failed.

The emphasis on dysfunctional families is also misleading on another count: Despite the massive shifts in family patterns during the last several decades, most students still come from intact families. But even traditional, two-parent, middle-class families contribute to the educational crisis because of their attitudes toward education and their own responsibilities.

In his cross-cultural studies of schools in the United States, Japan, and China, researcher Harold Stevenson attributed significant differences in achievement levels not simply to differing approaches to schooling, but also to the very different approaches to their children's education by Asian and American parents. "Chinese and Japanese children know that they will have free time only after they have completed the day's schoolwork," he found. "In American families, leisure activities and schoolwork compete for the child's time."[17] American parents do not like what they regard as excessive homework and frequently express distaste for schoolwork if it interferes with other activities they think should be given equal or even greater value.

The implications of this attitude are considerable. "Daily lessons cannot be mastered without review and practice," noted Stevenson, "and American students cannot gain this experience as long as teachers are reluctant to increase the amount of homework and parents and children hold unfavorable views about its value."[18] But the attitude about homework is merely one reflection of the different emphases Asian and American parents place on education. Americans, for instance, place heavy stress on preschool education, and American parents seem to be deeply involved in making sure their children get a reasonable head start. In contrast, Asian parents regard children under the age of six as enjoying an "age of innocence" and do not push younger children much at all. While nine of ten American mothers of kindergartners teach their children the alphabet at home, fewer than a third of Japanese and Chinese mothers teach symbols to their preschoolers. Only 36 percent of Japanese mothers teach numbers to their preschoolers, in sharp contrast to the 90 percent of American mothers who teach their preschool children numbers.[19] To an observer unversed in the cultural differences, it might appear that it is the American families that value education more highly, while their Asian counterparts pursue a far more casual and relaxed approach to learning.

But when children turn six and enter first grade, there is a dramatic change. For the Japanese and Chinese parents, the age of innocence is replaced by the "age of reason," when a child enters elementary school. Parents who were previously "nurturant and permissive become authorities who demand obedience, respect, and adherence to their rules and goals."[20] From their laissez-faire attitude toward education, Asian parents now become intensely involved with their children, helping and monitoring homework and providing a home environment in which schoolwork unquestionably is the highest priority.

At the same moment, however, that Asian parents are becoming more deeply involved with their children's education, American parents ironically are withdrawing. When a child turns six in Japan, his schooling becomes a parent's top responsibility; when a child turns six in the United States, parents tend to entrust their educational future to the schools and to his teachers.[21] Japanese parents see the task of learning just beginning at the same moment that American parents see their job as coming more or less to an end. For too many Americans, Stevenson found, "schoolwork is considered to be the responsibility of teachers and students, rather than a major concern for parents." In this country, the beginning of elementary school is "not accompanied by strong parental demands for academic excellence or devotion to homework and demands do not increase much during the succeeding years of elementary school."[22]

This perhaps explains the story one mother told me as I was working on this book: She had attended a parents meeting at her child's elementary school. At the meeting some of the other parents complained that their children were being given *too much* homework and that it was interfering with their sports, and even cutting into the time they had for watching television. Other mothers admitted—apparently without embarrassment—that they had done their children's homework for them, to spare them both time and anxiety. The assumption that seemed to dominate the parents' meeting, the mother said, was that schoolwork had become a distraction from things that many of the parents believed to be the main business of a child's life. They were not concerned that their children were not learning—they were annoyed because expectations were too high. Their views were probably not representative either of a majority of parents at the woman's school nor did they reflect the attitude of most American parents. But they are undoubtedly widespread; most teachers can tell stories of parents who complained about excessive homework, low marks, high standards.

Unless American parents raise those expectations, it is unlikely that America's schools will ever raise them unilaterally. Mediocrity, unfortunately, is contagious. But so is excellence.

NOTES

Scenes from the Front: "Mere Facts"

1. Vincent Carroll, "Jeffco Schools and Bill Spady: How Tight Is the Connection?" *Rocky Mountain News*, 7 March 1994. See also Vincent Carroll, "In Littleton, Colo., Voters Expel Education Faddists," *Wall Street Journal*, 18 November 1993.

Scenes from the Front: Andrea's Complaint

1. Keith Ervin, "Class Too Easy, Highline Teen Complains," *Seattle Times*, 6 July 1994.

2. Letter to the Editor, "Unchallenging Class Turning Students into Morons," *Seattle Times*, 13 July 1994.

3. Ervin, "Class Too Easy."

4. Jane Hadley, "Student Quits, Says Science Class All Fluff," *Seattle Post-Intelligencer*, 7 July 1994.

5. Ervin, "Class Too Easy."

6. Ervin, "Class Too Easy."

7. Hadley, "Student Quits."

8. Ervin, "Class Too Easy."

Chapter 1. Dumbing Down Our Kids

1. "First Things First: What Americans Expect from the Public Schools," Public Agenda, September 1994.

2. Arthur Bestor, *Educational Wastelands: The Retreat from Learning in Our Public Schools*, 2nd. ed., (Urbana, Ill.: University of Illinois Press, 1985, pp. 54, 55.

3. Hannah Arendt, "The Crisis in Education," *Partisan Review* (Fall 1958), pp. 494–95.

4. John Keats, *Schools Without Scholars* (Boston: Houghton Mifflin, 1958), pp. 83, 85.

Chapter 2: Losing the Race

1. Catherine S. Manegold, "41% of School Day Is Spent on Academic Subjects, Study Says," *New York Times*, 5 May 1994.

2. Harold W. Stevenson and James W. Stigler, *The Learning Gap* (New York: Summit Books, 1992), p. 55.

3. Ibid.

4. Seymour Itzkoff, *The Decline of Intelligence in America* (Westport, Conn.: Praeger, 1994), p. 55.

5. Stevenson, *The Learning Gap*, p. 31

6. Ibid., p. 33.

7. Ibid., p. 31.

8. Itzkoff, *The Decline of Intelligence*, p. 59.

9. Ibid., p. 34.

10. "What College-Bound Students Abroad Are Expected to Know About Biology," The American Federation of Teachers (1994), pp. ix, x.

11. Stevenson, *The Learning Gap*, p. 67.

12. Ibid., p. 25.

13. Ibid., p. 58.

14. Ibid., pp. 82–83.

15. Ibid., pp. 49–50. Stevenson concluded: "We found little overall difference in the levels of cognitive functioning of children across the three cultures. American children did not display lower intellectual abilities than Chinese and Japanese children. . . . The hypothesis that the academic weakness of American children is due to deficiencies in innate ineffectual ability is without merit."

16. Catherine S. Manegold, "Students Make Strides But Fall Far Short of Goals," *New York Times*, 18 August 1994.

17. Paul E. Barton, Richard J. Coley, "Performance at the Top: From Elementary through Graduate School," Policy Information Report, Educational Testing Service, Princeton, New Jersey, 1991, and Ina V. S. Mullis, "Trends in Academic Progress, Achievement of U.S. Students in Science, 1969–70 to 1990; Mathematics, 1973 to 1990; Reading, 1971 to 1990; and Writing, 1984 to 1990," Educational Testing Service, Princeton, New Jersey, November 1991. Mullis concluded that: "Overall, the trends suggest few changes in educational achievement levels across the two decades covered by NAEP assessments. However, some declines in science and mathematics for 17-year-olds during the 1970s and generally low performance levels across several curriculum areas prompted reform efforts. Improvements occurred in science and mathematics during the 1980s at all three ages. Particularly for science, there is a pattern of decreased proficiency in the 1970s followed by recovery in the 1980s. Conversely, the reading results show that gains made by 9-year-olds in the 1970s eroded during the 1980s, while the performance of 13-year-olds remained constant. Writing achievement also showed some decline in the 1980s for eighth graders."

18. Ibid.

19. Ibid.

20. National Assessment of Educational Progress, 1990.

21. Lynn Olson, "Writing Still Needs Work, Report Finds," *Education Week*, 15 June 1994, and Associated Press; NAEP 1992 Writing Report Card.

22. NAEP 1988 Writing Report Card.

23. Elizabeth Mehren, "Test Scores Are Low, but What Do They Measure," *Los Angeles Times*, 29 September 1993.

24. Itzkoff, *The Decline of Intelligence*, p. 63. Referring to this report, Secretary of Education Richard W. Riley said: "This report is a wake-up call to the sheer magnitude of illiteracy in this country and underscores literacy's strong connection to economic status. It paints a picture of a society in which the vast majority of Americans do not know that they do not have the skills they need to earn a living in our increasingly technological society and international marketplace."

25. "Student Preparation: the Faculty View," *Education Week*, 22 June 1994.

26. Karen Diegmueller, "Experts Decry Poor Grasp of Geography Among Children, Adults," *Education Week*, 8 June 1994.

27. *Philadelphia Inquirer*, 10 June 1987.

28. William Celis 3d, "Science I.Q. of Americans Is Not O.K., Survey Shows," *New York Times*, 21 April 1994.

29. David Maraniss and Bill Peterson, "U.S. Students Left Flat by Sweep of History," *Washington Post*, 2 December 1989.

30. Deirdre Carmody, "Many Students Fail Quiz on Basic Economics," *New York Times*, 29 December 1988.

31. Ibid.

32. Susan Antilla, "On Economics, the Teacher May Need Homework," *New York Times*, 17 August 1994. First-year graduate management students at Wake Forest University answered correctly only 17.2 percent of the time on a basic "cultural literacy" test. (Imagine trying to do business with Nicaragua, when 63 percent of the executives-of-tomorrow couldn't identify Managua.) But if their cultural ignorance was alarming, their ignorance of basic business terms was frightful. Fully 70 percent of the *graduate management students* could not define "amortization"; 45% were clueless about the meaning of "bear market"; 62 percent were unable to define "capital gains"; and 79 percent were stumped by "lien." See also Francis Flaherty, "U.S. Decline: A New Clue," *New York Times*, 30 May 1993.

33. The College Board.

34. Louis V. Gerstner Jr., "Our Schools Are Failing. Do We Care?" *New York Times*, 27 May 1994.

35. Ibid.

36. Edward B. Fiske, "Impending U.S. Jobs 'Disaster': Work Force Unqualified to Work," *New York Times*, 25 September 1989.

37. Itzkoff, *The Decline of Intelligence*, pp. 49–50.

38. Fiske, "Impending U.S. Jobs 'Disaster'," The study referred to is "Workforce 2000" by William B. Johnson and Arnold H. Packer.

39. John H. Bishop, "Is the Test Score Decline Responsible for the Productivity Growth Decline?" *American Economic Review*, March 1989.

40. Warren Brookes, "Public Education and the Global Failure of Socialism," *Imprimis*, April 1990.

41. Bishop, "Test Score Decline."

42. Eric Hanushek, "How Business Can Save Education: A State Agenda for Reform," Heritage Foundation Conference, 24 April 1991.

Scenes from the Front: An Endangered Species I

1. Adele Jones, "'F' Is For Fired," *NEA Today*, September 1994.

2. Grossman, Ronald, "A school system that's Fail Safe: Firing of teacher for flunking students offers a lesson to American educators," *Chicago Tribune*, 2 August 1993.

3. Jones, "'F' Is For Fired."

4. Grossman, "School system that's fail safe," Subsequent references are also to Grossman, unless otherwise noted.

5. "Grave Expectations," *Chicago Tribune*, 9 August 1993.

Chapter 3. The American Way of Denial

1. Seymour Itzkoff, *The Decline of Intelligence in America* (Westport, Conn.: Praeger, 1994), p. 63.

2. Harold W. Stevenson and James W. Stigler, *The Learning Gap* (New York: Summit Books, 1992), p. 116.

3. Ibid., 29

4. "52 Percent of Parents Give A or B to Public Schools, Survey Finds," *Education Week*, 13 April 1994.

5. "Schools Earning High Grades from Public, Poll Shows," *Education Week*, 4 May 1994.

6. Carol Innerst, "Violence called schools' top problem," *Washington Times*. 26 August 1994.

7. Cited in Chester E. Finn Jr., "Up from Mediocrity," *Policy Review*, Number 61, Summer 1992.

8. Ibid.

9. Ibid.

10. Stevenson, *The Learning Gap*, p. 114.

11. Carol Innerst, "Wordsmiths on wane among U.S. students," *Washington Times*, 25 August 1994.

12. Gene Maeroff, "My Ordinary Career," *Education Week*, 27 April 1994.

13. Chester E. Finn Jr., *We Must Take Charge* (New York: Free Press, 1991), p. 106.

14. Harold W. Stevenson, Chuansheng Chen, and David H. Uttal, "Beliefs and Achievement: A Study of Black, White, and Hispanic Children," *Child Development* 61 (1990), pp. 508–23.

15. John Keats, *Schools Without Scholars* (Boston: Houghton Mifflin, 1958), p. viii.

16. Lawrence A. Cremin, *The Transformation of the School* (New York: Alfred A. Knopf, 1962), p. 6.

17. Ibid., p. 7.

18. Ibid., pp. 341, 342.

19. Bestor, *Educational Wastelands: The Retreat from Learning in our Public Schools* 2nd. ed. (Urbana, Ill.: The University of Illinois Press, 1985), pp. 8–9.

20. Ibid., p. 9.

21. Ibid., p. 110.

22. Ibid., p. 111.

Scenes from the Front: How Did Einstein *Feel?*

1. "New Achievement Test Brings Sharp Questions," *New York Times,* 4 May 1994.

Chapter 4: Feelings

1. Debra Saunders, "Feelings . . . nothing more than feelings," *Milwaukee Journal,* 13 September 1994.

2. Ibid.

3. Debra Saunders, "Folly of feel-good schooling," *Milwaukee Journal,* 18 September 1994.

4. William Kilpatrick, *Why Johnny Can't Tell Right from Wrong* (New York: Simon & Schuster, 1992), p. 39.

5. Ibid.

6. Cited in the Final Report of the Senate Select Committee to Study the Michigan Model for Comprehensive School Health Education, December 1992, p. 35.

7. Ibid., p. 34.

8. Ibid., p. 37.

9. William D. Hedges and Marian L. Martinello, "What the Schools Might Do: Some Alternatives for the Here and Now," in *Feeling, Valuing, and the Art of Growing: Insights into the Affective,* Association for Supervision and Curriculum Development, 1977.

10. Charles C. Anderson, "A Canadian Critic on Teacher Education in Western USA," *School and Society,* 23 April 1960, p. 204.

11. James D. Koerner, *The Miseducation of American Teachers* (Boston: Houghton Mifflin Company, 1963), pp. 165–66.

12. The yearbook's authors were nothing if not ambitious. In the introduction ["What the Schools Might Do," p. vii.], they wrote: "Periodically a book is published that makes a difference in American education. *Perceiving, Behaving, Becoming,* published in 1962 by ASCD, was just such a book. It made a difference in public and private schools, in teacher education programs, in curriculum development, in supervision, and in teaching. From it, educators learned there is hope for all learners, that a

learner's self-concept is important in daily performance, and that self-concept can be enhanced.

"The impact of the book was broadened during the 1960's by writing of third-force theorists. . . . Most of these writers can now be grouped as supportive of what we call humanistic education. . . . Now ASCD publishes its 1977 Yearbook: *Feeling, Valuing, and the Art of Growing: Insights into the Affective.* Once again, we have a book that can make a difference in American education."

13. Cecil H. Patterson, "Insights About Persons: Psychological Foundations of Humanistic and Affective Education," in *Feeling, Valuing, and the Art of Growing: Insights into the Affective.*

14. *Feeling, Valuing,* p. 201.

15. Hedges and Martinello, "What the Schools Might Do."

16. Ibid.

17. Patterson, "Insights About Persons."

Chapter 5. The Religion of Self-Esteem

1. Lillian G. Katz, "Reading, Writing, Narcissism," *New York Times,* 15 July 1993.

2. "Teaching Self-Image Stirs Furor," *New York Times,* 13 October 1993.

3. Harold W. Stevenson and James W. Stigler, *The Learning Gap* (New York: Summit Books, 1992), p. 111.

4. Lauren Murphy Payne, *Just Because I Am: A Child's Book of Affirmation* (Minneapolis: Free Spirit Publishing, 1994) and Lauren Murphy Payne and Claudia Rolhing, *A Leader's Guide to Just Because I Am: A Child's Book of Affirmation* (Minneapolis: Free Spirit Publishing, 1994). Subsequent references will be to "Text" and "Guide" respectively.

5. Payne, Guide, p. 1.

6. Ibid.

7. Ibid.

8. Ibid., p. 5.

9. Ibid., p. 8.

10. Payne, Text, pages are not numbered.

11. Payne, Guide, pp. 15, 16.

12. Ibid., pp. 18, 22.

13. Ibid., p. 38.

14. Ibid.

15. Payne, Text.

16. Payne, Guide, p. 45.

17. Ibid., p. 14.

18. Katz, "Reading, Writing, Narcissism."

19. Martin V. Covington, "Self-Esteem and Failure in School: Analysis and Policy Implications," in Mecca, Smelser, Vasconcellos, *The Social Importance of Self-Esteem* (Berkeley, Calif.: University of California Press, 1989).

20. Thomas G. Moeller, "Self-Esteem: How Important Is It to Improving Academic Performance?" *Virginia Journal of Education*, November 1993.

21. B. C. Hansford and J. A. Hattie, "The relationship between self and achievement/performance measures," *Review of Educational Research*, No. 52, 1982.

22. V. Covington, "Self-Esteem and Failure in School: Analysis and Policy Implications," op. cit.

23. Quoted in Robert Coles, *The Moral Life of Children* (Boston: Houghton Mifflin, 1986), p. 93.

24. Sylvia Rimm, *The Underachievement Syndrome* (Watertown, Wis.: Apple Publishing, 1986), p. 4. Explains Rimm: "This is a competitive society and families and schools are competitive. . . . It is not possible to be productive in our society or in our schools until one learns to deal with competition, and dealing with competition means coping with losing in a productive way."

25. Quoted in Chester E. Finn Jr., *We Must Take Charge* (New York: Free Press, 1991), p. 108.

26. Covington, "Self-Esteem and Failure," op. cit.

Scenes from the Front: The Mission Statement

1. "Strategic Long Range Planning," School District of Lomira (Wis.), 1994.

Chapter 6. The Attack on Excellence

1. Lynda Richardson, "Public Schools Are Failing Brightest Students, a Federal Study Says," *New York Times*, 5 November 1993.

2. Andrew Ferguson, "Dumbing Down," *Washingtonian*, October 1993. See also Karen Diegmueller, "Growing Number of Schools Reject Class Rankings," *Education Week*, 15 June 1994.

3. "New Grading System Begun in L.A. Schools," *Los Angeles Times*, 9 September 1993.

4. Peter West, "Ill. School Barred from Team Science-Fair Prize," *Education Week*, 25 May 1994.

5. Quotes are taken from Tom Steward's report on Outcome Based Education, WCCO-TV, Minneapolis, Minn., Sept. 12–13, 1994.

6. Quotes are taken from Jayna Davis, "What Did You Learn in School Today?" KFOR-TV, Oklahoma City, Okla., 27 May 1993 and 6 June 1993.

7. Glynn Custred, "Onward to Adequacy," *Academic Questions*, Summer 1990.

8. Dennis Farney, "For Peggy McIntosh, 'Excellence Can Be A Dangerous Concept,'" *Wall Street Journal*, 14 June 1994.

9. Gillian Lee Weiss, "Brain Drain," *New Republic*, 28 February 1994.

10. Tony Mauro, "School 'tracking' to be challenged as biased," *USA Today*, 4 May 1994.

11. Patrick Welsh, "Staying on Track: Can We Teach Honors Kids and Hard Cases Together?" *Washington Post*, 7 March 1993.

12. Ibid.

13. Mark A. Mlawer, " 'My Kid Beat Up Your Honor Student'," *Education Week*, 13 July 1994.

14. Eugene Kennedy, " 'Do-gooders' don't when they eradicate competition from life," *Chicago Tribune*, 12 July 1993.

15. Melinda Henneberger, "New Gym Class: No More Choosing Up Sides," *New York Times*, 16 May 1993.

16. Alfie Kohn, *Punished by Rewards: The Trouble with Gold Stars, Incentive Plans, A's, Praise and Other Bribes* (Boston: Houghton Mifflin, 1993), pp. 204–5

17. Ibid., p. 204.

18. Ibid., pp. 208–9.

19. Margaret M. Clifford, "Students Need Challenge *NOT* Easy Success," *Education Digest*, March 1991.

20. William Glasser, *Schools Without Failure*, (New York: Harper & Row, 1969), p. 69.

21. Ibid., p. 72.

22. Ibid., pp. 59, 61.

23. Ibid., pp. 102–4.

24. Ibid., pp. 73–74.

25. Ibid., pp. 74–75.

26. Ibid., p. 104.

27. Ibid., p. 105.

28. Ibid., p. 106.

29. Ibid., p. 98.

30. Albert Mammary, "Fourteen Principles of Quality Outcomes-Based Education," *Quality Outcomes-Driven Education*, October 1991.

31. Ibid.

32. Ibid.

33. Ted A. Mueller, "Outcome Based Education: A Critique," (Madison, Wis., Christian Research Institute, 1993).

34. William G. Spady, "Shifting the Paradigm that Pervades Education," *Outcomes*, Spring 1991.

35. Ibid.

36. Ibid.

37. Tony Mauro, "School 'tracking' to be challenged as biased," *USA Today*, 4 May 1994.

38. Gillian Lee Weiss, "Brain Drain," *New Republic*, 28 February 1994.

39. "Teachers, Students Give Mixed-Ability Grouping a Mixed Review," *Christian Science Monitor*, 1 February 1993.

40. Welsh, "Staying on Track."

41. Ibid.

42. "Teachers, Students Give Mixed-Ability Grouping a Mixed Review."

43. Part of the problem with measuring what programs work for gifted and talented students is methodological. Because gifted students (who score in the top three to seven percent) tend to score near the ceiling on standardized tests, researchers say, the tests do not always reflect all of the improvement; researchers call this "the ceiling effect." This would also be true to a somewhat lesser extent of the top 33 percent of students classified as "high-ability." The ceiling effect tends to mask the improvement of bright students in studies that measure the effectiveness of special programs

44. Susan Demirsky Allan, "Ability-Grouping Research Reviews: What Do They Say About Grouping and the Gifted?" *Educational Leadership*, March 1991.

45. Cited in William G. Durden and Carol J. Mills, "Talent Derailed: The Education Establishment's Assault on Ability Grouping," *WI: Wisconsin Interest*, Winter/Spring 1993. Opponents of ability grouping often cite the research of Professor Robert Slavin of Johns Hopkins University, which found few academic benefits in grouping students by ability. But Slavin's research did not address the question of whether programs specifically created for gifted and talented students were effective. He left such programs out of his research since they "involve many other changes in curriculum, class size, resources, and goals that make them fundamentally different from comprehensive grouping plans." In other words, critics of ability grouping continue to cite studies comparing students "subjected to the same lock-step, grade-restricted curriculum and teacher-controlled pace of instruction," note William G. Durden and Carol J. Mills of the Johns Hopkins Center for Talented Youth, rather than studies that compare students in enriched programs with students in regular classes. Slavin himself has said that there are real benefits in ability grouping on a subject-by-subject basis, such as advanced math classes, where the pace of the instruction was matched to the abilities of students.

46. Chen Lin Kulik, "Effects of Inter-Class Ability Grouping on Achievement and Self-Esteem," paper presented at the annual convention of the American Psychological Association, Los Angeles, California, 1985.

47. Allan, "Ability-Grouping Research Reviews."

48. cited in Durden and Mills, "Talent Derailed." Hastings comments appeared in the October 1992 issue of *Educational Leadership*.

49. Kohn, *Punished by Rewards*, p. 214.

50. Marian Mathews, "Gifted Students Talk About Cooperative Learning," *Educational Leadership*, October 1992.

51. Elizabeth Blackburn Brockman, "'English Isn't a Team Sport, Mrs. Brockman': A Response to Jeremy," *English Journal*, January 1994.

52. Ibid.

53. Durden and Mills, "Talent Derailed."

54. In fact, it is doubtful that slow learners model themselves on fast learner in any case. A 1987 study found that slow and average learners do not look to gifted students as models after all. Instead, students appear more likely to be motivated by watching students of their own ability succeed.

55. Allan, "Ability-Grouping Research Reviews."

Chapter 7: The Making of an Educationist

1. Richard Mitchell, *The Graves of Academe* (New York: Simon & Schuster, 1981), P. 33.

2. James Koerner, *The Miseducation of American Teachers* (Boston: Houghton Mifflin, 1963), p. 18.

3. Among the dissertation titles Koerner cited:

"A Study of the Emotions of High School Football Players."

"A Study of the Relationship Between Certain Aspects of Clothing and the Ability to Handle Selected Clothing Construction Tools with the Developmental Levels of Early Adolescent Girls."

"Recruitment, Selection, and Training of Custodians in Selected Public School Systems."

"An Experimental Study of the Effect of Soothing Background Music on Observed Behavior Indicating Tension of Third Grade Pupils."

"A Performance Analysis of the Propulsive Force of the Flutter Kick."

"The High School Student's Perception of Most-Liked and Least-Liked Television Figures."

"A Study of Little League and its Educational Implications."

"The Relationship Between Personality Traits and Basic Skill in Typewriting."

"A Study of Factors Influencing Selection and Satisfactions in Use of Major Household Appliances as Indicated by Three Selected Groups of Married Women Graduates of the Ohio State University."

"The Cooperative Selection of School Furniture to Serve the Kindergarten Through Third Grade Program in the Garden City Public Schools."

4. Ibid., pp. 19, 32.

5. Quoted in Charles S. Silberman, *Crisis in the Classroom,* (New York: Vintage Books, 1971), pp. 441–42.

6. Koerner, *The Miseducation of American Teachers*, p. 35.

7. Theodore Brameld, *Cultural Foundations of Education* (New York: Harper, 1957), p. 256.

8. Silberman, *Crisis in the Classroom*, pp. 442–43

9. Koerner, *The Miseducation of American Teachers*, pp. 26–27.

10. See Charles J. Sykes, *ProfScam: Professors and the Demise of Higher Education* (New York, St. Martin's Press, 1988), pp. 109–110. See also Stanislav Andreski, *Social Sciences as Sorcery* (New York: St. Martin's Press, 1972), pp. 82–83.

11. All of the dissertations cited are listed in *Dissertation Abstracts International* between 1990 and 1994.

12. The record of those schools has been so poor, that in 1986, the Holmes Group—a consortium of graduate school deans—called for the abolition of the undergraduate major in education. In its place, they called for the restoration of liberal arts education, plus a fifth year of practice teaching and a smattering of education courses. The group also recommended a full-year's internship before teachers assumed full-time responsibilities. Similar recommendations were made by the Carnegie Corporation's Task Force on Teaching as a Profession. Reform efforts have, however, been spotty at best.

13. See Rita Kramer, *Ed School Follies: The Miseducation of America's Teachers* (New York: The Free Press, 1991), p. 209.

14. Ibid., p. 33.

15. Ibid., p. 209.

16. Ibid., p. 211.

Scenes from the Front: "I Wanted to Be a Teacher"

1. Letter from Beth Brooks Sailor to author, 14 October 1994.

Chapter 8: The New Illiteracy

1. All references to Beverly Jankowski, Joan Wittig, and their children are based either on personal communication with the author or from their unpublished manuscript, "Because We Care About Children: A Report on the Communications Arts Curriculum of New Berlin School District Using 'Whole Language Philosophy,' " 1994.

2. Sandra Wilde, "A Proposal for a New Spelling Curriculum," *Elementary School Journal*, vol. 90, no. 3, pp. 275–89.

3. Richard Mitchell, *The Graves of Academe* (New York: Simon & Schuster, 1981), p. 180.

4. Michele Schiesser, "Virginia's Writing Test Penalizes Correctness," *Richmond Times-Dispatch*, 20 October 1993.

5. Richard Mitchell, *The Leaning Tower of Babel* (Boston: Little, Brown and Company, 1984), pp. 41–42.

6. Wittig and Jankowski, "Because We Care About Children." Quotes are taken from official district documents describing the "Communication Arts" program.

7. Matthew Lipman, letter to *Basic Education*, April 1983.

8. Mitchell, *The Graves of Academe*, p. 82.

9. Mitchell, *The Leaning Tower of Babel*, p. 56.

10. Associated Press, 11 December 1994.

11. *A Guide to Understanding the Issues*, The National Right to Read Foundation, 1994, p. 2. See also "Illiteracy a Drag on Industrialized Nations'

Economies, Study Finds," *Los Angeles Times*, 5 April 1992; and "When Johnny's Whole Family Can't Read," *Business Week*, 20 July 1992.

12. Rudolf Flesch, *Why Johnny Can't Read*, (New York, Harper & Row, 1966). . . .

13. Lynn Smith, "A New Reading on U.S. Literacy," *Los Angeles Times*, 29 September 1993.

14. Rudolf Flesch, *Why Johnny Still Can't Read* (New York: Harper & Row, 1981), p. 3.

15. R. C. Anderson, et al., *Becoming A Nation of Readers: The Report of the Commission on Reading* (Washington, D.C.: National Institute of Education, U.S. Department of Education, 1985).

16. Harold Stevenson and James W. Stigler, *The Learning Gap* (New York: Summit Books, 1992), p. 47.

17. Gilbert Sewall, *Necessary Lessons*, (New York: The Free Press, 1983) p. 130.

18. Jeanne Chall, "The New Reading Debates: Evidence from Science, Art, and Ideology," *Teachers College Record*, vol. 94, no. 2, Winter 1992.

19. Ibid.

20. "Don't abandon phonics, say the British," *American Teacher.* vol. 78, no. 3.

21. Marilyn Jager Adams, *Beginning to Read: Thinking and Learning About Print* (Cambridge: MIT Press, 1990).

22. Jeanne Chaney, Reading Improvement Program Coordinator for the Chicago Public Schools, writing in "*Beginning to Read*: A critique by literacy professionals and a response by Marilyn Jager Adams," *Reading Teacher*, vol. 44, no. 6, February 1991.

23. Adams, *Beginning to Read.*

24. Jankowski and Wittig, "Because We Care About Children."

25. Jayna Davis, "What Did You Learn in School Today?" KFOR-TV, Oklahoma City, Okla., 27 May 1993 and 6 June 1993.

26. Mary Jett-Simpson, "Parents and Teachers, Partners in Helping Children Learn to Read," Wisconsin Department of Public Instruction, undated.

27. "An Interview with Harvey Daniels: Whole Language: What's the Fuss," vol. 8, no. 2, *Rethinking Schools*, Winter 1993.

28. Mitchell, *The Graves of Academe*, p. 44.

29. David P. Pearson, "Reading the Whole-Language Movement," *Elementary School Journal*, vol. 90, no. 2, November 1989, pp. 232–41.

30. Yetta Goodman, "Roots of the Whole-Language Movement," *Elementary School Journal*, vol. 90, no. 2, November 1989.

31. Ibid.

32. Kenneth S. Goodman, "Whole-Language Research: Foundations and Development," *Elementary School Journal*, vol. 90, no. 2, November 1989, pp. 207–21.

33. Dorothy Watson, "Defining and Describing Whole Language," *Elementary School Journal*, vol. 90, no. 2, November 1989.

34. Lois Bird, "What is whole language?" In "Dialogue": D. Jacobs, ed., *Teachers networking: The whole language Newsletter*, Number 1, 1987.

35. Watson, "Defining and Describing Whole Language."

36. Ibid.

37. Patrick Groff, "Seven Tragic Reasons Why Teachers Use Whole Language Instead of Phonics," *Right to Read Report*, September 1993.

38. Goodman, "Whole-Language Research."

39. "An Interview with Harvey Daniels."

40. Foyne Mahaffet, "The Hooked on Phonics Scam," *Rethinking Schools*, January/February 1992.

41. Cal Thomas, "Dismal report on American's education rooted in failure to teach reading," *Milwaukee Journal*, 16 September 1993.

42. Jeanne Chall, "The New Reading Debates: Evidence from Science, Art and Ideology," *Teachers College Record*, vol. 94, no. 2, Winter 1992.

Chapter 9: Why Johnny Can't Add, Subtract, Multiply, or Divide (But Still Feels Good about Himself)

1. "First Things First: What Americans Expect fom the Public Schools," Public Agenda, 1994.

2. Ibid.

3. Jean Merl, "Say Goodby to Chalkboard Math Drills," *Los Angeles Times*, 30 April 1994.

4. Ibid.

5. Ibid.

6. Constance Kamii, Barbara A. Lewis, and Sally James Livingston, "Primary Arithmetic: Children Inventing Their Own Procedures," *Arithmetic Teacher*, December 1993.

7. Quoted in Russell S. Worall and Doug Carnine, "Lack of Professional Support Undermines Teachers and Reform—A Contrasting Perspective from Health and Engineering," 19 September 1994, unpublished manuscript.

8. R. R. Heaton, "Who is minding the mathematics content? A case study of a fifth-grade teacher," *Elementary School Journal*, (93) 2

9. Worall and Carnine, "Lack of Professional Support."

10. *Curriculum and Evaluation Standards for School Mathematics* (Reston, Va.: National Council of Teachers of Mathematics, 1989).

11. *The University of Chicago Mathematics Project* (Evanston, Ill.: Everyday Learning Corporation, undated. This publication included articles from the *UCSMP Newsletter*, Winter 1988, and from the project brochure, Autumn 1989 and Autumn 1992).

12. Quoted in John Saxon, "The Coming Disaster in Science Education

in America," *Notices of the American Mathematical Society*, vol. 41, no. 2, February 1994.

13. Richard Bernstein, *Dictatorship of Virtue: Multiculturalism and the Battle for America's Future* (New York: Alfred A. Knopf, 1994), pp. 253–54.

14. Sacerdote, Mark, "The Board of Education Fails a Math Test," *New York Times*, 17 April 1993.

15. Ibid.

16. Ibid.

17. Ibid.

18. Saxon, "The Coming Disaster."

19. Ibid.

Chapter 10: Dumbing Down the Texts

1. *History Textbooks: A Standard and Guide 1994–95 Edition* (New York: American Textbook Council, 1994), p. 9.

2. William H. McGuffey, *The Eclectic Third Reader* (Cincinnati: Truman and Smith, 1837), p. 89.

3. William H. McGuffey, *The Eclectic First Reader for Young Children* (Cincinnati: Truman and Smith, 1837), p. 28.

4. Donald P. Hayes and Loreen T. Wolfer, "Was the Decline in SAT Verbal Scores Caused by Simplified Textbooks?" unpublished manuscript prepared for the *Journal of Educational Research*, 31 August 1993.

5. Frances FitzGerald, *America Revised: History Schoolbooks in the Twentieth Century* (Boston: Atlantic Monthly Press, 1979), p. 150.

6. Gilbert Sewall, *American History Textbooks: An Assessment of Quality* (New York: Educational Excellence Network, 1987), pp. 27, 28.

7. Ibid., p. 41.

8. Ibid., p. 32.

9. Ibid., p. 14.

10. Ibid., p. 1.

11. *History Textbooks: A Standard and Guide*, p. 19.

12. Sewall, *American History Textbooks*, p. 20.

13. Ibid., p. 20.

14. Isabel Beck, Margaret McKeown, and Erika Gromoll, *Issues That May Affect Social Studies Learning: Examples From Four Commercial Programs* (Learning Research and Development Center, University of Pittsburgh, January 1988, executive summary.

15. Sewall, *American History Textbooks*, p. 29

16. *History Textbooks: A Standard and Guide*, p. 24.

17. Quoted in William G., Durden, "The Deconstruction of American Education," *WI: Wisconsin Interest*, Fall/Winter 1994.

18. Sewall, *American History Textbooks*, pp. 59–60.

19. *History Textbooks: A Standard and Guide*, p. 24.

20. Stephen Bates, *Battleground* (New York: Poseidon Press, 1993), p. 220.

21. Ibid., p. 221.

22. Ibid., pp. 221–22.

23. Ibid., p. 221.

24. Ibid.

25. Paul C. Vitz, *Censorship: Evidence of Bias in Our Children's Textbooks* (Ann Arbor: Servant Books, 1986), p. 2.

26. Ibid.

27. Ibid., p. 3.

28. Ibid., pp. 3–4.

29. *History Textbooks: A Standard and Guide*, p. 33.

30. Ibid.

31. *Environmental Science: A Framework for Decision Making* (New York: Addison Wesley, 1989), p. 5.

32. Joan Luckman, *Your Health* (Englewood Cliffs, New Jersey: Prentice-Hall, 1990), pp. 541–42

33. Michael Sanera and Jane Shaw *A Parent's Primer on the Environment: How to Talk to Your Children About the Earth,"* draft copy, 1994.

34. Ibid.

35. Helen Cowcher, *Rainforest* (New York: Farrar, Straus and Giroux, 1988).

Scenes from the Front: The Political Classroom I

1. Bob Peterson, "Bias and CD-ROM Encyclopedias," *Rethinking Schools*, vol. 9, no. 1, Autumn 1994.

2. Bob Peterson, "Teaching for Social Justice," *Rethinking Schools*, vol. 8, no. 3, Spring 1994.

Chapter 11. Dumbing Down the Tests

1. John Jacob Cannell, "How Public Educators Cheat on Standardized Achievement Tests: The "Lake Wobegon' Report," Friends for Education, Albuqueque, New Mexico, 1989.

2. Ibid.

3. Ibid.

4. John Jacob Cannell, "Nationally Normed Elementary Achievement Testing in America's Public Schools: How All 50 States Are Above the National Average," *Educational Measurement: Issues and Practice*, vol. 7, no. 2, Summer 1988.

5. Ibid.

6. Ibid.

7. Gary W. Phillips and Chester E. Finn Jr., "The Lake Wobegon Effect: A Skeleton in the Testing Closet?" *Educational Measurement: Issues and Practice*, vol. 7, no. 2, Summer 1988.

8. Cannell, "Nationally Normed Elementary Achievement Testing."

9. Robert L. Linn, "Test Misuse: Why Is It So Prevalent," Office of Technology Assessment, U.S. Congress, September 1991.

10. Cannell, "How Public Educators Cheat."

11. Daniel Bice, "Many fail GED test in Wisconsin," *Milwaukee Sentinel,* 1 February 1994.

12. Michael Winerip, "SAT Increases the Average Score, by Fiat," *New York Times,* 11 June 1994.

13. Charles Krauthammer, " 'Recentered' scores just another step toward medicority," *Chicago Tribune,* 17 June 1994.

14. Winerip, "SAT Increases the Average Score."

15. Albert Shanker, "Standards in Ohio," *New Republic,* 23 May 1994.

16. Lonnie Harp, "Curriculum Is Focus in Probe of Ohio Exam," *Education Week,* 6 April 1994.

17. Ibid.

18. Shanker, "Standards in Ohio."

19. "RAND study points to problems in Vermont's portfolio assessment program," *Executive Educator,* February 1993.

20. George F. Madaus and Thomas Kellaghan, "The British Experience with 'Authentic Testing,' " *Phi Delta Kappan,* February 1993.

Scenes from the Front: The Political Classroom II

1. All references are to "Classroom Activities in Sex Equity for Developmental Guidance," Wisconsin Department of Public Instruction, Herbert J. Grover, State Superintendent.

Chapter 12: The "Values" Wasteland

1. Jane Gross, "Where 'Boys Will Be Boys,' And Adults Are Bewildered," *New York Times,* 29 March 1993.

2. J. Kikuchi, "Rhode Island Develops Successful Intervention Program for Adolescents, *National Coalition Against Sexual Assault Newsletter,* Fall 1988.

3. *USA Weekend,* 21–22 August 1992.

4. Garry Abrams, "Youth Gets Bad Marks in Morality," *Los Angeles Times,* 12 November 1992.

5. Ibid.

6. Michael Josephson, "Young American Is Looking Out for No. 1," *Los Angeles Times,* 16 October 1990.

7. Harold W. Stevenson and James W. Stigler, *The Learning Gap* (New York: Summit Books, 1992), pp. 85–86.

8. "Citizenship: 4th–6th Grade," xeroxed worksheets, undated. Several copies were provided to me by parents whose children had been given the assignment during class.

9. "PALS: Peers Always Listen Sensitively," a Curriculum for Teaching

Conflict Resolution, School District of West Allis–West Milwaukee, August 1993.

10. William Kirk Kilpatrick, *Why Johnny Can't Tell Right From Wrong* (New York: Simon & Schuster, 1992), p. 16.

11. Sidney B. Simon, Leland W. Howe, and Howard Kirschenbaum, *Values Clarification: A Handbook of Practical Strategies for Teachers and Students* (New York: Hart Publishing, 1972), p. 15.

12. Ibid., p. 16.

13. Ibid., pp. 18–19.

14. Ibid., pp. 155–157.

15. Ibid., pp. 143–150.

16. Ibid, p. 366.

17. Ibid., p. 288.

18. Kilpatrick, *Why Johnny Can't Tell*, p. 84.

19. Dennis Prager, conversation with author.

20. Nancy Gibbs, "How Should We Teach Our Children About Sex?" *Time*, 24 May 1993.

21. Ibid.

22. Bruno Bettelheim, "Our Children Are Treated Like Idiots," *Psychology Today*, July 1981.

23. "Mixed Messages," *Newsweek*, 12 April 1993.

24. Barbara Dafoe Whitehead, "The Failure of Sex Education," *Atlantic Monthly*, October 1994.

25. Sex Information and Education Council of the U.S., *Guidelines for Comprehensive Sexuality Education, Kindergarten–12th Grade*, New York, SIECUS, 1991. [SIECUS's National Guidelines Task Force included representatives of Planned Parenthood, the March of Dimes, the National School Boards Association, the American Medical Association, the National Education Association, the St. Louis, Missouri Public Schools, the Wesport, Connecticut Public Schools, and the Centers for Disease Control, among others.]

26. Joani Blank and Marcia Quackenbush, *A Kid's First Book About Sex* (Burlingam, California: Yes Press, 1983).

27. Ibid., pp. 11, 14.

28. Ibid., pp. 15–16.

29. Ibid., pp. 17–19.

30. Ibid., p. 26.

31. Ibid., pp. 28–29.

32. Ibid., pp. 31–33.

33. Ibid., p. 36.

34. Ibid., pp. 46–47.

35. David Elkind, *The Hurried Child: Growing Up Too Fast Too Soon* (Reading, Mass.: Addison-Wesley, 1988), p. 63.

36. Whitehead, "The Failure of Sex Education."

37. Ironically, opposition to the prescribed curricula of their children's schools by parents is the only issue where individuals challenging the power of government over their lives are *themselves* characterized as a threat to the Constitution. Usually, it is the usurpation of rights by the government that is regarded as the threat and the individual's resistance to that usurpation as a defense of constitutional liberties. Only in controversies that pit individual parents against government-run schools is the formula reversed. Civil libertarians who routinely side with individuals against government frequently align themselves with school districts against citizens who challenge the authority of the schools to impose some doctrine or another on their children. Often, this attitude is reflected in media coverage of controversies over "human growth" programs. While parents who might object to prayer in schools can generally expect a reasonably sympathetic press, parents who opt out of or object to sex education programs should not be surprised to find themselves covered under the headline, "The New Censorship," or included in stories about the threats to public education from the religious right.

38. *Final Report: The Senate Select Committee to Study the Michigan Model for Comprehensive School Health Education*, December 1992, p. 6.

39. Ibid., p. 23.

40. Ibid., p. 38.

41. Ibid., p. 29.

42. Whitehead, "The Failure of Sex Education."

43. Ibid.

44. Ibid.

45. Stan T. Weed, "Curbing Births, Not Pregnancies," *Wall Street Journal*, 14 October 1986.

46. Ibid.

47. Gibbs, "How Should We Teach."

48. John D. Hartigan, "Giving Kids Condoms Won't Work," *Wall Street Journal*, 19 December 1990.

Chapter 13: Telling on Mommy and Daddy

1. Kathleen Parker, "When counselors poke into family business," *Chicago Tribune*, October 21 1994.

2. "School District of Kettle Moraine K–5 Protective Behaviors: Approved by Kettle Moraine Board of Education," 13 October 1992.

3. Ibid., p. 61.

4. Ibid., p. 62.

5. Ibid., p. 93.

6. Ibid., pp. 96–97.

7. Ibid., p. 99.

8. Ibid., p. 64.

9. Ibid., p. 67.

10. Ibid., pp. 69–72.

11. Daniel Goleman, "Perils Seen in Warnings About Abuse," *New York Times*, 21 November 1989.

12. "School District of Kettle Moraine." p. 152.

13. Ibid., p. 153.

14. Ibid., pp. 125–26.

15. Ibid., p. 108.

16. Bittjane Levine, "The Forbidden Touch," *Los Angeles Times*, 18 November 1993.

17. Joy Sells, "Do not touch: Reaching out has been withdrawn as a safe option in the '90s," *Chicago Tribune*, 14 February 1993.

18. Daniel Goleman, "Doubts Rise on Children as Witnesses," *New York Times*, 6 November 1990.

19. Ibid.,

20. Richard Gardner, "Modern Witch Hunt—Child Abuse Charges," *Wall Street Journal*, 22 February 1993.

21. Douglas J. Besharov, "Gaining Control over Child Abuse Reports," *Public Welfare*, vol. 48, no. 2, Spring 1990. See also "Child Sexual Abuse," *CQ Researcher*, vol. 3, no. 2, 15 January 1993.

22. Goleman, "Perils Seen in Warnings About Abuse."

23. Ibid.

24. Ibid.

Chapter 14: Doctor, Doctor

1. Mary Jordan, "Push to Mainstream Disabled Students Gets a Mixed Report Card," *Washington Post*, 25 December 1993.

2. David Jackson, "Mainstreaming can put kids in over their heads," *Chicago Tribune*, 1 April 1993.

3. Catherine Manegold, "Special Pupils, Regular Classes, Thorny Issues," *New York Times*, 26 January 1994.

4. Sarah Lubman, "More Schools Embrace 'Full Inclusion' of the Disabled," *Wall Street Journal*, 13 April 1994.

5. Jordan, "Push to Mainstream Disabled Students."

6. Ed McManus, letter to the editor, "Inclusion works for disabled children," *Chicago Tribune*, 18 April 1993.

7. Junda Woo, "Disabled Student's Expulsion Draws Fire," *Wall Street Journal*, 18 July 1994.

8. Jordan, "Push to Mainstream Disabled Students."

9. Albert Shanker, "Inclusion and Ideology," 1994

10. John Leo, "Mainstreaming's 'Jimmy problem'," *U.S. News and World Report*, 27 June 1994.

11. Shanker, "Inclusion and Ideology."

12. Jackson, "Mainstreaming can put kids."

13. Joseph Berger, "Costly Special Classes Service, Many With Minimal Needs," *New York Times*, 30 April 1991.

14. Michael Winerip, "A Disabilities Program That 'Got Out of Hand,' " *New York Times*, 8 April 1994.

15. Peter R. Breggin, *Toxic Psychiatry* (New York: St. Martin's Press, 1991), p. 284.

16. Winerip, "A Disabilities Program That 'Got Out of Hand.' "

17. Gerald Coles, *The Learning Mystique* (New York: Pantheon Books, 1987), p. 195.

18. Ibid., pp. 196–97.

19. Ibid., p. 200.

20. Ibid.

21. Ibid., p. 203.

22. Winerip, "A Disabilities Program."

23. Ibid.

24. Ibid.

Chapter 15: The Attack on Learning

1. *Organizing the Elementary School for Living and Learning* (Washington, D.C.: Association for Supervision and Curriculum Development, National Education Association, 1947), p. 9.

2. Ibid., p. 167.

3. Ibid., p. 21.

4. Ibid., p. 208.

5. Ibid., p. 18.

6. Ibid., pp. 40–41.

7. Ibid., p. 41.

8. Ibid., pp. 65–67.

9. Ibid., p. 67.

10. Ibid., p. 27.

11. Ibid., pp. 48–49.

12. Ibid., p. 18.

13. Ibid., p. 15.

14. Ibid.

15. Ibid., p. 27.

16. Ibid., p. 15.

17. Jacques Barzun, *The House of Intellect* (New York: Harper & Row, 1961), p. 120.

18. Lawrence A. Cremin, *The Transformation of the School: Progressiv-*

ism in American Education, 1876–1957 (New York: Alfred A. Knopf, 1962), p. 328.

19. Robin Barrow, *Radical Education: A critique of freeschooling and deschooling* (London: Martin Robertson, 1978), p. 2.

20. Ibid., p. 5.

21. Ibid., p. 21.

22. Jean-Jacques Rousseau, *Emile,* p. 23.

23. Ibid.

24. Barrow, *Radical Education,* p. 38.

25. Cremin, *The Transformation of the School,* pp. 8–9.

26. Ibid., pp. 62–63.

27. Ibid., p. 75.

28. Ibid., pp. 118–120.

29. Harold Rugg and Ann Shumaker, *The Child-Centered School* (New York: World Book Company, 1928), p. 21.

30. Frances FitzGerald, *America Revised: History Schoolbooks in the Twentieth Century* (Boston: Atlantic Monthly Press, 1979), p. 174.

31. Cremin, *The Transformation of the School,* p. 138.

32. *The Nation,* CII (1916), pp. 480–81.

33. Richard Mitchell, *The Graves of Academe,* p. 73

34. Ibid., p. 80.

35. Ibid., p. 83.

36. Ibid., p. 88.

37. Cremin, *The Transformation of the School,* p. 142.

38. Ibid., p. 220.

39. Ibid., p. 275.

40. Ibid., p. 207.

Scenes from the Front: 1928

1. Harold Rugg and Ann Shumaker, *The Child-Centered School* (New York: World Book Company, 1928), pp. 3–4.

2. Ibid., p. 60.

3. Ibid., p. 69.

4. Ibid., p. 57.

5. Ibid., p. 35.

6. Ibid., pp. 7–8.

7. Ibid., p. 324.

8. Ibid., p. 65.

9. Ibid., p. 64.

Scenes from the Front: 1958

1. John Keats, *Schools Without Scholars* (Boston: Houghton Mifflin, 1958), pp. 25–26.

2. Ibid., p. 27.

3. Ibid., p. 28.

4. Ibid., p. 88.

5. Ibid., p. 29.

6. Ibid., pp. 39–40.

7. Ibid., p. 46.

8. Ibid., pp. 66–67.

9. Ibid., p. 35.

10. Ibid., pp. 36–37.

11. Ibid., p. 46.

12. Ibid., p. 43.

Chapter 16: Educational Wastelands

1. John Keats, *Schools Without Scholars* (Boston: Houghton Mifflin, 1958), pp. vii, 93.

2. Ibid., p. 83.

3. Arthur Bestor, *Educational Wastelands: The Retreat from Learning in Our Public Schools*, 2nd ed. (Urbana, Ill.: University of Illinois Press, 1985), p. 11.

4. Ibid., pp. 90–91.

5. Ibid., pp. 12–13, 14.

6. Ibid., p. 15.

7. Ibid., pp. 17–18.

8. Ibid., pp. 18–19.

9. Ibid., p. 21.

10. Ibid., p. 27.

11. Ibid., p. 49.

12. Ibid., p. 48.

13. Ibid., pp. 43–44.

14. Ibid., pp. 50–51.

15. Ibid., pp. 54–55.

16. Ibid., p. 64.

17. Lawrence A. Cremin, *The Transformation of the School: Progressivism in American Education, 1876–1957* (New York: Alfred A. Knopf, 1962), p. 338.

18. Gilbert Sewall, *Necessary Lessons: Decline and Renewal in American Schools* (New York: The Free Press, 1983), pp. 40–41.

19. Ibid., p. 51.

20. Bestor, *Educational Wastelands*, pp. 228–230.

Scenes from the Front: Mold

1. Videotape of School Board Meeting, Sun Prairie, Wis., 24 May 1993.

Chapter 17: The Blob

1. Arthur Bestor, *Educational Wastelands: The Retreat from Learning in Our Public Schools,* 2nd ed. (Urbana, Ill.: University of Illinois Press, 1985), pp. 101–2.

2. U.S. Department of Education, *American Education: Making It Work,* 1988.

3. "Cortines Says School Board Misstated Staff Size," *New York Times,* 11 February 1994.

4. "Improving Schools and Education," National Policy Forum, 1994.

5. Michael Fischer, "Why I Quit Teaching," *WI: Wisconsin Interest,* Fall/Winter 1993.

6. Charles Sykes, "Why the Schools Are Suffering," *Isthmus* (Madison, Wis.), 29 January 1993. See also 1993–95 Biennial Budget Request, Wisconsin Department of Public Instruction, 9 November 1992.

7. Peter Brimelow and Leslie Spencer, "The National Extortion Association," *Forbes,* 7 June 1993.

8. Ibid.

9. Gilbert Sewall, *Necessary Lessons: Decline and Renewal in American Schools* (New York: Free Press, 1983), p. 70.

10. Brimelow and Spencer, "The National Extortion Association."

11. Stephanie Chavez, "Teachers Gird for Voucher Battle," *Los Angeles Times,* 12 September 1993.

12. Henry Chu, "Teachers Fight Voucher at Work, Group Claims," *Los Angeles Times,* 24 September 1993.

13. Brimelow and Spencer, "The National Extortion Association."

14. "The NEA's Public Enemy #1," *Wall Street Journal,* 13 July 1993.

15. Brimelow and Spencer, "The National Extortion Association."

16. Ibid.

17. Ibid.

18. Matt Helms and Terry Birkenhauer, "MEA's Donations Lead Class: Teachers Union Counts on Grateful Legislators as Votes Near," *Detroit Free Press,* 15 November 1993.

19. Joan Richardson, "Tenure Reform Bills Make Firing Bad Teachers Easier," *Detroit Free Press,* 11 June 1993.

20. Michael Fischer, "A Betrayal of Teachers by Their Union," *WI: Wisconsin Interest,* Fall/Winter 1994, vol. 3, no. 2.

21. Sam Dillon, "Teacher Tenure: Rights vs. Discipline," *New York Times,* 28 June 1994.

22. Gerald W. Bracey, "Setting the Record Straight: Confronting the Myths of Public School Failure," *Phi Delta Kappan,* vol. 73, no. 2, October 1991, pp. 104–136.

23. Wisconsin Education Association Council, Division for Professional Development and Training, 1994.

24. Publication of the Division for Professional Development and Training, Wisconsin Education Association Council, 1994.

25. Donna H. Kerr, "Teaching Competence and Teacher Education in the United States," *Teachers College Record*, vol. 84, no. 3, Spring 1983.

26. Ibid.

27. Sewall, "Necessary Lessons," p. 123.

28. Ibid., pp. 123–24.

29. *A Nation at Risk*, The National Commission on Excellence in Education, 1983.

30. William Celis 3d, "10 Years After a Scathing Report, Schools Show Uneven Progress," *New York Times*, 28 April 1993.

31. Lawrence A. Cremin, *The Transformation of the School: Progressivism in American Education, 1876–1957* (New York: Alfred A. Knopf, 1962), pp. 348–49.

32. John P. Kaminski, ed., *Citizen Jefferson: The Wit and Wisdom of an American Sage* (Madison, Wis.: Madison House Publishers, 1994), p. 104.

33. Rita Kramer, *Ed School Follies: The Miseducation of America's Teachers* (New York: The Free Press, 1991), pp. 26–27.

Chapter 18: Outcome Based Education

1. Diane Spoehr, personal communication with author.

2. Cheri Yecke, in *To Tell the Truth: Will the Real OBE Please Stand Up?* PA Parents Commission, April 1993.

3. After her narrow re-election in 1994, the superintendent, Sandy Garrett, backed off from her enthusiasm for OBE and said she would ask the legislature to repeal legislation that requires an "outcome-oriented approach" to school accreditation in the state. Merely changing the name or the language, however, does not mean that the state's educrats have changed their underlying philosophy.

4. Jayna Davis, "What Did You Learn in School Today?" KFOR-TV, Oklahoma City, Okla., 27 May 1993 and 6 June 1993.

5. Ibid.

6. Charles J. Sykes, "Dumbing Down Our Kids," *WI: Wisconsin Interest*, Fall/Winter 1993.

7. In Virginia, for example, the state's Department of Education originally drafted a plan in 1992 called the "World Class Education Initiative," which included a "Common Core of Learning," which listed thirty-eight separate student "outcomes," under seven "dimensions of living": "Personal Well-Being and Accomplishment; Interpersonal Relationships; Lifelong Learning; Cultural and Creative Endeavors; Work and Economic Well-Being; Local and Global Civic Participation; and Environmental Stewardship. When opponents objected to the vacuity of such goals, the state drew up a second version in February 1993 that only slightly revised the "seven life roles" (fulfilled individual, supportive

person, lifelong learner, expressive contributor, quality worker, informed citizen, and environmental steward). In May 1933, the state Board of Education approved a revised version of the "outcomes," which, however, did not mute the controversy. In the fall of 1933, Governor Douglas Wilder ordered the withdrawal of the plan, acknowledging that despite his good intentions the plan had "become tied to other fashionable approaches to curriculum reform."

Researcher Bruno Manno notes that "In several other states this general pattern has been repeated: the governor or state legislature appoints a commission to establish learning outcomes for the state's public schools; well-intentioned elected officials blindly hand responsibility for specifying outcomes to groups dominated by education views antithetical to those the public officials thought they were mandating; the commission develops a laundry list of outcomes, many involving transformational OBE; a wide cross section of the public raises an outcry; and the state government cancels the plan or at least the most offending parts of it. States as varied as Colorado, Kansas, Minnesota, New Hampshire, Oklahoma, Pennsylvania, Washington, Ohio, Iowa, and Wyoming have had such experiences." (Bruno V. Manno, "Outcome-Based Education: Miracle Cure or Plague?" Hudson Institute Briefing Paper Number 165, June 1994).

One of the most enthusiastic efforts took place in Minnesota, where a statewide Outcome Based Education program was launched with the enthusiastic backing of the state legislature and Governor Arne Carlson. The governor was so intent on pushing OBE that he fired the state's school superintendent for being insufficiently enthusiastic. But in September 1993, Governor Carlson abruptly reversed himself, summoning the state's Board of Education to his office where he told them to drop fuzzy, vague and value-laden goals such as the requirement that students understand "the integration of physical, emotional and spiritual wellness." In April 1994, the Minnesota House voted to delay the state's outcome-based high school graduation rule for a year and placed conditions on the final approval of its content.

In June 1994, one of the state's biggest school districts, the Rosemont–Apple Valley–Eagan School District, scrapped its experiment with OBE. Although the Rosemont–Apple OBE program had been regarded as a model for other OBE programs in the state, critics had charged that bright students were being slowed down and that student admission to college was being jeopardized by the new grading philosophies (which awarded only A's, B's, and Incompletes). A local task force that studied OBE in the district recommended that it be scrapped because there was no consistency or standardization in the way standards were being implemented. (Joanna Richardson, "Minn. District Scraps OBE Experiment Seen as a Model," *Education Week*, 1 June 1994).

8. Letter from Jack Steinberg, PFT, director to educational affairs to the Honorable Ron Gamble, 16 March 1993.

9. George Judson, "Bid to Revise Education Is Fought in Connecticut," *New York Times*, 9 January 1994.

10. David P. McGrath, "Tracey Ullman," *Happenings Magazine*, 21 October 1993.

11. Karen M. Evans and Jean A King, "Research on OBE: What We Know and Don't Know," *Educational Leadership*, March 1994.

12. Proposed Education Goals, State of Kentucky.

13. Proposed Education Goals, State of Pennsylvania.

14. "K–12 Teaching and Learning: A Working Document," Department of Curriulcum and Instruction, Milwaukee Public Schools, September 1991.

15. Albert Mammary, "Fourteen Principles of Quality Outcomes-Based Education," *Quality Outcomes-Driven Education*, October 1991.

16. Albert Shanker, "Outrageous Outcomes," *New York Times*, 12 September 1993.

17. Mitchell, *The Leaning Tower of Babel*, p. 72.

18. See Robert E. Slavin, "Mastery Learning Reconsidered," Center for Research on Elementary and Middle Schools, Johns Hopkins University, January 1987.

19. Thomas R. Guskey, "The Theory and Practice of Mastery Learning," *The Principal*, March/April 1982.

20. Ron Brandt, "On Outcome Based Education: A Conversation With Bill Spady," *Educational Leadership*, December 1992/January 1933.

21. Ibid.

22. William G. Spady and Kit J. Marshall, "Beyond Traditional Outcome-Based Education," *Educational Leadership*, October 1991; see also William G. Spady, "Organizing for Results: The Basis of Authentic Restructuring and Reform," *Educational Leadership*, vol. 46, no. 2, 1988.

23. Jayna Davis, "What Did You Learn in School Today?" KFOR-TV, Oklahoma City, Okla., 27 May 1993 and 6 June 1993.

24. This is not merely speculation on my part. In Missouri, the state's educrats suggest that "Students . . . conduct a simulated Constitutional Congress, requiring them to draft and negotiate their own constitution" as one way to fulfill the educational "goal" that students be taught to "Make Responsible Decisions Individually and Within Groups as Students, Family Members, Workers and Citizens."

25. "Academic Performance Standards for Missouri Schools: An Interpretive Guide," Missouri Department of Elementary and Secondary Education, May 1994.

Chapter 19: Goals 2000 and the Counterreformation

1. Allyson Tucker, "Goals 2000: Stifling Grass Roots Education Reform," *Heritage Foundation*, Issue Bulletin #182, 14 July 1993.

2. Cited in Tucker, from minutes of the National Council on Education Standards and Testing, Implementation Task Force, 31 October 1991, pp. 72–73.

3. Debra Viadero, "Arts-Education Standards Set for Unveiling," *Education Week*, 9 March 1994.

4. Karen Diegmueller, "English Group Loses Funding For Standards," *Education Week*, 30 March 1994.

5. Jo Thomas, "U.S. Panel's History Model Looks Beyond Old Europe," *New York Times*, 11 November 1994.

6. Carol Gluck, "History According to Whom?" *New York Times*, 19 November 1994.

7. Lynne V. Cheney, "The End of History," *Wall Street Journal*, 20 October 1994.

8. Ibid.

9. Ibid.

10. John Leo, "The hijacking of American history," *U.S. News & World Report*, 14 November 1994.

11. Thomas, "U.S. Panel's History Model."

12. Stephen Arons, "The Threat to Freedom in Goals 2000," *Education Week*, 6 April 1994.

Scenes from the Front: An Endangered Species II

1. Debbie Stone, "This Teacher Commands Attention," *Wisconsin State Journal*, 1 May 1994.

2. "Much Ado About Alice," *Wisconsin State Journal*, 11 April 1990.

Chapter 20: Schools That Work

1. Gilbert Sewall, *Necessary Lessons: Decline and Renewal in American Schools* (New York: The Free Press, 1983), pp. 139–140.

2. Ibid., pp. 130–31.

3. Ibid., pp. 135–37.

4. Quoted in Sewall, "Necessary Lessons," p. 134.

5. Ibid., pp. 132–33.

6. Ibid., pp. 132–33.

Scenes from the Front: Barclay

1. Lavinia Edmunds, "The Woman Who Battled the Bureaucrats," *Reader's Digest*, December 1993. This account is also based on a presentation Gertrude Williams made in Milwaukee, Wis., on 8 October 1994, and personal discussion with author on the same date.

2. "Philosophy and Objectives," Calvert School, Baltimore, Maryland, undated.

3. Millicent Lawton, "Borrowing From the Basics," *Education Week*, 20 April 1994.

4. Ibid.

5. Edmunds, "The Woman Who Battled."

6. Ibid.

7. Ibid.

8. "Third Year Evaluation of the Calvert School Program at Barclay Elementary School," Center for the Social Organization of Schools, Johns Hopkins University.

9. Lawton, "Borrowing From the Basics."

10. Ibid.

11. "Third Year Evaluation."

12. "Course Survey," Barclay Elementary School.

13. Lawton, "Borrowing From the Basics."

Chapter 21: The Coming Educational Revolution

1. John E. Chubb and Terry M. Moe, *Politics, Markets & America's Schools* (Washington, D.C.: The Brookings Institution, 1990), pp. 28–31.

2. Ibid., p. 32.

3. Ibid., p. 35.

4. William Raspberry, "Set the highest goal for the brightest—they will achieve," *Chicago Tribune*, 19 July 1994.

5. "What Kids Need to Know," *Newsweek*, 2 November 1992.

6. E. D. Hirsch, "Teach Knowledge, Not 'Mental Skills,'" *New York Times*, 4 September 1993

7. "What Kids Need to Know."

8. Ibid.

9. Michael E. Hartmann, "Sometimes So Simple, It's Sad," *WI: Wisconsin Interest*, Spring/Summer 1994.

10. Peter Steinfels, "Why Catholic Schools Succeed: A Community of Shared Values," *New York Times*, 17 April 1994. See also: Anthony S. Bryck, Valerie E. Lee, and Peter B. Holland, *Catholic Schools and the Public Good* (Cambridge, Mass.: Harvard University Press, 1993).

11. Stephen L. Carter, quoted in Michael E. Hartmann, "Sometimes So Simple."

12. "Initial Results From Nationwide Survey Give High Marks to Home Schooling," *Home School Court Report*, December 1990.

13. Steve Strecklow, "Fed Up With Schools, More Parents Turn to Teaching at Home," *Wall Street Journal*, 10 May 1994.

14. Mary Jordan, "Tutoring Moves from Stigma to Status Symbol," *Washington Post*, 15 May 1994.

15. Rita Kramer, *Ed School Follies: The Miseducation of America's Teachers* (New York: The Free Press, 1991), p. 15.

16. James Q. Wilson and George Kelling, "Character and Community: The Problem of Broken Windows," in *Good Order: Right Answers to Contemporary Questions*, Brad Miner ed. (New York: Simon & Schuster 1995), pp. 90, 91.

17. Harold Stevenson and James W. Stigler, *The Learning Gap* (New York: Summit Books, 1992), p. 68.

18. Ibid.

19. Ibid., p. 76.

20. Ibid., p. 80.

21. Ibid., p. 73.

22. Ibid. p. 80.

INDEX